The Complete Book of
PET CARE

DR. PETER ROACH

Birds Cats Fish Dogs
Guinea Pigs Hamsters Horses
Mice Rabbits Reptiles

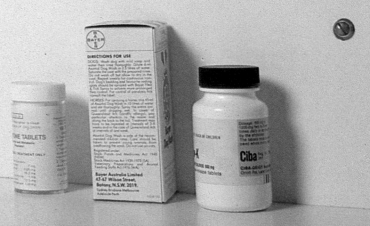

HOWELL BOOK HOUSE

New York

THIS BOOK IS DEDICATED TO MY WIFE, LYNNE.

First American Paperback Edition 1995
Distributed by Howell Book House
Macmillan Publishing USA
15 Columbus Circle, New York, NY 10023

Published by Lansdowne Publishing Pty Ltd
Level 5, 70 George St, Sydney NSW 2000 Australia
First published 1983
© Copyright Peter Roach 1983, 1995
Produced in Australia by the Publisher
Typeset in Australia

Printed by Kyodo Printing Co. Neythal Road, Jurong, Singapore

Illustrations by *Paul Geros* and *Ann Twells*
Designed by *Ann Twells*
Typeface: Set in Times Roman 9pt, 11pt; Helvetica Medium
Cover photography by *Reg Morrison*

CONTENTS

FOREWORD

During the past decade the public has shown a tremendous increase in awareness of the need to provide animals with proper care and attention. This has been particularly noticeable in the case of domestic animals. However, most of these owners have had no practical training in animal care and are at a loss to determine if their pet is in good condition or 'off key'. All too often, the owner receives dubious advice from fellow owners, frequently to the detriment of their animals. For these reasons, I was delighted when I was shown the manuscript of *The Complete Book of Pet Care*.

Here is a publication brimming over with good, sound, easily read information, providing the pet owner with a quick reference for clarification and reassurance. Indeed, it is almost as though the reader is consulting the Veterinary Surgeon, who is instructing his client in how to provide the necessities and extras which will give the pet animal every opportunity to enjoy a long life of good health, with mutual contentment. The reader is also advised of the sort of information which the owner should collect to assist the Veterinary Surgeon in arriving at a professional diagnosis.

This book is a significant advance in providing pet owners with an opportunity to appreciate the veterinary requirements of their animals which are dependent upon them for good health. After all, kindness brings satisfaction to the giver as well as the receiver.

Peter Roach is to be commended for his initiative in compiling *The Complete Book of Pet Care* and Lansdowne Press for undertaking its publication. I recommend this book to all those who have become, or are about to become, 'a pet owner'.

Colin F. McCaskill
Former Executive Director
The Royal Society for the Prevention of Cruelty to Animals
New South Wales

ACKNOWLEDGEMENTS

I should like to express my indebtedness to the following people for their assistance and advice:

Dr J. D. Burton, Dr H. Collins, Dr Harry Cooper, Prof. C. W. Emens, Prof. Brian Farrow, Prof. John Keep, Dr Peter Merkelbach, Dr K. R. Moulton, Mr Greg Parker, Dr Jeff Smith, Laurie Small at St George Aquariums, Rockdale,N.S.W.,Australia, Pets International, and Taronga Zoo.

Various clients who allowed me to photograph their pets.

Particular acknowledgement is made to the Post-graduate Committee in Veterinary Science, The University of Sydney. This organisation plays a vital role in keeping the Veterinarian up to the minute with the latest information by way of articles, cassettes and courses. Great reference has been made to this valuable source to ensure that readers of this book have the latest information.

In particular I would like to acknowledge the then director of the Committee, Dr T.G. Hungerford O.B.E., B.V.Sc, F.A.C.V.Sc., H.D.A., whose energetic and tireless activities through the Committee have helped both man and animals.

INTRODUCTION

During my 25 years as a practising Veterinarian and on my 'talk-back' radio programme I have been constantly asked questions by pet owners about their animals. Some owners feel that their question does not justify a visit to the Vet. Some pet problems occur at odd times and sometimes it is difficult to know whether a condition is serious enough to warrant consulting the Veterinarian. Often, even in a consultation, the Vet may be too busy to fully explain the background to a problem. Some pet owners like to follow-up their pet's problem by additional reading.

I felt there was a need for a book of this nature to act as a household reference book.

Some readers may find some of the photographs or illustrations a little disconcerting, but they are included to help you, the pet owner, to quickly and accurately identify your pet's problem.

The information within the book is based on the latest knowledge available to the veterinary profession, coupled with my own 25 years of intensive veterinary practice.

It is devoid of 'old wive's tales' and is written in plain English, so that you will find the facts, but will not be confused by technical or academic jargon.

Those owners who wish to pursue a certain subject in greater depth, should, as the next step refer to an academic text recommended by a Veterinarian.

This book covers the management, care, problems and common ailments of birds, cats, dogs, fish, guinea pigs, horses, mice, rabbits and reptiles: in fact, all the pets a household is likely to have. As well as being a pet owner's household reference it is an ideal text for the newly graduated Veterinarian, Veterinary nurse, animal breeder and zoo attendant.

Peter Roach

Dr. Peter J.G. Roach B.V.Sc., M.R.C.V.S., M.A.C.V.Sc.
1995

METRIC MEASURES

IMPERIAL TO METRIC			METRIC TO IMPERIAL		
1 inch	=	2.5400cm	1 cm	=	0.393700 inches
1 foot	=	0.3048m	1 metre	=	3.280840 feet
1 yard	=	0.91440m	1 metre	=	1.093613 yards
1 mile	=	1.60934km	1 km	=	0.621371 miles
1 sq. inch	=	6.45160 sq. cm	1 sq. cm	=	0.15500 sq. in.
1 sq. foot	=	0.09290 sq. m	1 sq. m	=	10.76391 sq. ft.
1 sq. yard	=	0.83613 sq. m	1 sq. m	=	1.19599 sq. yds.
1 acre	=	0.40469 Ha	1 Ha	=	2.47105 acres
1 ounce	=	28.349523 grams	1 gram	=	0.35274 oz
1 lb.	=	0.453592 kg	1 kg	=	2.20462 lbs
1 ton	=	1016.0469 kg	1 kg	=	0.000984 tons
1 pint	=	0.56826 litres	1 litre	=	1.7596 pints
1 quart	=	1.13652 litres	1 litre	=	0.87988 quarts
1 gallon	=	4.5609 litres	1 litre	=	0.21997 gallons

BIRDS

Selecting a bird

A few decades ago, caged birds within the house were very popular pets. In recent years, many people have changed their ideas on confining birds to small cages. The discovery of the disease psittacosis (carried by birds and transmitted through the air to cause pneumonia in humans) has also had some effect on the decline in popularity of indoor birds.

Nevertheless, many little birds are kept in small cages within the house and give their owners great pleasure.

In the last few decades, outdoor aviaries have become enormously popular. They provide, in my opinion, a much more humane method of keeping birds captive. Many aviaries are large enough to allow flight, and the inclusion of natural vegetation. This usually provides such a satisfactory environment that the birds will reproduce, despite being in captivity.

The most popular birds are canaries, tiny finches, budgerigars, small parrots and quail. The keeping of large parrots such as the Australian white sulphur crested cockatoo in small wire cages should be outlawed. These birds are very intelligent and in most cases can be set free to return as 'free roaming pets'.

Whether you obtain your bird from a pet shop, a breeder or a friend, make sure that it is in good condition, with a sleek plumage, bright eyes, and an alert manner. Examine the bird's cage for evidence of diarrhoea. The normal droppings are target-like with the centre white (urine) and the outer a dark brown (faeces). Check the cage for signs of moulting. If the bird is 'fluffed up' it is likely to be sick, especially if it is on the floor of the cage.

It is best to get a young bird so that it becomes attached to you. Newly hatched parrots, canaries and finches are blind and naked for the first month or so. After the first moult, which usually occurs at twelve months, it is not easy to determine a bird's age. Older birds tend to be fatter and their plumage is less smooth and sleek.

Sexing of birds is difficult unless the plumage of the male and female of the same species is different in colour.

Any bird locked in a small cage will get bored and this may cause health problems necessitating a trip to the vet. Include in the enclosure toys such as swings, chains, bells and mirrors, as well as some fresh vegetation. Above all, the bird will need your company, so place the enclosure (whether cage or aviary) in an area where there is plenty of human activity.

Birds can also be trained on the reward system to do various 'tricks', usually of the vocal type. Most canaries are bought for their song, and most members of the parrot family in the hope that they will develop an elaborate vocabulary. The best way to be assured of a songster or a mimic is to get a bird already showing its prowess in these fields.

Birds do not need any vaccinations. In fact, most birds, if kept in hygienic conditions with regular food and clean water, lead a healthy life without ever needing veterinary attention.

Housing

Of all the pets kept for the enjoyment of the human race, birds probably suffer the most restrictions. Birds, like any other animal, will live and breed successfully only if their environment is satisfactory. It is most important that intending bird purchasers obtain the type of aviary the particular bird requires. For all but canaries or budgerigars, substantial aviaries are needed. Plan and construct the aviary before the birds are purchased.

The large open aviary

All birds except the canary or the budgerigar (which seem to cope with small cages) should have room not only to stretch their wings but also to fly. If you have the space available it is best to build a large aviary 2 metres wide, 2 metres high and up to 2.5 metres long. The bottom of the aviary should

Small birds are very popular and give their owners much pleasure.

Here is the ideal aviary; most bird species can be kept in this environment.

be rodent-proofed with galvanised sheeting, each sheet about a metre long. Bury one end of the sheets 70 centimetres into the ground, so that rodents are discouraged from digging their way into the aviary, and so that 30 centimetres of sheeting protrudes above the ground. Overlap any joins in the sheeting. Corrugated iron is excellent for this purpose. The iron should be nailed or screwed to each corner post and to the timber frame.

The floor of the aviary should be soil in which grasses and other low shrubs are growing. Some dry grass, hay or twigs should be made available on the floor for nesting material. A compost heap can be kept in the aviary to attract insects for feeding. For the walls, wire netting is available as 'chicken mesh'. This gives an open netted flying area to the birds (but do make sure small birds can't fly through the holes in the wire netting!).

This is the ideal aviary and most species of bird can be kept in it as the environment is very similar to that in the wild.

One end of the aviary should be enclosed with solid walls and roofed, with a door that can be shut, to keep the birds inside during cold or windy weather. Any building material is satisfactory providing it affords protection.

During the breeding season those birds which prefer secluded nest sites may be confined to the indoor section while outdoor shrubbery nesting birds may be left in the open section.

In hot weather, aviaries can be cooled by a sprinkler system on the roof.

Tropical birds kept in temperate climates require a completely enclosed aviary.

The large enclosed aviary

Tropical birds kept in non-tropical climates require special conditions. Instead of having an open netted flying area, birds should be totally housed, with windows suitably placed for ventilation if necessary. In the southern hemisphere large windows should be placed in the northern and western walls to catch the morning and afternoon sun. Suitable bird-proof air vents should be placed in the eaves to provide ventilation when the windows are closed during very cold weather.

Whenever glass is built into an aviary it should have bird wire on the inside to prevent the birds flying into the glass and injuring themselves. Birds tend to fly at glass because they can see their reflections in it, presumably because they assume the reflection is an intruder to be driven off.

The small aviary

Where space is a problem and only a few small birds are kept, a small aviary is quite satisfactory. Because of the smaller space, hygiene becomes more important and it is advisable to have the aviary raised off the ground with a removable metal floor tray at the bottom of the cage to collect faeces for disposal. The floor of the aviary should be 60–80 centimetres above the ground so that it is completely rodent-proof.

Small indoor cages

These cages are very small, usually 50cm × 50cm × 30cm, and provide accommodation for only one or two small birds such as budgerigars or canaries. Because the cages are so small, they are available ready made at very reasonable prices. They usually have a self-feeding and watering system and a removable floor tray. These items make for a hygienic existence, which is necessary in such a small area.

Since the cage is so small, it must be placed where there is plenty of action so that the bird does not become bored. Once the bird has become domesticated, many owners let it out for short periods to fly in a closed room.

Breeding cages

Single breeding cages suitable for canaries and finches can be made by bird owners to any desired number. Or they can be purchased ready-made in multiple units. The units are separated by inserting a sheet of wallboard between the wire sections during the breeding season; the wallboard can be removed at the conclusion of the breeding season so that the cages can be used as small aviaries.

Because the breeding cages are so small, they should have a removable floor tray or a paper liner that can be laid on the floor and removed each day. Feed and water utensils should be attached to the outside of small cages to prevent water and feed being spilled on the cage floor.   This allows for easier cleaning, and discourages the bird from eating off the floor.

The large aviary will have all that is needed to meet the requirements of most bird species, such as running water for drinking and bathing, an earthen floor, twigs and shrubs on which to perch, and nesting materials

In hot weather a fine mist of water will refresh most birds.

This nesting receptacle is suitable for most medium to large-sized parrots.

During the breeding season nesting receptacles should be provided in the cage.

A wooden nesting box with perch for budgerigars.

A wicker nesting basket for finches.

available from the floor. It is in the smaller aviaries and cages that owners must pay particular attention to ensuring that the birds have everything necessary to make them feel at home and comfortable in their small environment.

Perches

Cages should be provided with shrubbery, either in pots or as cut pieces, for the birds to perch on, particularly in the case of finches. The shrub branches are preferable to dowel perches and must be provided during the breeding season anyway for the birds to nest in.

Where perches are used, they should not be the round hardwood dowels commonly used, but should be made of oval softwood. Hardwood should not be used because it invariably splits, allowing a hiding place for mites and lice, which can then withstand disinfection of the cage and attack the birds again at night.

Canary cages should have two perches, the first 7–10 centimetres from the ground and the second not closer that 15 centimetres to the roof of the cage; the perches should be at opposite ends of the cage. The distance of the top perch from the roof is critical during the breeding season, as mating may be impaired if it is too close to the ceiling. The cock bird must be able to mount the female, flap his wings to maintain his balance, and swing to the correct mating position freely.

Materials for nesting

During the breeding season, or when the hen (the female bird) restlessly hops or flies around the cage as if looking for nesting materials, a nest cup or box should be provided. However, only birds that have been bred in captivity for a few generations will use these. Some finches will not use nest cups or boxes at all. If they are provided they should be placed as high up in the cage or aviary as possible, but not so high as to cause difficulty for the birds entering.

For those birds that prefer to make their own nests completely, grass and other material should be provided together with a piece of shrub or other closely branched vegetation. Some birds may need special materials for

This finch has built her own natural camouflaged nest from twigs and grass. On the left is a vacated nest.

nesting, including grass stems, twine, coconut fibre, moss, soft grasses, leaves, cotton-wool, teased rope, down, gravel, stones and feathers. For further information on the nesting requirements of different bird species, it is best to discuss the subject with the pet shop or breeder from whom you purchase the birds. The larger the aviary, and the more natural the plants and shrubbery, the less difficulty the birds will have in choosing material and position to suit their needs.

Waterers

Select a drinking vessel that does not become fouled, cannot be spilled and which the birds cannot bathe in. The ideal system is an inverted bottle with a screw-on plastic salt-shaker top. It is secured to the wire on the inside of the cage. Alternatively a nipple-type, bent glass tube running through a cork in an inverted bottle serves the same purpose. This can be attached to the outside of the cage.

An inverted bottle with a screw-on salt-shaker top is the ideal waterer.

Large aviaries should be provided with a source of running water which should be 3–4 centimetres deep and controlled by a floating ballcock system at one end, or alternatively a tap which is only just on. Always provide the birds with something to stand on in the middle of the water, which will also prevent young birds drowning—this could be a stone or a brick. If running water is not provided, birds should be provided with separate bathing vessels, otherwise the drinking water will be fouled and the birds may become ill.

Feeders

There are many types of feeders, but the self-feeding system is the best. It requires little maintenance and provides the birds with fresh, clean material all the time. Big, commercial self-feeders are available. Points to watch for are that the bulk carrier is transparent and that the tray is small enough to prevent the birds perching on the edge or in the tray itself while feeding. Preferably a perch should be set up close to the feeding trough so that birds can perch there to eat, thus allowing droppings to fall to the floor of the cage rather than into the feed trough.

A water bowl for large birds needs some form of protection to prevent fouling.

Dirt baths

A container should be provided of fine, sandy, dry, loamy soil on the floor of the cage. It is a good idea to mix a small amount of insecticidal powder with the dust. This will control lice and other ectoparasites.

Location

Cages and aviaries should be in a sunny spot, particularly where they collect the winter sun. They should be in a draught-free area, sheltered by a fence or another building from the prevailing cold winds and rain. Aviaries with a shelter at one end should have the exposed end open to the direction of the sun while the three enclosed sides should be against the prevailing winds and driving rain. In the southern hemisphere the open end should face north. Finch and parrot aviaries in non-tropical areas should be partly enclosed, with an open section allowing the birds to take full advantage of the sunshine. The enclosed section provides shelter and privacy during nesting and rearing.

A self-feeding system provides fresh, clean food for birds.

The aviary should be located so that the birds are disturbed as little as possible, by noisy roads, playing children or any other noisy activity. Excessive disturbance may lead to refusal to nest, or desertion of eggs or young. Small cages containing canaries or budgerigars should never be left in the sun for long periods. If a position that affords partial shade and sunlight is not available, partially cover the cage with a cloth.

Another method of providing clean drinking water.

General care

Captive birds are subjected to an environment that is controlled by the aviarist. It is most important to provide clean food and water utensils daily. The birds' droppings should be removed from a large aviary at least once a week, and from cages or small aviaries twice weekly. This is most easily effected by having a removable tray in the bottom of the cage, or by placing several sheets of newspaper on the floor—one or two sheets and droppings can be removed at a time. Droppings should not be removed more frequently, as there is need for coprophagia (eating droppings).

Parasites

Birds are commonly affected by lice and mites which attack their legs and feathers. Several insecticides are available for painting the undersides of the perches. These insecticides are very poisonous and should be used strictly according to the instructions on the label. Painted on the undersides of the perches, the fumes rise and penetrate the birds' feathers, killing any lice.

Other effective methods of controlling vermin are to spray or paint perches and cages with kerosene or an insecticide such as Malathion. Birds should be removed from the cages or aviaries during this procedure and not returned to the cages for two or three days. The cages should be rinsed with water after the insecticide has had time to work.

Catching and handling

Remove all obstacles from the cage (perches, drinking bowls, feeding bowls, and so on).

When catching a bird inside a cage the main point to remember is that they are all very frail, especially the smaller ones. It is important that your hand closes right around the body of the bird, including the wings. Any attempt to take hold by one wing or one leg will injure the bird seriously. Move your hand slowly and deliberately towards the bird until it is very close, then seize the bird quickly, and arrange it so that the palm of your hand is over the back of the bird, with your first two fingers either side of the head and neck, and the thumb and last two fingers forming a loose cage around the body, holding all extremities (wings and legs) firmly together. This method is satisfactory for all small birds. Your index and second fingers can be used to guide the head and beak and prevent the bird from biting. The second finger can be slipped under the bird's beak to keep the head elevated, with the index finger at the back of the bird's skull. This way the bird will be prevented from pecking.

Small birds, such as budgerigars, canaries and finches, are particularly susceptible to shock and any rough handling or squeezing may cause death within seconds.

Large parrots and other birds should be approached as described above, but the neck only is grasped with one hand while your other hand seizes the body of the bird or both legs high up to prevent struggling. The bird should be quickly wrapped in a small cloth or towel to prevent wings or legs being injured.

With pigeons and similar birds, the tail, wing tips and feet may be grasped together to allow most of the body to be examined.

When handling a small bird it is important that your hand closes right around the bird's body, including the wings.

Large birds should be held with both hands.

Birds for the home aviary

Canaries

Canaries are seed-eaters and are known as hardbills, with the typical short, pointed beak of the predominantly seed-eating bird. They have four claws, the first pointing backwards, and the second, third and fourth forwards. They weigh about 16 grams and normal body temperature is 43.3°C.

Canaries can be mated at one year of age and used for breeding for two to three years. Some have been known to breed for as long as twelve years. They can live for between six and twenty years. It is very difficult to age birds once they are over twelve months of age, except by their appearance: young birds are well groomed, with feet and legs smooth, while the older birds become ragged. Leg rings give some guide to age.

A well-groomed young canary.

Sexing

At breeding time the lower portion of the abdomen and vent of the male becomes prominent and protrudes downwards. In the female the vent is swollen but is in line with the contours of the abdomen. At five weeks of age the cock may make feeble attempts to sing and his throat will begin to swell. Cocks generally sing but hens only cheep. Males have a stronger, more thickly set, masculine head. When sexing birds it is easier to compare with other birds in the cage than to make decisions on single birds.

Hybrids between canaries and finches (for example, the goldfinch–canary) are known as mules. Mules are usually infertile, particularly the male.

An older canary has more ragged feathers.

Breeding

Nests (round tins, or wooden, metal or earthenware containers) should be hung in the upper half of the cage. Nesting materials that should be placed in the cage include cow hair, meadow hay, grass, pieces of cotton-wool, felt or moss. The incubating period is thirteen to fourteen days.

When hatching commences, give egg food or proprietary nestling food three times a day. Egg food is arrowroot biscuit and hard-boiled egg yolk.

At hatching, the young are blind, and have little down. Eyes open at seven days and the nestling is completely feathered at three to four weeks of age. The young birds moult at six to eight weeks. Adult birds moult annually at the end of the breeding season. A canary under one year old that has not had an adult moult is said to be 'unflighted' and the wing feathers are paler than those of a full adult.

Feeding

In the breeding season, feed plain canary seed 14 parts, rape seed 2 parts, whole oats 2 parts, linseed ½ part, white millet 1 ½ parts. In addition, give them daily small quantities of fresh green feed such as thistle or lettuce.

While the young are being reared, continue feeding the egg food described above (a crumbled mixture of milk arrowroot biscuits and hard-boiled egg yolk); it may also be fed to breeding birds with poor mating. Grit and cuttlefish should be made available.

A pair of finches: the brightly-coloured one is the cock bird.

Finches

Finches are suitable for either cage or aviary and are, together with the budgerigar, most people's idea of the typical cage bird. Most finches are easy to manage, willing to breed, reasonably priced, dainty, colourful and ideal for the novice. Some finches are good songsters, while other types are not melodious at all.

Sexing

Finches breed easily in captivity though it is sometimes difficult to determine their sex from their colour. The zebra finch is an exception, and can be sexed by colour. The males have red bills, and chestnut flanks and cheeks. There are hundreds of different species of finches, so it is best to ask your local bird dealer to differentiate the sexes or refer to a colour plate book.

Breeding

Finches are generally easy to manage, and are very willing breeders. The breeding aviary should be protected from draughts and from frosty nights.

It is best to have an abundance of nesting sites. Most finches will use either cylinders of approximately 10 centimetres diameter (like a jam tin) or any enclosed area with an opening suitable for entry. Dry grass, hessian, straw and cotton-wool make excellent nesting materials. Leave a good supply on the bottom of the cage.

Feeding

Finches may be fed on panicum seed 15 parts, plain canary seed 3 parts, white millet 2 parts. Rolled oats can be provided for larger finches. Green feed or flowering grasses should be given daily, as well as cuttlefish bone and gritty sand. Finches also like live insect food. Nearly all finches, particularly when they are rearing young, relish white ants.

Pigeons and doves

Pigeons and doves are usually kept as show birds or for sport or racing. They have a long history of being beneficial to mankind, and have probably been domesticated for longer than any other animal.

The sport of pigeon racing grew out of the ability of pigeons to find their way home across land and water they had never seen before.

There is no real difference between pigeons and doves—the larger kinds are called pigeons and the smaller, doves. The incredible array of varieties has been produced from one common ancestor.

Pigeons tend to fly and perch up high, while doves spend more time on the ground. Aviaries, however, should be situated in a position which affords a good, high, all-round view. Sudden movements or noise should be avoided as pigeons and doves panic easily and can injure themselves.

A suitable nest for pigeons.

The type of nest a pigeon builds in its natural state.

Sexing

Males and females look very much alike. Often the only way to sex the birds is to see the males displaying. This entails the male pursuing the female, inflating his neck or chest to show off distinctive markings, and fanning the tail to reveal bold patterns.

Breeding

Once a true pair is established, nesting is assured. The nests are little more than a flimsy platform of twigs, even if better materials are provided. It is therefore best to assist by providing a piece of wire netting, or a wicker or wooden tray. Suitable trays for doves are 235 square centimetres with a lip of 3 centimetres, and for pigeons 524 square centimetres with a lip of 5 centimetres.

The majority of doves lay two white eggs that are incubated by both parents for twelve to eighteen days.

During the first few days, the sole food fed to the squabs (the young) is a nutritious curd-like substance known as pigeon's milk, which both sexes produce in the crop. The young develop rapidly and the lighter varieties can fly within two weeks.

Feeding

Most of the commoner pigeons and doves eat seed and grain. There are others that eat different types of food and some that feed exclusively on fruit, but the seed and grain eaters are most common. A normal pigeon mix available from feed suppliers is adequate.

Pigeons and doves also eat oats, wheat, corn and peas. All will eat linseed, rape and niger. Some will eat white ant larvae, wood lice, worms and cleaned maggots. All need some sort of grit.

Quail

Quail are small plump birds belonging to the pheasant family. They walk and run along the ground, rarely taking to the air. They are a great asset to many aviaries, adding interest and colour to the ground section.

Sexing

Most males have striking head and throat markings, but otherwise both sexes are coloured to blend with the grassland and undergrowth.

Breeding

Quail are prolific egg layers, but have a few problems. They are nervous, excitable birds whose actual chick production is very low. The painted quail, which is probably the commonest, regularly lays many more eggs than necessary in a random, haphazard manner. Some of these eggs, if fertile, can be incubated artificially.

Hen quail should be brought into a warmer environment during the winter. Otherwise, egg binding can easily occur. The consequences of this can be fatal, particularly as the hen will hide from view if she is outside.

For quail rearing young, the normal diet should be supplemented with eggfood, live insects and chick crumbs.

Quail add interest to the ground section of the aviary.

Feeding

Quail are seed eaters and eat the same mixtures as pigeons and doves.

Budgerigars

A great range of different colours has been produced in budgerigars by breeding in captivity. The cere, which is the rectangular, fleshy area above the upper mandible (bill), varies in colour with the bird's sex: the male's is a rich blue or flesh colour, and the female's is chocolate brown. In the very young female the cere is pale watery blue.

There are four digits, two pointing forwards and two pointing backwards, as in all members of the parrot family. Normal body temperature is 42.2°C. Adult weight is about 50 grams.

Budgerigars are bred in a wide variety of colours.

Development

The young are blind and naked when hatched. Eyes open at six days and at one month plumage is complete. Adult budgerigars moult irregularly throughout the year. However, control of light and dark and control of humidity can regulate moulting. There is no way of estimating age accurately, except by leg rings. Older birds tend to have longer upper beaks and their nails grow longer with age and become more friable. In immature birds the plumage markings are fainter, and the forehead shows faint, dark bars. Sexual maturity is reached at three to four months, but cocks should not be used for breeding under ten months, and hens under eleven months. The lifespan varies—females up to six years, males up to eight years, though some birds live to twenty years.

Budgerigars are hardy and can be kept outside all year round once they are acclimatised.

As pets they benefit from daily exercise and can be allowed to fly around the room or around the house, although care must be taken with glass windows and mirrors.

The male budgerigar has a blue cere at the top of the beak; the cere of the female is brown.

Breeding

Budgerigars will breed all year round if allowed. If possible have equal numbers of the sexes and pair them in separate cages before introducing them to the breeding aviary. Some pairs are incompatible.

Compatible birds rub their beaks and 'kiss' and the cock feeds the hen. If the hen declines the cock she pecks him and refuses to be fed by him. The nest box should be introduced some five to seven days after mating a pair. Most hens commence to lay at ten days after nest introduction. If they do not, they should be returned to the aviary and another hen substituted. Because eggs are laid every second day, the young hatch every second day. They are born bare of all feathers.

Budgerigars live in flocks naturally and hence may be kept in community cages. Breeding will take place in wooden nest boxes 15 × 15 × 23 centimetres. The entrance hole in each box should be 4 centimetres in diameter, with a perch provided in front of the entrance. Breeding boxes should be left uncleaned, as the excreta provides a good source of heat during its decomposition. Perches should be 12–17 millimetres in diameter, and the birds will also relish irregular twigs for perching.

Feeding

The cock feeds the hen while she is sitting on the nest. The young are fed by both parents by the regurgitation of partly digested seed. They leave the nest at six weeks of age and are fed for several more days by the parents. Young birds should be left with their parents for ten days, if compatible, after they have learnt to fly so that the older birds may encourage the youngsters to shell seed for themselves.

Male birds talk better than females, and it is best to remove young birds within a few days of actively leaving the nest if you wish to train them as talkers. An ideal feed for budgerigars is canary seed 7 parts, panicum 12 parts, whole oats 1 part. Green feed is essential, such as seeding grass, silver beet, carrots or apples. In addition, the daily use of a vitamin mineral drop in the water is recommended. Shell grit, cuttlebone, and iodised saltblocks are recommended additives. On leaving the nest, the young birds may be given canary seed in place of millet, as it has a higher protein content.

Other parrots

The commonest cause of illness in parrots is incorrect feeding and general management, particularly lack of exercise from too small a cage. Other factors are poor hygiene from placing perches over food and water, cluttering the cage with feeding utensils and toys, and exposure to draughts or marked fluctuation in temperature. In addition, marked variations in the length of time the bird is exposed to light and/or solitary confinement for long periods produce boredom and self-plucking of feathers. Exposure to direct sunlight for long periods without shelter, failure to remove stale food and provide plenty of water, and failure to provide green food are further causes of illness in the parrot family.

Parrots are capable of inflicting skin wounds and should be handled with gloves. When grasping the parrot always try to hold it by the neck with one hand allowing the head and beak to protrude through. The two legs and wings should be held by the other hand.

Feeding

A suitable feed for parrots is sunflower seed 5 parts, oats 3 parts, plain canary seed 1 part, panicum seed ½ part, white millet ½ part.

Parrots purchased as youngsters are often being fed from a teaspoon on a porridge-like mixture of powdered milk and cornmeal. The new owner must continue with this until the parrot is old enough to dehull its own seed.

For cockatoos an ideal feed is sunflower seed 5 parts, whole oats 3 parts, corn 1 part and wheat 1 part. Canary seed and linseed may be added if the bird enjoys them. Parrots will also eat green foods and peanuts. Smaller parrots may be fed with the mixture recommended above for budgerigars. All parrots can handle sunflower seed.

Beaks that are distorted or overgrown need to be ground back with sandpaper. Cuttlefish bone should also be supplied in the cage for the birds to do this naturally.

Parakeets are inquisitive and eat almost anything placed in their cage.

A cage that is too small is a common cause of illness in parrots.

The galah is especially suited to aviary life as it is a proven breeder in captivity. However, as it is one of the bigger members of the parrot family it requires a large aviary.

Parakeets need canary seed, millet seed and steel-cut oats in a ratio of 3 : 1 : 1 for young birds, and 1 : 2 : 1 for adults.

Grit is essential for all caged birds. Pulverised eggshell and 1 per cent iodised salt are also beneficial.

Sexing

Sexing the parrot family is very difficult and depends on the species of parrot. As there are hundreds of different species, it is impossible to describe the male and female colour differences in this book. Check with a parrot breeder, or with one of the reference books specialising in this subject.

Breeding

Breeding parrots is a specialised job. Parrots usually nest in shafts inside hollow trees. For the larger parrots these shafts are up to 2 metres deep. In captivity parrots' nesting logs should be lined with sawdust or wood shavings. Smaller parrots will use hollow logs suspended from the aviary roof or a larger version of a budgerigar nest.

Caring for the sick bird

A major problem with sick birds is that they all tend to show similar symptoms, no matter what the disease. The typical sign of a sick bird is that it is usually quiet, drowsy, rests with both feet on the perch, has its feathers ruffled and the head tucked under the wing or drawn back into the chest, with the eyes partly closed. Some may squat on the perch or floor of the cage and show excessive stretching of the wings and legs, together with shivering.

Immediately a bird is noticed to be sick, it should be isolated and placed in a warm environment, preferably 30–32°C for twenty-four hours. This warmth is easily provided by placing an electric light bulb immediately below the floor of the cage; it will provide a constant source of heat but will not illuminate the cage. The exclusion of draughts is very important.

Ruffled feathers, head drawn back into the chest, and eyes partly closed are all signs of a sick bird.

Note the droppings first. With the healthy bird these should be made up of a firm, black ring of faeces with a white soft centre of urine. In inflammatory intestinal conditions, droppings will be watery or pasty when mixed with the urine. Where there is a temperature or infectious disease, droppings are frequently yellow, and in other diseases the faeces sometimes change from yellow to green or sometimes bloody in terminal cases. Where these occur the bird should be taken to a veterinarian promptly.

Nectar- and fruit-eating birds have loose droppings normally. Lorikeets and lories, if fed fruit and green feed, may also have loose, wet droppings without their being abnormal.

Observe whether the cuttlebone is being properly used. When the bird has quietened down after being moved, check whether the plumage is normal or ruffled. Note whether the bird is bright or listless and whether there is evidence of a good appetite. Is the bird at all emaciated or weak? If you are confident in handling the bird, it should be examined for abscesses or swellings, or abnormalities of any kind. The nasal openings should be pressed gently to express discharges. If the condition is not obvious, the bird should be taken to a veterinarian.

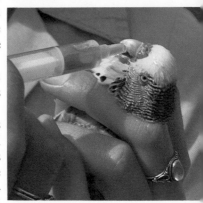

Giving fluids to a sick bird.

An injured bird needs to be handled carefully and as little as possible. Place it on a soft surface in a warm cardboard box, cover the box, and transport it as soon as possible to the surgery for the vet's examination.

Common injuries are grouped in the Common Ailments listing under INJURIES IN BIRDS.

Nursing care

Temperature is of critical importance in nursing birds. Sick birds should be excluded from draughts and should be kept in a warm cage. Cover the cage with two or three layers of cloth on three sides and heat it by placing a light

Correct environmental temperature is of critical importance in treating sick birds.

bulb beneath the cage. Have a thermometer near the bird's perch to check that the environmental temperature is kept constant at 30–32°C; keep the temperature high for one to two weeks or as long as the bird is ill. Birds under heated conditions such as this will drink more water.

Provision of heat for sick birds is of the utmost importance, particularly before they are handled or dosed. Before moving the bird to a colder environment, acclimatise it by reducing the cage temperature gradually over a period of at least six hours.

A good general antibiotic mix is 1 : 1 sulphadimidine (33.3 per cent sulphamethazine, I.C.I.) to chloramphenicol oral suspension, give two drops by mouth every four hours for seven to fourteen days or as needed. Ampicillin orally is also very useful.

Supportive therapy is important in nursing the sick bird. Fluids should be given orally. Depending on the bird's size, give 1–4 millilitres of a glucose-in-water mixture (flat lemonade is ideal) five times daily. In addition give 2–3 drops of a vitamin/mineral tonic once daily.

Common ailments

Abscesses

Abscesses are common in budgerigars and are usually encapsulated and can be opened surgically. An alternative treatment is to lance the abscess and irrigate it with a 50 per cent peroxide solution in water, three times daily for three days. Any debris in the abscess should be evacuated by massaging the area. (See also BUMBLEFOOT.)

Alopecia (Loss of plumage)

Loss of feathers, including self-plucking, is frequently incurable and very annoying. The causes are varied and can include deficient or unbalanced diet, boredom, external parasites, exhaustion, nervousness and hormone imbalance. Some hormone imbalances are a consequence of the birds being kept in areas artificially lit, resulting in abnormal day : night ratios. The condition can affect all bird species but caged birds of the parrot family are most commonly affected. Baldness occurs on the head and neck, and usually there is no inflammation.

A white sulphur-crested cockatoo with early feather plucking.

Feather plucking at an advanced stage.

It is important that the veterinarian searches for ectoparasites. In canaries, feather pecking of a cannibalistic nature may be caused by overcrowding, unhygienic conditions and sometimes parasitism. Sometimes parents may peck the nestlings. Mature canaries a month or so old may peck one another quite seriously. In these cases isolate the birds, treat the condition causing the problem (for example, worms) and remove all evidence of blood. Newly

introduced and sick birds are often the subject of attack. Where a nutritional origin is suspected, diets should be varied and supplemented with green, fresh seeding grasses and insects. Vitamins can be administered in the drinking water or in the form of yeast.

Self-inflicted feather plucking is characteristic of the parrot family. This is usually the result of boredom or dietary deficiency, viruses, rarely parasites, occasionally the preen gland, but probably most often psychotic disturbances. These conditions are rarely seen in free-ranging native birds. It should be remembered that most members of the parrot family are unfortunately kept in particularly small cages when compared to the size of the bird. Boredom can be relieved by allowing the parrot its freedom in the yard after wing clipping, or by use of a leg chain and wire runner—though there are risks that the latter device may break the bird's leg. Alternatively place the parrot out among other native birds in the garden, use a bigger aviary, or place some green shrubbery in the cage for the bird to chew on. In obstinate cases where the cause is diagnosed definitely as boredom or neurosis, the bird may need to be released, but always make sure that it can be self-supporting. Nervous exhaustion, another cause of self-plucking, may be caused by dogs, active children, mice, rats or other sources.

Feather rot caused by mites which can live in crevices of the cages and fittings.

External parasites should be eliminated as a cause (see PARASITES). Various injections can be given by the veterinarian for some conditions. The red mite common in poultry yards may trouble such caged birds as budgerigars, canaries and parrots. These mites live in crevices of the cages and fittings, which should be treated with Malathion powder or solution or with other insecticides.

Birds may need to be tranquillised during and after treatment to stop the self-mutilation.

Feather loss can also occur in beak rot (see BEAK DEFORMITIES).

Apoplexy (Coma)

This occurs fairly commonly amongst canaries and other seed-eating perch-sitting birds. Cerebral haemorrhage, possibly due to trauma or shock, is not unusual. If the bird does not die at once, paralysis and collapse may result. Apoplexy should be differentiated from the fainting fits suffered by some older canaries. The treatment for apoplexy is to place the bird in a quiet, dark box and leave it undisturbed.

Reduce the likelihood of head-on collisions by removing obstructions that tempt birds to fly into them, such as clear glass and mirrors.

Arthritis

See LEG DISORDERS.

Aspergillosis

This is one of the fungal diseases that are reasonably common in parrots, including (to a lesser extent) budgerigars. Affected birds show breathlessness, but very little else. Main lesions are in the air-sacs and the trachea. Treatment is 120–300 milligrams of potassium iodide dissolved in 60 millilitres of drinking water. A very successful therapy is to nebulise Amphoteracin B and use as an inhalant.

Asthma

See RESPIRATORY DISORDERS.

Beak deformities

Overgrown beaks

Budgies are frequently presented with overgrown top beaks to be trimmed. The beak can be trimmed with a pair of scissors or filed back with an emery board. It should be trimmed or filed back so that the upper mandible (the top beak) overlaps the lower mandible by 3 millimetres. There are several common causes for overgrown beaks:

Overgrown beak: the top beak should only overlap by 3 millimetres.

Mite infestation of the beak and surrounding tissues.

Mite infestation of the beak The burrows of the mite (*Cnemidocoptes* sp.) are visible with the naked eye. There are many topical treatments for the mite, such as paraffin and Dettol. Ivermectin orally or on the skin gives the best result. Sometimes long treatments are necessary to eradicate the mites. Regular trimming of the beak is necessary so that the bird can eat. (See also PARASITES.)

Infection Various infections of the air passages and the cere at the base of the beak result in inflammation which stimulates beak growth. There is usually either staining of the tiny feathers above the nostrils or a history of sneezing and respiratory infection.

Trauma Crash landings or flying into windows, mirrors or other obstacles within the cage can cause beak damage.

Beak rot/Beak split syndrome

Beak rot/beak split syndrome of parrots and cockatoos is usually accompanied by a plumage disorder. The splitting leads to underlying infection and impaction of food particles and eventual exposure of the bone of the mandible. Infection of the bone, osteomyelitis, debility and inability to eat are the end results. The disease in Australian cockatoos and other parrots is manifested by progressive deformity of the beak and/or progressive feather pathology. The commonly affected birds are the sulphur-crested cockatoo, galah, Major Mitchell cockatoo, little corella, quarion (or cockateil), especially the red mutation, the African peach-face parrot, the Australian pale-headed eastern rosella, the Australian smutty rosella and the Indian ring neck, and the blue masked lovebird mutant. There are many similarities between this disease and that commonly called French moult in budgerigars (see MOULT). Usually the sufferer shows diagnostic signs of the disease by or at the time of its first moult. Both beak and feathers become affected as the disease progresses but either may be deformed in early cases. The disease is thought to be caused by a virus, and may take three forms:

Mortality of unhatched chicks.

Gastroenteritis, causing vomiting, diarrhoea, and death.

Feather loss syndrome: Note stretch lines in primary feathers.

Combined beak and feather disease syndrome In this syndrome the disease is characterised by progressive changes in the beak. In the sulphur-crested cockatoo it shows as a dark, almost shiny beak, which becomes overgrown, develops a line across it, breaks off short, may regrow several times, but eventually becomes underrun with the typical rot at the core of the beak. The first feathers to be affected are the down feathers located over the tops of the legs, which fail to puff out. Patches of infected feathers extend backwards and across over the rump; at the same time stretch lines are evident on some of the primary or flight feathers and/or tail feathers, as well as on some of the comb feathers. Feathers that shed or fall out are progressively replaced by malformed feathers which often remain encased (in part, or totally) in their sheath. They often have bloodstains in the centre of the quill and often a deformed pointed quill. Most suf-

Beak and feather disease syndrome: Note *overgrown beak before it drops off.*

Bumblefoot: Note *the abscess (lump) at the centre of the foot.*

Mite infestation of the beak (Cnemidocoptes *sp.).*

ferers lose their tail and primary flight feathers before they lose their body feathers. Very few birds recover from the disease, the great majority of birds progressing to a bald stage—with some dying because they are unable to eat due to the beak deformity. Seek veterinary advice—but the condition is usually fatal.

Beak fractures are discussed in INJURIES IN BIRDS.

Blood poisoning

See SEPTICAEMIA.

Breathlessness

This is a common sign of sick birds and can be due to aspergillosis (a fungal infection), canary pox, asthma, infectious bronchitis, emphysema or a thyroid condition. For treatment see the various conditions, including RESPIRATORY DISORDERS.

Bronchitis

This is an inflammatory condition of the lungs, usually caused by a virus. The bird looks puffed up and listless, shivers and occasionally sneezes. An early symptom is a slight watery discharge from the nose. Droppings are often white and watery. Keep the bird in a constant temperature of 30°C. Administer oral antibiotics prescribed by the vet.

Bumblefoot

Bumblefoot is caused by a localised abscess of the ball (or soft pad) of the foot, which produces lameness. The main causes are dirty cages, rough perches, toe-nail trauma through overgrowth, and toe biting by other birds. Cut nails regularly and prevent other birds biting by installing

double wire between cages. Treatment is to surgically incise the abscess parallel to the floor of the foot, clean out the pus, cleanse with hot antiseptic bathing, and pack with antibiotic or antiseptic ointment.

Canary pox on the head.

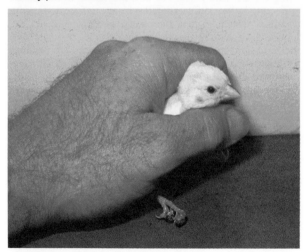

Canary pox: Note *red lump on the toe.*

Canary pox

Canary pox is a viral disease. In acute cases in canaries it causes gasping, followed by death. In sub-acute cases pox lesions (warts) develop on various parts of the unfeathered body, such as the comb, legs, feet and eyes. Inflammation of the eyelids, swelling of the margins of the eyes and closure of the eyes is common. Pussy sores develop at the corners of the mouth. Scratching and rubbing the eyes and beak on the perch or bars of the cage produce typical damage. In the canker form, yellowish plaque-lesions appear in the mouth. There is no treatment, although local lesions may be treated with antibiotic/cortisone creams. Warts usually disappear in 6–8 weeks if the bird survives.

Cancer
See NEOPLASMS.

Candidiasis (Moniliasis or 'thrush')
Birds affected by candidiasis—a fungal disease—are sick, show unsatisfactory growth, rough feathering, listlessness and could eventually die. On post mortem examination, the crop has a thin layer of whitish mucous loosely attached. Treatment involves vitamin B complex drops and a fungicide called nystatin.

Cataracts
See EYE DISORDERS.

Central nervous system disorders
Signs of nervous disease include circling and rolling, incoordination, loss of balance, convulsions, fits and paralysis of the wings and legs. Paralysis is common in budgerigars and is caused by a wide range of conditions, some of them affecting the central nervous system. Other causes include in the female a ruptured oviduct and consequent damage when the bird strains to lay an egg. In some cases budgerigars may be affected with a 'creeping paralysis', so-called because one leg becomes paralysed and then the other. This appears to be a genetically inherited defect of the central nervous system. In some cases tumour formation, particularly on the kidney, may be responsible. Curled toe paralysis may respond to a single injection of 25 milligrams of riboflavin. Concussion can be a cause of nervous symptoms. Concussion can be due to disturbances at night resulting in a sudden fright, or other factors causing birds to fly suddenly from their perches and collide with the walls of their cages. Concussion is not infrequent when a bird flies into a clear glass window which it did not see.

Cere abnormalities
Changes in the colour of the cere—apart from the normal sex reaction—occur in budgerigars, with progressive thickening and darkening of the cere. It may occur in both sexes and must be differentiated from infestation with cnemidocoptes (see BEAK DEFORMITIES). In cock birds, debility and cancerous growths of the testicles may produce the condition; in hens, cancer of the ovaries may produce a similar condition. Attention should be given to management and diet, but apart from this treatment is not satisfactory. Brownish, cheesy material may appear on the cere; it may be removed but it usually returns, because the bird usually has a respiratory infection.

Chills
See PNEUMONIA.

Claw overgrowth
Overgrown claws are due to lack of sufficient wear of the claws. It is common in the parrot family, especially in caged budgerigars. The claws become overgrown, curled and twisted and may become caught in the bars of the cage, leading to fractures. Treatment is to trim the nail with cutters, but avoid injuring blood vessels. Provide natural perches of varying diameters.

Claw-slipped
This condition (also known as slipped toe, or stiff claw) appears most often in the parrot family although it is also seen in other birds. Young budgerigars are most commonly affected. There is a curling of the digits in a clenched pos-

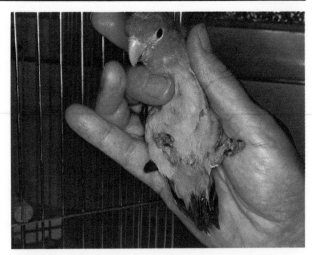
Curled claws may be due to a vitamin B complex deficiency.

When the claws are overgrown they should be carefully cut back to the normal shape.

ition which prevents perching. One or both feet may be affected. The disease may be due to a vitamin B complex deficiency, which can be rectified by providing yeast. The condition has also been reported in birds suffering from threadworm (capillariasis) infection of the intestine (see PARASITES).

Coccidiosis
This is an internal parasite which attacks the lining of the intestine. Birds have the typical sick look about them, with fluffed-up feathers, and they often rest on the bottom of the cage. Bloodstained droppings and diarrhoea may be closely followed by death in severe cases where conditions are damp, dirty and overcrowded. Treatment is ten drops of 16 per cent solution of sulphadimidine in 30 millilitres of drinking water. Amprolium in the drinking water is also very effective.

Conjunctivitis
See EYE DISORDERS.

Constipation
Constipation occurs in all birds from time to time, more particularly the parrot family, and follows faulty diet. The usual signs are straining, scanty and hard droppings, and general lethargy and sickness. Prevent by providing supplementary vitamin B-complex and fresh green feed. When necessary administer oil (liquid paraffin), at the rate of two drops three times daily for a large parrot. Be careful not to overadminister, or it may lead to feather clogging and feather picking. (See also EGG BINDING.)

Convulsions

Convulsions can be caused by viruses, bacteria and cancerous growths—their effects on the nervous system can result in depression, tail flicking, inability to fly, ataxia, paralysis, chorea, and convulsions. In addition, heart diseases, heart failure and poisoning cause convulsions.

The bird should be kept in a subdued light. Widespectrum antibiotics should be given, together with prednisolone (0.2 milligrams) twice daily for three days.

Coprophagia

The eating of faeces. A normal requirement among some birds.

Cramps (Curled-toe paralysis)

This condition responds to B-group vitamins. Add yeast to diet, or for quick results take the bird to a vet for an injection. (See also CLAW-SLIPPED.)

Crop impaction (Crop binding)

Crop impaction is seen most frequently in the parrot family, and particularly among debilitated birds. It is common in young cock budgerigars. Distension of the crop is caused by dough-like, fermented contents.

Failure to dehusk seed is a common cause. Parent birds usually dehusk seed for their young and when the young start to feed themselves they may not always do it. The condition is seen as a swelling of the crop, with severe vomiting. In bad cases the crop will need to be opened surgically for removal of the debris. Pigeons producing crop milk, however, cannot be operated on because of the vascularity of the crop at this time.

Sometimes, while the bird is under general anaesthetic, the crop may be massaged and the impaction relieved. Particular attention should be paid to a bird that has already suffered crop impaction, as it tends to recur if the bird's general condition remains poor. All that can be done to prevent crop impaction is to keep birds in good health, feed them properly and make sure adequate grit is available.

Crop necrosis

Crop necrosis is a digestive disease characterised by regurgitation of mucoid fluid, diarrhoea and general malaise. The majority of cases die within a few days but sometimes death is quite sudden and unexpected. Treatment is with broad-spectrum antibiotics.

A canary with feather cyst.

Cystic conditions

Feather cysts are quite common in canaries and can be single or multiple. The cysts, which involve feather follicles, occur mainly on the wings, back, breast and tail, and develop mainly during the bird's first or second moults. The cysts usually contain yellow, granular, cheese-like material. They should not be confused with cancerous conditions or skin abscesses. Their treatment is complete surgical excision under general anaesthetic, rather than mere lancing.

Deficiency diseases in birds

Because so little is known of the precise dietary requirements of many caged birds, it is likely that many disease conditions are due to deficiencies. For example, such conditions as French moult and other plumage disorders, gout, kidney disease, nervous conditions, poor hatchability, reduced fertility, failure to thrive and obesity are all influenced by diet.

Mixed vitamin supplements and increased fruit, green stuff and water intake have a beneficial effect in many conditions in canaries and budgerigars. In many illnesses the supply of live termites (white ants) can provide essential nutrients.

Diarrhoea

Normal droppings in the bird are black with a white centre. Diarrhoea is usually evidenced by profuse, greenish droppings. The birds are very thirsty, there may be straining and eversion of the cloaca, and a craving for grit. Diarrhoea can be caused by: faulty feeding; several organisms such as E. Coli, Salmonella, psittacosis and chlamydiosis; coccidiosis; access to poisonous garden plants such as violets, jonquils and gladioli. Sometimes stale wilted green stuff, or any other dirty food may induce intestinal inflammation and result in diarrhoea. The bird quickly goes into shock, becomes depressed, loses its appetite, and stands about in a typical sick bird attitude with ruffled feathers. Samples of the droppings should be examined by a veterinarian and suitable medication prescribed as quickly as possible. Supportive therapy includes providing warmth, electrolytes in the water and intestinal antibiotics.

Suggested treatment is 1 gram Terramycin soluble powder per litre of drinking water for five days. Nectar-eating birds can be fed on 175 grams honey, 175 grams Complan and 175 grams of bread per litre of water. The bird should be force fed initially and treatment continued for five days. Isolate the bird and keep it warm and quiet.

A second treatment regime is a teaspoon of Spectramycin soluble powder (55 grams oxytetracycline per kilogram) per 250 millilitres of water, plus 2–3 drops Lomotil syrup twice daily. Initially injections are needed. With any of these treatments it is important to supply grit. (See also TRICHOMONAS.)

Egg binding

Egg binding is common in caged birds, particularly in canaries and pigeons. It leads to excessive straining and a prolapse may occur. In canaries it occurs at the start of the breeding season and if not corrected may be quickly fatal. It often occurs in cold weather and in unhealthy or immature birds, who will be found fluffed up in the corner of the cage. Treatment is to place the bird in a warm cage at 26–32°C (80–90°F). This alone may relieve the spasm of the oviduct. Lubricate the egg and vent area with some warm paraffin oil. If this fails, pierce the egg with a needle, remove the contents and then the shell. An owner with confidence can perform this procedure.

Eye disorders

Irritation, inflammation and slight closing of the eye can be caused by the pox virus. Cataracts, which are often seen, may be due to inbreeding. Conjunctivitis caused by chlamydiosis is commonly seen in parakeets—symptoms are excessive drinking and partial closing of the eyes with mucous discharges. It is successfully treated with antibiotic eyedrops.

Faeces eating

See COPROPHAGIA.

Inflammation and closing of the eye; in this case caused by Periorbital granuloma cellulitis.

Fainting
See APOPLEXY, HEART DISEASE, CONVULSIONS.

Fatness
See OBESITY.

Feather loss
See ALOPECIA.

Feather picking
See ALOPECIA.

Feather wounds
See INJURIES IN BIRDS.

Feet disorders
See BUMBLEFOOT, CLAW-SLIPPED, CLAW OVERGROWTH, INJURIES IN BIRDS.

Fractures
A fracture in a bird is a serious problem, and not one for home remedies. Fractures of the major bones in large birds can be satisfactorily repaired by inserting a pin surgically. Smaller bones, and the legs of smaller birds, can be splinted while the bird is under a general anaesthetic with quite satisfactory results, using splints made of 12 millimetre strips of adhesive tape and fine plastic tubing. It is important that the bird be encouraged to perch, with the limb extending behind and resting on top of the perch.

Fractures of the toes are not uncommon but they invariably heal well when splinted by adhesive tape to the adjacent toe.

Fractured wings are very common. The typical sign is a drooped wing. To facilitate healing, the wing should be lifted back to its normal position. In large birds pinning can be done surgically and is one of the better remedies. In birds weighing less than 50 grams surgery is generally unwarranted, and the fracture can often be treated by manipulation of the conscious or sedated sufferer and the wing strapped in its normal position against the body which serves as a splint. Adhesive tape 12 millimetres wide is used to encircle both wings just behind the wing butt and connected to another strip holding the primary flight feathers together and to the tail base by a strip along the back of the bird. Free leg movement is essential. It takes time for the bird to learn to balance without the use of its wings. Splinting remains for twenty-one days. All primary and secondary flight feathers on the affected wing are cut off to remove any drag on the wingtip. In some cases wings may have to be amputated, but birds in captivity cope very well.

French moult
See MOULT.

Gangrene
Gangrene is sometimes reported among canaries. The feet become cold, black in colour, and slough off. The cause is unknown—but it may be due to bacteria ergot. The area should be treated with local applications of tincture of chloramphenicol daily. Cleanse and disinfect the cage and destroy and replace the perches. The condition can be confused with canary pox or simple inflammatory conditions.

Gastroenteritis
See DIARRHOEA.

Gout
Gout is usually a sequel to a kidney complaint (see NEPHRITIS). A bird with gout may be restless and may lift and lower the feet alternately. Joint lesions take the form of nodules on the feet and legs (budgerigars), and sometimes on the wing joints. The only treatment that can be suggested is manipulation of the joint while the bird is under general anaesthesia, the provision of narrow-diameter perches and control of any kidney disease.

Gout is a complex problem. Nutritional deficiencies of riboflavin, vitamin E and manganese may all play a part. A detailed examination of all factors such as husbandry, nutrition and evidence of disease needs to be made before specific treatment can be carried out. A change in diet to a mixed vitamin supplement, reduced seed intake, and an increased fruit, green and water intake are general recommendations in budgerigars and canaries where gout is occurring. The condition is usually progressive.

Heart disease
Heart disease is common in parrots. The signs are fainting fits, leading to collapse, followed (in older birds) by recovery. Older birds tend to recover because they have better compensatory ability than younger birds. The fainting fits increase in frequency and eventually result in heart failure, usually due to pericarditis.

In canaries aged seven years and older fainting fits and heart failure are common. The cause is usually a fibrinous pericarditis or gout. Signs are sudden fluttering about the cage followed by partial collapse with the wings held away from the body and weakness of the legs. Death may ensue, or the bird may recover after a few hours. Keep the bird quiet and warm, lower the perches and remove obstacles on which the bird may injure itself. Treatment is glucose at the rate of 30 grams per litre of drinking water and Nikethamide by injection 0.25 millilitres. A minute amount of strychnine may be given in drinking water. No alcohol should be given.

Heatstroke
Heatstroke can occur in any caged bird. If the cage is placed in direct sunlight without shelter, the bird becomes distressed, suffers prostration and eventually death from heart failure and shock. The bird suffering from heatstroke should be removed to a cool, shaded area or placed in a refrigerator for a minute to get rapid, dry cooling. Take care not to overdo this—some may recommend three minutes but one minute is safer. Afterwards place the bird in a cool, dark room. Taking the bird to the vet will only cause increased stress, so it is advisable to leave the bird quiet.

Hernia
Hernia is sometimes seen in caged birds but most often in budgerigars. It is a fluctuating swelling beneath the skin of the abdomen. The only method of repair is by anaesthesia and surgery. It may be confused with a tumour. The condition is most likely due to injury.

Impaction of the crop
See CROP IMPACTION.

Injuries in birds
Following injury to a captive bird or on capturing an injured bird, handle it as little as possible. Place the bird in a soft cardboard box and keep it dark (excepting larger parrots, which do not go into shock so easily).

While maintaining a warm environment for the bird,

take it as rapidly as possible to the vet's surgery.

External injuries

Flight and tail feathers   Broken or damaged primary and secondary tail and flight feathers are removed by traction. Regrowth time varies from eight weeks to four months depending on the species. Self-mutilation of feather wounds can be limited by fitting an Elizabethan collar or by releasing the bird into a very large aviary. Sometimes reduction of light intensity and improved husbandry eliminates the problem. An injured feather, though often difficult to locate, is best removed and the area cauterised with ferric chloride solution to stem the bleeding.

Puncture wounds and lacerations to the skin from the environment or other birds are common. Large wounds can be sutured and/or an Elizabethan collar used to prevent pecking at the wound.

(See also ABSCESSES.)

An Elizabethan Collar prevents self-mutilation of feather wounds.

Fractures of the beak   A common injury. In large species (the parrot particularly) the beak may be repaired by threading stainless steel wire through holes drilled in it. In small species the use of 'Super-glue' is sometimes effective. Fibreglass has also been used. All these operations require that the bird be anaesthetised first.

Foot conditions   Bumblefoot, previously discussed, is a major problem of the foot. Excess toe-nail growth and consequent snagging or toe biting by other birds are frequent. Often a nail strip occurs, but regrowth of the nail over the undamaged stump is rapid. If osteomyelitis (inflammation of the bone) sets in, antibiotics are required.

Soft tissue injuries

Leg rings   Most budgerigars and canaries bred for exhibition are fitted with closed aluminium rings on their legs, but the incidence of problems associated with these is low. If the ring is too tight the leg may be fractured and/or the blood supply to the foot restricted. The ring often becomes restrictive if there is swelling of the leg because of canary pox or cnemidocoptes mite infestation. Removal of the ring should be undertaken with extreme care and only while the bird is anaesthetised, as it is very easy to fracture a leg. As the ring is usually made of soft aluminium, it may be cut off with a pair of fine scissors, ideally by inserting one blade under the ring and cutting. If access by this technique is impossible, then a fine pair of tin snips is applied above and below the ring which is cut in two positions. The traumatised tissues of the leg are treated with local preparations and the bird is placed on antibiotics.

Emphysema   Emphysema is an accumulation of air under the skin. It can be caused by a penetrating wound that punctures the skin and creates a 'bellows' effect in the

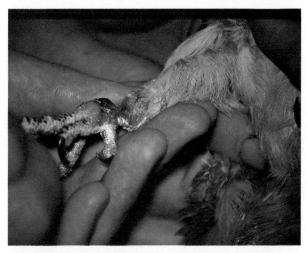

A leg ring which has restricted circulation has caused serious injury to this bird.

surrounding muscle tissue; air is 'pumped' in through the wound. Another cause is the rupture of an air sac which results in a massive accumulation of air in the head and neck region. Veterinarian treatment is required.

Crop fistula   Commonly encountered in large parrots and resulting from internal trauma or ulceration. In racing pigeons, injuries result from external trauma from trees, power lines and birds of prey. The opening usually comes from the crop to the outside skin. Treatment is surgical.

(See also ABSCESSES and BUMBLEFOOT.)

Internal trauma

Internal trauma results from eating a foreign body or from the migration of a sharp object (such as a needle or a piece of wire) through any part of the upper intestinal tract. Sometimes X-rays will reveal the foreign body. Part of it may be visible externally. Surgery can be done under anaesthetic to remove the problem.

Gunshot wounds

Gunshot wounds are common in racing pigeons particularly and produce a variety of lesions. Removal of pellets is difficult and often unnecessary unless they are affecting the bird's bones.

Prolapse

Collapse of the walls of the oviduct, and subsequent emergence of the tissue through the vent, may occur after egg-laying in immature or geriatric females. If the prolapse is attended to quickly, lubrication or gentle restoration using a blunt instrument is all that will be needed. Prolapse of a longer duration is more difficult to reduce, but patience and gentle pressure with thorough lubrication will restore the organ to its normal position. A purse-string suture around the vent for the next seven to ten days will prevent a recurrence. Laying birds should be checked daily. Antibiotic therapy is necessary.

(See also FRACTURES.)

Kidney disease

See NEPHRITIS.

Leg disorders

Swollen knees in lorikeets and budgerigars may be due to infectious arthritis or gout. Infectious arthritis can be treated with a mixture of 1 : 1 sulphadimidine and chloramphenicol palmitate suspension. Give two drops by mouth every four hours for seven to fourteen days. Nodules on the legs and feet may be the result of gout. If the swelling is due to canary pox, the disease can be identified by the typical pox lesions (warts) on the skin of the body and on the feet and legs, and the usual cycle of the warts (they will disappear in about six weeks).

(See also BUMBLEFOOT.)

Lice
See PARASITES.

Light birds
Going 'light' is a symptom, not a disease, and is common to many diseases. The bird sits listlessly with its feathers fluffed, and it loses weight as it picks disinterestedly at its food. It flies sluggishly and with increasing difficulty as breast and pectoral muscles waste away almost to nothing. Birds affected by this condition should be taken to a veterinary surgeon.

Loss of voice
Invariably there is some underlying problem with the bird. Observe it carefully to detect clinical signs of illness. See also MOULT.

Moult
Moulting varies in timing, but usually occurs towards the end of summer. Canaries moult more fully than budgerigars. Parrots moult more slowly than canaries and start earlier.

Canaries may lose their song, and there is reduced activity during the moult. Vitamins, fresh greens, fruit and canary seed—so-called moulting foods—should be supplied during the moult. When moulting is incomplete and the remaining feathers are dull, the bird may be treated by ultraviolet irradiation. The lamp should be positioned 1 metre from the cage for half a minute on the first day, one minute on the second day, and thereafter lengthening the time each day by half a minute until by the thirtieth day the bird is receiving a dose for fifteen minutes. Moulting will be erratic when the bird's diet is unsatisfactory. Some birds benefit from small pieces of raw meat, some benefit from soft corn meal mush seasoned with salt and pepper. Other diets that promote healthy moulting include slices of wholemeal bread soaked in warm milk and honey, sweet apple, fresh corn on the cob and a boiled egg occasionally.

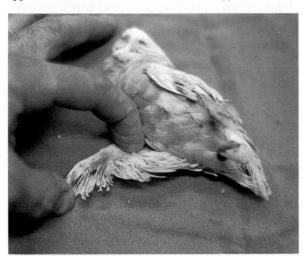

French moult 'runner'.

French moult
French moult is a condition of young budgerigars and some other parakeets. It is a condition of faulty plumage occurring in the nest or during the fledging stage, and is thought to be a deficiency disease induced by continuous breeding. It is associated with a deficiency of protein secreted by the female. Nestlings have excessive feather growth but are subnormal in size. Continuous moulting affecting the wing or tail feathers can give rise to the so-called 'runners' or 'crawlers'. The condition should be differentiated from parasitic disease or self-plucking. To prevent the birth of young that will continue the disorder, breeding adults should be rested from breeding for six months. Control apart from this is dietary. Some success has resulted from using high levels of vitamin E (80 i.u. per kilogram of foodstuff). Molasses, seaweed and B-group vitamins mixed in the drinking water are also helpful. The best response is to antibiotic therapy during incubation and rearing.

Soft moult
Soft moult is the continual moulting of a few feathers. This condition occurs in budgerigars and canaries where they are kept in cages under artificial light, such as the living room of an ordinary household. It is commonest in canaries under such conditions. The affected birds have a dishevelled appearance as they continually shed their feathers and produce new growth. The birds become debilitated and may die. Treatment includes varying the diet, providing constant temperature, and exposure to normal hours of daylight. It can take up to six months for the condition to be cured.

Muscle wasting
Muscle wasting is a sign of serious illness in the bird, and particularly of cancerous growths (see NEOPLASMS).

Neoplasms
Cage birds as they age become susceptible to a wide range of benign and malignant tumours. The incidence of cancers is very high in budgerigars. Treatment is seldom possible, apart from surgical removal of subcutaneous neoplasms. Neoplasms may also occur in the kidneys or in the pituitary

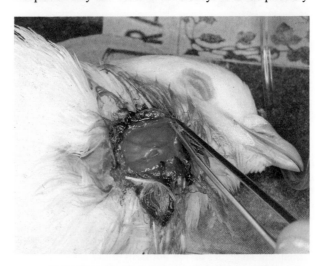

A crop fistula extending from crop to outside skin is shown on an anaesthetised bird.

Crop fistula — post-operative.

gland, and cause a quarter of all deaths. Cancerous growths lead to a variety of symptoms but externally all produce wasting and death.

(See also CYSTIC CONDITIONS.)

Galah with tumour.

Nephritis (Kidney disease)

Birds are commonly affected with nephritis due to the production of uric acid crystals which get caught in the tubules of the kidney. Sometimes there is associated gout. Symptoms are depression, thirst and watery diarrhoea which may be whitish with urates.

Swelling of the limbs can occur in canaries. The condition is commonly caused by a virus. Treatment is to use antibiotics such as Amoxil or Clavulox and check on the dietary protein. The surrounding temperature should be maintained at 24–26°C. If the canary becomes emaciated, increase the ratio of canary seed to millet seed from 1 : 2 to 3 : 1. If its weight does not increase, consult your veterinary surgeon for antibiotic therapy.

Obesity

Obesity is a serious problem, as it affects the liver, heart, lungs and kidneys, resulting in respiratory disturbance, lethargy, sometimes abdominal rupture, reproductive disorders and collapse if the bird is excited. Flight may be impossible and walking may be an effort. It occurs in birds between fifteen months and six years of age. Control is by strict dieting on a high-protein seed ration, giving only one level teaspoonful two or three times a day for about ten days.

Oil removal from marine birds

An oiled bird should be sprinkled with dry cornflour, which should be dusted off once it has absorbed oil. Repeat the dusting with fresh cornflour until the bird's plumage is normal. Allow the marine bird a test swim in a small tub before releasing to the wild. Birds should not be degreased with a detergent-type product as this also removes natural plumage oils which keep the bird buoyant while swimming.

Ornithosis (Psittacosis or Parrot's disease or Parrot fever)

This condition affects birds of the parrot family, budgerigars, canaries and other species of wild birds and pigeons. It is a danger to human beings, as it may produce respiratory symptoms that vary from mild to severe, sometimes total bronchopneumonia. The disease is readily transferred from birds to humans by inhalation, and kissing pet birds is for this reason extremely dangerous.

Symptoms in birds vary a lot and are not specific. Laboured breathing is the commonest symptom. Birds go off their food, show sleepiness, roughing of the feathers, greenish diarrhoea, breathlessness, discharge from the nose and eyes, loss of weight, drooping of the wings, general apathy and attacks of shivering. Treatment includes antibiotic therapy, but serious thought should be given to destroying the bird because of the danger to human health.

Osteomalacia

Budgerigars, parrots and cockatoos may suffer from osteomalacia, a gradual softening of the bones. The condition is dietetic in origin, being caused by a deficiency or imbalance of calcium and phosphorus and a deficiency of vitamin D. The bones become weak and may fracture. The easiest treatment is to feed with a commercial brand of bird seed. Seek professional advice regarding adequate and balanced calcium and phosphorus in the diet.

This condition is becoming more apparent among native birds fed by the public on bread and honey. If this diet accounts for a large proportion of a bird's total diet it will eventually suffer from osteomalacia. Bread is very poor in calcium and very high in phosphorus.

Paralysis

See CONVULSIONS, CLAW-SLIPPED, HEART DISEASE.

Parasites, external

Red mite

Red mites live in dirty cages in cracks and crevices and come out at night to suck blood from the bird. They may be discovered by placing a white bed sheet over the cage and observing the parasites on it next morning. Nesting

Mite infestation of a budgerigar's beak.

birds, particularly canaries, may be forced to leave their eggs. The blood-sucking mites bring weakness, anaemia and even death to the birds.

The cage should be scrubbed with a 1 per cent solution of hot caustic soda, 45 millilitres per 4.5 litres, followed by dusting with 4 per cent Malathion dust. The bird should of course be housed elsewhere during and for three days after the treatment. Be very careful not to cause poisoning with the caustic soda or do yourself an injury during use. Rinse the cage with water before any birds enter it. Install new perches painted with Malathion solution on the undersides. Mites are not a problem if there is good cage sanitation.

Scaly leg/scabies of the beak

These conditions are caused by the cnemidocoptes mite. The mites burrow under the scales of the legs, cause inflammation and a discharge which dries to produce a rough, raised, powdery appearance. Scabs are present on

Feather loss due to feather quill mite.

the feet. Lameness may result. The best treatment is Ivermectin orally or placed on the skin. A pest strip 0.5m from the cage is useful.

Lice
Lice infestation in caged birds spreads rapidly. The lice cause intense irritation, with the bird scratching and shedding feathers. Skin lesions (scabs) appear. Lice are yellowish–grey and can be observed with the naked eye, as they are about 2.5 millimetres long. They can be seen only in good light when the bird is examined carefully and the feathers ruffled backwards to expose them. Affected birds should be treated by dusting with Pyrethrin or Carbaryl powder.

Feather quill mite
Feather quill mites attack canaries. Infestation is indicated by skin irritation which induces self-pecking, moulting and loss of feathers in the back, the tail and the wings. The mite can be identified in the quills of the undeveloped feathers only. Treatment is as for lice infestation.

Parasites, internal
Roundworm
At times roundworms become a serious problem and cause loss of condition, diarrhoea and enteritis, particularly in parrots. Emaciation, weakness and anaemia occur in severe infestations. Use piperazine preparations at manufacturer's directions. An ideal alternative treatment is Nilverm (I.C.I.); levamisole is the active ingredient (20 per cent w/v) and is administered neat or preferably diluted to the beak of a six-hour-starved bird using a small disposable syringe. The dose is 0.025 to 0.5 millilitres per 120 grams of the bird's body-weight. (A healthy adult budgerigar weighs only 40–50 grams.) At this dose rate there is 100 per cent kill of roundworms, including immature and mature capillary worms as well.

Even if the correct level of dosage is calculated and administered, the occasional parrot is knocked out for an hour or so and many may vomit. Regurgitation of the medicine is a problem with parrot species of the *Polytelis* family (such as the rose-throated parrot, superb parrot, regent parrot) but not with other birds encountered. Panacur is another medication which is now being used with considerable success.

Threadworm (Capillariasis)
In advanced cases of infestation birds have a white diarrhoea, dehydration, wasting of muscles, and may be unable to grip or perch due to the claws knuckling together. Di-

agnosis can be made by microscopic examination of the faeces for the eggs of the worm.

Treatment is to keep the bird warm; give 3 drops twice daily of Penbritten oral suspension; 1–2 millilitres of glucose in water (that is, a pinch of glucose in 2 millilitres of water); and 2–3 drops of a mineral and vitamin tonic once daily. Do this for two days and then worm the bird.

Worming procedure Birds to be treated must be made thirsty, so remove all water for twenty-four hours. Medicated water is then provided for twenty-four hours. Use Nilverm at the rate of 60 millilitres per 4.5 litres of water. Honey may be added to improve the bitter taste.

Tapeworm
Tapeworm can reduce the bird's natural ability to thrive. Dose affected birds orally with Droncit or Oxphendazole.

Paratyphoid infection
Salmonellosis is relatively common among caged finches, young parrots, budgerigars and canaries. In paratyphoid epidemics, 50 per cent of birds may be lost among canaries and young parrots. Predisposing causes to paratyphoid infection include chilling, draughts, stress during transport, overcrowding and faulty feeding. These will all trigger off or augment the severity of an outbreak. The incubation period is four to five days and death occurs after two to four days' illness. In the acute form the birds may be found dead. Usually there is a greenish–yellow diarrhoea and in some cases there is dysentery (bloody diarrhoea), particularly in parrots. The bird is breathless, pants, is depressed, is obviously ill and sometimes goes into convulsions. Vomiting has been recorded in parrots. The course of the disease extends for three to five days and if the bird survives it may become a carrier. Treatment is by the administration of antibiotics.

Parrot's disease/Parrot fever
See ORNITHOSIS.

Pellet wounds
See INJURIES IN BIRDS.

Pneumonia and chills
Pneumonia may be brought on by severe chilling in cold wet weather if birds are in the open and unprotected. Caged birds are more susceptible than wild birds as their feathers do not possess the same protective wax layers. Aviaries should be protected and (in the southern hemisphere) face the north, and the back and sides should be protected from winds. Shifting birds from a warm district to a cold district or to an exposed cage may produce chilling. Symptoms are ruffled feathers, drooped wings, dejection, excessive drinking and sometimes vomiting. Treatment is by antibiotics.

Poisoning
Poisoning can occur accidentally by feeding greens or other vegetable materials that have had an insecticide applied to them. Lead poisoning can occur from nibbling paint on toys. Strychnine poisoning has occurred when birds accidentally eat strychnine grain that had been placed outside to poison sparrows or starlings. There is no treatment, except supportive therapy of warmth and nursing.

Prolapse
See INJURIES IN BIRDS.

Psittacosis
See ORNITHOSIS.

Regurgitation/vomiting
Vomiting may occur physiologically when a bird (say, a budgerigar) attempts to feed its image in a mirror. Vomiting may also occur from irritant and unsuitable foods or from drinking alcohol. Crop impaction and crop stasis can cause regurgitation; liquid paraffin and massage may re-

solve it. Frothy crop contents may cause vomiting. Vitamin B complex, sulphonamides, antibiotics, 0.1 per cent gentian violet by mouth, or a weak solution of potassium permanganate, all have been suggested as cures. Ulcerative gizzard syndrome, which is of viral origin, causes vomiting. This disease has a poor prognosis.

Respiratory disorders

Respiratory disorders are common in caged birds, particularly in parrots, although all birds are susceptible to respiratory diseases. These include sinusitis, bronchitis, congestion of the lungs, pneumonia, infection of the air-sacs and asthma. The conditions can be caused by various bacteria, fungi and viruses. Chilling and draughts are predisposing factors. The signs include nasal discharge, restlessness, gaping, conjunctivitis, contracting and extending the neck, emitting high-pitched squeaks, loss of voice, holding wings away from the side of the body and a pumping twitch of the tail. Treatment depends on the cause and should be dealt with by a veterinary surgeon. It will require antibiotic therapy.

Rickets

Rickets is due to a deficiency or an imbalance of calcium and phosphorus and vitamin D in young birds. It occurs occasionally in budgerigars but can occur in all birds, (see also OSTEOMALACIA). Prevention and treatment are by supply of vitamin D3, and of calcium and phosphorus by means of fish or bone meal and milk.

Rings on birds' legs

See INJURIES IN BIRDS.

Salmonella infection

See PARATYPHOID INFECTION.

Scaly face

See PARASITES, EXTERNAL.

Scratching

See PARASITES, EXTERNAL.

Septicaemia

Septicaemia can be caused by a variety of organisms that invade the bloodstream and organs, causing very serious illness. The bird shows signs of depression with plucked-up feathers; it may be on the bottom of the cage. The disease is serious and requires veterinary attention.

Shock

Shock occurs in all birds, but more particularly in the parrot family, as a result of a severe fright by dogs, cats, humans, predatory birds (for example, a bigger bird trying to get into a canary's cage), headlights of cars at night and severe handling. Loud noises may cause shock. Such occurrences are common, particularly in small birds, and the result is death. Very little can be done except to provide warmth, darkness and oxygen by artificial respiration if the bird is still alive.

Sore feet

See BUMBLEFOOT.

Starvation

This is a very common cause of death in caged birds, particularly of budgerigars and canaries. It may be due to overdieting of fat birds, neglect during holidays, careless husbandry or accidental starvation. Birds die very rapidly if deprived of food, even for periods as short as twenty-four hours. They have a very high metabolic rate and have very little storage of energy and food.

Thrush/Moniliasis

See CANDIDIASIS.

Trichomonas infection

Trichomonas infections are common in pigeons, doves, and budgerigars. The infection, which produces yellow deposits in the throat, is seen in both young birds and older birds. Infected birds show ruffled feathers, and they gasp for breath. The droppings may be thin and yellowish. Losses from the disease may be quite heavy in an aviary. Treatment is by dosing with Emtryl or Ronivet.

Tumours

See NEOPLASMS.

Vertigo

See HEART DISEASE.

Vomiting

See REGURGITATION.

Warts

See CANARY POX.

Wing damage

See FRACTURES.

Worms

See PARASITES, INTERNAL.

Wounds

See INJURIES IN BIRDS.

CATS

Selecting a cat

The cat is a fastidiously clean animal quite content to be independent and aloof. While loving affection, it is not the faithful companion that has made the dog man's best friend.

The desexed cat is usually content with the territorial limitations of the urban backyard and very satisfied to spend the major part of the day basking in the sun. It will rarely come when called—unless food is in the offing. It is much happier on someone's lap in front of a winter's fire than accompanying a jogger on a rainy night.

Cats are ideal for people living in flats or units—in fact, anywhere a pet is desired but the territory is limited (although, as cats are not allowed in some apartment buildings, do check first). Cats are less costly to keep than most dogs.

When selecting a cat, there are a great variety from which to choose. The sex of the cat doesn't matter so long as you have it desexed. Next you should think about long hair versus short hair. The colour combinations are now so numerous that all cat owners' tastes can be satisfied.

The age of the cat is a consideration but it doesn't really matter whether you select a mature cat or a young kitten, providing you give it sufficient time to establish a relationship with you. Young kittens will demand more of your time because they need to be fed four times a day and toilet trained. Generally, however, the pleasure derived from observing the antics of a young kitten far outweigh any disadvantages.

Breed

If you haven't had a cat in the family before, each member of the family should check they are not allergic to the animal. Handle the cat; even bring its fur in contact with your face. An allergic reaction causes watering and irritation of the eyes, accompanied by snuffling and sneezing. If a member of the family is allergic, it is much easier to be sensible about the situation before the cat has become part of the family.

The most trouble-free breed of cat is the common short-haired tabby type. They need a minimum of grooming, and in warm climates are the obvious choice. On long-haired cats ectoparasites such as fleas and ticks are more

If a member of the family is allergic to the animal be sensible and act before the cat has become part of the family.

Young kittens will demand more time, but their antics are a delight to behold.

Cats are quite content to spend the major part of the day basking in the sun.

Cats with 'pushed in' faces
frequently have tears washing
down their faces.

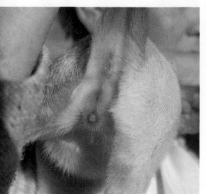

The male kitten: Note the 'dot'
of the penis. The testes are
between the penis and the
anus.

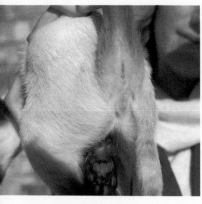

The female kitten: Note the long
'slit' of the vagina.

difficult to eliminate. Long-haired cats require frequent grooming to prevent the development of matted areas along the belly and flanks. Badly matted hair can lead to dermatitis serious enough to require treatment under a general anaesthetic. The ordinary tabby or alley cat makes an excellent house cat and pet and it has no peer as a rodent exterminator. The tabby comes in all sizes, shapes and colours. Because it is crossbred, it is less susceptible to diseases, particularly to the upper respiratory tract viral infections which are so common in other breeds. The tabby has virtually no hereditary or congenital abnormalities.

Pedigree cats can be divided into long-haired and short-haired varieties. Some of the long-haired varieties, particularly the creams and chinchillas, have been bred to accentuate the 'pushed-in' face. Unfortunately, this has led to problems: many of these cats have tears constantly washing down their face, marking their hair, and causing chronic conjunctivitis.

Siamese and Burmese cats are particularly sensitive to cat flu viruses. Blue-eyed white cats are usually congenitally deaf. Tortoise-shell or calico cats are usually female; the few males are usually sterile. White-eared cats are subject to sunburn and skin cancer of the ear tips.

Sex

In the male both openings are round and separated by the swellings of the testes. In cats older than two months the testes can be felt. In the female the openings are closer together and resemble an upside-down exclamation mark. In the male the prepuce, which is the bottom hole, can be pulled back on both sides to expose the tip of the penis. Similar examination of the female reveals a vertical slit, rather than a circular hole.

Any cat that is not to be used for breeding should be desexed, whether it is male or female. Male cats, after reaching maturity at six months, develop a very offensive urine odour. As it is their nature to spray their environment with urine (called 'marking' their territory), and this can include furniture in the house, they can be unpleasant to have around. Undesexed males may also roam looking for queens (female cats) on heat, leading to territorial encounters with other male cats and inevitably fights, which result in injuries and abscesses.

Female cats, if not desexed, will come on heat each twenty-one days until they are mated. While on heat they can be particularly vocal and sexually active. A cat may have up to twelve kittens a year if left undesexed, which means you are faced with the problem of finding twelve homes! Desexing of both toms and queens should take place before they reach sexual maturity, at five to six months. Desexing does not alter the cat's personality, nor does it cause obesity. A desexed female or a desexed male makes an equally good pet.

Selecting from a litter

Wherever you get your cat, keep the following points in mind. Note the appearance and sanitary condition of the establishment from which you are purchasing the animal. Is it clean and free of odours? Are the cages clean and in good condition? What is the general appearance of the animals in the cattery?

One advantage of dealing directly with a breeder is that a history of the mother and her management during the pregnancy can sometimes be very helpful in choosing the right cat. If the mother has had two or three litters in the space of twelve months, it is possible that her bones are starting to become deficient in the essential vitamins and minerals necessary for proper bone formation in the kittens. If she has been fed a meat diet only, without calcium supplementation, this will increase the possibility of weak bones in the kittens. Worming should have taken place before the mother became pregnant and she should have been wormed two or three times during the pregnancy. The mother should have been vaccinated against infectious feline enteritis and cat flu within the previous twelve months and preferably midway through the pregnancy also. Kittens infected with fleas are a good indication of lack of care on the breeder's part. If the breeder has taken the trouble to care properly for the mother, then you can be sure that the litter has the best opportunity for survival.

Don't base your selection of a kitten entirely on a cute expression or an appealing look. Never be tempted to feel sorry for the runt of the litter or a sickly kitten. Observe the whole litter at a distance. Select a kitten that is alert and playful. It should have a glossy coat and be well and robust in condition. Avoid the very shy kitten, particularly if you have small children in your family, as such a pet will require careful handling and will not submit to being handled by young children.

Once a kitten has been selected at a distance, pick it up and compare its weight to the others in the litter. Hold the kitten in the palm of your hand and feel its activity and weight. Look for dry scurfy skin, lice and fleas. Check under the tail to see if the kitten has had any diarrhoea.

Examine its mouth and check that the gums are a good pink colour. Check the roof of the kitten's mouth for a cleft palate (this is a slit in the roof of the mouth). Check the eyes for discharge. If the third eyelid (a mucous membrane at the corner of the eye) is protruding more than one-sixth towards the centre, it indicates that the kitten is in ill health. Blindness can be checked by darting the fingers towards the eye; the kitten should blink. Check the ears for any smell or discharge. Kittens with infected ears will shake their heads and paw at the outsides of the ears. Ear infections can be cured but do consider the veterinary expenses. Deafness can be determined by snapping your fingers or clapping your hands behind the cat. If it fails to respond the chances are that it is deaf. Examine the belly of the cat for hernias. The kitten should have five toes on each front foot, and four on each hind-foot.

The kitten's sex should be determined (see above). Pedigree cats should come with papers documenting their pedigree. In the case of a cat already registered, a transfer form signed by the breeder should be available. Weaning of the kitten should have started at four weeks of age. At six weeks the kitten is ready to leave its mother, but some breeders prefer to wait till the cat is nine weeks old.

Housing

In many cases the kitten will be leaving the comfort and security of the litter and its mother for the first time. At your place there will be strange new smells, different people and perhaps different pets. It is essential that the new kitten has human company, warmth, ample food and something to distract its attention during the night—for example, a clock wrapped in a blanket. Give the kitten a well-wrapped hot-water bottle for warmth. Keep the kitten on the foods that the breeder was using for at least four or five days. Any change in diet should be made slowly. Some kittens are allergic to cow's milk, so if diarrhoea occurs, the milk should be stopped until the kitten is well. Milk can then be gradually reintroduced if watered down fifty-fifty with water, with the concentration being increased over the following four to five weeks. If milk is reduced, ensure that the cat is on a balanced commercial diet or has supplementary calcium.

Young kittens are usually happy sleeping in baskets or boxes on the floor. Don't be overenthusiastic about preparing special sleeping quarters for cats, as they usually make their own arrangements. Older cats like to sleep above floor level or ground level. If convenient, set up a shelf for your cat to use as a perch. Otherwise it will climb on chairs and other elevated places.

Most young kittens, and even older cats, enjoy playing with toys, particularly ones that move. A few simple toys will keep a kitten contented in the

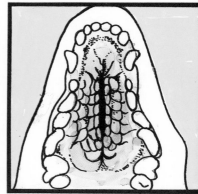

Illustration of cleft palate.

Cats like to be elevated, with a good view of their surroundings so that they can maintain their alertness and independence.

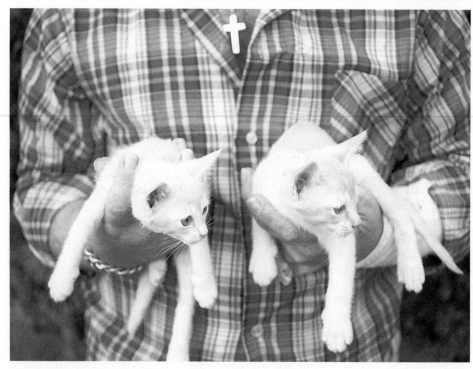

Once a kitten has been selected, compare its weight with others in the litter.

A suitable cat door; a slide can be bolted across to keep the cat inside.

Whether the cat is housed indoors or outdoors the area should be warm and draught-free.

first few days in a strange environment—for example, ping-pong balls, a spool with a piece of string on it, a dangling piece of wool or even a small twist of newspaper hung on a string from a doorknob. Cats also enjoy crawling into cardboard boxes or tunnels made out of large paper shopping bags.

The best way to stop the kitten or mature cat from wandering during the first few days in a new home is to confine it to the house or an enclosed space. Your cat will become used to being fed at the one place, and when it is left free it will return for its food. It has been said that placing butter on the cat's paws will hasten its acclimatisation. By doing this the cat leaves traces of its own scent wherever it goes in the house, thus making the surroundings seem more familiar.

Whether the cat is housed indoors or outdoors, it is important that the area is warm and draught free. Cats like to be elevated, with a good view of their surroundings so that they can maintain their alertness and independence and be safe from dogs and young children. They also appreciate being able to come and go as they please, so it is ideal to fit a cat door to the shelter your pet regards as its own (be it in the kitchen or an insulated garden shed). The door is a flap on a two-way hinge at the top, just big enough for the cat to fit through. A bolt on the flap is useful in case you wish to keep the cat in—for example, when it is ill or when a queen is in season.

The best bedding for the cat is newspaper; it is cheap and disposable, which means it is hygienic. Fleas, lice and worms can be thrown out and burned on a regular basis. It is also very warm.

If a cat basket is used, the ideal style is one with a waterproof base and an elevated wire surface on which the cat lies. If a kitten does have an accident, it is not then standing or lying in its own mess. The basket should be wide and shallow so that the cat can see what is going on. A minority will prefer a closed-in basket, but they still like to keep an eye on things.

If a cat has to be kept indoors for lengthy periods, a litter box is essential. This should be a waterproof tray measuring approximately 30 × 38 centimetres with 5-centimetre side walls. Line it with a few sheets of newspaper, then fill it with commercially prepared litter or with soil or sawdust. The litter should be changed each day and the tray washed thoroughly with a non-irritant detergent and rinsed well. Don't use strong-smelling antiseptics, otherwise the animal may not use the tray. Some antiseptics, soaps and disinfectants are poisonous to cats. Check the label.

Feeding and drinking utensils should be solid and have flat bottoms. The traditional saucer is not ideal, since it is easily tipped over by a hungry kitten stepping on the edge. Some cats will pull the food from the bowl, particularly if there are strands of meat to play with, so it is a good idea to set the bowl on a sheet of newspaper.

Feeding and drinking utensils should have flat bottoms.

Feeding

Most of the nutritional diseases seen in cats result from reliance on a single food or type of diet, which usually occurs for reasons of convenience, economy or because the cat refuses any other food. When cats are restricted to a single diet it magnifies marginal deficiencies and may result in nutritional disease. Cats are fussy eaters and easily become addicted to a particular diet or type of food. They establish their eating patterns at a very early age and if not exposed to a variety of food as kittens they may be very restricted in the food they accept as adults.

The complex nutritional requirements of a cat can be met best and most economically by using a commercially prepared cat food. Home diets can be made up, but when the time and cost of ingredients are taken into account they cannot be compared with commercially prepared rations. These factors are becoming more important for the average pet owner. Recent research has demonstrated that the cat has many unique nutritional requirements which are quite different to other species, such as the dog. It is most important that the very best diet is fed when maximum performance is expected, such as reproductive efficiency or showing.

When a cat is first changed to dry food from either meat or tinned food, it is most important to teach it to drink more water. This can be done by mixing water into the food or by salting the food. Dried food should be introduced gradually so the animal can adjust to the increased drinking requirements.

Protein

Cats have an unusually high requirement for dietary protein—nearly double that of dogs and several times that of humans on a body-weight basis; cats will refuse food with less than 19 per cent protein. The protein offered must be of a high biological value and easily digestible. Blindness can be induced if a cat is fed a protein-deficient diet. The recommended dietary protein levels for cats are a minimum of 21 per cent (dry basis) for adults, and 33 per cent (dry basis) for kittens. Dry basis means that the calculation is made after all water is extracted and only dry food is left.

Fat

The cat has a high energy requirement, making a diet with a high calorie density necessary. The cat's high fat requirement in its food is made necessary by these energy demands.

Dietary fat is a concentrated source of energy; it provides essential fatty acids and fat-soluble vitamins and adds palatability to the diet. However, many owners and breeders reduce the fat in the erroneous belief that cats cannot tolerate dietary fat. Recent research has shown that the cat prefers a high level of dietary fat and should have at least 30 per cent in the diet (dry basis). Cats digest and absorb fat very efficiently even at such high levels. Cats fed diets deficient in essential fatty acids become listless, their coats become dry with severe dandruff, and they show other abnormalities such as infertility.

Carbohydrates

Experimental feedings and analyses indicate that cats are able to efficiently digest most types of carbohydrates. Diarrhoea sometimes occurs in kittens that are unable to digest the lactose component of cow's milk. (The alphabetical listing of 'Common Ailments' of the cat includes this and other causes of diarrhoea.)

Vitamins

Vitamin A

Several features of the cat's vitamin A requirements and metabolism are unusual among the animal species:

The cat stores large quantities of vitamin A in the kidney as well as in the liver.

Cats have a relatively high requirement of vitamin A for their size.

Because they cannot make vitamin A, they must be provided with vitamin A in the diet.

Adequate amounts of dietary fat are necessary for normal intestinal absorption of vitamin A.

The usual sources of dietary vitamin A are liver, eggs and milk. Acute and chronic vitamin A deficiency can cause blindness, sterility, reduced litter size, weak or dead kittens, skeletal deformities, neurological defects, cleft palate, hare-lip, emaciation, weakness of the hind legs and respiratory problems. Major losses of vitamin A occur during pregnancy and lactation, reducing the queen's stores by up to 75 per cent. If her stores are already low, the kittens will have low vitamin A stores at birth and through the suckling period. It is recommended that liver be fed occasionally—feeding particularly during pregnancy to replenish stores of vitamin A. Hyperkeratosis is a skin disorder of vitamin A deficiency.

Excessive vitamin A is also dangerous. Diets consisting mainly of liver have been responsible for bone abnormalities attributable to excess vitamin A. Too much cod-liver oil and multi-vitamin preparations may also be sources of excessive vitamin A. Affected cats show stiffness of the neck, foreleg lameness and paralysis, sensitivity to touch and abnormalities of gait and posture. Other signs include depression, irritability, reversible testicular degeneration in tom cats, premature loss of incisor teeth, and excessive gum tissue production. The length of time an excess intake of vitamin A will take to produce clinical signs depends on the level of intake and the age of the cat. Younger cats show signs sooner than older ones. In most clinical cases, affected cats are at least two years old and have been on a high vitamin A intake, usually in the form of a predominantly liver diet, for at least a year. Removal of the source of the excess results in marked clinical improvement within a few weeks. But while skeletal lesions are halted and undergo remodelling over the following year, they do not resolve completely and the cat may remain lame.

Vitamin B

Most balanced diets contain adequate quantities of B-group vitamins, but under certain circumstances (such as pregnancy and lactation) B-group requirements may increase. If the cat has a fever or is off its food for more than a few days, supplementary vitamin B-group therapy is advised because body stores are not substantial. Since failure to eat may be the effect of an acute deficiency of several of the B-group vitamins, the signs may be masked and aggravate the primary complaint. A convenient source of oral supplementary B-group vitamins is provided by brewer's yeast. Many cats will voluntarily eat the tablets. The recommended dose is 0.5 to 1.0 gram per kilogram body-weight.

Thiamine (Vitamin B1) Thiamine is destroyed by heat, usually from cooking or processing. In commercial foods, extra thiamine is added before cooking to compensate for the predictable losses. Clinical signs of thiamine deficiency are usually the result of long-term dependence on a deficient or marginal commercial product, unless raw fish has been fed to the cat. Signs of thiamine deficiency can appear within six to eight weeks. Pregnancy, illness, loss of appetite or fever may cause the onset of signs more quickly.

The clinical signs include: convulsions precipitated by handling; marked dilation of the eyes; characteristic flexion of the head and neck downwards; irritability; wobbliness of the back legs; walking with paws extended.

A cat suffering from thiamine deficiency may previously have been off its food, lost weight, vomited, become weak in the hindquarters. The oral administration of thiamine in the form of brewer's yeast tablets at a dose rate of 1 gram per kilogram body-weight per day produces noticeable improvement within twelve to twenty-four hours. However, in severe cases where there have been convulsions for several days, brain lesions may be irreversible. After clinical improvement the offending diet should be changed and oral thiamine supplemented in the form of brewer's yeast tablets.

Vitamin D

The cat's requirements for vitamin D are low, and its own production is probably adequate for its needs. Signs of deficiency are rare.

Vitamin E

Steatitis (yellow fat disease) has been reported in cats as a result of diets high in unsaturated fatty acids, usually from fish or fish oils. The most common offending diet is canned red tuna, but other fish, cod-liver oil, liver and horsemeat have also produced the disease. When high amounts of unsaturated fatty acids are present in the diet, adequate amounts of vitamin E are required to prevent the development of steatitis. When the oils are combined with adequate vitamin E supplies, they are not harmful even in large amounts. Affected cats are irritable, reluctant to move and fevered, and being touched causes them pain. Veterinary treatment consists of specific vitamin therapy, with oral administration of alpha-tocopheral at the rate of 50 milligrams per day.

Minerals

Calcium and phosphorus

A newborn kitten has a very small amount of skeletal calcium, which may be related to the low levels of calcium in its mother's milk. When the queen receives inadequate dietary calcium, her kittens show less skeletal mineralisation at weaning time than would occur with normal diets. Calcium deposition in the bones is not greatly increased even when supplementary calcium is given to kittens during the suckling period and only increases significantly when the kitten is fed a complete diet after weaning. The calcium required for bone growth and accumulation of skeletal stores must be derived from dietary sources. While growing, kittens require 200 to 400 milligrams of calcium per day.

The best utilisation of dietary calcium takes place when the calcium : phosphorus ratio is 0 9 : 1.1. Very large quantities can be safely given if this ratio is constant. For the pet owner, there is great difficulty in trying to estimate this ratio in home diets. It is therefore easier to select for the cat a complete commercial ration, which will have been balanced for calcium and phosphorus.

The problem occurs because in the wild the cat catches and eats the whole prey—a balanced diet. The home diet may consist of minced meat—one section of the prey. When growth is completed, intestinal *absorption* of calcium decreases to about 30 per cent of intake if the diet has previously been adequate and skeletal stores are normal.

In pregnancy and lactation, calcium loss increases to the point where a queen may lose one-third of her calcium reserves when raising five to six kittens. A daily intake of at least 600 milligrams of calcium is recommended to meet these requirements. With a continuing intake of a calcium-deficient diet, severe depletion of skeletal stores occurs, resulting in a generalised porous condition of the bones of both queen and kittens and consequent reduced bone growth and mineralisation.

Other minerals

Iron and copper deficiencies are uncommon, as cats are able to obtain the required amounts from a meat-based diet. The normal diet of the cat is rich in magnesium, so cats suffering from feline urological syndrome (a urine disorder) usually need a special low-magnesium diet.

Dangers of an all-meat diet

Nutritional secondary hyperparathyroidism (N.S.H.) disease is seen most often in healthy looking, well-grown kittens at four to six months of age which are being fed a basically all-meat diet. The protein content, caloric value and palatability of meat initially produces rapid growth, which increases the kitten's calcium requirements during the peak bone growth period. The problem is that in skeletal meat the calcium content is low and the phosphorus content relatively high (calcium to phosphorus ratio 1 : 10). At this ratio little calcium is absorbed, and body hormones stimulate the kitten's bones to dissolve to provide sufficient blood calcium.

Early signs of N.S.H. include behavioural changes, irritability and reluctance to run, jump and play. Affected kittens prefer sitting to standing and may show deviation of the paws inwards and lameness or weakness in the hindquarters (sometimes caused by fractures). Secondary complaints are respiratory difficulties, constipation and (at adulthood) difficulty giving birth. Even in severe cases, clinical improvement is obvious within a few weeks, once the diet has been corrected.

The most important step in treating nutritional secondary hyperparathyroidism is to provide the cat with a diet containing adequate amounts of calcium and phosphorus in the ratio of 1 : 1. The ideal way is to replace the meat diet with a completely balanced commercial ration. Cats being choosy eaters, however, will often refuse to change. Enforcing the change by starving the cat into submission is usually unsuccessful and does not provide the intake of minerals required for improvement. In this case, the meat diet may be supplemented with calcium to achieve the same purpose. Supplement each 100 grams of meat with 1 gram (1 level teaspoon) of calcium carbonate during the treatment period.

Once symptoms have subsided, administer half a teaspoon of calcium carbonate per 100 grams of meat. Where female cats have been affected by N.S.H., have them desexed to save them from difficulties giving birth, as the pelvis is usually permanently narrowed. The erroneous use of the name 'rickets' for this disease infers that a deficiency of vitamin D plays a role in its cause and suggests the use of the vitamin in its treatment. Although vitamin D enhances intestinal absorption of calcium, large doses actually increase demineralisation of skeletal bone. The use of combined injections of vitamin D and calcium is to be discouraged as they usually provide large doses of vitamin D and insignificant amounts of calcium, a dangerous combination in cats.

A pet's diet

Commercial products available for feeding your pet can be classified as moist foods or dry foods.

Moist foods usually contain 75 per cent moisture, 25 per cent solids. They may be complete rations, providing all requirements for the cat, or incomplete rations requiring supplementation with meat. Always read the label to ensure your cat is receiving a properly balanced diet.

Dry foods are 10 per cent moisture and 90 per cent solids. They can be mixed with each other or with other foods to satisfy the owner's preferences and the cat's taste.

Supplementary meat, eggs, table scraps, gravy, and so on, may be used, but in small quantities that should not exceed 25 per cent of the total diet;

otherwise you run the risk of upsetting the balance of nutrients in the commercial product.

Where a home preparation is preferred, additional calcium, iodine, vitamin A and possibly trace elements are desirable. A five-month-old kitten being fed meat could have calcium carbonate and a daily egg (at least, the yolk) and some milk, if tolerated, to improve its diet. Meat should be cooked or, if the cat prefers it raw, deep frozen for at least fourteen days to prevent parasite transmission. Whole eggs should be cooked also, as uncooked egg white is indigestible and it does contain half the protein content.

How much food?
Recommended amounts and frequency of feeding for kittens and cats.

How Much Food?				
Recommended amounts and frequency of feeding for kittens and cats				
Age	Average Weight	Total Daily Ration		Feedings per Day
		Canned	Dry	
During weaning	0.8 kg	⅓	½–⅔ cup	3–4
At 6 months	2.5 kg	½–⅔	¾–1 cup	2
Adults	3.0 kg	½	1 cup	1–2
During pregnancy	3.5 kg	¾–1	1–1½ cups*	2
During lactation		1½	1½–2 cups*	2–3

*Dry foods should not form the entire diet of a female cat during pregnancy and lactation.

Water
Cats in the wild drink only small quantities of water, usually once a day. The water content of their natural food is about 70 per cent. Cats, in addition, have the ability to utilise water from their dietary fat and can also concentrate their urine (that is, they can excrete large quantities of waste products in a very small quantity of fluid—this is what makes their urine so strong-smelling).

A cat fed on commercial tinned food (approximately 75 per cent water) will consume about 30 millilitres (3 dessertspoons) of water daily. If the cat is fed dry foods (approximately 10 per cent water), its water requirements increase tenfold.

The small quantity of water consumed by cats on a moist diet leads many owners to believe that water does not have to be provided. Even when water is available, cats will often prefer to drink from sinks, basins, bathtubs, showers, toilet bowls and plant containers. Beware, as cats are liable to ingest toxic substances from these sources (for example, disinfectants, plant sprays, fertilisers, and insecticides).

Special diets
Prescription diets for health problems such as obesity, cystitis, pancreatitis are available. Consult your veterinarian.

Cats that are exceptionally active, are kept in a cold environment or are used for breeding have higher energy requirements than most. (The opposite applies to inactive, confined cats, old animals or those known to gain weight easily.) Growth, pregnancy and lactation are the most frequent indications for increased energy, protein, vitamins and minerals. If a balanced diet containing good-quality protein is offered, the increased quantity of the food consumed will ensure increased quantities of all the nutrients to meet these requirements. In some cases, however, particularly during pregnancy, additional protein supplementation may be necessary. Eggs or small quantities of meat are then suitable. Feeding liver occasionally—that is, once weekly or fortnightly—provides additional vitamin A and is recommended during

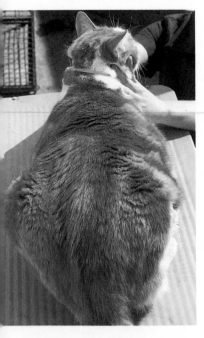

An overweight cat is an unhealthy cat.

Matted hair should be cut away from the ears.

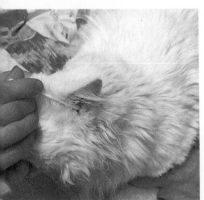

Cotton buds can be used to clean debris from the ears.

Grooming tools for cats should include a stiff brush.

Metal combs and scissors are necessary to cut away matted hair.

pregnancy. Illness, fever or loss of appetite increases requirements of B-group vitamins; add brewer's yeast (see Vitamins, pp. 42–3).

When the animal is ill, some foods may be more attractive than others, especially those with strong odours such as fish (tuna, sardines, pilchards), chicken and baby foods. Most foods should be warmed at least to room temperature. This enhances the odours, although cats with oral ulcers, as in upper respiratory tract infections, gain some relief from eating cold foods. Ice cream can also be attractive to these sick cats.

General care

Exercise
Cats by their nature require very little exercise to keep lithe and fit.

Grooming
Cats are fastidious and hygienic animals; they keep themselves clean. At times, however, they need some help—particularly the long-haired types. Grooming makes the animal feel better as it stimulates the circulation and removes any debris and loose hair. Grooming can be pleasurable for the cat if it is done on a regular basis and the cat's hair kept in reasonable condition, but it can easily turn into a fight if it is left until long hair becomes matted and knotted.

Matting can become so severe on the sides and belly that the cat needs a general anaesthetic before the thick wads of hair are removed. In this case, there is no alternative but to take the mat off at skin level. Grooming tools required are a stiff brush, a metal comb with close-set teeth, a smoothing glove or cloth and a pair of blunt-ended scissors. Place the cat on a table or bench, preferably out of the sun. Brush and comb the cat both with and against the lay of its hair. If the hair is matted, gently push the scissors between the skin and the hair mat and snip.

Sometimes a cat gets so dirty it needs a bath—though this must be approached with caution. Choose washing days at random; find the cat and lock it up before you prepare the bath or—invariably—no cat! Three-quarters fill a 10-litre plastic bucket with warm water. Use a recognised cat shampoo, preferably one that contains an insecticide; shampoos containing 20 per cent coconut oil are very satisfactory. Bath the cat in a confined area, such as the bathroom or the laundry, with the door shut. You will need two people. The first person should take the cat by the scruff of the neck in one hand and the back legs in the other and place it backside first into the bucket of warm water. The second person then runs his or her fingers through the cat's hair to make sure that the skin is wet right up to and including the neck. This should be done quickly and efficiently. Remove the cat from the water, place it on a bench and lather with shampoo; after massaging the shampoo into its coat, return the cat to the water and rinse the shampoo off. If the cat is particularly dirty, the process may need to be repeated.

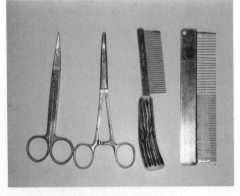

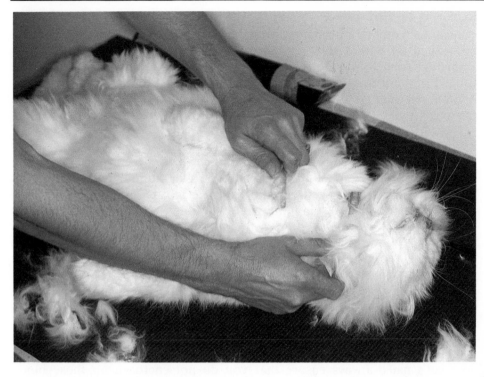

A general anaesthetic is often required to remove matted hair from the underside of Persian cats.

If the cat reacts violently to this technique, wrap a towel soaked in water around it to wet its fur. Hold the animal firmly as you do this, leaving its head out of the towel. Again, you will need two people—one to wrap the towel around the cat while the other holds its scruff and the back legs. Once the cat is thoroughly wet, remove the towel and lather its coat in the usual way. Talk reassuringly to the animal. After rinsing is complete, press any excess water from the coat using your hands. Rub the cat down vigorously with a towel to dry the hair. In cold weather, do the job in a warmed room.

Short-haired cats should not be brushed. Instead, use a chamois or smoothing cloth, rubbing the hair with the lie towards the rear of the animal. This will bring out the sheen.

Long-haired cats that are being exhibited at a show should be washed with a good shampoo no fewer than three to four days before the show, as it takes several days for the natural oils to return to the coat. Newly washed cats will often have a dull coat. Pour Johnson's Baby Powder liberally over the coat while brushing it back against the lie, towards the head. Do this daily until twenty-four hours before showing, when all the powder must be removed. Black cats should not be powdered, as it dulls the coat. Instead, rub some bran (warmed in the oven) into the fur twenty-four hours before the show. Once the bran has dried, comb it out carefully. With Persian cats, trim the hair around the tops of the ears to round off the outline.

Cats are fastidious and hygienic animals; they usually keep themselves clean.

Whatever other beauty tricks you use to make your cat look its best at a show, don't resort to using blue rinses to produce a silver-grey Chinchilla, or black boot polish to darken the tips of the Seal-point Siamese. This is illegal and if detected may mean disqualification.

Removing paint

A cloth dipped in turpentine will remove oil-based paint before it has dried. Never let turpentine come into contact with the cat's skin. If the paint is already dry, it will have to be clipped off. It is important to remove paint or any other chemical from your cat's coat, as cats are very sensitive to insecticides and other chemicals, not only from absorption through the skin but particularly from the constant licking at the area when attempting to clean itself. Water-based paints can be rinsed off while wet; once dried, clip the cat's hair.

Some cats are allergic to flea collars; the signs are local loss of hair and a moist dermatitis.

Removing tar and grease

Tar can be removed with paraffin which, however, is a skin irritant and must be washed off with a shampoo as quickly as possible. Lard or any other animal fat rubbed into the region will also loosen the tar which can then be rubbed off with a rough towel and shampoo.

Fresh chewing gum can be removed with paraffin or acetone (nail polish remover), but be sure to wash these dissolving agents off quickly.

Losing hair

Cats living indoors shed hair all year round because of the artificial light and various other factors, including dryness of the skin, humidity and cold. A cat normally sheds hair according to the seasonal light pattern; as the day gets longer, the hair stops growing and begins to fall out, and new hair replaces the old. When the days get shorter, the new coat grows faster and less hair is shed. All cats with artificial light shed some hair all the year round, but usually it is more predominant during spring. Regular combing will help prevent hair from accumulating on furniture and clothes.

Care of the nails

Each of the cat's nails has a hard outer covering, with blood vessels and nerves inside. Close observation will reveal a pink area (the blood vessel) running down to within 3 millimetres of the tip of the nail. When clipping your cat's nails, always ensure that you do not encroach on those blood vessels. Although ordinary scissors can be used, they are not as gentle as nail clippers with the guillotine-type action.

Hold the cat in your lap to cut its nails. If it is nervous or if it struggles, put it into a bag or wrap it in a towel leaving the feet exposed. Grasp the toe firmly with your finger under the pad on the bottom of the toe and your thumb on the fur at the top. Exert gentle pressure until the claw is exposed. Clip the nail and file or sandpaper the rough edges. If the blood vessel is cut, pressure and the use of a styptic pencil will soon stop the bleeding. (A styptic pencil contains a substance such as alum or tannic acid which causes contraction of blood vessels.)

When clipping your cat's nails do not encroach on the blood vessels. One nail has been cut to the correct length.

Correct positioning and use of the nail cutters.

Training

House-training

Kittens and cats are naturally clean and fastidious animals. The majority will have been taught by their mothers where to go to the toilet, either in a litter box or outside in the garden. Because cats are so clean in their habits, it is important to clean the litter box frequently—if it remains soiled too long, the kitten may start to look elsewhere.

Do not use the same litter in the sanitary box and the sleeping box—this creates confusion. If you use shredded newspaper in the sleeping box, use shavings, sawdust, soil or commercial cat litter in the sanitary tray.

When you first bring the kitten home, put its sanitary tray near the sleeping box for a few days, gradually moving it away a short distance at a time. If you want the kitten to learn to pass urine and faeces in the garden, gradually move the tray to an area outside. The next step is to put a small quantity of soiled litter in a cultivated area of the garden and to take the kitten to this spot after meals for a few days. If the odd accident occurs and you see it happen, don't knock the kitten or rub its nose in it, but chastise it firmly with your voice, and take it to the tray or the garden.

Kittens learn very quickly what is expected of them. It is most important if an accident occurs to clean it up carefully and to spray the area with a powerful deodorant, preferably something that has a smell totally obnoxious to the cat. Examples include ammonia products or strong-smelling household disinfectants. If you do this, the kitten will usually avoid the same spot.

If the spot is left uncleaned or half-cleaned, the kitten thinks that it is a toilet and returns there. If the cat persistently offends inside the house, lock it outside for a couple of days and then gradually allow its return.

Protecting household furniture

It is a natural instinct for a cat to seek high places to perch. Particular firmness may be required of you to stop your cat jumping on the table at meal-times. Pushing the cat down each time it jumps up will not, in most cases, break the habit. A firmer approach is necessary. Put the cat in another room or outdoors at meal-times or when food is being prepared, or discourage jumping by making a loud noise on the table when it looks like making an attempt.

While clawing at curtains, rugs and furniture is an enjoyable activity for a kitten, it is an expensive pastime for an owner. Most cats can be discouraged by substitutes—a wooden log with the bark left on it is ideal. Simply fasten a rough-barked post on to a wide heavy base. Fasten a small toy or piece of wool to a string embedded in the top of the post—this will also amuse the cat.

Some cats constantly claw the furniture despite being provided with a scratching post. Persistent offenders can have their front claws removed by surgery. This is neither disfiguring nor disabling, but it should be done only as a last resort. The animal can still defend itself, but not as well as before. The main argument for declawing is that it allows many people to keep their cats instead of having them put down.

Travelling

Never attempt to transport a cat in an insecure container—this includes wicker baskets and cardboard carrying boxes which can rapidly develop holes if soaked by urine. Instead, use a firmly fastened basket, a carrying case, zip bag or pillow slip.

Moving house

The cat's natural instincts are acute, especially the homing instinct. It is often reported that a cat has travelled 50 kilometres or more from its new home back to the old one. It has been recorded, incredible though it may seem,

Never try to transport a cat in an insecure container. This carrying basket has an elevated wire bottom, a waterproof base, and allows the cat good vision.

that a cat has found an owner's new home which it has never seen before, even though it was quite some distance away. Cats do become very attached to their homes. When moving, put your cat in a safe carrier box before the removalist arrives or even before you begin to pack up. This is particularly important if you are not returning to the area. When you arrive at your new home, keep your cat confined to the house for a few days, and place butter on its paws. This will help its scent disseminate throughout the house and it will quickly acclimatise to the new home. Make sure that all your pets get plenty of attention in the first few weeks of moving to a new home. Sometimes with nervous animals which are not used to travelling, sedation or tranquillisation may help.

Boarding

Always book ahead at a reputable cattery during holiday periods. Start checking your cat about four weeks before it is due to go to the cattery. Particularly check your cat's teeth and its ears to make sure they are in a satisfactory condition before your holiday period. If the cat has not had vaccinations against cat flu and infectious feline enteritis within the previous twelve months, these should be done at least fourteen days before the cat enters the cattery (this is an ideal opportunity for a veterinary inspection). Worm the cat one week before your holiday and four weeks after it comes home. If the cat tolerates flea collars or medallions, ensure that it has a current collar for the duration of its boarding period.

The gums and teeth of the cat need regular checking for disease.

Once you have found a satisfactory boarding place, continue to take your cat there as it will acclimatise much better. The staff will know your cat, and vice versa. If permissible, take a familiar toy or blanket for your pet—this will help it settle in. Cats are finicky and will go off their food easily if not completely happy.

Leave your next of kin's address and phone number if you are travelling a long distance. Give the name of your veterinary surgeon or at least give the cattery permission to call a veterinary surgeon if your cat becomes ill. If the cat will eat only specific types of food, make sure you have told the cattery what they are.

Problems arising from boarding cats are usually of two types:

Upper respiratory tract infection   Much can be done in a boarding establishment to eliminate or reduce the incidence of this disease, but even in the cleanest and best-run cattery respiratory tract infections may develop.

Cats losing weight during the boarding period   Cats are very finicky; the combination of being in a strange environment and being away from its usual companions can be traumatic. This is not necessarily the fault of the boarding establishment. Loss of weight should not be of much concern; once home, your cat will soon pick up.

Vaccinations

Feline panleukopaenia ('feline enteritis') can affect cats of any age but is more often seen in kittens and young adult cats. The virus enters the bone marrow and intestine and symptoms range from depression through to violent vomiting, diarrhoea and death. Death may be so sudden that the cat may appear to have been poisoned. The death rate due to this disease is very high.

Feline viral upper respiratory tract infection ('cat flu') is caused by two viruses. 'Snuffles' is another common name. The symptoms include sneezing, running or blocked nose, running eyes, ulcers on the tongue and mouth causing dribbling, and occasionally coughing—the symptoms will vary according to which virus is causing the disease. Although usually not fatal in itself, the disease causes considerable discomfort and may lead to serious and often fatal complications such as pneumonia. Siamese and Burmese cats seem to be more particularly affected. Cats that recover do not become permanently immune and may develop the disease again at a later date.

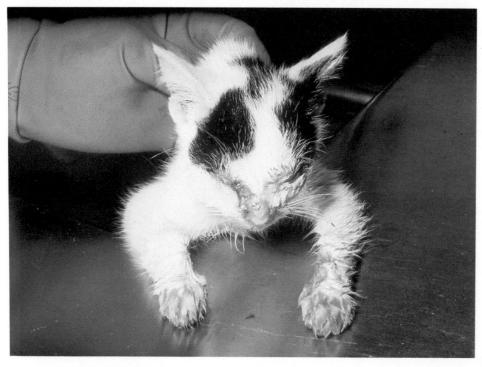

Cat 'flu' can be a fatal disease or at best leave the cat a chronic snuffler.

Vaccination is the best prevention against fatal diseases. Consult your veterinarian about requirements in your area.

Feline leukaemia is a blood cancer which results in tumors in various parts of the body (see p.68).

Rabies — See pp.96, 134.

There is no effective treatment for these diseases. Antibiotics are not effective against viruses though they may help in preventing complications. All the owner of a sick cat can do is to give careful and attentive nursing, but ultimately we have to rely on the cat's own constitution to pull it through.

Prevention is the best approach. These diseases are transmitted by infected cats; in the case of panleukopaenia, the disease often occurs as epidemics in urban areas, as the population of susceptible cats builds up. Any cat or kitten that goes outside the house is likely to come in contact with other cats and is therefore in danger of becoming infected. The feline respiratory diseases most often show up where there are concentrated groups of cats, such as at cat shows or in catteries. Some cats can become carriers of both diseases. Obviously, disease can be avoided by keeping your cat isolated, but more often than not this is impossible. Very few cats live inside the house all the time; show cats have to go to shows, and from time to time cats have to go to catteries. Some degree of control can be achieved in catteries by careful hygiene (the use of quarantine and disinfection programmes and good design). But whatever precautions are taken, there is always a possibility of your cat coming into contact with infection.

Vaccination is the best prevention.

Antibodies pass in the mother's milk to the kitten and thus make it difficult for the kitten to respond properly to vaccines until it's about ten weeks old, so try to keep your kitten isolated from other cats until it can be vaccinated against panleukopaenia at ten weeks, and for two weeks afterwards. A booster vaccination twelve to eighteen months later is recommended for lifetime protection.

Vaccination against feline respiratory disease is more complicated. Your cat may not need to be vaccinated until it goes into a high-risk situation, such as a cattery or a show. In addition, the protection against respiratory disease is not generally as long-lasting as that against panleukopaenia, and annual vaccinations may be necessary. The first time a cat is vaccinated against feline respiratory disease it will need another dose of vaccine three or four weeks later. If your cat has to be vaccinated for the first time for a special event, be sure to go to your vet early enough to allow at least three weeks for the full course. After that a single injection annually will keep up a high level of protection. Your vet will advise you of the best programme for your cat.

There are some circumstances under which kittens cannot be isolated until they are old enough to be properly vaccinated against panleukopaenia and cat flu. In these cases, some degree of protection can be given to the kitten by administering a vaccine at about six weeks of age. This should be considered as only a temporary vaccination. It is essential that kittens are vaccinated again at twelve weeks.

Worming

Some of the many parasitic diseases of the cat can be transferred to man, includine visceral larva migrans (roundworm), cutaneous larva migrans (hookworm), the tapeworms, toxoplasmosis and the flea.

Roundworms

Roundworms are very common, occurring in 35–85 per cent of young adult cats and in about 60 per cent of kittens. Young kittens become infested by eating eggs from the environment. In the adult cat, infestation occurs when the cat eats rodents, such as mice and rats, earthworms and cockroaches. The adult cat can also be contaminated by licking and cleaning kittens.

Because intrauterine infestation does not occur in cats, clinical illness in the kitten may not appear until it is four to six weeks old. Symptoms are manifested as digestive disturbances causing a rough and dry coat, general depression, inability to thrive, diarrhoea, abdominal distension and loss of weight. Adult worms may be vomited or passed in the faeces. They are 6 centimetres long, the thickness of a pencil lead, and usually curled like a spring. They are pointed at both ends and white in colour.

In the adult cat, heavy infestation may follow consumption of carrier hosts such as mice; the main clinical signs here are loss of condition, protrusion of the third eyelid and vague abdominal pain.

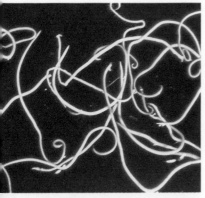

Roundworms are the most common worms seen in kittens.

Hookworm

Some surveys indicate that up to 80 per cent of cats may be infested with hookworm. The female hookworm lays 10 000 to 30 000 eggs daily. The cat may become infested by eating the eggs, or the larval stages may penetrate the cat's skin. Larval stages may enter mice, rats or insects; their development is arrested in the tissues of these transport hosts until eaten by the cat, when the parasite resumes a normal life cycle. Some larval stages pass into the female cat's uterus where they can establish an infestation in unborn kittens. Very few adult cats show clinical signs of hookworm infestation, but in young kittens infestation is demonstrated by a loss of appetite, depression, inability to thrive and marked anaemia.

Hookworm infestation is best treated with Drontal tablets.

Tapeworms

Infestation of tapeworms is recognised by the presence of mature segments in the faeces or under the tail of the cat. They are about 5 millimetres long, flat and a pinkish–grey colour. These mobile segments may not be found on every faecal sample, because they may have moved from the stool by the time the owner looks at it. (In some species of tapeworm, segments are not seen at all; only microscopic eggs are found in the faeces.) Ripe segments are passed in the faeces or crawl actively from the rectum, disseminating the eggs as they move over the anal region of the cat.

Fleas are also involved in the tapeworm's life cycle. Larval stages of the flea swallow the egg, which hatches and develops after the flea has reached the adult stage. The cat swallows the infested flea when cleaning itself. It is

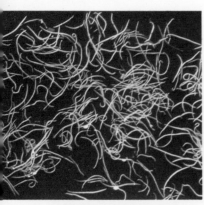

Hookworms can cause severe anaemia and death.

Life Cycles of Common Worms Affecting Cats

Roundworms

Kitten

Cat
Adult Roundworm
in small intestine

Paratenic Host

Ingested

Egg

(Via) Milk)

In Utero

Ingested by

Ingested by
Queen
Larvae in Tissues

Larvae Infective

Man Visceral Larva
migrans

Hookworms

Newborn Kittens

Egg

1st Stage Larvae

Larvae in Milk or in Utero

Egg

2nd Stage Larvae

Larvae in Tissues

Skin Penetration

3rd Stage Larvae

Cat
Adult
in small intestine

Ingested

Tapeworm

Cat
Adult Tapeworm

Eggs Ingested by

Flea Larvae

Infected Flea Ingested

Cysticercoid
Formed
in Adult Flea

Man
Adult Tapeworm

Infected Flea Ingested

Lungworm

Enters Lungs

Eggs coughed up and swallowed

Passed in Faeces

Eaten by Snails. Slugs

Cat Eats
Cats Intestine

Enters Bloodstream

Transport Hosts
Frogs. Birds. Rodents

---

therefore unwise to deflea a cat by crushing the fleas with your fingers, as in this way humans become infected.

Lungworm

Surveys indicate a 40 per cent incidence of lungworm in many cat populations. Adult worms, which measure 8 millimetres, are found in the air passages of the cat's lungs. Hatching larvae migrate to the windpipe and pass through the alimentary tract to be voided in the faeces. Snails and slugs eat the larvae and are eaten in turn by transport hosts such as rodents, frogs, lizards and birds. When the cat eats the transport hosts, the lungworm larvae penetrate its stomach and intestine and reach the lungs. In heavy infestations coughing, diarrhoea and death may occur.

Treatment for lungworm is best left to the discretion of your vet.

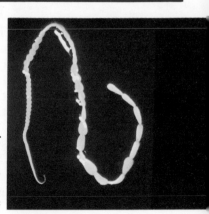

The individual segments of tapeworm are passed in droppings.

Worm control
- Mother cats should be wormed at three and six weeks during pregnancy.
- Kittens at three weeks and each two weeks until 12 weeks of age and then three times per year for life.
- Dispose of cat litter daily.
- Keep cats clean, well groomed and flea free.
- Eradicate rodents.
- Wash hands after handling animals.
- Avoid contact with cats faeces e.g. in children's sand pits, by fondling or kissing the cat or letting it sit on eating surfaces.

Treatment
Seek your veterinarian's advice because worm preparations vary in their efficiency against each species. Your veterinarian can diagnose if your cat has worms by examining a faecal sample microscopically. The egg shape identifies the species.

Breeding

The male (Tom)
Sexual maturity is reached in the male at about eight months. Toms under six months of age may show sexual interest, tussling with another kitten (female or male), mounting its back and perhaps simulating sexual motions. When a female on heat is nearby, the tom will cry and try to get out of the house to reach her. He may spray foul-smelling urine around the house. This is normal behaviour; an expression of his sexual ability and an advertisement of his availability.

Impotence is rare in the cat. Lack of virility can be caused by a vitamin A deficiency or a change in environment. Vitamin A deficiency can be corrected by two or three drops of good-quality cod-liver oil in the diet daily.

A male cat in which one or both testicles have failed to descend into the scrotum is known as a cryptorchid. Where both testicles are undescended, the cat is usually sterile. A male cat in which one testicle remains undescended is known as a monorchid and is usually fertile. Cryptorchidism is regarded as an hereditary abnormality. These cats should be desexed.

Any tom that is not going to be used for breeding should be castrated to prevent roaming, to eliminate the strong odour of the urine and to prevent unwanted kittens. Desexing also tends to make the male more docile and softens his appearance. It is best done at six months of age.

The female (Queen)
The queen is generally sexually mature at six months of age. While the male cat is interested sexually for the whole year, the female is sexually interested only when she is in season. This occurs at fourteen-day intervals and usually lasts for three to six days. It may be prolonged for up to ten days if mating does not occur. The two main breeding seasons are spring and summer but the cat may cycle at other times of the year.

Compared to the dog, the cat shows few physical signs of heat (such as swelling of the vulva or vaginal discharge). Behavioural changes, however, are unmistakable.

The queen on heat shows the following signs: increased restlessness (she may be absent for days at a time, if not kept confined); increased vocal activity, particularly in the Siamese breed; affectionate behaviour towards owners; constant rolling and crying; hollowing of the back; raising of the hindquarters; deflection of the tail to one side; treading movements of the hindlegs.

Ovulation in the queen does not occur automatically when the follicles ripen in the ovary, but requires some stimulus to trigger it off, such as mechanical stimulation of the cervix. A fairly prolonged period of courtship (three or four days) is necessary to stimulate the follicles to ripen to the point of rupture. During the courtship period, the female will reject male advances; then follows a period of about twenty-four hours when she will accept service from the selected male (or males) several times.

In contrast, lactating queens, which usually come into heat within a few days of giving birth, will disappear briefly and accept service without the courtship period. These matings are usually fertile and account for the feline species' ability to proliferate. It is important for people already saddled with an unwanted litter to remember that the cat can become pregnant again while lactating. Desexing three weeks into the lactation period will not dry up the mother's milk.

During mating, the male grasps the loose skin of the scruff of the female's neck with his teeth; this seems to be an essential part of the mating ritual. Because of the anatomical arrangement of cats' genitalia, the full co-operation of the female is essential for mating. Oestrus behaviour continues for twenty-four hours following mating, though a male is no longer accepted. Because a change in environment can affect the virility of the male cat, it is best to bring the queen to him.

Failure to cycle

Failure to cycle has several causes, the main one being nutritional deficiencies. Deficiencies of vitamin A and essential fatty acids are more common than is generally realised. Iodine deficiency is seen in cats on a mainly meat diet.

Illumination is important; it is recommended that breeding queens should be exposed to at least fourteen hours of light in each twenty-four, preferably a combination of daylight and artificial light. Contact with regularly cycling queens also promotes oestrus.

'Silent' oestrus is a newly recognised condition found in cats that are normally allowed to leave the house but kept confined during oestrus periods. Such queens develop the ability to conceal their status until leaving the owner's area of control and observation.

If fertilisation does not occur after ovulation, a state of pseudo-pregnancy lasting thirty to thirty-five days follows. This is not easily recognised, because the cat is perfectly normal but simply fails to cycle.

Birth control

Unless you have your female cat desexed or your male cat neutered, you will always have to contend with the animal's vigorous sex life. Females possess great sexual energy and will copulate with more than one tom during the heat period, which is usually short but very noisy, with both male and female yowling till the mating is over. Three or four heat periods a year are not uncommon.

Methods of contraception, apart from keeping the cat confined, are:

Contraceptive tablet or injection This method is not commonly used because of inconvenience. Lengthy use of these drugs may cause side effects and the cat may put on weight.

Desexing (spaying) is the usual choice. A surgical procedure to remove the ovaries, spaying is best done at six months of age. It prevents the cat from having heat cycles and prevents the birth of unwanted kittens. It also stops the female becoming involved in fights and eliminates visits by tom cats. The cat's tubes can be tied instead of removing the ovaries, but as this does not eliminate the nuisance problem of the cat on heat it is not recommended.

Breeding systems

A pedigree cat is one having both parents of the same breed. A breed is a group of cats with common characteristics which distinguish them from other groups. The following is a brief summary of some breeding systems (for further details, consult a book specialising in breeding systems).

Inbreeding

Inbreeding is the mating of very closely related cats, such as father and daughter, mother and son, brother and sister. This type of breeding is not recommended for the novice cat breeder, since many undesirable traits may be produced. It is used when there is a desire to accentuate certain characteristics in the offspring.

Line breeding

Line breeding is the most common and reliable system of breeding cats (and other animals). It is similar to inbreeding, but the animals are not so closely related—for example, mating cousins with cousins. Inbreeding and line breeding tend to concentrate characteristics, whether they be good or bad; great emphasis should therefore be placed on the selection of animals used in these systems. Bad features can be just as firmly fixed by these methods as good features.

Out crossing

Out crossing is the practice of mating unrelated or remotely related cats within a breed.

Cross breeding

Cross breeding is mating a pedigree cat with a pedigree cat of a different breed. When this is done scientifically, new breeds are established.

Pregnancy

Gestation in the cat usually averages sixty-five days; it is unlikely that kittens born before the fifty-sixth day will survive. Between days twenty-one and thirty-two, some pregnant queens show signs of oestrus, which can be confusing to an owner. This false oestrus is of no consequence.

At twenty-one to thirty-five days diagnosis of pregnancy can be made by abdominal palpation by your veterinary surgeon, but it will not tell you the number of kittens. X-rays of the abdomen after day forty are the only precise way of determining the number of kittens before birth. The nipples of a cat pregnant for the first time become more prominent and pink after the first fourteen days.

After about the thirty-fifth or thirty-seventh day, abdominal distension occurs in cats with litters of several kittens. The mammary glands become enlarged during the last week of pregnancy and milk secretion commences two or three days before the birth. The average litter size is four.

The cat requires little special treatment during normal pregnancy. Normal exercise, even jumping and climbing, is allowed and in fact is beneficial in maintaining muscle tone. Food intake does not increase very much till about the sixth week. It then increases until the queen is eating about twice her normal food intake at the eighth week. As the cat gets larger, it is best to divide the daily ration into two or three smaller meals. (For special nutritional requirements during pregnancy, see pp. 42-6.)

As the birth approaches, provide a suitable place for the queen to have her kittens. Select a spot that is protected on at least three sides and is in partial darkness. Find a small cardboard box and place several thicknesses of torn-up newspaper inside. Such consideration on your part is no guarantee that the queen will use the box, however.

Foetal death

The vast majority of cats have a completely normal pregnancy, but some pedigree cats, especially the so-called thoroughbreds such as the Siamese and Burmese, have a quite high incidence of abortion, foetal resorption, still-born kittens and weak failing kittens. (In many cases the kittens may be suffering from the effects of a vitamin deficiency.) The types of abortion are:

Sporadic abortion This is associated with hormonal and nutritional deficiencies, poor husbandry and other poorly defined causes.

Infectious abortion This may arise from bacterial, viral, mycoplasma or protozoan origin.

Habitual abortion This occurs most commonly in breeding catteries, causing abortion between the fourth and seventh weeks of pregnancy. This type of abortion is associated with the presence of a bloody vaginal discharge lasting five to six days. The queen appears clinically normal, with no temperature rise. Oestrus follows within four weeks of the abortion and a subsequent conception will be normal but there is a high probability that abortion will recur. The feline leukemia virus has been incriminated as a major cause.

The birth

During the first stage of labour, which lasts from twelve to twenty-four hours, the queen becomes restless, occasionally crying and making frequent trips to the nesting box where she may indulge in some bedmaking. There is a sharp drop in rectal temperature early in this stage.

Obvious straining marks the beginning of the second stage, and the first kitten is usually born within thirty minutes. Quite a high proportion of kittens are born tail first; this is of little consequence. Intervals between births may be ten to fifty minutes, depending to some extent upon the number of kittens in the litter. The birth of each kitten is normally followed by membranes, although it is possible for two or three membranes to come out together.

An interrupted type of labour has been described in the cat. Here a part of the litter is delivered normally, followed by a period of twelve to twenty-four hours when the queen behaves as though birth has been completed. Examination reveals that further kittens are present but the cat is resting. Labour is resumed at the end of the period of rest and the remainder of the litter is delivered without difficulty.

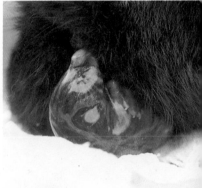

A new kitten is born, still in the foetal membranes.

Dystocia

This is the term to describe difficulty in giving birth. Abnormal births are usually caused by small openings in the pelvis, the result of healed fractures from motor vehicle accidents or spontaneous fractures and deformities resulting from calcium deficiencies; this is more common in Siamese cats. All queens suffering from pelvic deformities should be speyed at the earliest opportunity. Some birth difficulties result from abnormal presentation of the foetus sideways, oversized kittens or foetal monstrosities. Caesarian section in the cat is very rarely necessary. However, where the queen has been straining without result for more than one hour, a veterinary surgeon should be contacted.

Clear the mouth and nostrils of membranes but leave the cord intact .

Eclampsia

When a queen is suckling a large litter, there is the danger that she may suffer from calcium deficiency. In extreme cases she may suffer from the disorder eclampsia, when the kittens are three to eight weeks old. Symptoms include shivering, heavy breathing, staggering, high temperature and eventual coma. Take her immediately to the vet, who will administer an injection of calcium. The kittens, at that age, can be weaned.

After 15 minutes tear the cord 1 centimetre from the abdomen.

A normal, well-fed, warm kitten will lie on its tummy with its limbs relaxed.

A proud mother and her healthy kittens.

The newly born kitten

If the queen does not free the kittens from the foetal membranes, tear the membranes from the kitten's face with your fingers to allow it to breathe. Do not sever the umbilical cord for at least ten to fifteen minutes, as a valuable amount of blood is expressed from the foetal membranes into the kitten's bloodstream after birth. If it is necessary, the umbilical cord should be torn between your thumb and forefinger about 1 centimetre from the kitten's belly. Take great care not to pull on the kitten's stomach, as a severe hernia could result.

Occasionally, an apparently lifeless kitten is revived by the licking activity of the queen. If a kitten appears lifeless, active steps must be taken to revive it. Test for heartbeat by feeling the kitten's chest between your thumb and forefinger. Clear its airways by swabbing out the mouth and throat with cotton-wool attached to tweezers. Gentle mouth-to-mouth resuscitation can be attempted, but there is a danger of overexpanding, and possibly even rupturing, the lungs. A safer method is to hold the kitten between your hands and slowly swing it round in a circle with the head at the circumference two or three times. Another method is to rub the chest with a soft towel. Don't be 'heavy-handed'—you risk crushing the bones.

Once revived, the kitten should be placed in the mother's box with a well-padded hot water bottle warm enough so that you can keep it against the soft part of your arm comfortably. The importance of warmth for newborn kittens cannot be overemphasised. If the cat remains calm during the birth of her kittens, they should be allowed to remain with her and encouraged to suckle, as this tends to stimulate her uterine contractions.

Kittens usually suckle every two hours in the first week of life, and after this the frequency falls off to about every four hours. If the milk supply is inadequate, the kittens will appear to be hungry and will nose around the mother, crying continually. A normal, well-fed, warm kitten will lie on its tummy with its limbs relaxed. There is no crying. If there is any doubt about the mother's feeding ability, the kittens should be weighed. At birth a normal kitten weighs between 90 and 130 grams, depending on the breed and the number in the litter. An adequate milk supply should result in a gain of 10 grams each day. After the first week, weighing should be performed weekly; kittens should gain on average between 80 and 100 grams per week.

Orphaned kittens

Where the kittens are orphaned (or the mother's supply of milk is inadequate) a milk as close to cat's milk as possible must be supplied. The difference between cow's milk and cat's milk is that the latter contains about twice as much protein, which is essential for the normal high rate of growth of the kitten. A suitable substitute for cat's milk is one cup of evaporated cow's milk plus a quarter cup of water, or cow's milk to which has been added egg yolk at the rate of 1 part beaten egg yolk to 4 parts milk. There are also commercial substitutes.

Orphaned kittens can be fed by stomach tube.

Orphaned kittens will require feeding every two to three hours for the first week; the intervals between feeds can be gradually increased to four hours. Feeds can be given by stomach tube—a length of soft polythene tubing about 2 millimetres in diameter attached to a disposable syringe. Measure the distance between the kitten's nose and the rear of its rib cage when its head and neck are stretched out, and cut the tubing slightly longer (this is sufficient to reach the kitten's stomach). Pass the tube through its mouth and gently push until the indicated length has been reached. Initially about 3 millilitres (about half a teaspoon) of milk should be given at each feed. Increase the amount to 4 millilitres (nearly 1 teaspoon) by the end of the first week and to 10 millilitres (2 teaspoons) by the third week. You can also use a pet nurser bottle for the kitten to suckle. All equipment must be kept scrupulously clean; sterilise it as you would for a baby.

Keep orphaned kittens in a large cardboard box lined with torn newspaper, at a temperature of about 30°C; this can be effected by the use of infra-red lamps or electric light bulbs. By four weeks the kittens should be lapping and eating. A mother cat usually stimulates defecation and urination by licking her kitten's anal area. This can be simulated in orphaned kittens by gently rubbing with a paper tissue. Wipe the kittens clean afterwards. Keep them clean all over by daily wipe-downs with a soft damp towel. If the kittens are unable to suckle their mother in the first twenty-four hours to receive colostrum, it is advisable to take them to a veterinary surgeon who will dose them with a small quantity of normal cat serum to give them antibody protection against disease.

Checking the length of the tube.

Weaning

Weaning of all kittens should commence at about four weeks. Add Farex and dissolved meat jelly (obtained from any proprietary tinned cat or dog food) into the milk feed, gradually increasing the consistency and adding more cat food till the kittens are eating normally. It is important during weaning to accustom kittens to a wide range of foods. Siamese cats especially seem to become easily addicted to the one type of food.

Death of newborn kittens

The newborn kitten is incapable of regulating its body temperature by shivering. Even in quite high room temperatures, the kitten must be near a source of radiating heat such as the mammary area of its mother or on top of a warm water bottle, otherwise it will lose heat and become hypothermic. The early stages of hypothermia are marked by increased activity, high-pitched crying and an increased respiratory rate. The body surface feels cool. Later the crying becomes more plaintive, muscle tone is poor, attempts to suck are weak, and milk is not ingested. The kitten may fall on its side frequently. Later, crying ceases and the kitten lies motionless. Often these kittens are thought to be dead and discarded by the breeder. However, they can often be revived, even after a period of twelve hours, simply by warming them. Hypothermia may occur when the queen is a poor mother and denies the kittens access to the mammary area.

Kittens will also suckle the bottle.

Nutritional deficiencies in the pregnant queen can result in abnormal or weak kittens. Vitamin A deficiency may cause a high death rate without any other apparent cause. The main abnormality is a misshapen chest.

Iodine deficiency in the queen may cause difficulties at birth and a tendency to produce kittens with congenital deformities such as cleft palates.

Administration of certain drugs to pregnant queens may produce congenital defects in their kittens. For example, cortisone in early pregnancy may lead to the production of cleft palates, and penicillin late in pregnancy appears to cause gangrene of foetal extremities and the tip of the tail.

Viral infections contracted early in pregnancy may lead to abortion or to resorption of the foetus. Viruses contracted later in pregnancy can cause meningitis in the kitten after birth. This can also occur in kittens up to four weeks old that contract viruses after birth. Other viruses have been incriminated as a cause of fading and death associated with severe diarrhoea and ulceration of the mouth in young kittens.

Navel hernia can be congenital (or due to excess force while breaking the cord). Infection of the umbilicus is caused by bacteria. A condition that has been termed toxic milk, or acid milk, has been described as a cause of illness in young kittens. The characteristics include a crying, bloated kitten with a rough coat. The kitten usually lies with its feet tucked under its body and has a sore, raw-looking anal region. In such cases examination of the queen will usually reveal the presence of a vaginal discharge and an enlarged uterus, indicating a womb infection.

Caring for the sick cat

The first signs of sickness noticed by the owner are usually decreased appetite and listlessness. As long as a cat looks bright and has missed only a couple of meals, there is generally no need for concern—the cat may be eating at a neighbour's house, or having success hunting. If it appears listless, keep a careful eye on it and try to confine it; sometimes it is best to lock the cat up, as cats will go into old sheds or under houses or into other inaccessible places when they are ill.

Other signs of early illness are prolapse of the third eyelid, vomiting, diarrhoea, sneezing, runny eyes, straining, crouching, ear scratching, head shaking, bad breath, yowling, dribbling from the mouth and spitting. With any of these symptoms, the animal should be taken to a vet for a complete examination.

More than any other animal, a sick cat needs familiar surroundings. Its owner should give it plenty of attention. Often loving care can be more beneficial than medicine. Siamese and Burmese in particular will lose the will to live if they do not get a lot of attention from the owner. Because the owner's tender loving care is so important, most vets will keep a sick cat in the surgery only until it is over the critical stage, even if this means daily return visits to the surgery for further treatment. The combination of veterinary care and home attention is the best way to speedy recovery in the cat. Cats recuperating and convalescing from an illness will eat better if returned home. Cats can be difficult patients—their nervousness and tendency to bite and scratch in unfamiliar situations often makes treatment hazardous. When the cat returns home, put it in a warm, draught-free semi-dark room, where it can observe the activities of the family.

Your veterinarian will rely heavily on the cat's history and any observations that you can relay. It is best to record the cat's temperature, medical history and current symptoms, and any other abnormalities or relevant information the cat may show. This should be written down in a notebook. A sick cat's temperature should be taken twice a day, in the morning and again in the evening, when it will be at its highest point.

To take its temperature, use a narrow-bulb human thermometer. Shake it down below 38°C, lubricate the tip with soap, lift the animal's tail and insert the thermometer into the rectum. The mercury bulb should lie against the rectal wall to get a correct reading. Leave the thermometer in the rectum for about a minute. Normal temperature is about 38.5°C, but kittens might have a slightly higher reading. A slight fever is about 39–39.5°C, and a serious temperature is 40°C and higher. If the fever is due to a bacterial infection, it will be twenty-four hours before antibiotics reduce the temperature by even half a degree. As long as the temperature is falling, it is worthwhile persevering with the drug. If the temperature does not drop within thirty-six hours, contact your vet. Cats that are ill, have a fever or are off their food need increased vitamin B in their diet. This can be provided by brewer's yeast (see Vitamins, pp. 42–3.)

Foods with strong odours, such as fish (tuna, sardines, pilchards) chicken or baby food, are more attractive to the sick cat. Odours can be enhanced by warming the food—although cats with mouth ulcers, as in respiratory tract viruses, gain some relief from discomfort by eating cold foods.

Cats suffering from cat flu (feline respiratory disease) will sometimes get relief from inhaling human decongestants. Hold the cat's head over a bowl of steaming water and decongestant, with a towel over cat and bowl, and hold it there firmly for a few minutes to inhale the vapour. Hold the cat in such a way that it cannot struggle and hurt itself with the hot water.

Sick cats, particularly those suffering from upper respiratory tract infections, respond to the 'purring therapy'. This involves handling the cat and cuddling it to induce it to purr. The increased heart rate and respiratory involvement tends to clear out the sinuses, allowing the cat to smell its food and thus eat better.

Emergencies

The Common Ailments listing includes information on artificial respiration, drowning, motor vehicle accidents and shock.

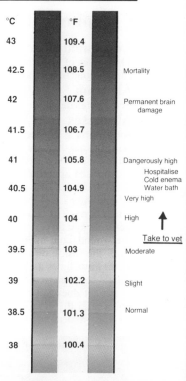

°C	°F	
43	109.4	
42.5	108.5	Mortality
42	107.6	Permanent brain damage
41.5	106.7	
41	105.8	Dangerously high
		Hospitalise
		Cold enema
40.5	104.9	Water bath
		Very high
40	104	High
		Take to vet
39.5	103	Moderate
39	102.2	Slight
38.5	101.3	Normal
38	100.4	

Temperature chart

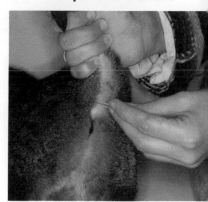

Shake the thermometer below 38°C, lubricate the end with soap, lift the animal's tail and insert the thermometer 2 centimetres into the rectum. Leave the thermometer there for about a minute.

Common ailments

Abdominal distension
The causes of abdominal distension are tumours, fluid accumulation, fatness and pregnancy.

Abortion
See Foetal death, p. 57.

Abscesses
An abscess is an accumulation of pus usually under the skin. In cats they are usually the result of a cat bite some three to four days earlier. The cat becomes listless and has a depressed appetite while the abscess is building up. The usual locations are around the head, on the back and around the base of the tail. If the abscess has burst, leaving a hole, irrigate it two or three times a day with 50 per cent peroxide and 50 per cent water for three to four days. Keep the wound hole open, using a cotton bud, until it heals from the inside out. After three days irrigate with clean water three times daily. If the abscess has not burst, the cat should be taken to the vet so that the abscess can be lanced. If the cat does not regain its appetite within twenty-four hours, visit the vet for antibiotic shots. (See also SKIN DISORDERS: PYOGENIC DERMATITIS, and TAIL DISORDERS.)

Abscesses around the head are commonly caused by fights with other cats.

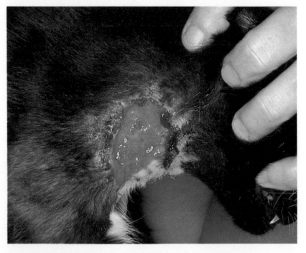

A healthy abscess wound 8 days after treatment.

Allergies
Cats can be allergic to certain foods, plants and other substances. An allergy may reveal itself in several ways: it can be accompanied by dermatitis, swelling of the local area, itchiness or sores. Tracing the cause of the allergy is frequently very difficult and is a job for your veterinary surgeon. Cats do not suffer from acute allergic reactions as do dogs.

Cats, unlike dogs, very commonly cause an allergic reaction in humans (see Selecting a Cat, p. 37).

Alopecia
See SKIN DISORDERS.

Anaemia
Anaemia is detected by pale mucous membranes of the mouth or the eyes. It can be caused by feline infectious anaemia (a blood parasite), feline infectious peritonitis (a virus), internal parasites (such as coccidiosis, roundworms, hookworms and tapeworms), dosing with antibiotics, chronic liver disease, poor nutrition and as an associated problem with many debilitating diseases. The exact cause of the anaemia should be determined by a veterinarian and appropriate treatment commenced. Supplementation of the diet with liver and B-complex vitamin drops helps.

Appetite, decreased
Decreased appetite has a number of causes. The cat may walk up to the food and attempt to eat, but cease, indicating that a condition of the mouth is causing the problem, such as ulcers, sore gums, or a cracked or decayed tooth. A fussy eater may be refusing a change of diet. If the cat is apparently well but misses one or two meals, do not worry particularly. The cat may be eating at a neighbour's place, it may be full of lizards, birds or other small life, or you may be overfeeding it. If the decreased appetite is accompanied by lethargy, the cat may have a fever and be incubating one of the infectious diseases or an abscess. If its temperature is normal but the animal is lethargic, then constipation, ticks or feline infectious anaemia should be considered. It can be seen from the range of illnesses mentioned—and these are only some—that a decreased appetite is only a symptom indicating the cat is unwell.

Appetite, increased
Increased appetite can be caused by an unbalanced diet, malabsorption syndrome, chronic pancreatitis, sugar diabetes, pregnancy, lactation, an extreme worm burden, nervous diarrhoea, anxiety, chronic bleeding, a cold environment, kidney disease or hormonal problems.

Artificial respiration
When artificial respiration is necessary, place the cat on its side in the fresh air with the four legs stretched out. With a handkerchief, pull out the animal's tongue and then with your hands on its rib-cage press down gently, release and wait. Repeat this sequence rhythmically at about fifteen beats per minute. When the cat revives, treat for shock and take it to a vet.

Bad breath
See MOUTH DISORDERS.

Baldness
See SKIN DISORDERS.

Behavioural problems
Cats do not seem to develop as many neuroses from urban life as dogs do, possibly because they can escape over the back fence and extend their territory. Behavioural abnormalities are confined to 'spraying' in the male cat and to aggressiveness. These traits are almost eliminated if the cat is desexed. When a tom starts spraying in the house he usually has a good reason (for a cat); maybe a new cat in the neighbourhood has become dominant over him, or there is a new pet or a new baby in the household. Your cat is trying to re-establish his territory by marking it with urine. Control over spraying and aggressiveness can be helped by the administration of progesterone or by desexing. Discuss this with your veterinary surgeon.

Birth difficulties
See Breeding, p. 57.

Bites
Puncture wounds on a cat are usually from another cat. Lacerations, tears and rips usually indicate involvement with a possum or a dog. If the wound is gaping and has gone through the skin, it is best to seek veterinary attention for antibiotic therapy and stitches. Open wounds should be irrigated three times daily with a 50 per cent peroxide and water solution for four days. After this period, irrigation with clean water is satisfactory. Keep the wound open with cotton buds so that it heals from the inside out. To prevent your cat fighting, feed it in the evening and lock it indoors until morning. This will reduce the incidence of fighting because most aggressiveness occurs at night. If the wound becomes infected, and your cat is off its food, veterinary attention should be sought for the administration of antibiotics. (See also ABSCESSES.)

Bleeding
If severe bleeding occurs on an extremity, a tourniquet can be applied between the laceration and the trunk of the body. The tourniquet must be released for several seconds every three or four minutes. If bleeding occurs from a wound on the body, apply a pressure bandage. Take the cat to the nearest veterinary surgeon in either case. If it is difficult to bandage the area, simply use a clean handkerchief and apply pressure over the bleeding point.

Blindness
See EYE DISORDERS.

Bones
Bone problems are dealt with in the section on Common Ailments of dogs.

Breathing problems
Shallow, rapid breathing can be caused by tick paralysis, snake bite, spider bite, pus in the thorax, pneumonia, hernia of the diaphragm, bronchitis, pleurisy, anaemia or fever. (See also Vaccinations, pp. 50–2, and Caring for the Sick Cat, pp. 60–1.)

Bronchitis
The bronchi are the two main branches of the trachea (windpipe). They extend into each lung where they break up further to form the lung tissue. Bronchitis is simply an inflammation of the mucous lining of these tubes.

It can be caused by allergies, bacteria, dust, parasites or viruses. The usual symptoms are coughing and distressed breathing. There may also be a temperature rise.

Treatment depends on diagnosing the cause. A vet will usually prescribe antibiotics and antihistamines to control the problem.

Burns
Cats can be severely burned by lightning (if up a tree during a storm), electric shock, chemicals, open flames or hot ashes. Watch open fire-places—cats will often crawl in there for the warmth and get burned by hidden embers. Many cats are scalded by hot liquids in busy kitchens. If the cat has first-degree burns, where the skin is red or blistered or the hair is singed in a localised area immerse the cat immediately in cold water, then trim away the hair and apply a thick grease such as petroleum jelly, butter, lard or commercial burn ointment. Do not apply antiseptic. Wet tea leaves (which contain tannic acid) will help reduce pain and loss of fluid; however, they should not be used on large burns or scalds, as too much tannic acid is toxic to cell tissue. In cases of more severe burns, where the hair is burnt off and the skin charred or black, it is imperative to get the animal to a vet.

Calcium deficiency
See Feeding, pp. 41–6.

Cancer/carcinomas
See SKIN DISORDERS.

Castration
See Birth Control, p. 55.

Cataracts
See EYE DISORDERS.

Some cats and birds are able to live together in one family.

Cats and birds
It is natural for a cat to be a hunter, even though it may have access to plenty of food. In the peripheral areas of cities, where there are reserves and national parks, domestic cats frequently venture for a day's hunting. Unfortunately there are practical limitations in trying to stamp out this kind of activity. Cats have also fallen into disfavour with the increasing number of city and suburban bird lovers who maintain feeding trays.

Bells on a cat's collar may work sometimes, although it is quite possible for cats equipped with this alarm system to stalk so quietly that the bells don't ring until the bird is well and truly caught. If you intend feeding birds, try to place a cat guard (or other animal guard) around the feeding area. But even then tragedies will occur—the bird lands on the ground to pick up a fallen seed and the cat will spring out from a hiding place.

A recent survey of cats' stomach contents in urban areas indicated that much of the wild fauna consisted of small lizards rather than birds.

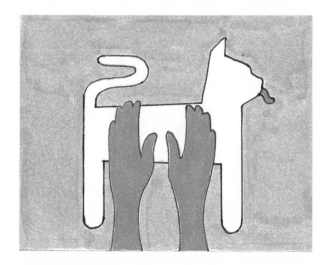

Artificial respiration

Cats and dogs

If there are cat-hating dogs in the neighbourhood you will have to protect your cat. Most cats are quicker than dogs; where there is a one-to-one challenge, the cat can usually look after itself. When there is more than one dog, the cat can sometimes be in trouble, particularly if it is cornered. The cat usually adopts a defensive role and the dog at worst ends up with a scratched nose or a punctured eye. In the worst situations a cat can be torn apart and killed.

Cats and dogs of the one family nearly always get along very well. This is particularly the case if one or the other has been introduced as a young animal. The older animal mothers the other one. It is a common sight to see cats and dogs of the same family playing with each other in the garden. If you have no fences or your own dog is a problem with your cat, the best idea is to have accessible high areas in the garden where your cat can escape. Alternatively, have a small cat door which only allows the cat through.

Cats and dogs of the one family nearly always get along well.

Cats and fish

Goldfish swimming in a neighbour's garden pool are another source of interest for your cat. This may provoke some 'communication' between you and your neighbour. Although there is no law to stop a cat from going fishing, your neighbour may take steps to stop your cat from roaming near the goldfish pond. The simplest method is to cover the pond with a wire grill.

Chin sores

See SKIN DISORDERS.

Clawing furniture

See p. 49.

Coccidiosis

A microscopic organism, coccidiosis lives and multiplies in the cells of the intestinal tract. It affects mainly young animals and is particularly prevalent where overcrowding exists, such as in breeding establishments or pet shops. It causes diarrhoea, lethargy, weight loss and rough coat. The diagnosis can be made by examining faeces under a microscope. The disease must be specifically treated; ordinary anti-diarrhoea treatments have only a temporary effect.

Congenital defects

Unlike the dog, the cat has very few congenital defects. For those it does have, see Selecting a Cat, pp. 37–38.

Conjunctivitis

See EYE DISORDERS.

Constipation

The signs of constipation are straining, listlessness and de-

creased appetite. In serious and chronic cases, vomiting may also occur. One of the commonest causes is an all-meat diet and consequent nutritional secondary hyperparathyroidism (N.S.H.) which results in the narrowing of the pelvic outlet, in turn causing constriction of the bowel. Faecal build-up forward of this constriction results in distension of the intestine. Even though faecal matter may escape from this distended area initially, the muscle layers in the intestinal walls stretch so that the bowel is permanently ballooned. The type of diet is important in resolving the condition. (See pp. 41–6.)

Dried food or food high in calcium content, such as bone, tends to aggravate the problem. Treatment is by oral faecal softeners such as Dilax or Coloxyl tablets combined with paraffin oil at the rate of one teaspoon twice a day. In addition, commercial enemas or warm, soapy water can be used to evacuate the lower bowel. In cases where conservative treatment is unsuccessful, surgery can be performed to remove the faecal contents from the intestine and to widen the pelvic outlet. Twice-weekly applications of oil, faecal softeners and diets with high moisture, such as tinned foods, will help to prevent the condition. Liver, milk and kidneys tend to have a laxative effect in cats. The amount of medication or the degree of change of diet is governed by the relevant activity of the bowel.

Contraceptive tablets, injection

See Birth Control, p. 55.

Convulsions

See FITS.

Coughing

A persistent cough is an indication that something is wrong with the cat and it should not be ignored. Coughing can be due to irritation of the throat, the windpipe or the lungs. It can be caused by:

lungworms, which are caught when the cat eats lizards, grasshoppers or cockroaches (see Worming, pp. 52–4);
migrating roundworms (see Worming, pp. 52–4);
congestion caused by cat flu (see Vaccination, pp. 50–2);
pneumonia;
bronchitis;
tight collars;
foreign bodies in the windpipe.

Hair-balls cause regurgitation rather than a cough.

If coughing is persistent, the cat should be taken to the veterinary surgeon for diagnosis, as home remedies may suppress the cough without curing the problem.

Cycling

See Breeding, pp. 54–6.

Dandruff

When dandruff occurs it is most obvious along the back line of the cat. If the hair in the affected area is sparse and the remaining hairs are bristle-like, the dandruff may be due to a hormonal deficiency. If the hair coat is normal and glossy, the dandruff may be due to a diet deficient in essential fatty acids. These can be replaced by the addition of fat to the diet or by adding butter or margarine at the rate of one teaspoonful per day to the cat's diet. (See also DRY COAT.)

Deafness

See EAR DISORDERS.

Dehydration

See DRINKING, DECREASED.

Depression

Depression is a symptom of many diseases and of many problems. It may be caused by a fever, incorrect diet (particularly vitamin B-group deficiency), any disease situation, incubation of viral diseases such as cat flu, kidney complaints, tooth decay or fight wounds. It may also be caused by constipation or a blocked bladder. Cats can also become depressed by a change in environment—for example, being put in a cattery, being banned from the house for some reason, the introduction of a new animal to the household. These are some of the common conditions causing depression in the cat, but there are many others. Unless the reason for the depression is obvious, it is best to consult a veterinary surgeon.

Dermatitis
See SKIN DISORDERS.

Desexing
See Breeding, pp. 54–5.

Diabetes
There are two types—water and sugar. The former is rarely seen. Sugar diabetes is occasionally diagnosed. (See p. 124.)

Diarrhoea
Diarrhoea occurs when something irritates the gut and makes it push the food through the intestines at such a fast rate that water and nutrients are not able to be resorbed in the large bowel. This can lead to dehydration, loss of weight and the loss of important electrolytes. Diarrhoea must always be controlled as quickly as possible.

Diarrhoea can be caused by: bacteria; coccidiosis; diet; nervousness; viruses, such as feline enteritis; worms, especially roundworm infestations in young kittens (see Worming section).

Some tinned foods might disagree with your cat and cause diarrhoea. Milk has a component called lactose which requires the presence of an enzyme called lactase to break down (digest) the lactose. Cats deficient in the enzyme have a persistent diarrhoea when fed cow's milk. Take the cat off milk, but ensure that you replace the calcium content with calcium carbonate in the food at the rate of half a teaspoon per 100 grams of red meat. If the cat is on a commercial diet this is unnecessary. Once the cat's stools are back to normal, cow's milk may be restarted at the rate of 50 per cent concentration with water, or a commercially prepared lactose-free milk which may be obtained from the pharmacy. Liver and kidney can also cause soft stools.

If the diarrhoea is smelly or has blood in it, veterinary attention should be sought immediately. If the cat appears normal but the stools are liquid, the diarrhoea should be controlled by starchy foods, boiled milk, cooked rice, barley or cottage cheese. The administration of half the child's dosage of commonly used anti-diarrhoea treatments can be tried for twenty-four hours. If the diarrhoea persists, seek veterinary attention.

Dietary imbalance
Feline nutrition is discussed throughout the section on Feeding.

Dilated pupils
See EYE DISORDERS.

Dribbling
See FITS, MOUTH DISORDERS and POISONING. See also Vaccinations, p. 50.

Drinking, decreased
Some cats, particularly Siamese, do not drink milk. Others do not seem to find it necessary to drink fluids at all. In some cases these cats get their water from other sources such as garden taps or baths. Cats have the facility to concentrate their urine very highly and so long as they are on a moist diet which contains 70 per cent water (such as tinned commercial meat), their fluid requirement is quite minimal. Where the cat is transferred to a dry food diet it is important to teach the cat to drink. This may be done by moistening the food or adding a small amount of salt to it.

Decreased fluid intake in the unwell animal is a real problem. The average adult cat weighs about 4 kilograms. Small body weights dehydrate very quickly, and it is important in any illness to keep the cat's body fluid up from the first day. This can be done by orally feeding the cat glucose and water, at the rate of one tablespoon of glucose per 600 millilitres of water; the cat should receive about 40 millilitres (4 tablespoons) of this fluid orally per day, in four or five doses. If the cat refuses to drink, it will become dehydrated. Dehydration is evidenced by the skin failing to return when lifted from the body. Lift the skin at the scruff of the cat's neck; it should return by the count of three. The earlier dehydration is detected, the less damage will be done. If the cat continues to refuse to take fluids orally, it should be taken to a veterinary surgeon for intravenous administration of fluid.

Drinking, increased
Increased drinking can be caused by dried food diets, fever, kidney disease, vomiting, diarrhoea, pyometron or diabetes.

Drowning
Although most cats dislike water, they can swim for a short while before becoming exhausted and drowning. After rescuing your cat from the water, hold it by the back legs, upside down, allowing the water to drain out. Swing the cat around your head, three times, holding by the back legs, centrifugally forcing out excess water. Then place the cat on its side and apply artificial respiration. When it revives treat for shock and take it to the vet.

Dry coat
A dry coat can be due to any debilitating condition. It can also be due to worms or diet deficiencies, especially essential fatty acids which can be supplied in the form of additional butter or margarine or by increasing the fatty content of the food. Vitamin A deficiencies can be rectified by adding liver to the diet, but the liver should not constitute more than 10–15 per cent of the diet. Hormonal deficiencies can lead to dry coat. (See also DANDRUFF.)

Dystocia
Difficulty in giving birth. See p. 57.

Ear disorders
Ear disorders in cats are not as prevalent as in dogs because they have short-pricked ears with little hair. This allows good air circulation to keep the ear dry.
Cancer of the ear
This occurs in white cats or white-eared cats. (See SKIN DISORDERS.)

Deafness
Deafness is a congenital and hereditary problem in blue-eyed white cats. Deafness in old age is caused by senile calcification within the middle ear. Temporary or partial deafness may be associated with ear infections. Apart from clearing any ear infections, nothing can be done for deafness. When cats become deaf, it is important to keep them away from motor vehicles.

Haematoma
Haematoma (in this instance, cauliflower ear) is seen far less often in the cat than in the dog. It is caused by a burst blood vessel in the ear lobe. The ear will need veterinary attention so that it can be drained and sutured for about a fortnight. It usually follows extensive head shaking or scratching because of irritation caused by an infection of the inner ear canal.

Infected ears
Head shaking, scratching and odour from the ears all in-

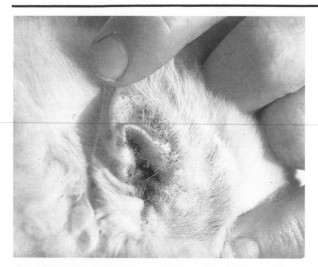

Ear mites are a common occurrence; they burrow and produce inflammation of the skin of the ear canal.

dicate infections. Ear infections are usually started by mites in the ear canal. In a recent survey, some 25 per cent of cats were found to have ear mites. The mites burrow and produce inflammation of the skin of the ear canal, which paves the way for secondary bacterial infection. The canal is usually moist and warm, and the leakage of serum from the attacking mites provides an excellent medium for bacteria and fungi to grow. In some cases of severe infestation, fits may occur.

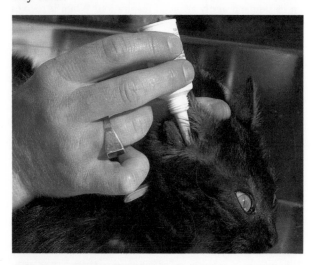

Even if the condition has improved, always complete the prescribed course of ear drops.

After cleaning the ears thoroughly with a 1 per cent Hibitane solution, control the mites by treating with one of the commercial ear drops that are available from your veterinary surgeon. It is important when treating your cat's ears to clean out any residual debris before the next treatment. This can be done with cotton buds (or cotton-wool on a matchstick) dipped in methylated spirits. Also clean the nozzle of the eardrop container before and after application to each ear to prevent transfer of infection. Shake the container well first. Place the prescribed number of drops in the ear and massage the ear canal down behind the jawbone for about thirty seconds to ensure that the drops go to the bottom of the ear (otherwise the cat will shake them out). Always complete the prescribed course. Many drops contain a local anaesthetic which gives immediate relief from the pain but does not mean the infection is cleared up. After a cat has had an infection of the ear, watch it carefully for a month to six weeks in case the infection returns. In severe cases, seek veterinary attention as the cat may have to be anaesthetised to allow the ear to be syringed clean before the first treatment.

Hair loss

Partial hair loss immediately in front of an ear in the temple region may be due to ringworm, grass mites or notoedric mange. If the skin appears normal although sparsely haired and the cat is not scratching at the area, the lack of hair is probably normal for that cat.

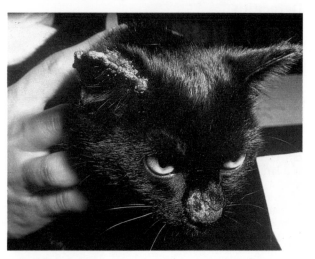

Mange can cause hair loss around the tip of the ear and on the forehead.

Eclampsia

Eclampsia is a rare condition in the cat. The cause is calcium deficiency due to suckling an excessively large litter. The symptoms appear when the kittens are between three and eight weeks old. The queen starts to stagger, shiver and breathe heavily. Eventually she loses the power of her legs and may go into a coma. This is very serious. Her temperature may rise to 41°C. Sometimes she vomits and has a rapid, shallow respiration. The kittens should be removed and immediately weaned, and the cat taken to a veterinary surgeon for an injection of calcium.

Electrocution

When the cat has received an electric shock, apply artificial respiration (see ARTIFICIAL RESPIRATION) to revive it, treat for shock and take it to the vet.

Enteritis
See FELINE ENTERITIS.

Epilepsy
See FITS.

Eye disorders
The appearance of the eyes is very important in reflecting the condition of your cat. The most common abnormality indicating sickness is prolapse of the third eyelid, which is often referred to by owners as a skin growing over the eye from the corner. This condition can be caused by tranquillisation or, more commonly, is a non-specific indication that the cat is in ill health. It can be caused by worms, viruses, including cat flu (panleukopaenia) or feline leukemia virus, dietary abnormalities such as vitamin A deficiency, fatty acid deficiency and anaemic conditions. If the cat has prolapse of the third eyelids but is in perfect health otherwise, do not be alarmed—it may be incubating a disease which its body will overcome without help. If other signs are present, consult your veterinary surgeon.

Blindness

Blindness is rare in cats and usually occurs only in the very aged animal. Providing the cat remains in its own environ-

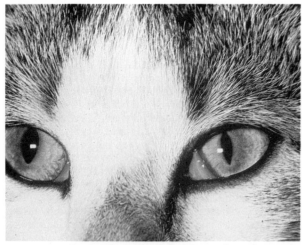

A common abnormality indicating sickness is prolapse of the third eyelid; 'skin growing across the eye from the corner'.

ment, its other sensory mechanisms will permit it to live quite a normal life.

A reversible inflammatory condition of the nerve of the eye can cause sudden temporary blindness in young cats. Vitamin A deficiencies and low protein diets can also cause blindness. Because of the complexity and interconnections of many of the eye diseases, treatment is best left to your veterinary surgeon.

Cataracts

These are rarely seen in cats, but when present may be associated with sugar diabetes.

The narrow black vertical slit of normal pupils.

Dilated pupils

Full dilation of the pupils from the normal vertical slit to a large circular black area in the eyes is a non-specific sign that the cat is unwell. This is particularly the case if the pupils fail to constrict when a torch is shone in the eyes. It is commonly seen in vitamin B-group deficiencies, tick poisoning, ocular neuritis (inflammation of the optic nerve) and many other debilitating sicknesses of the cat.

Keratitis

Keratitis is an inflammatory condition of the glassy part of the eye (the cornea). It starts as a blue haze and can progress to ulceration, pigmentation and finally, with the growth of blood vessels, can give the appearance of a red, fleshy sore. The most common cause of keratitis in the cat is the feline respiratory virus. It is a common and serious disease in cats, particularly in kittens. In young cats four to six weeks of age it is not uncommon for this condition to continue for six to eight weeks, despite intensive treatment.

Dilation of the oval black pupils, in this case coupled with third eyelid prolapse.

As with the feline respiratory diseases, Siamese and Burmese cats are the most susceptible. Because of the difficulty of treatment, veterinary attention is essential. Otherwise blindness may result.

Runny or pussy eyes

Runny or pussy eyes can be caused by conjunctivitis (which is an inflammation of the mucous membranes of the eyes caused by infection), a foreign body in the eye, dust or dirt. Home treatment includes rinsing the eye with an eye wash or boracic acid solution. If the condition does not resolve itself within twenty-four hours take the cat to the vet.

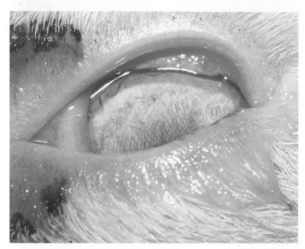

An acute viral conjunctivitis; in this case caused by the cat 'flu' syndrome.

Runny eyes can also be caused by a blocked tear duct. These ducts normally take excess tear production from the eyes to the inside of the nose. They can be permanently damaged in Persian cats or any breed with a pushed-in face. They may also become blocked with the cat flu virus or by infection. Sometimes the cat is born with the end of the tear duct covered by a fold of skin. The veterinarian will administer a dye to the eye and note its appearance at the nostril. Sometimes the duct can be flushed clear.

Acute conjunctivitis is indicated by a sensitivity to light; the eye is closed and there is a watery, profuse discharge. The mucous membrane of the eye is red. In chronic cases there is less watery discharge, less sensitivity to light and the eye is usually open. Conjunctivitis may also be caused by entropion, an inward turning of the eyelashes which rub on the eye. Ectropion is an outward turning of the eyelids, allowing accumulation of dust in the eye.

Entropion, especially of the cat's left lower eyelid, causing conjunctivitis.

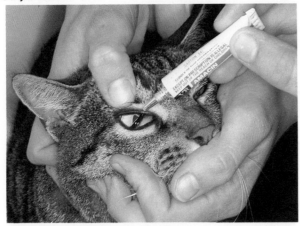

To apply eye ointment: push the two lids towards the nose and place the ointment in the corner.

Euthanasia

Euthanasia (painless death) usually involves the administration of an overdose of anaesthetic. The cat dies within six seconds. (This is covered more fully on pp.125-6.)

Facial paralysis

Injuries to the nerves controlling the facial muscles cause droopiness on the side of the face affected. Sometimes saliva runs from the paralysed corner of the mouth. If secondary to a wound or abscess, it is then a matter of time after these have been corrected to ascertain whether the nerve has recovered.

Feline aids

Is an immuno-deficiency disease allowing the affected cat to succumb to other diseases. It is transmitted in the saliva, usually by biting. There is a higher incidence in undesexed males, because they fight more. It is not sexually transmitted and will not cause aids in humans. There is no vaccine.

Feline enteritis

Feline enteritis is a major infectious disease of cats, usually known as feline panleukopaenia. There is no effective treatment for this viral disease. Prevention is by vaccination of kittens at ten weeks and again twelve to eighteen months later. See pp. 50-2.

Feline infectious anaemia

This is caused by a blood parasite which attacks the red blood corpuscles. Many cats carry this parasite without ever showing adverse symptoms. A flare-up only happens when a cat's natural resistance is markedly lowered by stress, starvation or disease. The cat gets a high persistent fever with loss of appetite and a rapidly developing acute anaemia noticeable in its very pale mucous membranes. Because of the anaemia, the cat becomes depressed and weak. The cat should be taken to your veterinary surgeon.

Feline leukaemia virus

Feline leukaemia virus infects cats of all ages. It is a blood cancer which results in tumours in various parts of the body and is ultimately fatal. There is a very long incubation period, during which time the cat becomes run down and susceptible to other diseases. Leukaemia virus may also be associated with anaemia, breeding problems and deaths in young kittens. Infection can become a serious problem where numbers of cats are housed together, as in a breeding cattery. Evidence at this stage shows that the leukaemia virus of cats cannot cause disease in humans. Cats that are infected shed the virus in their saliva, urine and nasal discharges. Other cats become infected by taking these excretions into their mouths. This can happen by sharing feed bowls, licking, biting or merely being in close contact with other cats. Queens can also transmit the virus to their kittens before they are born or afterwards in their milk. In dry situations the virus does not last more than a few hours. Some cats develop a resistance to the virus although sometimes the resistance is only enough to prevent disease symptoms from appearing but not enough to eliminate the virus. This results in a symptomless carrier-state. Although there is no treatment for the disease, there is a special blood test which can be done to detect contaminated cats. A vaccine is available.

Feline respiratory disease

A viral infection of the upper respiratory tract, also known as 'cat flu' and 'snuffles'. It is easily transmitted, but can be prevented by a course of vaccination. The importance of vaccinating your cat against this disease and feline panleukopaenia is discussed on pp. 50-2.

Female disorders

See Breeding section.

Fever

Fever is a rise in body temperature and can be caused by: viruses, such as feline enteritis, feline respiratory disease, feline leukaemia; bacteria, such as those from infected cat bites (abscesses), septicaemia or kidney disease; muscular contractions caused by convulsions or excitement; paralysis of the respiratory system (for example, from tick poisoning) resulting in inability to ventilate properly; heatstroke. The cat's normal temperature is 38.5°C. Dangers of temperatures higher than this are shown in the chart on p. 61..

Fights

See ABSCESSES, BEHAVIOURAL PROBLEMS.

Fish hooks

Fish hooks are a common problem; fishermen arrive home with a bait on the end of their line; the cat eats the bait and the hook as well. If the cat will remain still and the hook is in an accessible place—for example, the lip—the shaft of the hook closest to the line should be cut with a pair of pliers or snips. The hook is then continued on its path and out. Don't try to pull against the barb. Fish hooks usually have to be removed under general anaesthetic.

Fits

If the fits are due to a flea wash or other skin contaminants, wash the cat immediately in copious quantities of water.

A cat that is having a fit should be placed in a bag or other container and kept as quiet as possible in a semi-dark room until the fit has passed. Then take it urgently to a veterinary surgeon. It is very difficult to make a cat vomit—don't try. Go to the vet.

Fits in the cat, although not common, are usually accompanied by frothing at the mouth. Fits are caused by:
Concussion—after an accident.

Poisoning—from organo-phosphorus compounds or chlorinated hydrocarbons, which are used in many modern insecticides and other pesticides. Common poisonings in this category are due to bathing cats in Malathion, or tick and flea rinses of an incorrect dosage. Another poison causing problems is strychnine. This is usually from baits laid intentionally for noisy dogs in the neighbourhood.

Encephalitis, inflammation of the brain—caused by bacterial or viral infections.

Epilepsy—which is uncommon in cats.

Low blood *glucose* level or low blood *calcium* —particularly in females that have just had a litter of kittens and are in heavy lactation.

Ear mites—see EAR DISORDERS.

Vitamin B-group deficiency—particularly thiamine. (See also POISONING.)

Fleas
See SKIN DISORDERS.

Flies
See SKIN DISORDERS.

Flu
'Cat flu' is another name for feline respiratory disease.

Fractures
Fractures in the cat are rare. They usually occur as a result of motor vehicle accidents or falls from heights. The most common reason for fractures is nutritional secondary hyperparathyroidism (N.S.H.), which is a dangerous consequence of an all-meat diet. This causes the cat to have thin-walled bones. Cats with this condition can fracture a leg by merely jumping from a table. To handle a cat with a fracture, lift the cat by the scruff of the neck and support its body but leave the fractured area dangling. Place it in a box or blanket and take it to the vet.

F.U.S. (Feline urological syndrome)
See URINE DISORDERS.

Grass eating
Grass eating is normal and is done for two reasons: the first is to take in essential vitamins and minerals; the second is to cause the cat to vomit stale food.

Grass itch
See SKIN DISORDERS.

Groaning
Groaning is usually due to the cat having severe pain, as in a blocked bladder. The cat has a deep yowling cry. (See URINE DISORDERS.)

Gums
See MOUTH DISORDERS.

Haematoma
A haematoma can cause cauliflower ear. See EAR DISORDERS.

Hair-balls
Much fuss is made about hair-balls, particularly by breeders. As a practising veterinary surgeon I have rarely seen them cause problems in cats. Usually the cat copes quite well by regurgitating the ball of hair. Certainly the administration of paraffin or vegetable oil will help the cat pass the hair-balls. This should be administered at the rate of half a teaspoon twice a week.

Hair loss
See SKIN DISORDERS, and the general section on Grooming.

Handling cats
In their normal domestic situation most cats are quite calm and placid, but sometimes the veneer of domestication wears thin—for example, during travelling, or after injury. When transporting a cat, confine it in a firmly fastened basket, carrying case, zip bag or pillow slip. Ensure that the cat has sufficient air. When restraining a cat, take it by the

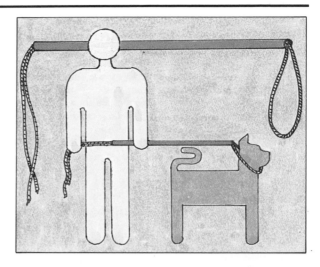

Vicious cats can be caught by using a cat-catcher.

scruff of the neck (the loose skin behind the ears) and the back legs; hold it firmly. An injured cat will sometimes bite its owner. Keep the cat's mouth away from you.

Vicious cats can be caught by using a cat-catcher, which is a 1.5-metre length of hollow pipe through which a rope loop has been passed. The loop is placed over the cat's head at a distance and pulled tight through the pipe. The cat can then be placed in a bag, basket or case. Once captured, a vicious cat is best handled by a professional such as the vet.

Hare-lip
Iodine deficiency in the pregnant cat or cortisone administered to a queen during pregnancy may produce deformity in her kittens—where there is a cleft in the roof of the mouth.

Head down
Flexion of the head downwards. (See the section on Feeding: Vitamins, Thiamine.)

Head shaking
Head shaking is usually a sign of irritation in the ear. See EAR DISORDERS.

Head to one side
See EAR DISORDERS.

Heat cycle
See Breeding, pp. 54–5.

Heatstroke
Cats suffer greatly from excessive heat and should not be left in hot rooms or cars. Long-haired cats, especially, will become overheated very quickly. Cats have a very small body weight at 4 kilograms, and a high surface area per unit mass of body. This means the cat's thermostatic mechanism has a much more difficult time controlling fluctuations in the outside temperature than that of most other animals. Symptoms of heat exhaustion in a cat are fever, heavy and laboured breathing, vomiting, prostration and eventually coma. Remove the cat to a cool place, wet it thoroughly and place it in a draught or in front of a fan. Do not give it any liquid while it is unconscious. When it regains consciousness, give it a stimulant, such as a teaspoonful of made coffee, which contains caffeine. Take it to a veterinary surgeon, as it will require further treatment for the next few days.

Hernia (Ruptures)
Four types of hernias are seen in cats:

Diaphragmatic hernia—caused when the diaphragm ruptures, allowing the intestines and other abdominal organs (such as the liver) to invade the thoracic cavity. This makes it difficult for the cat to breathe. This condition is usually the result of a motor vehicle accident.

Inguinal hernia—appears as a soft swelling in the groin, on one or both sides. The swelling may vary in size from time to time and usually disappears on pressure. This condition is hereditary, and treatment involves surgery.

Scrotal hernia—occurs when part of the bowel descends into the scrotum with the testicles. This condition is very rare in the cat and does require surgery.

Umbilical hernia—located in the centre of the abdomen in the region of the navel. Small ones contain only fat and are best left alone. Surgery on larger ones should be left to the discretion of your veterinary surgeon.

Hormonal problems

Hormonal imbalance in the cat manifests itself in strange behaviour and in skin disorders. Consult your vet for diagnosis and treatment.

Hyperkeratosis

See SKIN DISORDERS.

Inco-ordination

Lack of co-ordination can be of a general nature and caused by an ear infection, a central nervous system disease such as meningitis or encephalitis, or vitamin A or thiamine (vitamin B1) deficiencies. General illness can cause weakness. Weakness in the hindlegs can be due to ticks, fractures of the spine or limbs, dislocated hip joint or infections caused by cat bites.

Infertility

See Breeding section.

Insect stings

See STINGS.

Irritability

Irritability can be caused by a general disease situation, but it is more usually caused by a dietary deficiency of vitamin B, especially thiamine (vitamin B1). It can also be caused by vitamin E deficiencies (when high unsaturated fatty acids have been fed—for example, canned red tuna, cod liver oil, liver and horsemeat). Excess vitamin A, in high liver diets, can also cause irritability.

Jaundice

The causes of jaundice in the cat are similar to those in the dog. See Common Ailments of Dogs.

Keratitis

See EYE DISORDERS.

Kidney disease

See URINE DISORDERS.

Lameness

Lameness can be due to abscesses, fight wounds, fractures of the leg, a dislocated hip, foreign bodies in the pads (such as glass, burrs or thorns), infections between the toes, and ruptured ligaments in the knee joint. Stiffness in the foreleg may be due to excess vitamin A in the diet, particularly where liver is fed. (See also INCO-ORDINATION.)

Leaking

See URINE DISORDERS: INCONTINENCE.

Leprosy

A bacterial skin infection in the cat, affecting mainly the skin on the head. See SKIN DISORDERS.

Leukaemia

See FELINE LEUKAEMIA VIRUS.

Lice

See SKIN DISORDERS.

Lick dermatitis

See SKIN DISORDERS.

Lip ulcers

See SKIN DISORDERS: RODENT ULCER.

Listlessness/lethargy

See COCCIDIOSIS, DEPRESSION, FEVER.

Loss of balance

Middle ear infections can cause loss of balance. It can also be an indication of ticks or of vitamin B deficiency, especially thiamine (vitamin B1) deficiency. (See also INCO-ORDINATION.)

Malabsorption syndrome

Malabsorption is the end result of any disease affecting the small intestine or its lymphatic drainage to the extent that there is interference with the passage of digested nutrients into the appropriate circulatory system. It is a very complex syndrome and can only be diagnosed and dealt with by a vet.

Mange

Inflammation of the skin caused by mites. The condition is usually referred to as grass itch. See SKIN DISORDERS.

Mastitis

Mastitis is an inflammation of the mammary glands which usually occurs during lactation—although occasionally a tom may suffer from the same condition. The mammary gland is a hollow, moist, warm organ where bacteria can multiply rapidly, causing a high temperature and making the gland hot, swollen and painful. Suckling kittens may become unwell as the milk is watery, blood tinged, clotted and contains pus. Abscess formation and rupture of the wall of the gland may also occur.

It is important to seek veterinary aid immediately. Where possible the gland should be milked out continually and the animal put on to antibiotics. Hot compresses on the outside of the gland will increase circulation of the antibiotics and give some pain relief. Retention of milk after losing a litter can precipitate mastitis.

Meat diets

The dangers of an all-meat diet are discussed in the section on Feeding.

Milk for kittens

Cat's milk contains about twice as much protein as cow's milk, so care needs to be taken when feeding orphaned kittens (see Breeding section). Weaning should commence at about four weeks.

Mineral imbalance

The calcium : phosphorus ratio (see Feeding section) is an important factor in the health of the cat, particularly pregnant and lactating queens.

Cats susceptible to feline urological syndrome (see URINE DISORDERS) will probably need a diet that is low in magnesium. Average magnesium contents of cat foods are listed in the table in URINE DISORDERS.

Mites

See SKIN DISORDERS.

Moniliasis

See SKIN DISORDERS.

Motor vehicle accidents

If the cat runs away from the accident on all fours it can be assumed that its skeletal structure is unharmed. The cat should be caught and checked by a vet for internal injuries. If the cat is lying on the road gently move it to safety, allow it sufficient time (say, five or ten minutes) to recuperate from the shock of the accident before moving it. Then take the scruff of the cat's neck in one hand and slip the other hand under the cat's body. This should be done from behind the cat in order to avoid your being bitten. Be warned: cats in this situation will bite their owners. Take the cat immediately to a veterinary surgeon. If the cat has severe respiratory difficulty, do not leave it to rest but hold it upside down by the hindlegs to allow any blood to drain

Injured cats can be dangerous; carry a cat in this manner to avoid being bitten.

from the lungs. Apply artificial respiration and take it to a vet. If there is any bleeding of an extremity, place a tourniquet between the wound and the heart. If the bleeding is coming from the body where it is difficult to apply a tourniquet, use a clean handkerchief and apply pressure to reduce the blood flow.

Mouth disorders

Disorders of the mouth in cats are now extremely common. It is particularly concerning that few cats reach middle age without severe dental caries—usually resulting in extraction of their teeth. This may be a reflection of the soft diets that they are fed.

When it is still a kitten, the cat should be encouraged to tear and strip meat from large bones. Dry food also has a good effect on reducing the build-up of tartar on the teeth. See also TEETH DISORDERS.

Bad breath

Bad breath can be due to the type of diet being fed, particularly fresh meat. Any one of the following conditions can also cause bad breath.

Bleeding

The mouth is a very vascular cavity and sharp objects can easily lacerate the blood vessels. Take the cat to a veterinary surgeon, as a general anaesthetic may be needed to locate the damaged vessels.

Dribbling

Dribbling can be caused by convulsions, poisoning, stimulation of the salivary glands by infection or by chemical substances, bad teeth, infections of the mouth caused by viruses, bacteria or other organisms, trench mouth or infections of the gum. Some cats may dribble when purring—this is normal.

Inflammation of the gums

Inflammation of the gums is also associated with kidney disease (see URINE DISORDERS). Imbalances of calcium in the diet will cause the gums to recede from the teeth, leaving gaps in which food can accumulate. This food will decay, causing bad breath. (See also SKIN DISORDERS: THALLIUM.)

Lip ulcers

See SKIN DISORDERS: RODENT ULCERS.

Trench mouth

Trench mouth is a complex of organisms which cause inflammation in the arches of the back of the mouth. It leads to salivation and bad breath. There is a theory that the condition is perpetuated by dietary deficiencies. Trench mouth is a very difficult condition to treat. The B-group vitamins may help, although for effective treatment veterinary advice should be sought.

Nails

Paronychia is a disorder in which the ends of the toes are swollen and pus is visible in the claw fold. See SKIN DISORDERS.

Techniques of cutting the nails are given on p. 48.

Nose disorders

The sense of smell in the cat is very important to the animal's eating habits. Cats will only eat if they can smell their food. Sick cats, especially those with upper respiratory diseases, should be offered smelly foods such as sardines, pilchards or tuna. In addition, the nose should be kept free of discharge by regular cleaning and the use of decongestants. (See Care of the Sick Cat.)

Cancer of the nose

Cancer of the nose follows rodent ulcer of the lip (see SKIN DISORDERS) and spreads to the nose area. In the early stages it is seen as a wet, weeping chronic sore. The cat is very sensitive in the nasal area. As the cancer invades further into the nose, the lesion becomes more inflamed. The cat's face becomes so sore that it will not eat and it tends to snuffle. The earlier therapy can commence the better chance the cat has of survival. Failure to respond to conventional therapy indicates that a cancerous change has taken place and radiation treatment is indicated.

Discharge

If a nasal discharge is watery, it may indicate an allergic sinusitis. If it is accompanied by sneezing it indicates feline respiratory disease. A pussy discharge may indicate a later stage of the viral disease or an infection of the sinuses or lower areas of the respiratory system, such as pneumonia. If the discharge is coming from one nostril only, the condition is localised to one side of the sinuses; it may indicate a cheek tooth-root abscess, or a local infection.

Nutritional secondary hyperparathyroidism (N.S.H.)

See p. 44.

Obesity

Obesity is less of a problem in the cat than it is in the dog. However, more cats are now becoming overweight as a result of leading a sedentary life and being fed good-quality commercial rations. It is unhealthy for any animal to be overweight. The most effective way of dieting a cat is to choose a nutritious food which is relatively unpalatable for the cat. If the cat has been on a moist or fresh meat diet, convert it to a dry food diet or try different brands of tinned cat food. Frequently, cats have a very narrow range of foods that they find palatable, so keep trying until you find an unpalatable one.

Some cats in urban areas are always in the kitchen, always waiting for high-calorie food dropped by a sympathetic owner. Cats in the wild need to be slim and lithe in order to catch their prey. If they become overweight they are not fast enough to catch their food and they starve until they slim down. Domestic cats are handed their food even when overweight. This is unhealthy and unnatural. Apart from selecting an unpalatable food, feed the cat only one meal a day. It is important to remain steadfast and not give in to the temptation to supplement the cat's diet with more appetising food. When the cat becomes hungry, the relatively unpalatable food will be appetising enough for it to eat. Another diet for slimming a fat cat is to feed it on alternate days with its usual highly palatable diet and leave dehydrated food or unpalatable food around for it to eat on the other days.

However, despite these measures, a cat's natural agility allows it to scale high fences and beg food from a soft-hearted neighbour.

Oestrus
See Breeding section.

Old age
The average lifespan of a cat is fifteen years, but cats can live into their twenties. The most common problems affecting older cats are dental decay and associated gum problems, and kidney disease.

The dental problem can be largely avoided by veterinary check-ups on a twelve-monthly basis.

The kidney problem arises because cats eat large amounts of protein, and the kidney of the cat has a remarkable capacity to concentrate urine. This no doubt takes its toll towards the end of the cat's life.

In many cases the kidney and mouth problems are directly related. The cat usually dribbles, drinks excessively, and gradually loses weight. (See also URINE DISORDERS.)

Orphans
See Breeding section.

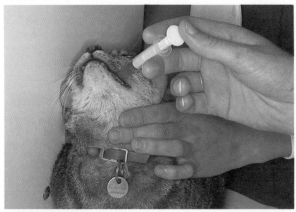

Liquids given orally must be given slowly to allow the cat to swallow.

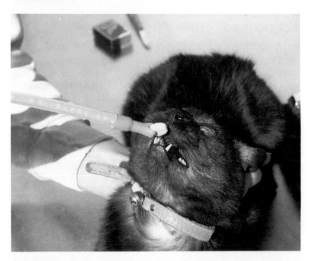

Tablets must be placed at the very rear of the mouth.

Painful all over
Sometimes cats react painfully to touch over large areas of their body. This can be due to multiple cat bites or to a condition called steatitis caused by diets high in unsaturated fatty acids, such as canned red tuna, any sort of fish, cod-liver oil, liver and horsemeat. If the cat's diet is also low in vitamin E, it will produce steatitis. Most commercial manufacturers are now aware of the problem and add vitamin E to the food. Affected cats are irritable, reluctant to move and have a fever. They have a generalised pain from inflamed body fat which takes on a yellow colour. The history of a diet mainly of fish or large amounts of fish oil

suggests the diagnosis. Treatment consists of vitamin E therapy, 50 milligrams per day, plus a change in diet. (See also SKIN DISORDERS: THALLIUM.)

Paint removal
See Grooming section.

Panting
See BREATHING PROBLEMS.

Paralysis
Paralysis is most commonly caused by tick poisoning. Other causes are severance of the spine after a motor vehicle accident; dog attack; an abscess over the back which causes such severe pain that the cat refuses to use its back legs; snake bite; and spider bite. (See also INCO-ORDINATION.)

Parasites
The larger parasites are worms (roundworms, hookworms, tapeworms, lungworms), fleas, mites and ticks.

Penis licking
This can be a sign of feline urological syndrome in the male cat. See URINE DISORDERS.

Poisoning
The most common type of poisoning in the cat is caused by washing it in flea rinses. In these cases a cat salivates profusely and may convulse. First aid measures are to wash the cat thoroughly in copious quantities of clean water to dilute the insecticide remaining on the coat and skin Prevent the cat from licking the coat and take it to a veterinary surgeon immediately. (See FITS.)

The causes of poisoning in the dog are also relevant to the cat. (See Common Ailments of Dogs.)

Pregnancy
See Breeding section.

Pus
See ABSCESSES, SKIN DISORDERS, and the relevant part of the body.

Pyometron
This is an infection of the womb (uterus). It normally occurs after a pregnancy. The queen becomes dull, listless and off her food. She may drink excessively and vomit. There may be a pussy discharge from the vagina.

Surgery to remove the puss-filled womb (hysterectomy) should be performed urgently.

Rabies
See p. 134.

Respiratory problems
Respiratory disease in the cat is almost entirely confined to cat flu (feline respiratory disease). This is described in the Vaccinations section. (See also BREATHING PROBLEMS and COUGHING.)

Restraint
See HANDLING CATS.

Ringworm
See SKIN DISORDERS.

Rodent ulcer
See SKIN DISORDERS.

Rough coat
See DRY COAT.

Roundworm
See Worming section.

Salivation
See DRIBBLING.

Scratching
See SKIN DISORDERS.

Sex of kittens
See p. 38.

Shaking the head

This usually indicates an irritation in the ear. (See EAR DISORDERS.)

Shock

Shock can follow severe injury, as from car accidents, burns or snake bites. The cat may not be conscious; its eyes may be glassy, staring and vacant; the body may shiver or tremble; and breathing may be shallow and irregular. The animal may also vomit and have diarrhoea. Firstly, check for serious bleeding and apply artificial respiration as the case warrants. Keep the cat warm with a blanket, sweater or water bottle and tilt the head down. Tilt the whole body into a head-down position to assist the flow of blood to the brain. Take the animal to a veterinary surgeon as soon as possible. (See also MOTOR VEHICLE ACCIDENTS.)

Skin disorders

The overall incidence of skin disease in the cat—particularly when compared to that in the dog—is relatively small, probably because of the cat's fastidious habits of cleanliness. However, when a skin disease is present, the cat's habits of licking and grooming lead to great difficulties with treatment and therefore delay healing. Sometimes the medication is swallowed, giving rise to side effects, as many medications are toxic to the cat. The range of substances that can be used with safety in treating skin diseases in the cat is therefore somewhat limited. In general, lotions and tinctures are better accepted than greasy oils and creams.

Bacterial skin infections

Cat leprosy affects mainly the head and lips, but the condition may be found anywhere on the body. It occurs as small painless, usually multiple, discrete ulcerated lumps varying from 1 to 3.5 centimetres in diameter and extending from the surface of the skin to the subcutaneous layer. Surgical excision is best.

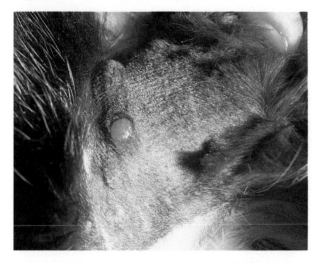

M. Lepraemurium (cat leprosy) indicated by an early lesion on the cat's neck.

Feline acne occurs on the chin and margins of the lips. There is hair loss, and pustules and small cysts are present. In severe cases there is swelling of the entire chin and pus on the surface. The cause is the cat's failure to clean the chin, particularly a cat with excessively greasy skin. Dirt and surface fats accumulate, leading to secondary bacterial skin infections. Clean the area daily with mild soap and water or with alcohol. If there is an infection, rub in an antibiotic cream.

Paronychia is a condition where the ends of the toes are tender and inflamed, and the paws appear malformed. The cat has difficulty extending the claws because of swelling,

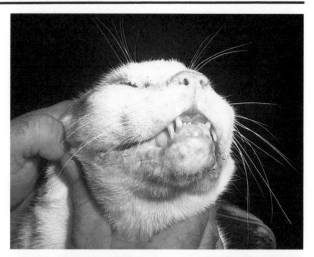

A severe case of feline acne on the cat's chin.

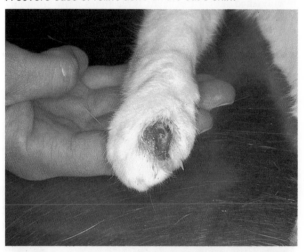

Inflammation of the skin-nail margin indicates paronychia; eventually the whole toe will be tender and inflamed.

and a sticky, pussy material is visible in the claw fold. The condition is usually chronic. The cause is secondary bacterial invasion following damage to the claw fold. Extend the claws and remove the pussy material with 50 per cent water/50 per cent hydrogen peroxide solution and a cotton bud. Then apply 2 per cent gentian violet solution well into the skin nail fold. Antibiotics are also very effective. In chronic cases the nail may have to be removed under general anaesthetic to provide good drainage. The infected nail is usually loose and comes away easily. In most cases it grows back after the infection has cleared up.

Pyogenic dermatitis occurs at the base of the tail, on the head and the ears, on skin over bony prominences and between the toes. In superficial cases, this condition appears as small, crusty sores. Under the crust is an inflamed sticky base. Deep cases appear as single or multiple raised acute and inflamed red or reddish-blue pustules, varying in size from 1 to 5 centimetres. They may have two or more openings, discharging a thick yellow pus. The cause is contaminated wounds resulting from fighting and other types of trauma. The sharp canine teeth of the cat are responsible for most sores, particularly at the tail. Clip the hair around the sore. Some wounds may need to be lanced. The cat should be put on antibiotics. Irrigate the wounds three times daily with 50 per cent hydrogen peroxide and water for four days, then with clear water for three days. (See also ABSCESSES.)

Fungal skin infections

Moniliasis affects the external ear canal, nail folds, anal, oral and vaginal membranes. Sores on the mucous membranes appear as grey–white areas with a foul-smelling discharge; external sores are covered with a brown crust. Diagnosis and treatment of these sores are best left to your veterinary surgeon.

Ringworm is very common, particularly in young kittens, and affects the head and legs, with a tendency to become generalised. The classic case begins as one or more pinkish, scaly areas which spread outwards. The condition is caused by a fungus (not a worm) which invades the wall of the hair. The hair becomes brittle and breaks off close to the skin. The mature sore is well-defined, round, discrete and covered with adhering grey scales. Diagnosis and therapy are best left to a veterinary surgeon. Ringworm can be transferred to humans; it is common for young children to get ringworm from kittens.

Ringworm of the claws is very similar in appearance to paronychia. The claws become misshapen and have a mottled appearance. The claw shell becomes loose and is usually shed. Local treatment three times daily for fourteen days with tincture of iodine is often satisfactory. Otherwise see your vet.

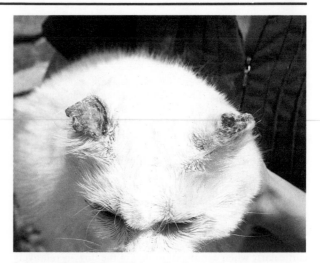

Sunburn (Solar Dermatitis) on the tips of the ears.

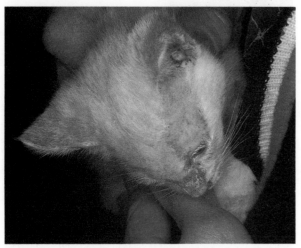

A kitten with ringworm: Note *in addition the dirty ears.*

Physical and chemical skin conditions

Acute contact dermatitis can affect any part of the body, but the common sites are eyelids, ears and neck. Symptoms include discrete, hot, weeping areas. In many cases itchiness and self-trauma are evident. Old lesions become thickened, crusty and scaly. In the acute stage there may be a generalised swelling of the skin in the area. Causes include contact with irritant chemicals such as tar compounds, kerosene, cement powder, lime, insecticides, turpentine, paints and sometimes flea collars. These conditions usually require veterinary attention.

Cancer involves the ear tips and margins of cats with white ears. Sometimes the lower eyelids and the nose are affected if they are unpigmented. The condition is caused by sunburn. The area takes on a typical sunburnt appearance, with swelling, thickening, inflammation and peeling of the skin. Later the area becomes itchy and self-trauma causes more damage. The problem worsens each summer, until finally cancer develops. In the early stages, keep white-eared cats out of the midday sun by bringing them indoors before 10 a.m. and allowing them out after 4 p.m. The tips of the ears can be tattooed or stained with potassium permanganate solution (Condy's crystals) or any other suitable dye. In addition, human suntan lotions and blockout creams can be used on the tips of the ear. Once cancer has developed, excision of the whole ear lobe is recommended.

Hyperkeratosis affects firstly the neck and withers (the area between the shoulder blades), but later the condition becomes generalised. The skin becomes thickened, wrinkled and inelastic, with gradual accumulation of hardened skin. Deep wrinkles form which cannot be reduced by stretching. There is hair loss over the affected areas. This condition is caused by the ingestion of wood preservatives, lubricating oils, floor finishes and varnishes that contain chlorinated naphthalene derivatives. These interfere with the metabolism of vitamin A and in the early stages the condition can be reduced by vitamin A therapy. If left, the cat could die.

Physical and chemical alopecia (or scars) are usually white or pinkish–white to grey, glistening, parchment-like, hairless areas. They are sharply defined from normal skin and hair. The cause is usually boiling water, chemical or thermal burns. The condition can also result from healed areas of dermatitis and extensive wounds. If the condition has settled down, no further treatment is required. If the animal is valuable and the owner wants repair for cosmetic reasons, plastic surgery and/or skin grafting can be done.

Thallium poisoning dermatitis affects the skin around the mouth, eyes, armpits and groin, which becomes dry, inflamed, hairless and crusted. Cracking of the crust and bleeding may occur. The hair of the face and body pulls out easily. The cat will also vomit, have diarrhoea, wobbliness in the back legs, a high-pitched wailing cry and will be sensitive to the touch. In some cases the cat will have very bad breath, due to ulceration of the mouth cavity. Poisoning occurs by eating baits or rodents poisoned by thallium. Veterinary attention is recommended but the future of the animal is extremely poor.

Parasitic skin infections

Feline flea dermatitis can either be localised to the inside of the thighs, the abdomen, under the forelegs and sometimes the base of the tail, or be more generalised and include the lower back, the spinal region and the neck. In severe cases it may extend to cover the entire body. Two forms of the condition occur:

Localised, inflamed, small, moist areas up to 2 centimetres across, which later develop into discrete, oval, weeping areas with intense itchiness; a generalised form which shows numerous, small, reddish-brown, moist crusted areas.

The skin may become thickened, wrinkled and scaly. Partial hair loss may be evident and the areas will be obviously itchy. The lesions are due to the cat being highly sensitive to the flea saliva. This condition is very common in cats, and its prevention and control is by removal of fleas both from the cat and from its environment. This can present problems of its own, as most insecticides are toxic to cats. Malathion and carbaryl are the only two that offer some degree of safety. They are most conveniently used in the form of powders or aerosol sprays, because cats do not like being bathed. Powders should be rubbed well into the hair and the surface powder removed by smoothing the hair in its natural direction with a damp cloth. Alternatively, combing the hair after a few minutes will remove comatosed fleas as well as excess flea powder. It is important when using any insecticide to read the instructions on the containers. Malathion can be used as a 2 per cent powder or a wash (20 per cent Malathion solution, diluted to 1 dessertspoon to 600 millilitres of water). It should not be used on kittens. Dichlorvos-impregnated collars are 90–100 per cent effective on cats, and the incidence of allergic reaction is low. Oral insecticides in the form of tablets or liquids are available. These should be used only as a last resort—as you would be feeding an insecticide to the cat! However, it doesn't seem to cause them much harm. The liquid can be added to the food, which is ideal for difficult cats.

Instead of having the cat attracting fleas from the surrounding environment to its body (and then trying to eradicate the fleas), it is much better to treat the cat's surroundings. Use the insecticide in the environment, particularly under houses and in sandy spots where the cat may rest. A suitable insecticide is 30 per cent Malathion spray. In the house, residual insecticides may be sprayed around the skirting boards and under furniture. In severe cases the services of professional pest exterminators may be required. Because cats are extremely sensitive to insecticidal preparations, they should be kept away from the treated area for at least forty-eight hours.

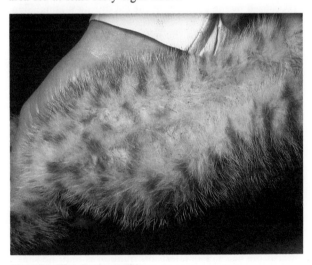

Flea-bite allergic dermatitis.

Fly strike usually occurs in incontinent, paralysed or sick animals which are unable to groom themselves or attend to their wounds. The usual sites are around the anus and other body openings. The hair is moist and matted into clumps and can be pulled out easily. The skin is inflamed and usually has small holes which overlie pockets filled with numerous small white larvae. The area should be clipped and any dead tissue removed, then cleaned with a mild antiseptic solution and as many larvae as possible removed. Insecticidal powders will kill remaining larvae.

Grass itch (from mites present in the grass) usually involves the external ear canal and the ear lobe, particularly the small cleft on the outer edge of the ear. The area between the ear and the eye may also be affected. Occasionally the condition may be generalised. The lesions appear as discrete, red, crusted lesions up to 2 centimetres in di-

ameter. Small, bright red to orange-coloured mites can be seen in the crust. Itchiness and self-trauma are also evident. Remove the crust and mites from the lesions and apply an insecticidal dust such as 5 per cent carbaryl powder at regular intervals. Keep the grass short in the cat's environment by regular mowing, particularly in late summer and autumn.

Lice infestation occurs around body openings. Lice do not penetrate the skin, but gain moisture by congregating around the bodily orifices (for example, ears, mouth, anus). Infestation can also be generalised. Signs include intense itchiness and a dry, matted, neglected coat with loose hair. Lice can be effectively treated by insecticidal powders.

Skin infections

Allergic skin infections are usually a generalised condition, with intense scratching, biting and licking at the skin. The condition can also be accompanied by diarrhoea. It is an allergic response—various foodstuffs such as milk, canned cat food, raw and cooked beef, rabbit, chicken, whale meat and penicillin have been incriminated. The diagnosis of this condition is a veterinary matter.

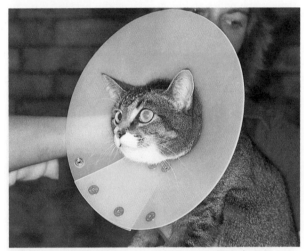

An Elizabethan collar is used to prevent the cat from mutilating areas of its body.

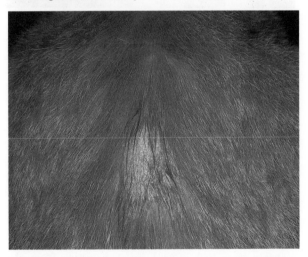

The typical lesion seen in early flea or hormonal deficiency dermatitis along the backline above the tail.

Metabolic skin conditions

Endocrine dermatitis affects the hindquarters and abdomen of the cat. It affects both sides symmetrically and results in partial hair loss, with the remaining hair short, dry and brittle. The skin appears normal; there is no redness, scaling or itchiness. The animal is usually a castrated male or a desexed female; it is rare in unaltered cats. The condition can be rectified by treatment with thyroid tablets and appropriate hormone therapy.

Nutritional alopecia usually appears as a short, ungroomed coat which is harsh and lustreless, accompanied by excessive shedding and generalised dandruff, but no itchiness. It is usually seen in undernourished animals and in females under the strain of late pregnancy or heavy lactation. A good response is achieved by providing the animal with an ample and adequate high protein (30 per cent) diet with mineral and multi-vitamin supplements. Where possible, wean her kittens.

Neoplasms of the skin

Squamous cell carcinoma commonly appears on the tips of the ears, the eyelids, nose and other skin areas sparsely covered by hair. It is more frequent in unpigmented skin and lightly coloured cats. The lesion is usually single and discrete, irregular in size and shape, and appears as a red, slightly raised, ulcerating area, with a thickened border. The speed of invasion of surrounding healthy tissue varies greatly, and in the latter stage a secondary spread to the local lymph nodes and lungs is common. Because it is cancer, take the cat to your veterinary surgeon immediately for a diagnosis.

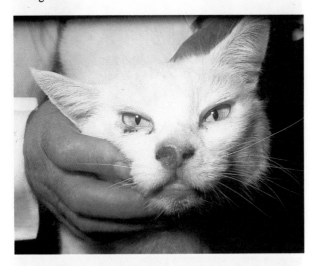

Cancer of the nose (Squamous cell carcinoma). There is also a cancer on the cat's right lower lid. Note the light colour of the cat.

Basal cell carcinomas may appear anywhere on the cat's body but the neck is the most frequent site. The tumour is usually a single, discrete, rounded, rubbery, hairless elevation, and the surface may ulcerate. This condition requires veterinary attention immediately.

Miscellaneous dermatoses

Lick dermatitis occurs on the inside of thighs, the lower abdomen, back and tail, and any other area that the animal can lick conveniently. It is more common in short-haired thoroughbred cats. The signs are well-defined areas of complete hairlessness. The surrounding hair is usually stained brownish-red by the saliva in light-coloured cats. Various degrees of inflammation are seen in the hairless skin. The cat continuously licks the area. The condition probably starts with a local irritation arising from any number of causes, but boredom and nervousness are psychological factors that do contribute to the condition. In many cases, response to therapy is disappointing. Sometimes a change in the animal's environment and routine is all that is necessary.

Rodent ulcer (eosinophilic granuloma) usually develops in the upper lip opposite the canine tooth. It can occur on the hard or soft palate and occasionally on the skin of the

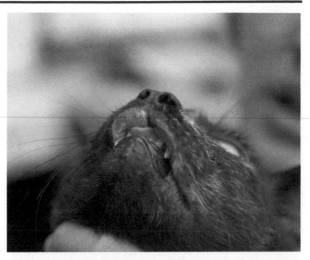

The typical lesion of a rodent ulcer. There is a lesion on either side of the upper lip.

abdomen, legs and feet. The lip usually shows an early localised zone of inflammation with a raised edge, progressing to a yellowish-pink ulcerated area with a glistening surface. It can occur elsewhere on the body as circumscribed, multiple, hairless, granulating, pink, moist areas on the abdomen and the inside of the thighs and feet. The cause is uncertain, though it is generally thought to be caused by the cat's rough tongue. The lesion may eventually develop into a cancer. This condition should be seen by a veterinary surgeon immediately.

Stud tail occurs on the top side of the tail, along the midline of the back, and occasionally extends to the head. It is caused by the activities of the cat during mating. Signs are scant or profuse, dry or oily, white or yellowish–white flaky scales throughout the hair. They vary in size from 1 to 3 millimetres. There is no complete cure, but the condition can be kept under control by regular bathing in hexachlorophene or Seleen shampoo.

Snake bite

Although cats in urban areas are rarely bitten by snakes, it is a problem in the peripheral areas of the city and in rural areas. Snake bite usually appears as two small punctures of the skin. The symptoms include swelling, intense pain, weakness, shortness of breath, vomiting, poor vision and eventual paralysis. Try to keep the cat still by wrapping it in a blanket or coat, as excitement or motion tends to increase the movement of the venom in the bloodstream towards the heart. If the bite is on an extremity, such as a leg, apply a firm bandage to the whole of the leg. This is a constriction band to prevent the venom from flowing towards the heart. The latest information is that the snake bite should not be cut. Get the cat to a veterinary surgeon as soon as possible.

Sneezing

Continuous sneezing is one of the symptoms of feline respiratory disease.

Sores

See ABSCESSES and SKIN DISORDERS.

Spaying

Removing (or destroying) the ovaries of a female. (See Birth control, p. 55.)

Steatitis

See PAINFUL ALL OVER.

Sterility

See Breeding section.

Stiffness

This can be caused by deficiencies of vitamin E or excesses

of vitamin A, by bite wounds, abscesses or motor vehicle accidents.

Stings

Insect stings are common in cats. They can be painful and even dangerous, particularly if the cat is allergic. When bitten or stung, the animal usually cries out, leaps into the air, and tries to escape by climbing the nearest tree or building. Examine the swollen area, and if a sting is visible remove it with tweezers. Ice packs or cold wet cloths applied to the swelling will help to reduce the pain and swelling. Calamine lotion or ammonia preparations can be applied to relieve itching, but an injection of antihistamine gives greater relief, particularly where the bite involves a vital area. Where the sting is from a venomous insect or spider, the symptoms are similar to snake bite.

Stones

In the early stages of feline urological syndrome (F.U.S.), a hard swollen area can be felt in the male cat's abdomen. The cat will have difficulty in urinating and will constantly lick its penis in an attempt to ease the irritation. The condition worsens rapidly, and if the bladder ruptures death may follow. See URINE DISORDERS.

Straining

See CONSTIPATION and URINE DISORDERS: FELINE UROLOGICAL SYNDROME.

Sugar diabetes

See DIABETES MELLITUS.

Tail disorders

Bleeding tail tip

Usually a consequence of the cat chasing its tail and biting it. This is an indication for an Elizabethan collar around the cat's neck so that the tail is inaccessible (the Elizabethan collar is more frequently used on dogs, to stop them licking themselves). If the condition occurs often, a quick, permanent solution is to amputate the tail at the base. Amputating the tip of the tail does not stop the problem.

Kinks in the tail

Kinks in the tail are due to dislocation of the vertebrae in the tail, usually when the cat is immature. Splinting will rectify the problem in many cases.

A limp tail

This usually indicates a fracture of the pelvis or the base of the tail, or infection from cat bites.

Skin infections on the tail

Skin infections can be due to flea dermatitis. In these cases there is hair loss with a pussy superficial sore over the base of the tail, extending down over the first 5–8 centimetres. If it is a very deep infection, it is due to cat bites, the most common site being the first 5 centimetres of the base of the tail. Close examination will reveal one or two holes about 3 millimetres in diameter, surrounded by devitalised skin which has lost its hair. If the area is squeezed, it sometimes releases pus. These wounds should be irrigated three times a day with 50 per cent peroxide and water. The cat also requires antibiotic therapy for at least five days. Failure to use antibiotics can result in gangrene of the tail.

Tapeworm

See Worming section.

Teeth disorders

A cat has its full mouth of 30 permanent teeth by seven months of age—the twelve incisors appear at four months, the four canines at four and a half months, and the fourteen molars between six and seven months. For the next couple of years a cat's teeth are usually trouble free.

Discoloration

A yellow discoloration of the teeth is due to the cat's mother receiving medication during pregnancy, particularly tetracyclines. Nothing can be done to restore the nor-

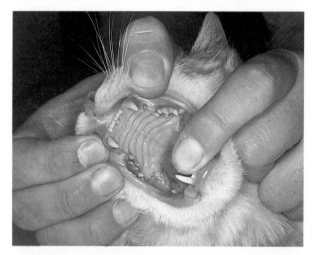

This kitten is losing the upper molars on both sides: Note the inflamed gums.

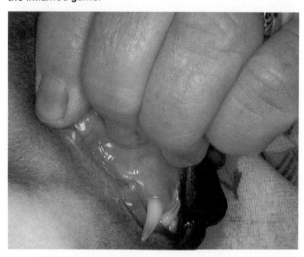

Some antibiotics, especially the Tetracyclines, when given during pregnancy can cause yellow enamel on the teeth.

mal colour of the teeth. Discoloration can also be due to tartar build-up.

Loose teeth

Multiplication of gum tissue and a premature loss of incisor teeth in front is seen in cats on diets that consist mainly of liver or are high in cod-liver oil, or where excess multi-vitamin preparations have been given. The problem is excess vitamin A.

Tartar

Dental plaque and tartar may start to form from the age of three years. The cause is not fully understood, but it is thought to be associated with a degree of alkalinity or acidity in the saliva. There must also be some predisposing factor in individual cats, since the majority of cats do maintain clean, healthy teeth in their old age. Tartar build-up is seen much more frequently since the introduction of soft, commercial foods. To prevent it, feed the cat dry foods occasionally and obtain some large meaty shank bones from the butcher on which the cat can exercise its teeth and gums. (For further information on bones, see the dog section, pp. 121–2.) Inspect the cat's teeth each six months, and if necessary take it to the vet. Very few cats will allow the tartar to be removed, so a general anaesthetic is usually required.

Temperature

See FEVER. A temperature chart is given in the section on Caring for the Sick Cat.

Thirst
See DRINKING, INCREASED.

Ticks
The adult female tick is flat and oval and about 0.5–1 centimetres long. She can lay between 2000 and 3000 eggs, the larvae becoming active within a week. Most native fauna (including bandicoots and possums) and domestic animals can act as host. Only the female tick causes paralysis, four days after becoming attached to the cat. The first sign may be a change in the voice, particularly in Siamese and Burmese cats, due to partial paralysis of the vocal cords. This may be accompanied by gagging or a cough. Lack of co-ordination in the hindlegs may progress to the front legs. The pupils usually dilate, and the cat may adopt a growl. This usually occurs about the fourth or fifth day following attachment of the tick. As the ascending paralysis progresses, the diaphragm becomes paralysed and respiration becomes laboured and depressed. There is a frothy salivation and vomiting may occur. Paralysis of the respiratory system and heart causes death.

Cats are less frequently affected by ticks than dogs because of their cleaning habits. When a cat is bitten by a tick, it is usually on a part of the animal that is difficult for it to clean, such as under the chin, or the chest, on the shoulder, or between the shoulder blades. The development of immunity following a tick bite is variable and often short-lived.

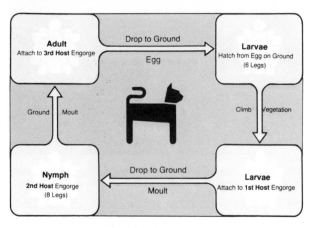

Locate and remove the tick with a pair of forceps (pincers or tweezers) by grasping the head of the tick as close to the skin as possible and gently pulling it out. It does not matter if some of the tick's mouth parts are left behind in the skin—damaged mouth parts will remain as a foreign body in the host and fester out at a later date. Do not fiddle with the tick by cutting it or applying chloroform, ether or methylated spirits. This only gives the creature more time to inject toxin. Search the cat thoroughly for any more ticks, and bathe it in 1 per cent Malathion solution. If the cat is affected in any way it should be taken to a veterinary surgeon for anti-tick serum.

Tick bite is now felt to be as dangerous as snake bite. The longer the injection of anti-tick serum is delayed, the less effective it will be. If the tick is quite a large one, it is sometimes advisable to give the anti-tick serum to the cat anyway, because the full effects of the toxin injected may take three or four days to become apparent. By this time anti-tick serum may be useless.

Toilet training
See House-training, pp. 48–9.

Toxoplasmosis
This organism is transferable to man. In any given population about 25 per cent of adult humans have been exposed to this infection. The most serious effect of toxo-plasmosis in the human is its ability to cause birth defects if the disease is contracted during pregnancy. Pregnant women should avoid contact with cat faeces, and should not eat raw or lightly cooked meats.

Toxoplasmosis is an intracellular parasite which is neither host specific nor tissue specific. The organism invades the cell, multiplies until the cell ruptures, then moves on to invade a further cell. Toxoplasmosis has been reported in animals and humans throughout the world.

At the onset of the disease in cats, non-specific signs include lethargy, loss of appetite, weight loss and persistent high fever. This is followed by shortness of breath and acute abdominal disorders, such as vomiting, tenderness, liver enlargement and mild jaundice. As the toxoplasmosis egg has a three-day incubation period, daily disposal of the faeces is recommended (wear plastic gloves). The cat excretes infective eggs for about two weeks after it has become infected. Cats should be fed on cooked or sterilised meats to reduce the possibility of contamination. Treatment should be left to the vet.

Urine disorders
Cystitis (Inflammation of the bladder)
The first indication of cystitis is often that the cat is becoming dirty about the house—urinating in places other than its sanitary tray. There is increased frequency of urination, with small quantities being passed. Frequently the urine is bloodstained and contains small whitish crystals, and the cat may strain. The area around the genitals tends to become contaminated with urine and has an ammonia odour. Cats with this condition remain bright, however, and continue to eat in the majority of cases. Sometimes there is increased thirst and occasionally an attack may be ushered by fever and vomiting.

The condition is best treated with specific antibiotics which are excreted in high concentration in the urine. If the patient's urine is alkaline the use of acidifiers is recommended. The alkalinity can be determined in the laboratory. The general treatment of cystitis includes increasing the water intake by the administration of common salt either in the food or in the drinking water. Eliminate dry cat foods from the diet, as these tend to decrease overall water intake, resulting in more concentration of the urine. Although dry foods (10 per cent water) tend to increase the thirst of the cat more than tinned foods (80 per cent water), the overall water intake on dry foods is less than with tinned food because of the different percentages of water in the food.

Feline urological syndrome (F.U.S.)
F.U.S. is characterised by cystitis with blood in the female cat, and a blockage of the urinary tract in the male cat. It is more common in males. The condition appears to have been increasing in incidence in recent years—the increase is ascribed by some to the growing popularity of dry cat food. The condition is comparatively rare in cats under one year but peaks at two years of age. Affected cats are more likely to be neutered, lazy males that have restricted access to outdoors. They are more likely to live in households with more than one cat and long-haired breeds seem to be more susceptible. Affected cats tend to drink less. A recent survey indicated that the feeding of dry food is numerically associated with the occurrence of F.U.S. in clinical cases of the condition; but of these cases, 25 per cent had received no dry cat food in their diet.

In the early stages of the condition the male cat licks his penis frequently, occasionally producing sufficient trauma to cause bleeding. The penis is often protruded from the sheath for considerable periods of time. The cat may often become dirty about the house, squatting in odd corners of the room attempting to urinate and avoiding his sanitary tray. Attempts at urination with vigorous straining efforts are often accompanied by a loud groaning cry. Sometimes the owner attributes this to constipation and treats the cat for this, with a resultant loss in valuable time. In early cases, a hard, swollen area the size of an orange can be felt in the abdomen. This is the distended bladder. Sometimes one can see a yellowish, chalky material in the eye of the penis.

After twenty-four to thirty-six hours, the cat may go into shock—almost a comatose condition—showing no sign of tenderness in the abdomen. In these cases, the bladder may rupture if handled. Signs of coma, vomiting, dehydration and collapse precede death. Treatment by a veterinary surgeon is therefore essential.

By the time the owner realises the cat is in trouble, the disease has usually progressed to a serious stage, and even on removal of the urinary plug causing the problem the cat must be hospitalised for some days. Intravenous electrolyte fluid therapy, together with appropriate antibiotics, is necessary.

Straining, and licking the tip of the penis, are signs of F.U.S.

Prevention of recurrence is very important, for once the cat has suffered an obstruction it is highly probable that the condition will recur, often with an increasing frequency. It is suggested that there is some physiological difference between stone-forming and non-stone-forming cats. In stone-forming cats preventative measures are aimed at reduction of the urinary magnesium concentration by provision of a diet low in magnesium, at dilution of the urine, and lowering the specific gravity of the urine.

The cat should be fed foods low in magnesium for at least fourteen days to allow the excretion of any excess magnesium from the body. Following this, they should be fed with milk and low-magnesium food. Water should be available to the cat at all times.

The normal diet of the cat is rich in magnesium. Consult your vet for information on local brands.

When cats are introduced to dry foods it is important to teach them to drink. This can be done by adding water to the dry food to make it mushy or by adding salt to the food. Initially the dry food should form only a part of the diet, not the entire diet. A cat transferred from a wet diet containing 70 per cent water (such as canned food) to a dry food diet would require ten times as much fluid intake. One reason for the increased incidence of F.U.S. might be that cats transferred to a dry diet do not increase their water intake sufficiently.

Stone-forming cats should be allowed easy access to outdoors for the purpose of urinating, as it is known that retention of urine within the bladder helps to produce F.U.S. Fat cats appear to be more prone to develop this condition, so dietary measures should be aimed at reducing the body weight—always providing that magnesium rich foods are not a part of such dietary measures.

In the female cat F.U.S. does not result in obstruction, as the female's urethra is short and larger in diameter. The clinical signs in the female are a tendency to urinate around the house instead of in its sanitary tray, and increased frequency of urination with only small quantities passed. The act of urination appears to be painful, with the cat squatting and straining for several minutes at a time. Usually the urine becomes bloodstained and has a strong ammonia odour. Veterinary treatment is still important.

Kidney disease

Kidney disease is very common in cats, particularly in old age. The signs include loss of appetite, weight loss, increased drinking of water to the point of sitting over the water bowl, vomiting, diarrhoea or constipation, dehydration, ulceration of the tongue and gums, brownish scum on teeth, increased frequency of urination, occasionally increased respiratory rate, anaemia and depression. In many cases, the disease has progressed to a serious stage by the time the cat is brought for veterinary attention and permanent damage may have been done to the kidneys. Because of the complexity of the different types of urinary diseases and the different methods of treatment for each of them, early veterinary attention is advised.

Once the kidney disease crisis has been controlled, conservative medical management can be instituted. This includes maintaining fluids, electrolytes and acid/base balance by providing unlimited access to water. The excretory load of waste products in the blood presented to the kidneys should be reduced. Protein intake must be lowered to reduce the excretory load on the kidneys. The caloric value of the diet must be raised to compensate for the reduced protein content and to ensure that body proteins are not used for energy purposes. Experiments have shown that cats will accept up to 64 per cent fat in their diet and remain healthy. Apparently cats find such a diet very palatable, so it may be preferable to give more fat than starches. Protein content of the diet should be of high biological value—lean meat, chicken, eggs, cottage cheese, milk and cream. As the kidneys eventually lose their ability to conserve sodium, salt should be given in the drinking water at the rate of ¼ teaspoonful per 500 millilitres.

Cats with kidney disease must be allowed unrestricted access to water. Only if significant vomiting occurs after drinking should the supply of water be regulated and then only until vomiting has been brought under control by the use of drugs. Maintain the animal's appetite by using appetite increasers (anabolic agents), treat all infections properly, and eliminate any vomiting or diarrhoea. Care must also be taken when prescribing drugs for cats with kidney diseases, as the kidneys are the major route of excretion of drugs.

Urinary incontinence

This has two major causes: disturbance of nerves supplying the bladder, and severe cystitis.

Disturbance of the nerves supplying the bladder can result from fractures of the back, or dislocation or inflammation of the spinal cord, or damage to the brain. In these cases there is a lack of voluntary urination, with the result that the bladder becomes distended with consequent overflow-type dribbling of urine. Bacterial infection of the stagnant urine often occurs, so the condition is usually complicated by bacterial cystitis.

Severe, long-standing cystitis causes replacement of the muscle tissue of the bladder by either fibrous tissue or cancerous elements. This results in the bladder wall becoming hard and inelastic, so that urine overflow is a fairly constant dribble. There is no treatment. Unless the owner is prepared to cope with this problem, the cat should be euthanased.

Urinating in the house
See BEHAVIOUR PROBLEMS, and URINE DISORDERS above.

Vaccinations
See Vaccination section, pp. 50–2.

Vitamins
See Feeding, pp. 41–6.

Vomiting
Excessive vomiting causes a severe fluid deficit together with a loss of electrolytes. Classifying the cause of vomiting is difficult and the following list serves only to emphasise the complexity of the problem.

Infectious diseases—feline panleucopaenia and hepatitis.

Acute abdomen—acute pancreatitis, peritonitis, intestinal obstruction, penetrating wounds and ruptured organs within the body.

Indigestion, pancreatitis, overeating, spoilt foods, poisons.

Deformities of the gastro-intestinal system.

Metabolic disorders resulting in retention of by-products (nephritis).

Drugs—such as digitalis, morphine and certain antibiotics.

Nervous problems—motion sickness, injuries to the head and nervousness.

Throat irritations—caused by enlarged tonsils, or by a piece of string with one end caught around the base of the tongue and the other end in the food pipe, stomach or small intestine.

Bites—from ticks, snakes or spiders.

Projectile vomiting—caused by increased pressure on the brain, high intestinal obstructions or foreign bodies.

If your cat is behaving normally and appears healthy but vomits once a week, this is considered normal and nothing to worry about. Because of the complexity of the vomiting sign, cats with a problem should be taken to a veterinary surgeon for differential diagnosis.

Water
See DRINKING, INCREASED, and p. 45.

Weakness
This usually accompanies depression or lethargy and is associated with a generalised infectious process. It can also be associated with poor diet, including vitamin A deficiencies, vitamin B-group deficiencies (particularly thiamine), worm burdens, and weaknesses of the hindlegs, including tick paralysis, snake bite, abscesses and infectious processes of the hindquarters. See also INCO-ORDINATION.

Weight loss
The average adult cat weighs about 4 kilograms. It is difficult to assess weight loss if the diet varies, if the animal is overweight to begin with or if previous weight records are unavailable. The two major considerations in weight loss are changes in food consumption and evidence of a disorder of gastrointestinal functions, such as vomiting or diarrhoea. The magnitude of the weight loss and the time in which it has taken place are important.

Loss of appetite can occur in such a wide variety of conditions that this sign in itself is not fruitful in reaching a diagnosis of the cause of weight loss. However, decreased absorption of food may occur in pancreatic or liver disease. Weight loss may accompany general illness, such as feline panleucopaenia, hepatitis, kidney disease or cancer of the alimentary tract. Fever, itself a sign of disease, increases the metabolic requirements of the animal and may result in severe weight loss. Weight loss accompanied by increased urination suggests sugar diabetes, water diabetes or chronic kidney disease. Weight loss may frequently occur without a significant change in food consumption. This suggests hyperactivity or a psychosis, such as extreme nervousness created by a new environment or the introduction of competition, such as a new baby or a new pet into the household.

Weight loss sometimes occurs because of underfeeding. The animal may be receiving large quantities of food but the caloric density of the food and total calories may not be enough to fulfil the animal's need. An animal's caloric requirements fluctuate with its activities, the environment, body temperature, environmental and emotional stress and specific conditions such as pregnancy. Diagnosing the cause of weight loss demands a careful investigation of the animal's diet, how much the animal is fed, how much it eats, its environment and its general health.

The common causes of weight loss in cats are diarrhoea, vomiting and kidney disease—the latter usually occurs in the older animal and is accompanied by the cat drinking excessive amounts of water. Parasites such as roundworms, lungworms and tapeworms also cause weight loss.

Wobbling
See INCO-ORDINATION.

Worms
See the section on Worming.

FIRST AID BOX

The number of things that could be kept in an emergency first aid box is limitless. The following is a basic list.

Acriflavin, mercurochrome, triple dye, zinc cream
Wound dressing powder (preferably one containing an antibiotic)
Antibiotic/cortisone skin ointment
Antibiotic dispenser
Antibiotic eye ointment
Eye wash
Antiseptic wash (e.g. chlorhexidene)
Hydrogen peroxide 3%
Flea powder
Flea rinse
A roll of 5-centimetre wide adhesive bandage, such as Elastoplast
Two rolls of conforming gauze bandage or clean white cloth
Cotton-wool
Scissors
50 millilitres liquid paraffin
Tweezers
Thermometer
Cat carry basket

Opposite: A Siamese cat uses a scratching post provided by the owner.

DOGS

Selecting a dog

Once you have decided to take on the responsibility of a pet dog, the next step is to decide how old a dog you want—a six-weeks-old puppy or a grown dog. The ideal is a newly weaned puppy about six weeks old. At this age the puppy is dependent on its owner for feeding, companionship and protection, and your fulfilling of these requirements will build a strong bond between the puppy and you. If there are young children in the family an especially strong bond will be formed between puppy and children, mainly because of the long periods each day they will spend in each other's company. If possible, defer getting a pup until your family is complete, as some dogs become very jealous of a new baby.

There are, of course, some disadvantages to purchasing a pup. Toilet training, for example, can be quite time-consuming (and frequently frustrating). Also, for the first eight to twelve months, during their teething phase, puppies have a habit of chewing toys, socks, shoes and sometimes furniture.

One way to overcome these annoyances is to choose an older dog, but then you may be getting somebody else's problems. The dog may have irritating traits which will take considerable re-education. Tender loving care, however, will win the hearts of most pups (and adult dogs).

Sex

A female desexed will make the best pet. Desexing takes place at five to six months before the bitch has her first season. Desexing makes the bitch less likely to wander; and it eliminates the problems caused by the bitch coming on season every six months and attracting hordes of male dogs to the house. (It is an offence to allow a bitch 'on heat' to enter a public place, even on a lead.) Desexing prevents unwanted litters and it reduces the possibility of mammary tumours and an infected womb.

Contrary to popular belief, desexing does not alter the personality of the dog. The only disadvantage is that some dogs become fat—invariably this is because the owner has not thought to reduce the dog's diet since it reached maturity.

A male dog should be desexed if breeding is not contemplated. Domestication and confinement to urban territorial limits are completely unnatural to the male dog's natural needs; dogs are naturally pack animals and undesexed male dogs tend to roam, gathering in public places such as schools and shopping centres where they frequently become involved in fights with other male dogs over bitches on heat in the area. A frequent consequence of this is that the dog finishes up in the pound, where it may contract diseases requiring expensive veterinary treatment. If the dog is not collected within a stipulated time, it may be destroyed at the pound.

Male dogs away from home are not fulfilling the requirement for which they were acquired—namely as a pet or as a guard dog. In addition to roaming, sexually frustrated male dogs may begin 'riding' children or the outstretched legs of visitors (very embarrassing to some). In order to reduce the stray dog population, it is therefore important to desex male dogs as well as female. Unfortunately, there is considerable (and illogical) reluctance on the part of dog owners to have male dogs desexed. Perhaps they should take a tip from horse owners: any male horse not wanted for breeding is always desexed (gelded) at the earliest opportunity.

Conformation

Dogs come in many shapes, sizes and colours. Those conforming to fixed standards are classified as breeds. Various breeds have been developed over generations for specific purposes—for example, for sport, work, guarding or appearance or as lap dogs. Each breed has a number of different characteristics which set it apart from others.

During their teething phase puppies love to chew.

Size

It is important for a prospective owner to consider the size of the territory that will be available to the dog. Small dogs will be satisfied by urban blocks of land, while large dogs require much more territorial space. Small dogs require less food; they therefore excrete less faeces, which are becoming a problem in inner-urban areas. They also require less medication, because it is administered on a per-weight basis. In most cases the small pet will satisfy the companionship and watch-dog needs of the average urban family.

Temperament

Most dogs were bred for specific purposes, and it is only recently that many have been chosen as pets. Some breeds were developed to be aggressive hunting or work dogs. It is important to understand the temperament of a particular breed. Some breeds are prone to biting, such as Dobermans, Cocker Spaniels, Terriers, Dachshunds, Corgis, Border Collies and Cattle Dogs. It is rare for a dog to bite its owner, but it is the owner's responsibility to ensure that the dog doesn't bite visitors.

Long hair

In most cases long-haired dogs were bred in cooler climates, but during the past hundred years or so they have been transported to all parts of the world, including some very hot climates. In these areas fleas and ticks are much more prevalent and they can be a severe problem for long-haired dogs. In countries where ticks are a problem (especially the paralysis tick, which can kill a dog in a matter of days) the long hair makes it particularly difficult to search the dog. In some cases the dog may have to be clipped all over, which can be quite expensive and ruins the appearance.

Long haired dogs require a lot of attention.

Unhealthy skin conditions are also much more prevalent in long-haired dogs. Fleas, which cause an allergic reaction, are better protected under the long hair. Grass seeds, burrs, sticks and other irritating objects are more easily held within long hair to irritate the skin. Skin problems in long-haired dogs are usually at a serious stage before the owner spots them.

In general, long-haired dogs require much more grooming, care and maintenance than short-haired dogs. Matted hair around the anal area frequently prevents the dog from passing faeces, and this calls for the hair to be clipped. Long-haired dogs usually have an abundance of hair in the ear canal and this, together with long, floppy ears, will predispose the animal to poor circulation in the ear canal. A moist environment ensues, allowing bugs to breed and causing 'canker' or infection of the ear.

Colour

In general, light-coloured animals have weaker skin and are more susceptible to skin infections than darker-coloured animals. In hot climates, they are more susceptible to sunburn and 'hot spots' or dermatitis.

Long backs

Dachshunds are one of the main sufferers of back trouble.

Corgis and Dachshunds are the main sufferers of back trouble, which may lead to paralysis of the hind legs. Bassets rarely have trouble with their backs. Paralysis of the back legs may be of a temporary nature, lasting one or two weeks, or it may become permanent, necessitating euthanasia.

Congenital abnormalities

Many purebred dogs have abnormalities, some serious, others minor. They are usually confined to a specific section of the breed where there has been close inbreeding. The whole breed should not be condemned.

The following breeds, however, do have a consistently high incidence of serious abnormalities:

Poodles have an array of congenital abnormalities, including dislocating

Common Genetic Disorders of the Dog
(see 'Common Ailments' listing, p. 118)

Disorder	Breed	Symptom
Bones and Joints		
Cervical vertebral deformity (wobbler)	Basset, Great Dane, Doberman	Weakness in hindlegs
Hip displasia	Most large breeds, notably German Shepherds, Labradors	Difficulty raising hindquarters, lameness and weakness in hindquarters
Intervertebral disc degenerated	Cocker Spaniel, Dachshund, Pekinese, Beagle	Weakness in hindquarters
Legg-Perthes disease (degeneration of hip joint)	Most toy breeds	Lameness in one or both hindlegs, weakness in hindquarters
Overshot and undershot jaw	Cocker Spaniel, Long-haired Dachshund, Shetland Sheepdog, Chihuahua, Collies, Whippets	Top row of incisor teeth do not oppose bottom row
Patella luxation (dislocating knee-cap)	Many toy breeds, especially Poodles	Lameness in one or both hindlegs
Deformities of spinal cord	Boxer	Inco-ordination
Digestive System		
Cleft lip and palate	Staffordshire Terrier, Dachshund, Cocker Spaniel, English Bulldog, Beagle, Shih Tzu	Failure of the top lip and or roof of the mouth to join. Puppies with cleft palate cannot suckle and have milk in the nostrils
Dentition abnormality	Boxer, English Bulldog	Irregular setting of the teeth
Gingival hyperplasia	Boxer	Wart-like tumours of the gum
The Ear		
Deafness	Dalmation, Collie, Foxhound, White dogs of various breeds	Cannot hear (best test is to clap hands behind the dog's head)
Metabolic Disorders		
Diabetes mellitus (sugar diabetes)	Dachshund, Miniature Poodle	(See 'Common Ailments' listing)
The Eye		
Cataract	Cocker Spaniels, Poodles	(See 'Common Ailments' listing)
Corneal ulceration Entropion Glaucoma	Boxer, Pekinese, Basset Hound, Wire-haired Fox Terrier, Cocker Spaniel, English Cocker Spaniel	(See 'Common Ailments' listing)
Wall eye (a section of the iris is a different colour to the other eye)	Collie, Shetland Sheepdog, Dachshund, Great Dane, Old English Sheepdog	(See 'Common Ailments' listing)
Progressive retinal atrophy	Cardigan Welsh Corgi, Miniature and Toy Poodles, Cocker Spaniel, some Labradors	(See 'Common Ailments' listing)
Nervous system		
Behavioural abnormalities	Several breeds including Poodle, Cocker Spaniel, German Shepherd, Dachshund and some Terriers	Nervous, aggressive, biting, hyperactive
Epilepsy	Poodles, other toy breeds, some German Shepherds	Convulsions
Other structural malformations		
Elongated soft palate	Boxers, Pekinese, Maltese Terriers	Snores when sleeping, difficulty in breathing
Hernias	Collies, Cocker Spaniels, Bull Terriers, Basenjis	(See 'Common Ailments' listing)

knee-caps, cataracts, heart conditions and a predisposition to ear infection.

The long, hairy, floppy ears of the *Cocker Spaniel* make them susceptible to ear infection. They also suffer from eye conditions such as ectropion, an outward deflection of the eyelid. Dirt and dust accumulate, causing chronic conjunctivitis. Cockers are susceptible to cataract formation.

The very short snout of *Pekinese* predisposes them to respiratory problems; they are a bad anaesthetic risk. Their eyes bulge so that frequently the hair from the facial fold touches the eye, causing corneal ulcers.

Type of dog needed

Before you purchase a dog, ask yourself why you are buying it. Is it to be a watchdog, a companion or a sporting dog? How much time will you have to exercise and care for it? Will it live in an urban community, or in a country area where there is plenty of territory for the dog to run free? When you have considered these factors, together with the characteristics described earlier, you will be able to select a breed of dog that will suit your particular purpose and set of circumstances.

Selecting from a litter

Your own veterinary examination of your prospective purchase, particularly a puppy, is most important.

Once you have selected a pup, compare its weight with others in the litter.

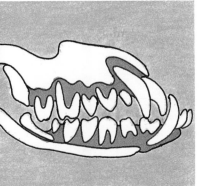

Undershot jaws are common in the short-snouted breeds.

Make the first night comfortable for the puppy.

The kennel should just exceed the size of the dog.

The type of care the mother received while carrying the pups—that is, vaccinations, worming and nutrition—will determine the health of her pups. She should have had a vaccination booster midway through the pregnancy to confer a good immunity on the newborn pups and should have been wormed during the pregnancy to eliminate the possibility of worms in the new-born pups. A well-balanced diet—with particular attention to calcium—is important. (For further information, see the section on Feeding.)

Check the number of litters the bitch has had in the preceding couple of years. Bitches should not have more than one litter per year, as too many litters deplete the mother's bones of essential vitamins and minerals and the puppies will therefore be weak.

At the kennels, check the surrounding area for hygiene. Check the other animals in the breeder's establishment to ensure that they are all healthy with glossy coats.

Once you are satisfied that the breeder's credentials are up to standard, examine the pups. Ask the breeder about their diet and the worming and vaccination programme. Examine the pups at first from a distance and don't be fooled into taking the weakest pup out of sympathy. Always select the strongest looking pup—the one with the glossy coat and bright eyes. Check around the anal area to ensure there is no evidence of diarrhoea. If you are selecting a dog for showing, take along someone familiar with the ideal characteristics of the particular breed. Don't select a sleepy pup. Once you have selected the pup at a distance, pick it up and feel its weight in the palm of your hand. Pick up the other puppies in the litter and compare their weight. The pup should feel firm and heavy.

Examine it for abnormalities such as a cleft palate, overshot or undershot jaw. An overshot jaw is particularly common in Collies and Whippets, and undershot jaws are common in the short-snouted dogs, such as Boxers, Maltese Terriers, and Pekinese. Check the puppy's abdomen at the umbilicus for hernia. Count the number of digits on the toes. There should be four main digits, with a dew claw in some breeds. If the dew claw is missing, don't be concerned as in most breeds these are snipped off when the pup is one to two days old. The puppy's gums should be pink in colour, not pale. Examine the internal area of the ear and smell this area. Some puppies have ear mites which they have contracted from their mother. Ear mites cause a smelly inflammation of the ear. In most cases this condition can be cured by the vet.

Puppies under six weeks of age should not be taken from their mother. Before taking the pup get a written copy of the diet the puppy is on. Do not change this diet for about a week to ten days, as the stresses of a change in environment are enough to upset the pup without a change of diet at the same time. Also get from the breeder the puppy's worming history and find out when the pup should next be wormed. Collect any vaccination cards that indicate what vaccinations have been done and when the next ones are due.

If possible, obtain from the breeder a piece of cloth or blanket that has been used in the puppy's bedding, so that on the first few nights the puppy will at least have a familiar smell around it. Make the first night comfortable for the puppy. A hot water bottle should be placed in the bed clothing, a ticking clock in his box, plus something of a smelly nature, either the piece of bedding from the breeder or perhaps a pair of used socks. And remember, nothing makes a puppy happier than a full tummy before it goes to bed.

Housing

Dogs can be accommodated in a number of ways. In temperate climates, a kennel is not essential, provided the dog has access to the house, a garage, underneath the house, or some other suitable shelter which protects it from direct sunlight, wind and rain. In cooler climates, a kennel is essential. The kennel should just exceed the size of the dog so that body heat can warm the surrounding air. The kennel should be located in the shade and should be well-ventilated, warm in winter and cool in summer. It should be weather-proof, draught-free and elevated from the ground, with a wooden floor. Bedding should be disposable—for example, sawdust, shavings or newspapers—as this helps eliminate a breeding site for fleas and mites. Rinse the kennel once a month with an insecticidal preparation, put in new bedding and burn the old. All feeding utensils should be washed daily, and clean water provided daily in a shady spot.

Feeding

Before dogs were domesticated they used to catch their prey and eat the whole of it. It supplied them with a balanced, nutritious diet of bones, muscles and internal organs such as the heart, kidneys, liver and lungs. It also provided various vitamins and minerals from the vegetative matter in the gut of the animal eaten. Dogs had to be fit and slim enough to chase and catch their prey. After eating a large meal they would lie down and sleep it off. If they became obese they would not be fit enough to chase and kill more prey.

Dogs are very adaptable in terms of diet and because of this they have thrived in a wide variety of environments and on a wide range of diets. As a result, they are probably less subject to serious dietary disease than most other animals. In the past decade, dogs have benefited from our increasing knowledge of their nutritional requirements and the application of that knowledge to prepared, commercial dog foods. Dog feeding is now much less haphazard than it was in the past, when the dog was dependent on its owner's variable and often rudimentary understanding of nutrition.

The dangers of overfeeding

Excess food intake with resultant obesity is becoming an ever-increasing problem for dogs in urban areas. The dog is often hand-fed two or three times a day, at the owner's meal-times. Dogs only need to be fed once a day.

Urban restrictions on the animal's territorial horizons mean the dog leads a rather sedentary life, not using up a great deal of energy and therefore going to fat. Obese animals have an increased susceptibility to various diseases including osteoarthritis, sugar diabetes, skin disease and impairment of body-heat regulation, pulmonary, cardiovascular, hepatic and reproductive functions. Recent scientific evidence indicates that chronic underfeeding of a complete diet is the only means known for increasing the length of life of laboratory animals beyond the limits characteristic with the species. At the other extreme, chronic overfeeding or other dietary excesses or imbalances curtail the animals' life span.

Obesity is becoming an ever-increasing health problem.

Inadequate feeding

Inadequate food intake is not uncommon, particularly among breeders trying to get their animals into show condition. The animals are thin but healthy, yet won't put on weight. This can be a complex and difficult problem, although more often it can be rectified easily.

If the animal is otherwise healthy there are two possibilities: lack of opportunity and lack of motivation. Lack of opportunity may simply be that another dog is taking the larger share, or that the dog is unable to eat enough of the food with which it is fed to attain a satisfactory body weight. Where this occurs and the food is too bulky for the animal to accommodate its energy requirements at one meal, it may be necessary to feed the dog three or four times per day instead of once a day. This situation is particularly relevant to a bitch losing weight with a large litter of puppies.

Boredom may be another cause of reduced food intake. While dogs and cats can subsist more or less indefinitely on one type of food (providing it is nutritionally complete), most animals will show some boredom with the same diet after a period of about a week. If increased palatability and food intake is desired, it is advisable to vary the type of food that is fed to the animal. This should be done slowly, avoiding abrupt and major changes to the diet. Food that is fed cold is also of low palatability.

Canine nutrition

The ideal diet is a mixture that supplies daily all the elements needed for the dog's bodily development and functions. It should be balanced and palatable, in a form that is easy and pleasant to handle. The amount of water contained in the food can influence its keeping qualities. As a general rule, the higher the percentage of water the poorer the stability of the food.

Vitamins and minerals

While supplements—in particular calcium and vitamin A—are essential to most meat-based diets formulated in homes and kennel kitchens, they are not always used correctly. While one mineral deficiency is minimised or avoided, other imbalances may be created. Sometimes these supplements are used and recommended despite the fact that commercially prepared dog foods, containing adequate amounts in correct proportions of the required vitamins and minerals, are available.

The average nutritional requirements of dogs are known and most commercial foods are formulated to meet them. When a properly formulated, carefully produced product is available, no further nutritional supplements are necessary for the average dog. Special situations, such as those imposed by pregnancy, strenuous exercise or disease, may benefit from certain types of supplements. However, during periods of increased requirements, the greater intake of food relative to body weight provides the additional nutrients required. A pregnant bitch at full term eats one-and-a-half to two times the normal amount of food and will thus be getting more vitamins and minerals in the correct proportions—if the diet is balanced. Indiscriminate supplementation will upset this balance. Excessive amounts of vitamins and minerals will not be beneficial to a dog already nutritionally replete. In fact, the difference between the required amounts and toxic levels of some is small, and overdosing is dangerous.

In sickness, particularly in diseases of the liver or pancreas, or where there has been an inadequate diet of fat, supplementation of the fat-soluble vitamins A, D, E and K may be advised.

Most of the B-complex group of vitamins are found in varying quantities in types of foods included in the diets of most dogs. Liver and yeast are particularly rich sources. Additional amounts of some of these vitamins are synthesised by bacteria in the intestine. Sometimes this activity may be diminished if intestinal bacteria are disturbed or destroyed by disease or by antibiotic therapy. Under these circumstances, additional amounts of B vitamins should be given. Fever, a prolonged loss of appetite and chronic kidney disease are other conditions in which B vitamins should be given.

At this stage, scientific experiments have failed to substantiate that vitamin C plays any part in the therapy of disease in the dog. The most common supplements in use are those containing calcium, often in combination with phosphorus, other minerals and vitamin D. (See Common Ailments, Bone Problems, All Meat Diets.)

In summary, most dogs receiving a nutritionally complete basic diet do not require supplements.

Commercial dog foods

Commercially prepared dog foods are very commonly used (feeding about eight of every ten dogs). These fall into two main categories: complete diets (the bulk of the dog food sold on the market), and incomplete diets, which require meat added to them. Pet foods are also divided into three large groups, depending on their moisture content.

DOG FOOD CHART

Moist or canned foods, which contain 70–75 per cent moisture

Semi-moist foods, which contain 25 per cent moisture

Dry foods, which contain 8–12 per cent moisture

There are three groups of *moist* foods: frozen, fresh meat or canned meat products, which are packed as an incomplete diet and are best used as an ingredient in a home-mixed formula where cereals and possibly calcium supplements are added. There are, in addition, completely balanced canned products which have been fortified with minerals and vitamins or a combination of meat, cereals and other ingredients. When buying a moist canned food, read the label to ensure that you are buying a balanced food. Canned foods are usually highly palatable because of their high water and moisture content, which means they are expensive per calorie. Generally they have a poor-quality protein source.

Semi-moist foods are sold in plastic wrappers. They look like chunks, patties or packets of fresh meat and are made from meat, meat by-products, soya beans, vegetable oils, sugar and preservatives. Semi-moist foods are a complete balanced diet, highly palatable, easily digested, with a high kilojoule density. All of these points make them well suited to young, growing or pregnant pets, but for the same reasons they may promote obesity in mature or sedentary dogs. They should not be fed to dogs over six months old. Many of these foods contain a high density of cereals, which may promote allergic skin conditions in some dogs.

Dry foods are a mixture of ground cereals, meatmeal, soya beans, cheese, vegetables and animal fats, with trace ingredients and preservatives. They are usually presented as meals, biscuits or kibbles, pellets or expanded chunks (listed in order of increasing palatability and expense). They tend to have a low-quality protein. In general, dry food products are not very palatable, but they are inexpensive. They are ideal for feeding mature dogs or dogs that tend to become overweight. Their unpalatable nature, coupled with a low protein level, renders them ideal for self-feeding, as the dog is unlikely to overeat and become fat.

The highest number of calories and food value come from high-protein dry foods. This is because moist foods or canned foods contain about 72 per cent water, while high protein dry foods contain only 8 per cent water.

Which commercial ration is best? This is difficult to answer, because each dog is an individual, with its individual metabolism. Each commercial ration is different in its make-up. Nutrition is such a complex business that the best method of choosing a dog food is to observe the animal's performance after feeding one particular food for a period of a month or six weeks. Contents labels on cans are of little use, as they don't tell you what biological value the meal will have for your pet.

Palatability can be rated in decreasing order: fresh meat or canned, fortified meat, semi-moist foods, canned rations (which have cereal and meat mixtures) and dry foods. Preferences for fresh meat show a ranking from high to low of beef, lamb, chicken and horse meat. Cold meat straight from the refrigerator is generally less acceptable than cooked or warmed meat. Ground meat is preferred to cubed or whole meat. Animal proteins and fats are much more favourably accepted by most dogs than vegetable oils and cereal proteins. Many dogs also like human condiments such as salt, garlic and onions. Some prefer their food soft and wet, while others like it dry and crunchy. Appetite appeal is often moulded by habit.

Special diets   Complete commercial diets are available in dry and moist form for puppies, working dogs, and geriatrics. Prescription complete foods are available for various health problems such as obesity, pancreatitis, bladder stone formation.

Bones are a rich source of nutrients. As well, bone chewing exercises the dog's jaw and keeps its teeth clean.

Bones

Bones are important for several reasons. The first is that they prevent boredom. Chewing on bones also exercises the dog's jaws and keeps the teeth clean and free of dental caries and tartar build-up. They are a rich source of nutrients—particularly calcium and phosphorus—and contain proteins and minerals essential for the dog's development and general maintenance.

However, bones can cause two problems. They can form obstructions or pierce the food pipe. And if fed in large quantities, they can cause constipation. Their high concentration of calcium carbonate can create rock-like masses when water is resorbed in the large intestine.

Bones should form only about 10 per cent of the dog's diet. Fish, chicken and chop bones should *never* be given to your pet, as they can splinter or fracture easily and lodge in the food pipe. The best bones are shin of beef or soft crumbly bones such as knuckles or boiled breast of mutton. Whichever bone is given, ensure that your dog is nibbling small crumbs from the end of the bone, not shattering it into large fragments.

Milk

Milk is an essential part of the pup's diet but can still be fed to older dogs without harm. It is a rich source of protein, fat and minerals, as well as having a pleasant taste. Milk can either be given as the raw product, slightly warmed, or reconstituted from either tinned or dehydrated milk. If the dog or pup is not accustomed to straight cow's milk, it is advisable to commence by using watered-down milk (50 per cent water, 50 per cent milk). The concentration of milk should gradually be increased over a period of five to six days. Some puppies are allergic to cow's milk and this will induce diarrhoea. It is a fallacy that milk transmits worms.

How much food?

The amount of food required by any dog has to be determined by trial and error and each dog is different. Exercise affects the amount of food required. Some breeds are hyperactive, others lead a more sedentary life. The more energy used while running about, the more food will be required. As a rule of thumb you should be able to feel your dog's ribs through a thin layer of fat lying just under the skin. Look at dogs of similar breed to see how your dog compares.

If a dog is overweight, it is usually because it is fed too much energy-giving food. A two-pronged approach is necessary; reduce (or even eliminate) the energy part of the food, and try to introduce a ration that is less palatable, such as a dry food. Increased exercise for the dog will also help reduce weight. Only feed the dog once a day, and every now and again miss a day.

Weigh your dog regularly. If it gradually gains weight, then it is eating too much. As a rough guide, an adult dog requires about 14 grams of food per 450 grams of body-weight. About two-thirds of this ration should be protein and the balance should be cereal food such as biscuits or meal. Table scraps can also be included.

Any type of human food is suitable for your dog: cooked vegetables, fruit, apples, bananas, table scraps—in fact, anything that people eat is suitable for the dog. If the dog refuses to eat some particular food or begins to vomit or have diarrhoea, eliminate that particular substance.

A bitch that is feeding puppies requires extra attention to her diet. She must have more food, which should be given as an additional meal rather than by increasing the amount given at her normal feeding time. The pregnant bitch requires twice her normal amount of food during the last half of her pregnancy.

The normal adult dog should be fed one main meal a day with possibly a small snack in the morning. Feed at a regular time, preferably in the evening. Always use a clean food bowl, always provide clean water, and do not leave any food that is not eaten within a reasonable time. One good way of measuring the average dog's appetite is to place its ration in front of it and wait. When the dog walks away from the plate it has usually had sufficient food for that meal. This should be the limit of the food given at subsequent meal times.

HOW MUCH FOOD?	
Age	**Meals Per Day**
6 weeks (weaning)	4
2–3 months	4
3–6 months	3
6–9 months	2
9 months and over	1
Pregnancy (last third)	2–3
Lactation	2–3

Feeding a puppy

The diet programme for pups is more complex, as they are growing rapidly and require frequent meals because of limited stomach capacity.

At two to three months, puppies require four meals a day: a morning meal, which could be minced meat or a suitable commercial ration, particularly a semi-moist type of food, together with a granular dog meal. The midday meal and the mid-afternoon meal should consist of milk with cereal, baby foods or breakfast cereals. The evening meal should be the same as the morning meal, and given an hour before bedtime to encourage the puppy to empty his bowels and urinate on his last trip outside. Water should be available at all times.

From three to six months, three meals a day are adequate; eliminate the late afternoon meal and gradually increase the evening meal. Between six and nine months, when the puppy has nearly matured, two meals a day are adequate: morning and evening.

From nine months of age on, one meal a day is all that is necessary. It is important to realise that at this age the dog has finished growing and its nutritional requirements will change. If the dog is still fed a number of times a day, it will become obese.

General care

Exercise

Young puppies up to six months of age should be allowed to exercise themselves. This is particularly important in the larger breeds, which are those that reach 15 kilograms by the age of three months. Forced exercise during the early growing phase can do damage to the hip joints and promote hip dysplasia. It is just as important, however, not to confine dogs for long periods. The dog in its natural environment is a roaming animal and requires plenty of territory.

The amount of exercise is also dependent on the breed. Sporting and hunting dogs require much more exercise and territory than smaller breeds or lap dogs. These factors should be taken into consideration before purchasing the dog. A large number of domestic dogs get very little organised exercise and not only keep happy and healthy but even reach a ripe old age.

Hard exercise, such as following a jogger or a bicycle, is not good for a dog and may be injurious to its health. A dog is a very loyal companion and will do its utmost to keep in contact with its master in these situations. But in doing so it may become liable to injury. If you can, take the dog for a walk each day; the dog will exercise itself running three or four times the distance that you walk, and by doing this will exercise within its own limits.

Fallacies

Fresh meat makes a dog savage. It does not.

Milk given to young puppies causes worms. This myth has been perpetuated by the fact that puppies begin to drink milk at three to four weeks, at about the same age as they start to pass round white worms ('milk worms') from infestations acquired in the mother's womb.

Meat gives worms. Any meat, other than that purchased from a butcher's shop, can give worms, even meat from a reputable pet shop. The best approach is to cook all meat bought from a pet shop.

A purebred bitch is ruined for breeding when she has pups to a mongrel or dog of another breed. This is false. Once a bitch has had a litter of pups, the womb is cleaned out and free to accept the next pregnancy. It is biologically impossible for the previous sire to exert any genetic influence on subsequent pregnancies.

More than one father to a litter of pups is impossible. This is incorrect. A bitch may be promiscuous during her heat cycle so that different eggs within her womb may be fertilised by sperm from different dogs, the result being a mixed bag of pups.

Grooming and washing

Your nose will generally tell you when a dog should be washed—as a rule, about every three weeks or whenever the dog becomes smelly. Choose a warm day and a warm draught-free location. A small dog may be washed in the laundry tub or the bath.

Pour warm water over the animal to wet the hair, being careful not to get water in its ears, then apply an insecticidal shampoo, or a bland soap if the dog suffers from any allergic dermatitis. Wash any gross dirt from the coat and relather, leaving the shampoo on for about ten to fifteen minutes to allow the insecticide to work.

Rinse the dog, using warm water, and then apply an insecticidal rinse to the coat. Insecticidal rinses, used to protect the dog against fleas and mites, are also partially effective against ticks. Remember that insecticidal rinses are poisons; the manufacturers' instructions must be followed carefully.

Towel the dog down and leave it in the sun to dry. Dogs naturally roll to dry themselves, so tie up your dog on a surface where it will not get dirty.

Dogs that have a lot of hair around the ear canal should have their ears plucked with a small pair of tweezers. Cleaning the ear lobes is done with a piece of cotton wool soaked in diluted methylated spirits to dissolve any wax. Cotton buds can safely be used to clean the ear canal, as the ear canal in the dog has a right-angled bend before it reaches the ear drum, making penetration of the drum almost impossible.

Adult dogs change their coats once a year, usually in spring. The process takes about six weeks. To groom, use a fine-toothed metal comb or pluck the hair out with fingers and thumb when it is loose enough to do so without hurting the animal. Occasionally the dog will scratch as if troubled by skin

Wash on a warm day and in a draught-free location.

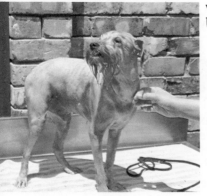

Leave insecticidal and medicated shampoos on for 10 minutes before rinsing.

Towel the dog down and leave it in the sun to dry.

disease or insects, but this is just nature's way of hastening removal of the old coat. Dogs also shed their coats during serious illness or after whelping.

The first (or puppy) coat is soft and woolly and is different from the second and subsequent coats. It is usually much darker. Pups generally change their coats for the first time at nine or ten months, but if born in winter they will change their coats in spring.

For those owners wishing to enter their dogs in dog shows, good grooming is imperative. Grooming tools include:

Brushes Always use a bristle brush, soft, medium or stiff on short-haired dogs, and a pin brush on long-haired breeds to remove the loose undercoat.

Combs A regular size, coarse steel comb should be used on long-haired breeds and a fine comb on smooth-coated dogs.

Nailclippers Nails need cutting if they touch the ground when the dog is standing upright, as the pressure can cause a painful condition in the joints of the toes. Outdoor dogs, particularly those running on concrete or other hard surfaces, rarely need their nails cut. Indoor dogs, or those kept on soft ground, should have their nails checked regularly and cut when necessary. Long nails, particularly dew claws which do not touch the ground, can grow too long, and curl and embed themselves painfully in the footpads. Ordinary scissors should not be used. Use proper nailclippers of the guillotine type. The flat surface of the guillotine blade should be parallel with the bottom of the pad. If the pink quick is visible, cut the nails to within 3 millimetres of the end of the pink.

Scissors A sharp pair of scissors will be suitable for grooming most breeds, but in the case of poodles, or other breeds which need a curved effect on their coats, used curved scissors.

Fine stripping knife This is a tool that should be used instead of a brush on the sensitive areas of the body such as the ears and head.

Tweezers Use tweezers regularly to pluck hair from inside the ears to stop dirt and debris collecting and thus protect the dog from ear infections by allowing proper air circulation to dry out the ear canal.

Velvet pad or soft handkerchief Essential for rubbing the coat of white short-haired breeds to give a gloss. A velvet pad rubbed over the coat of other short-haired breeds such as Boxer or Dachshund gives a good sheen.

Tooth scraper Teeth should be kept fairly white by using a tooth scraper to remove excess tartar. If the teeth are bad, take the dog to your vet.

No-tangle shampoo Knotted hair can largely be prevented by using a no-tangle shampoo. If knots occur, you may have to cut them out. Use blunt scissors. You may have to go right to skin level and leave the dog with various bare patches, but this is better than subjecting the dog to a very painful experience if you comb the knots out.

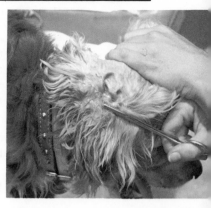
Plucking hair from the ear canal.

Cleaning wax and debris from the ear.

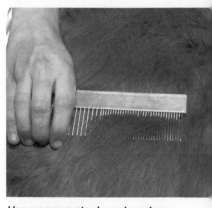
Use a coarse steel comb on long-haired dogs.

Proper grooming tools are essential for hair care.

Dew claws.
Use proper nail clippers to cut a dog's nails.

The quick can be easily identified on a light coloured nail: Note the cutting position.

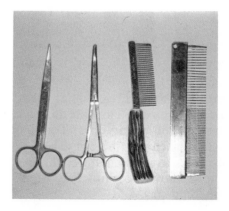

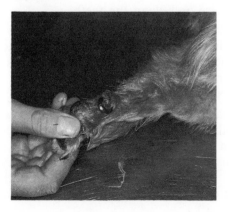

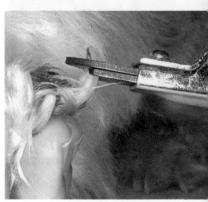

Teeth

A puppy is born without teeth, but by five to eight weeks it will have twenty-eight puppy or 'milk' teeth, which seldom give trouble while being cut. At about four months—sometimes a little sooner—puppies other than toy dogs begin to change their teeth. The forty-two or forty-four permanent teeth are usually through by five months.

Toy dogs change their teeth a little later. It is generally the toy breeds that have trouble at this time; sometimes they appear unable to cast their milk teeth, which should be extracted when the permanent teeth come through.

Overcrowding can be a problem, particularly in dogs with short muzzles. Discoloration of teeth can be caused by the administration of certain antibiotics to the puppy or the mother before the teeth erupt.

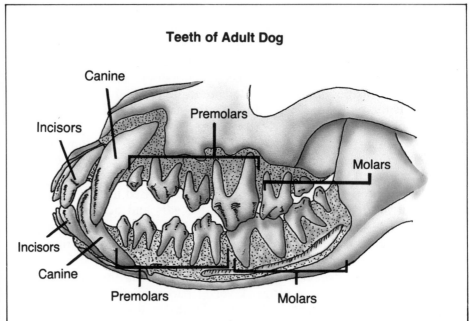

Teeth of Adult Dog

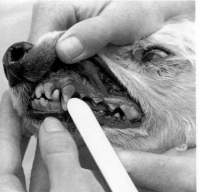

Some dogs will allow teeth cleaning, others need an anaesthetic.

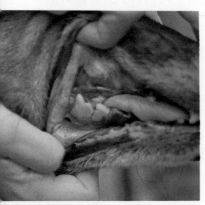

Check your dog's teeth regularly for tartar.

Teeth troubles have become more common since the introduction of soft commercial foods, which allow accumulation of food debris (plaque) between the teeth and between the tooth and gum margin. Plaque in turn allows tartar to build up, causing discoloration and decay of the tooth. Sometimes gingivitis (inflammation of the gums) and bad breath follow. Dry biscuits, fed at least once a day as part of the ration, will help keep the dog's teeth in good order. A large shank bone with some tissue and tendon sheaths attached will help, as the time spent tearing and gnawing the bone will exercise and clean the teeth.

Check your dog's teeth annually by pulling back the lips to expose the teeth at the rear of the mouth. Any accumulation of tartar (a yellow substance) should be removed. If this is impossible, or if the dog is uncooperative, visit the vet.

The only teeth that regularly cause a problem are the carnassial teeth, situated on either side of the upper jaw, towards the rear. They are massive teeth with triple roots which are subject to decay in ageing dogs. The first sign of trouble is usually a swelling in the cheek, beneath the eye. The dog will show signs of discomfort and may go off its food; sometimes the eye will be inflamed. If the offending tooth is not removed, a sinus may break out over the swelling, discharging a foul-smelling pus.

Training

A well-trained dog is a delightful companion and an intelligent member of the family. Training is a rewarding occupation requiring patience and kindness, which will bring you closer to your dog.

Puppies have short memories and must learn by repetition. In the early stages aim for short daily training sessions with the minimum of distraction and preferably just before feed time. Encourage the puppy when it has done well; give the occasional titbit, always a word of praise and a pat. Never smack the dog with your hand for punishment, other than on the rump, and never use any physical force on its nose—this is its most sensitive part and the dog's sense of smell can easily be impaired. If the puppy must be punished, catch it in the act of wrongdoing; otherwise it will not know what it has done wrong. Dogs understand differences in the tone of your voice, so make your initial reprimand by deepening the tone of your voice and speaking severely. If this does not work after repeated attempts, use a folded piece of newspaper to smack the animal; this makes a lot of noise, indicates to the dog that it is being punished but does not hurt it physically. Do not expect too much too soon; many pups will not learn commands until they are five or six months old and remain mischievous and destructive until then.

The same basic principles of reward and punishment apply to all forms of training.

House-training

From the time it is weaned a puppy can be taught to be clean and to go to a tray containing dirt, sand or ashes to empty its bladder and bowel. Put it on the tray several times a day, and always after it has been fed, and praise any action. It will quickly learn to go there regularly. As the puppy grows older, put it outside five or six times a day, especially first thing in the morning and last thing at night, as well as immediately after eating. If possible, select a spot in the garden and take the puppy there regularly, as the odour emanating from its toilet will stimulate its desire to pass urine or faeces. If possible, stay with the puppy until it has performed and then praise it; it will soon learn what is expected.

Older puppies or dogs that have not previously been trained are sometimes more difficult. They require careful watching and frequent putting out. If they misbehave in the house, scold them with words.

If a trained dog has an accident in the house it usually means the dog has a problem. It may be an antisocial jealousy behaviour pattern, it may indicate an infection of the bladder, or in older dogs it can be urinary incontinence. Never rub your dog's nose in the mess when it has made a mistake; take it to the spot, hold it near and say 'no' or 'bad dog' several times in your scolding voice, then put the dog straight outside for some time as an indication of punishment.

Travelling

Domestic animals that are unused to travelling should be tranquillised or sedated for journeys, as they can get very upset. To prevent travel sickness, do not feed the animal within four hours of travelling and allow the dog adequate ventilation away from exhaust fumes. Keep your dog on the floor of the car so it cannot see moving objects outside. Travel sickness in dogs is usually demonstrated by salivation and vomiting. Specific anti-sickness tablets are available for dogs.

Boarding

Dogs to be boarded should be fully vaccinated and wormed fourteen days beforehand. Once a satisfactory establishment has been found, continue to patronise it because it and the staff will become familiar to the dog. The dog should be re-wormed four weeks after returning home.

Vaccinations

The six major infectious diseases of dogs are distemper, hepatitis, parvo disease, rabies, para influenza (kennel cough), bordatella and leptospirosis. Distemper, hepatitis, parvo disease and rabies are all caused by viruses, and all four can kill.

Canine distemper can affect dogs of any age. It produces a range of symptoms varying from loss of appetite and high temperature, to fits and death. The few dogs that do not die from distemper usually suffer long-lasting side effects, including paralysis, nervous twitches and deformed pads.

Canine hepatitis can also affect dogs of any age. It is less common than distemper but just as dangerous. The virus affects the liver; animals that survive an attack usually suffer from permanent liver damage. The virus of canine hepatitis does not cause human hepatitis.

Parvo disease is a new viral disease which can affect any dog. It is particularly fatal in young and very old dogs. The virus attacks the heart muscle and the intestinal tract, causing a fatal bloody diarrhoea.

Rabies is a viral disease affecting the brain and making the animal aggressive towards other animals and humans. There are two types: furious rabies, and dumb or paralytic rabies. In both the animals become very excited and aggressive, but in the dumb or paralytic form this phase is very short and the disease progresses rapidly to paralysis and finally death. It is almost impossible to eradicate rabies once it exists in a country—hence the strict quarantine laws by rabies-free countries such as the UK, Australia and New Zealand.

Para influenza (kennel cough) (see p. 123.)

Leptospirosis is caused by an organism that can penetrate the skin or mucous membrane, multiply rapidly in the blood and cause fatal anaemia.

There is no effective treatment for any of these diseases. Antiserums are available, but by the time an animal is seen to be sick the diseases have often progressed to the point where treatment is ineffective. Antibiotics are useless against viruses. The only safeguard is prevention by vaccination.

Because these diseases are transmitted by infected dogs through contact with their urine, saliva and faeces, or through contact with the dogs themselves, you can protect your dog by keeping it in isolation. This is essential for the pup too young to be vaccinated, but is obviously impractical for the older dog, whether it is a working dog, a sporting dog, a show dog or just

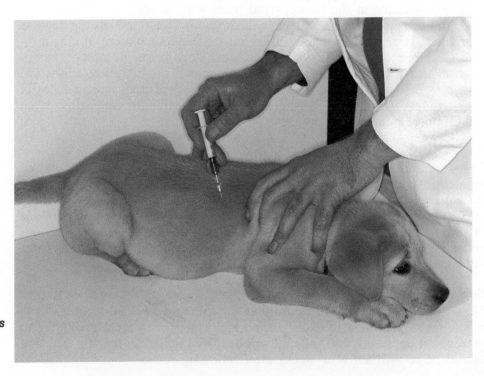

Vaccination against fatal diseases is vital for your dog's health; check requirements with your veterinarian.

the family pet. The only practical and effective way to protect your dog is to have it vaccinated by your veterinary surgeon.

Modern-day vaccines do not generally have any after-effects and most can be given from six weeks on. Because various vaccination programmes are available, it is best to consult your veterinary surgeon about the best time to start the vaccinations and the frequency of booster shots. Pups under twelve weeks of age require a special course of vaccinations. Vaccination causes the production of antibodies which circulate in the blood and protect the dog against infection.

A whelping bitch passes antibodies to her pups in the first milk (colostrum) within twenty-four hours of whelping. This is why it is so important that pups suckle immediately after birth. The antibodies the pups receive from their mother disappear gradually over a twelve-week period, leaving them unprotected unless immediately vaccinated. Some breeders have their pups injected with gamma-globulin at three weeks of age as a temporary protection against distemper and hepatitis. This is not vaccination. It protects the pups against infection for two to three weeks only.

When purchasing a pup it is always important to find out what immunisation it has had and, if possible, obtain its vaccination card so your own vet can determine which of the several different varieties of vaccine it has been given and when it needs the first booster.

As vaccinations do not work immediately, but take from three to seven days to build up adequate protection, keep your dog away from other dogs for a couple of weeks after vaccination.

Visits to the vet

Dogs can't talk, so the vet depends heavily on the owner's observations. If it is a non-urgent problem, watch the dog for twenty-four hours and make a list of any abnormal signs. Check its eating habits and toilet activities (take samples of urine and faeces). Is the dog vomiting or doing anything else unusual? Do not attend to minor discharging wounds or skin lesions for at least twenty-four hours before the visit, so that the type and colour of the discharge is obvious.

If possible, make an appointment, as this will reduce the length of time your pet is confined in a waiting room with other animals and will thus reduce the risk of fights. Take the dog for a walk outside first and let it sniff the local smells to stimulate it to go to the toilet—this lessens the likelihood that the smells of other dogs in the waiting room will cause an 'accident'.

Make sure that the dog's collar is a firm fit and cannot slip over its head if the dog pulls back, and use a strong secure lead. Don't let a child hold it—you are taking the dog into a strange place with strange smells, some of which may be offensive to it; there will be other animals present, and the vet's surgery is no doubt alongside a busy road.

Worming

The four main categories of worms that affect the intestinal tract are hookworm, roundworm, tapeworm and whipworm. In the tropical climates heartworm is also a problem (it lives in the right ventricle of the heart).

Hookworms

Hookworms are 10–20 millimetres in length, and the adult forms are found firmly attached to the lining of the gut. Surveys indicate that in many canine populations the incidence is about 35 per cent.

The life cycle of hookworms is direct—there is no intermediate host, although transport hosts (for example, mice) can play a part in the worm's transmission.

Female hookworms are prolific egg producers, averaging an output of 10 000 to 30 000 eggs per female per day. A heavily infected puppy can pass

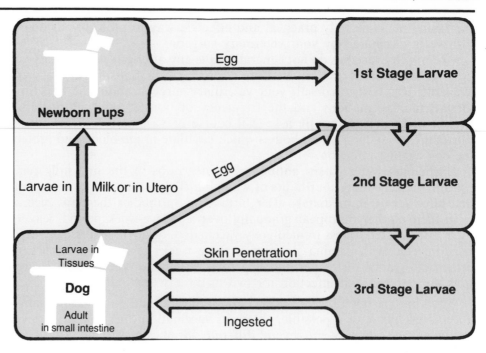

Life Cycle of the Hookworm.

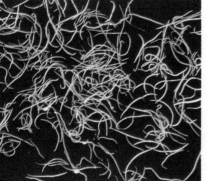

Hookworms can cause fatal anaemia.

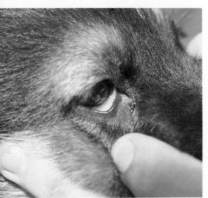

This pup had a massive hookworm infestation at 8 weeks of age: Note the pale mucous membrane of the eye.

a total of five million eggs per day for more than four weeks at a time. Infection is by five routes:

Skin penetration—where the larval stage penetrates the skin and migrates via the blood system to the lungs and then to the intestinal tract.

Oral infection—where development takes place exclusively within the gastro-intestinal tract.

Intrauterine/transmammary infection—occurs when migrating larvae are carried to the uterus to establish a prenatal infection in a pregnant bitch, or are carried to the mammary glands to infect suckling puppies.

Ingestion of hookworm-infected paratenic hosts—for example, mice infected with the larval stages of the hookworm.

Arrested development in the gastro-intestinal tract—occurs when inhibited larval stages provide a protected reservoir of infection which complicates treatment and control programmes. Conventional worming preparations are ineffective against the hookworm in its dormant tissue stages. Susceptible adult worms removed by worming treatment may be replaced by worms growing from these inhibited larval stages. If this happens, rapid reinfestation occurs and the response to the worming treatment is only temporary. The presence of these arrested forms of hookworm within the host dog cannot be detected by faecal examination for worm eggs, and this complicates the diagnosis.

Diagnosis of hookworm infestation is by detection of microscopic eggs in the faeces, or by the appearance of bloody diarrhoea and anaemia in puppies less than three weeks old.

To prevent reinfestation, treated dogs must be housed in an environment that can be readily cleaned and which is unsuitable for the development of hookworm eggs and larvae. Faeces should be removed regularly and, particularly in earth-floored runs, at intervals of no more than one to two days. In large areas, soil can be treated periodically with salt at the rate of 160 grams per litre of boiling water, or sodium borate at the rate of 14 kilograms per square metre. Sodium borate at this concentration is toxic and dangerous to pups.

Young puppies are highly susceptible to worm infestation. They should always be provided with clean areas (for example, concrete-floored kennels and runs, or wire floors out of contact with soil) which are treated weekly to remove any infected larvae. In kennels where there are severe problems, consideration should be given to early weaning and worming treatment of puppies, together with housing of the dogs on suspended wire floors.

It is possible that a vaccination against hookworm will be produced in the foreseeable future.

Roundworm

Surveys indicate that 40-50 per cent of most dog populations are affected by roundworm. Infection may be by one of five routes:

Direct infection—when a puppy eats the eggs directly from faecal matter. Within one month adult female worms will be present in the dog's body although eggs may not be present in the dog's faeces for six to eight weeks. The eggs hatch in the intestine, releasing small larval stages of the roundworm which migrate to the liver within two days. The larval stages also migrate to the lungs and are coughed up and reswallowed into the intestinal

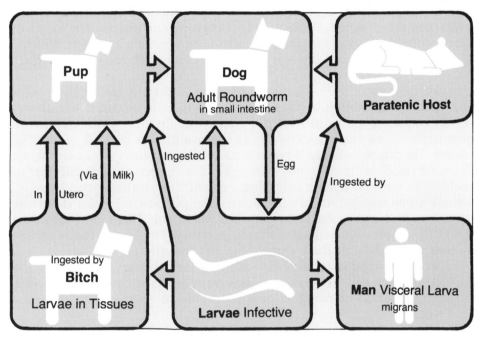

Life Cycle of the Roundworm.

tract. During this phase they may go to the uterus of a female dog and, if the bitch is pregnant, infect her unborn puppies.

Intrauterine infection—which occurs when female dogs older than one to three months eat infective eggs and the larval stages become arrested in the bitch's uterine tissues. If the bitch becomes pregnant, the larval stage is mobilised during the last fourteen days of the pregnancy and migrates through the placenta to the developing foetus, thus initiating an intrauterine roundworm infestation. Infected puppies have larval stages in their lungs when they are born. Eggs of the roundworm can thus appear in the faeces of puppies as early as three weeks after birth, and the production of these eggs from the mature female roundworms in the intestinal tract increases up to six months. Not all the dormant larvae in the uterus may be mobilised at the first pregnancy after infection. Some larvae may still be available for foetal infection in subsequent pregnancies.

Roundworms are the most common worm found in the dog population.

Transmammary infection—takes place when roundworm larva stages are transmitted through the milk of the bitch.

Post-parturient infections in bitches—these are caused either by the resumption of the development of dormant roundworm larval stages, or by the ingestion by the bitch of larval stages shed by her prenatally infected pups. During the suckling period the bitch ingests most of her puppies' faeces and any eggs therein have not had time to reach the infective stage; the eggs therefore pass through the bitch and are disseminated in her faeces. After a period in the environment they reach the infective stage—and then when eaten they complete their life cycle.

Infections through hosts—may occur when dogs eat the carcasses of rodents and other animals containing larval stages of the roundworm.

The principal symptoms associated with roundworm infection are: coughing, nasal discharge, frequent vomiting (especially after meals), stunted growth, intermittent diarrhoea, failure to eat, distended and painful stomach, and sometimes convulsions. If the condition is severe, puppies may die within twelve hours to a few days after birth. Postmortem examination of the puppies will confirm the diagnosis. In older animals the diagnosis is made by the faecal flotation test.

The most important aspect of roundworm treatment is to control and limit the effects of prenatal infections in young puppies. Puppies should receive two worming treatments during the first three weeks of life, ideally at two weeks and three weeks. Subsequently, between four and twelve weeks of age, puppies should have fortnightly treatments to ensure complete removal of the infection, because the worming preparations currently available are not completely effective against migrating larval stages.

In addition, puppies less than one or two months old are highly susceptible to direct infestation by roundworm eggs from infected bitches or previously contaminated kennel environments. Puppies may acquire infection from larval stages which are known to be transmitted in the milk of infected bitches. The puppies should be examined at four and eight weeks after birth to ensure freedom from roundworm eggs. It is important to realise that as bitches can become temporarily reinfected in the suckling period and so become a potential source of infection for the puppies, they also should be treated when the pups are three and four weeks old. This treatment of the bitch will not prevent later intrauterine infection. The bitch's faeces should be collected and burnt daily throughout the suckling period.

Eggs of the roundworm may be found on the coats of both bitches and pups, so children should be discouraged from handling the animals during the suckling period—if possible, puppies should be reared in an enclosure until weaning.

The female roundworm produces an enormous number of eggs which unfortunately are highly resistant to the environment and can survive and remain infective for years. The complexity of the roundworm life cycle makes control difficult. The particular susceptibility of young dogs to roundworm means that they are the most important sources of infection for other animals and for human beings. The bitch has an especially important role as a reservoir of infection for successive generations of dogs.

Tapeworms

There are many species of tapeworm, but the one most commonly seen by pet owners is the flea tapeworm. The most important tapeworm to avoid in terms of human health is the hydatid.

The flea tapeworm

Surveys indicate that up to 65 per cent of dogs in city areas may be affected with the flea tapeworm. Segments of the tapeworm are passed in the faeces or may leave the dog spontaneously. They move actively on the dog's anal area or on the ground and bedding, disseminating egg capsules which are swallowed by the maggot-like flea larva. When the flea larvae mature into adult fleas, dogs become infected by ingesting them while scratching and biting themselves.

The flea tapeworm is of little significance in dogs, except that it causes itchiness around the anal area; to relieve this the dog will scoot (rub its anal

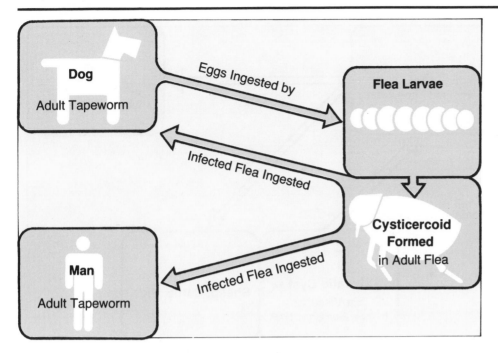

Life Cycle of the Tapeworm.

area on the ground). Anal itchiness with scooting and rubbing is common.

Segments of the tapeworm are often seen on the surface of the faeces. They are about 1 centimetre long, flat, pinkish-grey in colour and active.

Unless preventive measures are taken dogs will rapidly become reinfected and may be passing large numbers of segments in their faeces within weeks of treatment.

The tapeworm has an indirect life cycle involving fleas and lice as intermediate hosts, and this complicates prevention. Unless fleas are controlled, reinfection can occur rapidly and repeatedly. Children may become infected by the accidental ingestion of fleas; and the habit of picking fleas from dogs and crushing them between the fingernails is most unhygienic.

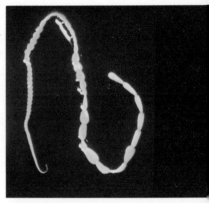

Usually small segments of the tapeworm are passed.

Hydatids

The occurrence of this tapeworm in dogs is widespread in rural areas in many countries.

The adult hydatid worm lives in the intestine of the dog. The eggs are passed in the dog's faeces. Intermediate hosts include a wide range of animals—sheep, cattle, goats, pigs, kangaroos, wallabies, and human beings—but sheep are by far the most important. In some countries, the domestic dog/sheep life cycle ensures the survival and transmission of the parasite. The eggs, when ingested by an intermediate host, pass to the small intestine and hatch to release a small cyst. The cysts penetrate the tissues of the small intestine, enter the blood vessels and are carried to the liver. Some pass through the liver to the lungs and central nervous system.

Human infection occurs only from the accidental ingestion of embryonated eggs of the hydatid tapeworm which are passed by the dog in its faeces. The worm itself is of little significance to the dog.

However, the intermediate or cystic stage is important, firstly in relation to sheep and the economic loss associated with condemnation of hydatid-infected livers at slaughter, and secondly as a cause of hydatid disease in human beings.

The eggs of the hydatid tapeworm can be seen in the faeces under the microscope.

To control hydatids all canine infections need to be eradicated. Prevent reinfection of dogs by adequately disposing of infected offal and sheep carcasses. Control strays and free-roaming farm dogs.

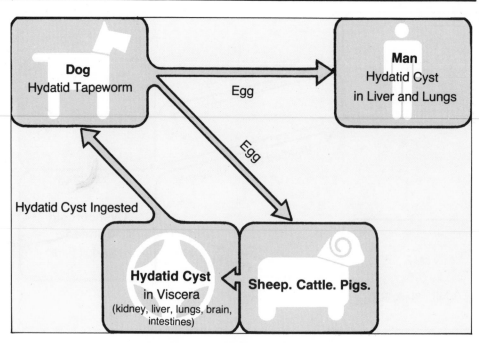

Life Cycle of the Hydatid Cyst.

Whipworm

Whipworms, 4–7 millimetres long, get their name because the first part of their body is long and slender and the back part is short and thick. In many city dog populations there is an incidence of approximately 15 per cent. Whipworms are particularly common in areas with a heavy concentration of dogs.

The worms have a simple life cycle with no intermediate host.

Diarrhoea, often associated with abdominal pain and dehydration, may indicate the presence of whipworms. The diarrhoea is characteristically dark and foul-smelling. Sometimes there are signs of central nervous excitation. In heavy infections, fresh blood may be seen in the faeces and there may be generalised jaundice associated with anaemia. Positive diagnosis is made on finding whipworm eggs in the faeces under the microscope.

The most important factor in the control of whipworm is the remarkable longevity of the eggs. They remain viable within a wide temperature range and thus an important source of reinfection for up to five years. This means that even dogs with light whipworm infections held in confined spaces such as kennels or training areas will seed the area with eggs that will be a continual source of reinfection. It may therefore be necessary to treat such dogs every ten weeks for a year or more before the residual source of eggs is exhausted.

Although whipworms are not common, when present in the dog they frequently cause persistent diarrhoea.

Worm control

- Pregnant dogs should be wormed at three and six weeks
- Puppies at three weeks and each two weeks until 12 weeks of age and then three times per year for life
- Dispose of dog faeces
- Keep dogs well groomed and flea free
- Wash hands after handling animals
- Avoid contact with dogs faeces. Don't foul public places.

Treatment — Hookworm, Roundworm, Tapeworm and Whipworm

- Seek your veterinarian's advice because worm preparations vary in their efficacy against each species
- Your veterinarian can diagnose worms by examining a faecal sample microscopically. The egg shape identifies the species.

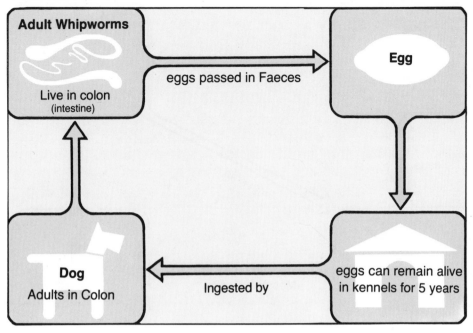

Life Cycle of the Whipworm.

Heartworm

Heartworm affects dogs in tropical and subtropical areas of the world. As the name implies, heartworms live in the chambers of the heart, and feed on the blood. The worms are thin and 12–30 centimetres in length. The number of worms that occupy an infected dog's heart may vary from a single worm to more than a hundred. In small numbers the presence of the worms may have little effect, but as the number of worms increases, so does the mechanical effect on the heart. Gradually the heart becomes less efficient until the dog begins to show the symptoms of chronic heart failure, namely coughing, low exercise tolerance and fluid accumulation resulting in a swollen abdomen. Severe heartworm infection may result in death.

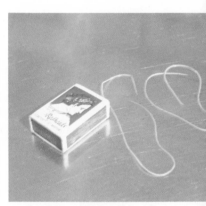

Heartworms are thin and very long; they cause mechanical blockage of the heart.

The heartworm is transmitted by mosquitoes. The adult worms in the heart of an infected dog produce larval stages called microfilaria which circulate in the blood and are picked up by biting mosquitoes. The microfilaria go through another stage of development in the mosquito and can be transmitted to another dog that is bitten by the infected mosquito. In the newly infected dog the microfilaria go through more stages of development, becoming adult worms in the heart about six or seven months later. The adult worms then repeat the cycle. Heartworm is not considered a human health hazard. Other animals, including cats, have been reported with heartworm infections, but this is extremely rare.

In most cases heartworm can be diagnosed by a simple blood test. In more complex cases, further examination by X-rays, electrocardiograms or additional blood tests may be necessary. Because heartworm produces specific symptoms of chronic heart failure and congestion, the veterinarian who sees a dog with the symptoms of heart disease will consider heartworm as a possible cause and carry out the necessary tests. Dogs that live in heartworm areas should be checked regularly, even if they are not showing signs of heartworm disease, to ensure they are not in the early stages of infection. A single blood test or two tests at a short interval will usually indicate the presence of adult heartworms.

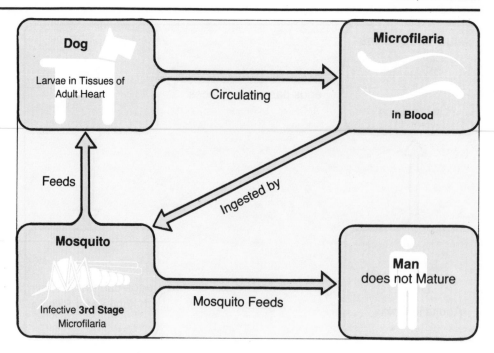

Life Cycle of the Heartworm.

Treatment

Infected dogs are usually hospitalised for treatment. Drugs are then administered which kill the adult heartworms. The break-up and dislodgement of worm segments can cause side-effects necessitating urgent veterinary attention. The course of treatment may be dangerous depending on the number of worms.

Heartworm prevention

- Control mosquitoes by preventing their access to their still water breeding grounds. Rain water tanks, buckets and stagnant ponds should be covered or drained.
- Administration of heartworm preventative medication. (H.P.M.)
  - Puppies should commence H.P.M. as soon as they commence solids. They can start without a prior blood test.
  - Dogs over six months require a blood test confirming they are negative prior to commencing H.P.M.
  - Dogs entering a heartworm area for holidays etc. should commence H.P.M. 4 weeks before and continue 8 weeks after.
- H.P.M. can be given as a syrup, tablets or chewables. Scientists are working on a vaccine. Currently, depending on the drug chosen, H.P.M. can be given either daily or monthly. Because heartworm can be so dangerous to your pet it is best to consult with your veterinarian.

Breeding

The male dog

Male dogs mature sexually at about six months of age. When both testicles are descended, theoretically the dog can mate, but it is best to wait until the dog is nine to twelve months old before using it for breeding. This is to allow the dog to fully mature; a heavy breeding season may stunt his growth.

In today's urban society where most male dogs are confined to limited territory and most bitches are desexed, the male dog has less opportunities for mating than he did in the wild. I believe this causes behavioural changes in many male dogs. Undesexed male dogs are more likely to bite, to fight with other dogs, chase cars, exhibit sexual deviations (such as riding legs, mounting children), be excitable, bark excessively, and display too much aggressiveness. If it is not to be used for breeding, a male dog should be castrated at five to six months of age. This is a simple procedure, requiring a general anaesthetic, in which the testicles are removed. The dog is usually only in hospital for twenty-four hours.

The Common Ailments listing includes some of the problems encountered in male dogs.

The female dog

The female dog first comes into heat anytime from six months of age on, depending on her breed and size. The small toy breeds usually come on heat at about six to seven months; the larger breeds usually at nine to ten months. This period of sexual activity usually occurs twice a year. At oestrus (Day 1), the bitch's vulva becomes swollen and there is a bloodstained discharge. Male dogs are attracted to the bitch, but she will not let them mate at this stage. About nine days later the discharge loses most of its bloody content, signifying that the female is entering the fertile and receptive stage of the heat cycle, when she will stand quietly, ready for service, with her tail raised. The breeding bitch should be mated on the eleventh and thirteenth day.

After the first few thrusting movements by the male, the two animals normally 'tie' together when a special section of the penis swells and 'locks' inside the vulva. Tying together is natural and indicates that the service has been successful. The dogs gradually untie after about fifteen minutes. It is possible for the dogs to turn back to back, but this is quite normal, and generally nothing to worry about. Never try to force the dogs apart, as this could cause injury.

The fertile, receptive stage may last for seven to nine days, after which the vulva gradually returns to a normal size and the discharge ceases. During the receptive phase the bitch may mate with several dogs, which can lead to puppies sired by different dogs.

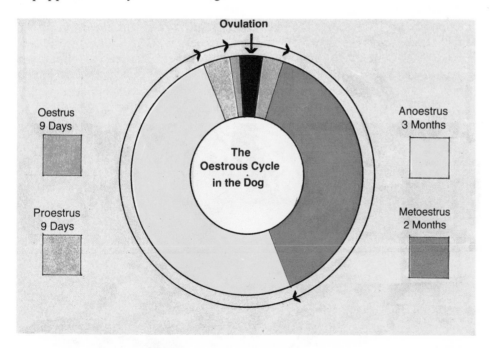

The female dog's breeding cycle.

Contraception

The problems associated with keeping a bitch include bleeding and soiling, attracting male dogs, roaming and change of temperament, unwanted pregnancies, and false pregnancies. All this leads to management problems twice a year. So oestrus control is desirable.

Methods of oestrus control can be surgical or medical.

Surgical control includes ovarihysterectomy (spaying), and tying the tubes.

The advantages of spaying are that it is a once-only, effective, relatively low-risk method of inducing sterility. It overcomes the nuisances associated with heat and keeps the bitch healthy by eliminating false pregnancy and the possibility of pyometra. It may help to reduce the chances of mammary tumour development. The disadvantages, apart from anaesthesia and post-surgical complications, include urinary incontinence and obesity. Urinary incontinence occurs in a very small proportion of bitches in later life and can easily be rectified by the administration of stilboestrol tablets. Obesity tends to occur in certain breeds, such as Labradors and Retrievers, if their diet is not strictly controlled. Obesity frequently occurs in sedentary animals and is blamed on desexing because desexing takes place when the animal has matured and the owner continues to feed the mature dog a growing dog's diet. Despite these disadvantages, spaying is probably the best method where owners have no intention of breeding from the animal.

Tying the tubes has very few advantages because some of the main problems—bleeding and attractiveness to male dogs—are not eliminated. Neither does it prevent false pregnancy, the possibility of an infected womb or mammary tumours.

Medical control is by injection or tablets. Injections are not often recommended because of side effects such as infected wombs. Tablets are quite effective and are used in two forms:

1. A course of tablets given over eight days when the bitch comes into season. These take the bitch off heat within three or four days, before she reaches the fertile phase of the cycle, but the course of tablets must be continued for the full eight days.
2. A prolonged dosage regime, where the bitch is given a very low dose of tablets over a period of twenty days.

Pregnancy testing

Many pet owners are under the impression that having a litter will improve their bitch in some way. This is a fallacy. Owners who are not interested in breeding their bitch are well-advised to have her desexed at about six months of age before she has her first season.

Once you have decided to breed your bitch, your veterinary surgeon should check her for any abnormalities or diseases that might endanger her

Do not overfeed the pregnant bitch; many overweight bitches have whelping problems.

pregnancy or make breeding inadvisable. During this preliminary examination, ask for advice on feeding, worming, mating procedures, and any problems associated with the breed. Some bitches require longer preparation for pregnancy than others, perhaps because of poor physical condition or the presence of parasites or reproductive tract infections.

Once the bitch has been mated, the best time to confirm pregnancy is between four and six weeks after mating, although it can be confirmed by palpation of the foetuses from three weeks, if the bitch has a supple abdomen. Keep careful records of all dates of mating, as most bitches whelp within sixty to sixty-five days following mating.

In the pregnant bitch, the vulva may stay enlarged following mating; this is a good early guide to pregnancy. In the non-pregnant bitch, the vulva will go back to normal size following the heat period. By five to six weeks most pregnant bitches will be obviously heavier and their abdomens will take on a full appearance.

Foetal death

Pregnancies may fail at any stage with the death of the foetuses. A dead foetus is then either resorbed or aborted. In early embryonic death, before implantation in the uterine wall, resorption is usual. Later on, abortion is more likely to occur, because the dead object is larger. (Abortion can also occur with a living foetus, although the mechanism that triggers uterine contractions, relaxation of the cervix and vagina, and extrusion of the foetus, are not fully understood.) There are five possible causes of foetal death:

Genetic faults   Foetal death followed by resorption may be associated with some genetic fault.

Infection   Viral and bacterial infections or, more rarely, fungal infections and parasites can cause foetal death.

Toxic causes   These may include drugs given by injection or orally for the treatment of disease, or skin and coat dressings ingested by licking, or polluted food, water or air.

Physical factors   These factors range from accidents to exposure to heat or cold. Extreme heat has recently been recorded as causing foetal resorption in guinea pigs.

Vitamin E deficiency   While it may be incorrect to list vitamin E deficiency as among the causes of resorption, it has been found that many bitches that have lost foetuses through resorption do not do so again if kept on a high dosage of vitamin E throughout oestrus and pregnancy. The correct dosage must be advised by a veterinarian.

Care during pregnancy

Diet during the first half of pregnancy should be at normal maintenance level. At five weeks the diet should increase about 20–30 per cent in total kilojoules and 2–4 per cent in protein. It is advisable to add liver, at the rate of 1 gram per kilogram of the dog's weight, eggs, dairy products or other good-quality animal protein daily during late pregnancy and lactation.

During the latter part of pregnancy, the nutritional needs of the foetus are provided by the bitch and if extra nutrition is not provided in her diet, foetal demands on her body stores will leave her in a depleted state to begin lactation. The bitch should gain about 10 per cent above the weight of the pups during pregnancy to be ready for lactation.

A fairly practical rule is to feed a maintenance level of high-protein, commercially balanced diet during pregnancy and increase the amount fed in proportion to the bitch's increase in weight. Since most of the weight increase occurs in the last four weeks, dietary needs are easily calculated. Nervous bitches or toy breeds usually eat small volumes and therefore need a diet of high energy value to receive proper nutrition during pregnancy—this means high protein and fat compositions. For most dogs, except the small breeds, a litter of two or three is only a moderate stress during pregnancy; more than four pups can pose problems for the bitch.

If marginal diets, especially those relying on meat scraps as the protein sources, are fed, the results will be a reduced litter size, poor viability of pups and excess weight loss for the bitch. From the nutritional standpoint, a bitch can be rebred when she has recovered any weight loss and is once more in good physical condition.

Do not overfeed a pregnant bitch; many overfat bitches have whelping complications. Exercise for the pregnant bitch is most important. This should not be too strenuous, but enough to keep her muscles in tone. Plenty of walking is ideal.

Worming

Breeding bitches should be wormed three or four times a year, including a treatment midway through pregnancy, with a safe worming preparation that covers roundworm, whipworm, hookworm and tapeworm.

Vaccinations against distemper and hepatitis midway through the pregnancy will give the pups a healthy, passive immunity which will last them to the age of six to nine weeks. The antibodies developed against the vaccination will be passed to the young pups in the colostrum in the first twenty-four to thirty-six hours of suckling.

Preparation for whelping

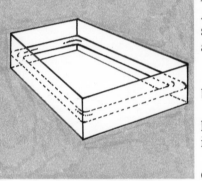

Whelping box.

About a week before the puppies are due, start encouraging the bitch to sleep where she is to whelp. This may be a box, a basket or even a clean area of the room. The essentials of a satisfactory whelping area are:

Size   It must be large enough for the bitch to lie fully extended.

Lighting   The area should be dimly lit and so arranged that the bitch can be observed without being disturbed.

Heating   The area should be warm, dry and draught free. Some form of heating should be provided in cold weather, but make sure it is not an 'oven' in summer.

Safety rails   A whelping box should be fitted inside with rails about 5 centimetres above the floor all round. The rails provide a safety area where a puppy can lie without being crushed if the bitch rolls. This is particularly important in large breeds of dogs.

Bedding   Ideally provide some form of absorbent, disposable paper as a bedding material, as this is easy to clear away afterwards. Torn newspaper is ideal.

Stages of labour

Sixtieth day, until labour

From the sixtieth day it is wise to take the bitch's temperature twice a day, as the normal temperature of 38.5°C will drop by about 1°C just before whelping commences. The vulva swells considerably and becomes very soft. At this stage, and sometimes for twenty-four hours before whelping, a whitish mucous discharge may be noticed.

First stage of labour

The first stage of labour lasts approximately six to twelve hours, or up to twenty-four hours in a bitch having her first litter. The bitch becomes restless, refuses food, may vomit, pants a great deal and may start nesting procedures, tearing up her bedding and often becoming very excited in the process. She may go into cupboards or under beds. Uterine contractions at this stage are very slight and may not be noticed.

Second stage of labour

During this stage contractions become stronger and the bitch is obviously straining. This stage usually lasts between fifteen to thirty minutes. The membrane around the pup ruptures with her straining and releases fluids that serve to lubricate the passage of the pup which is born soon afterwards.

The bitch should lick away the membranes from around the puppy and chew through the umbilical cord. She will continue licking the puppy, nudging it towards her abdomen and away from her vulva. Usually the afterbirth for each pup is passed next, but this is not always the case. The bitch usually eats the afterbirth. It does her no harm, and she may be upset if prevented from following her normal instincts. It is important at this stage not to interfere unless absolutely necessary.

Many dog breeders are not happy unless they have to 'help' the bitch whelp in some way or other. In the vast majority of cases, human interference is not only unnecessary, but is actually harmful. Many of the whelping problems presented to veterinarians are caused by the owners of the bitch being overzealous in their attentions. Some bitches prefer to be left alone, others prefer human company while they whelp, but none appreciate noise, fuss, floodlights, bowls of steaming smelly, disinfected towels, scissors, rolls of cotton wool for tying off cords, the neighbours and their kids, and the helpful expert who comes around to offer confusing advice at the worst possible moment.

Second stage labour; the appearance of the foetal sac.

Third stage of labour

The bitch will normally rest between each pup for fifteen to thirty minutes, with slightly longer intervals towards the end of the whelping as she tires. After the pups are born, the bitch rests and allows the litter to feed. She cleans them less constantly and becomes more relaxed in attitude.

The size of the litter usually varies with the size of the dog. The very small toy breeds may produce between one and three pups; intermediate-size dogs, four to six pups; while the larger breeds may produce anything up to a dozen.

Moments later the pup is born, the cord/placenta is still inside the mother.

Complications of pregnancy

False pregnancy

This is the most common breeding problem. At five to six weeks post-mating, the bitch gains weight and may make milk, but she is not pregnant.

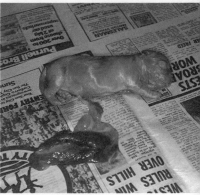
The cord/placenta is completely expelled; time must be given for the blood within the cord and placenta to enter the pup.

A proud, protective mother with her newborn pups.

The problem is likely to occur each heat period and is due to a hormonal imbalance in the ovaries. A normal pregnancy will not prevent the problem recurring at subsequent heat periods. Bitches prone to false pregnancies tend to be candidates for infections of the womb and the development of mammary cancer. The only cure, apart from the administration of hormone tablets to eliminate the milk and the psychological disturbances associated with the problem, is to have the bitch sterilised.

Bitches usually whelp without trouble. However, a knowledge of possible complications may save the bitch much discomfort and may save the lives of her pups. Dystocia (difficult birth) may be caused by any of the following:

Uterine inertia

The bitch fails to strain after breaking water, and generally looks uncomfortable. After a few hours she passes a blackish-green discharge, but no pups. This is a sign that the afterbirths are separating and she should be taken to a vet immediately. Contractions of the uterus may be stimulated by injections, but if this doesn't work, a caesarian section is necessary to save both pups and bitch.

Unproductive labour

As distinct from uterine inertia, this condition is generally due to an obstruction by a twisted or deformed pup. The bitch strains repeatedly and strongly, but is unproductive. Again, a caesarian section is necessary.

Slow birth

If the bitch has not severed the cord after 10 minutes it can be torn.

Some bitches are unable to expel the pups from the vagina easily and the pups may asphyxiate before they are born. Help should be given by gently grasping the protruding part of the pup with a clean towel and pulling gently outwards and downwards, towards the bitch's hocks, as she contracts and strains. When the pup is born, the membranes should be torn away from its mouth with the fingers and the umbilical cord left intact for at least fifteen to twenty minutes, so that the blood in the placenta can be recirculated into the pup's body. After this time, grasp the umbilical cord firmly between the fingers as far from the pup's body as possible and separate it from the afterbirth with a firm pull. It should not be necessary to tie off the cord. Avoid putting any strain on the pup's abdomen where the cord enters the body as a large and sometimes fatal hernia can be produced.

If the bitch passes one pup normally, she will generally need no further help. It is normal for pups to be presented either head first or tail first, and the latter usually presents no problem to the bitch.

The lactation period

Lactation is a period of maximum stress for the bitch. Her energy requirements start at the peak gestation levels and rapidly increase to a maximum of approximately 300 per cent of maintenance at about the third or fourth week. Her exact needs depend on the number, size and age of the puppies and whether they are eating on their own in addition to nursing. Eating should be encouraged as early as possible, at fifteen to twenty days.

A rough guide for estimating the increase in the bitch's food during lactation is to give her 920 kilojoules of extra food per kilogram of litter weight. The diet should be high in protein, up to 30 per cent, but must have adequate non-protein calories or the protein will be used for energy, not milk production. This means a high fat percentage is necessary too.

The daily ration should be divided into three or four portions. The best solution is to self-feed a high-protein dry food (one of the commercial rations) or feed a moist food with added fats two or three times daily. Water deprivation stops lactation quickly. Don't be tempted to add fresh meat to dry and canned foods as this will disturb the calcium balance.

Milk fever or eclampsia

Milk fever is a calcium deficiency in the blood of the bitch, caused by loss of calcium in the milk to the pups. It is more commonly seen in smaller breeds with large litters but can occur in any breed. Milk fever most commonly occurs two or three weeks after the birth of the pups, although it can happen much earlier, and can be rapidly fatal if immediate treatment is not given by a vet. The first symptoms are weakness and trembling of the limbs; it then progresses to convulsions, paralysis and heart failure. An all-meat diet (see Common Ailments listing) will aggravate the condition because of the low calcium and high phosphorus content of meat.

Giving the bitch milk to drink helps by supplying calcium, but a balanced dry food diet is more helpful in preventing calcium deficiency. It also provides the calories necessary to make milk. There is some evidence that heavy oral calcium supplementation before lactation may actually increase the likelihood of calcium deficiency during lactation, as it causes a depression of the mechanism whereby the bitch dissolves the calcium in her bones to supply the calcium in her blood.

Care of the pups and bitch

When the bitch and pups have had several hours together, have your vet check the bitch to ensure that there are no more pups or afterbirths inside her. The vet will usually give injections to ensure complete contraction of the uterus and to minimise post-partum infections. The pups can also be checked to ensure that they are healthy and free from congenital defects such as cleft palates, hernias and abnormal digit numbers which may necessitate early euthanasia. The vet will also advise on vaccination procedures. (Owners of puppies at this age should read the Worming section.)

The tail before docking.

There is no single cause of neo-natal mortality in pups. In a typical case, puppies appear vigorous and healthy at birth and suckle avidly for the first twenty-four hours. Thereafter, they become progressively weaker, make no further attempt to suckle and lose weight rapidly. Their heads may sway from side to side, they paddle feebly with their paws, and lack the strength to find or hold on to the teat. Spasm, with extension of the forelimbs and spine, may occur just before death. Very often the affected puppies become restless and cry continually, and the bitch may push them to one side. Eventually, respiration becomes difficult and the pup dies. Sometimes bleeding from the urinary passage may occur. Not all litter mates are necessarily affected and the bitch concerned may or may not produce failing litters in subsequent pregnancies. The causes fall into five main groups:

Micro-organisms   These consist of bacteria and viruses.

Parasites   As many as 90 percent of all pups are affected by worms. Infestation may also occur via the colostrum. In the course of migration, the larvae can give rise to pneumonia and the adult worms can lead to bowel disturbances such as diarrhoea, vomiting and obstruction of the intestine from the fourteenth day onwards. Jaundice from blocked bile ducts is sometimes a feature. Weekly dosing of pups with a piperazine citrate syrup at the rate of 100–200 milligrams per kilogram of body-weight from two weeks onwards is recommended, or canex puppy worming syrup.

The tail after docking.

Hypothermia   There is no doubt that chilling, which leads to hypothermia, accounts for a high proportion of puppy deaths. This is because puppies are incapable of generating heat by shivering, and have little subcutaneous fat to provide insulation. Consequently, if the room temperature is allowed to drop during the first few days after birth, a disastrous, irreversible chain reaction can be set up. The normal body temperature of a day-old pup is only 37°C and takes four weeks to rise to the normal adult level. However, no puppy should be given up, even if deeply hypothermic, without an attempt to resuscitate it by warming. If hypothermia is suspected, hot water bottles at approximately 44°C should be placed in the nest or the ambient temperature should be maintained at around 30°C. Radiant heat (that is, heat from a radiator) is acceptable as long as it does not draw cold air over the puppies by convection.

Bad mothering   Apart from cannibalism which can be accidental during excessive licking (especially in short-nosed breeds such as Boxers), crushing and laceration may occur. Starvation of a litter may also come about because of inadequate milk supply or because the bitch's nipples are too large or too tender, or the pups are premature. Many mothering problems can be avoided by paying attention to the design of the whelping accommodation and by allowing the bitch to become familiar with the surroundings well in advance of the birth. Dystocia (difficulty in giving birth) may account for the loss of as many as 8 per cent of viable puppies after birth.

Congenital defects   Conditions such as cleft palate, which can lead to inability to suckle or inhalation pneumonia, and obstruction of the anus or urethra and neo-natal jaundice frequently lead to puppy mortality.

The importance of thoroughly examining puppies that have faded cannot be overstressed. Where such problems are occurring regularly in a kennel, time should be spent examining pedigrees and discussing the breeding programme with your vet.

Suckling

The bitch should be checked to ensure she has a sufficient number of functional nipples to feed her litter. A normal large breed of dog can rear ten pups with ease providing early weaning is adopted. Many bitches of the larger breeds have litters in excess of this number. It is very important that the pups be allowed to suckle undisturbed for the first six to twelve hours, as it is during this period that they acquire their antibodies against disease from the colostrum. Pups deprived of this milk have a much greater risk of dying in the first six to twelve weeks of life.

Orphaned pups

Hand rearing is needed when a bitch is unable to feed her puppies for any reason and an alternative form of milk must be supplied. This may be cow's milk (adapted to suit the pups), goat's milk or special preparations obtainable from your vet. It is essential to adopt a routine so that the feeds are given regularly and the same type of milk is always used. Give as much to the pup as it will take in ten minutes or until it falls asleep.

Special pet feeders are available for nursing young pups.

Small puppy-feeding bottles with teats are available from veterinarians. For larger puppies, a baby's bottle with a small teat is suitable. Although a plastic dropper can be used, the puppy tends to swallow too much air this way. A glass dropper should never be used. All bottles, teats and other utensils used must be thoroughly cleaned and sterilised before each feed. The milk should be given at body temperature.

A puppy cannot empty its bladder or pass a motion when it is first born, unless stimulated by the licking action of the mother. It is therefore necessary to stroke the puppy's stomach and back of hindlegs before and after each meal, either with the finger or with a cotton bud. The puppy should pass water each time and should pass a motion after every two or three meals. The pup's coat should be wiped after each meal with cotton wool dipped in warm water, and dried with soft towelling before it is returned to its bed.

After each feed, stroke the orphaned pup's belly.

As soon as the puppy can lap, at about two-and-a-half weeks of age, milk can be given in a shallow container. At three weeks of age, solid food can be added gradually to the diet. Finely minced meat can be provided once a day at first with a calcium supplement (see Diet at weaning). By five weeks the puppy should be receiving four or five small meals a day, two with a meat basis, the remainder a milk mixture with some form of carbohydrate, either cereal, porridge or biscuits. All changes in the diet should be introduced gradually. A hand-reared puppy may at times suck air into the stomach which can cause pain. If this occurs hold the pup in a vertical position and gently massage the abdomen.

Diet at weaning

Weaning the pups should start when they are three to four weeks old. This is especially important where there are a large number in the litter or the pups are particularly big. Use one of the pre-packed brands of dry dog food and some good-quality canned food or finely chopped meat. By six weeks of age the puppies can be nutritionally self-sufficient.

The bitch will lose condition while lactating unless she is fed well on foods of high calorie content. The best and most balanced foods to feed at this stage are the dry, complete dog foods, as they are a balanced ration in a form that allows the bitch to obtain sufficient calories to produce the milk the pups need. Calcium can be fed to the bitch at this stage with some benefits. The most suitable type is calcium carbonate.

Dry dog foods have the correct calcium balance but many breeders disturb this balance by feeding meat as well. Canned dog foods provide meat protein with the correct levels of calcium and when fed in place of meat no additional calcium supplements are needed.

Tails and dewclaws

These can be removed to breed requirements by the vet when the pup is four to five days old, before it becomes old enough to suffer too greatly from the procedure. The dewclaw is equivalent to the thumb in humans and in the adult dog is approximately 2½ centimetres above the ground on the inside of the front legs. Some dogs may have them on the hindlegs as well.

Caring for the sick dog

Signs of disease present in two ways: a general disease condition where the dog is off-colour and won't eat; and the local problem, for example, a tooth decay, local abscess or fracture of a limb. With local problems it is usually very obvious what is wrong and how extensive it is.

In the general disease situation, the dog is usually lethargic, in many cases because of a fever although it might be because of a subnormal temperature. Lethargy is usually accompanied by decreased appetite, and subsequent loss of weight. Loss of weight can also occur while a dog is taking its normal diet, in cases of diarrhoea, kidney disease, sugar diabetes or bleeding into the intestinal tract.

Variation in the thirst of the animal can indicate a problem. Increased thirst can accompany a fever, or may be present in a dog with a normal temperature which is suffering from sugar diabetes or a kidney complaint. A lack of thirst can produce dehydration, particularly in small animals.

Sometimes an increased respiratory rate is a sign of disease. Frequently, the coat looks harsh and dry and the third eyelids may slip across, making the dog look as though it has a skin growing over the eyes.

A thermometer is indispensable when treating a sick dog; thick-bulb-end thermometers are the best type. Normal temperature for a dog is 38.5°C, considerably higher than that of a human. The rectum is the best place to take the temperature because the dog can't bite the thermometer. Shake the thermometer down to below 38°C, lift up the dog's tail, slide the thermometer in about 4 or 5 centimetres and leave it against the wall of the rectum for about one minute. A slight temperature is 39°C, a high temperature is 40°C. With a high temperature, the dog will usually be off its food and showing signs of lethargy. It should be taken to a vet.

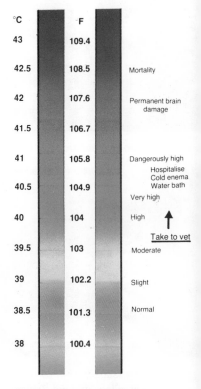

°C	°F	
43	109.4	
42.5	108.5	Mortality
42	107.6	Permanent brain damage
41.5	106.7	
41	105.8	Dangerously high
		Hospitalise
		Cold enema
		Water bath
40.5	104.9	Very high
40	104	High
		Take to vet
39.5	103	Moderate
39	102.2	Slight
38.5	101.3	Normal
38	100.4	

Temperature chart

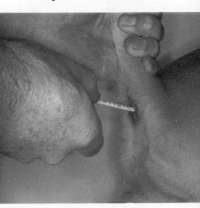

The rectum is the best place to take the temperature.

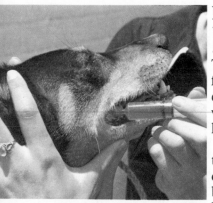

Liquids should be given slowly.

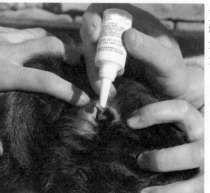

Applying ear drops.

Massage the ear canal for 15 seconds after applying drops.

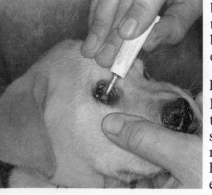

Place eye ointment or drops in the corner of the eye.

Nursing care

When a dog is not well, the following points are important. The dog requires a dry, draught-free place to rest, one that has a fairly constant temperature. The kennel or living area must be kept clean at all times and all things used for the dog's treatment must be kept clean. It must be left undisturbed, except for feeding, treatment and cleaning. Children should be allowed to visit their dog only at prescribed intervals; they must be quiet and not handle the dog.

Treatment must be carried out thoroughly, regularly and at the correct time. Fresh, clean water must always be available. Select food you know the dog likes, preferably barbecued chicken meat and red meats. Dressings, bandages and so on should only be reused if boiled. Dressings that have been soiled by a wound or discharge must never be reused.

Bed sores are caused by the dog lying on hard surfaces; the skin over bony prominences begins to die which allows surface bacteria to invade and cause sores. Bed sores *can* be prevented by lying the dog on a mattress of foam rubber. Bed sores should be treated with astringent agents such as mercurochrome, triple dye, or acriflavin.

It is most important that the dog, no matter how sick, gets fluids on a daily basis. The fluid requirement of the dog is approximately 20 millilitres per kilogram body-weight daily. If the dog is not taking this orally, veterinary advice should be sought so that it can be given the fluids intravenously. Failure to take in this amount of fluid per day will result in kidney shutdown and permanent kidney damage.

Administering medicines

To some people, giving the dog medicines is an awesome task. Here are some helpful hints.

Make sure the dog finishes the course prescribed. In ear cases, for example, treatment often contains a local anaesthetic to give the dog immediate relief and the dog may appear well very quickly, simply because the anaesthetic has removed the pain. If you stop the course at this point the problem will reappear because the medication has not had time to work. Similarly with antibiotics—sometimes an infection will appear to be better but has, in fact, not cleared up completely.

Ear drops

Shake the vial for at least a minute. This resuspends any particle matter in the solution. Clean the dog's earlobes with methylated spirits and cotton-wool. Using a cotton bud, clean out the ear canal. The ear canal is fairly long, with a right-angled bend at the bottom leading to the ear drum, so it is very difficult to touch (and consequently damage) the ear drum. Cleaning in this way allows the medication to get right to the infection, rather than be deactivated by debris. After administering the required number of drops to the ear, hold the dog's head firmly while massaging the ear canal down behind the jaw. This will allow the drops time to reach the depths of the ear canal before the dog begins to shake its head.

Eye ointments and drops

Medication should be given six times daily because constant secretion of tears washes away medication within forty minutes. Always follow the instructions exactly. Take advantage of the dog's third eyelid and place the medication in the conjunctival sac. With the forefinger and thumb of one hand, gently push the upper and lower eyelids towards the nose. The third eyelid will cross the eye in the opposite direction and form a membranous sac. In this way the dog cannot see the ointment or medication being administered. After the medication has been administered to the eye, hold the eyelids together and massage gently.

Powders and granules

Most medications designed to be put in the food are palatable, but sometimes a fussy eater will reject them. To solve this problem, starve the dog for twenty-four hours and then place the medication in about a quarter of the normal food allocation. When the dog finishes, feed another quarter to let it lick the bowl along with any remaining medication. For future meals, keep the appetite keen until the medication programme has been completed. In this way the dog will be so hungry at each feed that it will be prepared to eat the medicated food.

Solutions

Solutions are best administered with a plastic disposable syringe. Elevate the dog's head to 45 degrees and tilt the head to one side. Introduce the tip of the syringe to the corner of the dog's mouth on the upper side. Always administer the solution very slowly into the pocket between the lip and the teeth so the dog has time to swallow. Fluid administered too quickly, without the dog having time to swallow, can enter the lungs and cause pneumonia and possible death.

Tablets

Before administering any tablets, make sure that the dog has had a small portion to eat, otherwise the medication may be rejected by the stomach and the dog will vomit the tablets. A few dogs will take tablets in some minced meat, mush or sweets, but always observe the animal for ten minutes or so afterwards to make sure that it did in fact swallow the tablets. The surest method of administration is to open the dog's mouth wide by placing your thumb and forefinger around the upper lips and pushing the lips over the dog's teeth with your fingers, so that if the dog tries to bite or clamp its jaws

Opening the mouth: Note position of fingers.

Popping the pill.

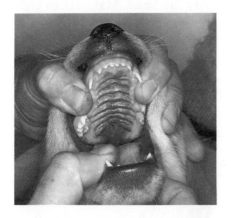
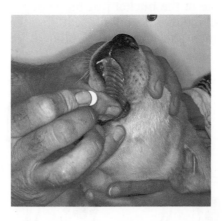

Pushing the pill over the back of the tongue.

its lips will be pressed uncomfortably against its teeth. Pull the dog's head back and place the tablets at the back of the tongue as if you were trying to push them right down the throat (it is impossible to push them into the windpipe). Close the dog's mouth, keeping it elevated, and allow the dog to swallow. If it does not swallow, tickle its throat. Lock the dog in a confined space for fifteen to twenty minutes to ensure that the dog does not regurgitate the tablets. If it does, try again till they stay down.

Bandages

The most effective bandage for the dog is a 5-centimetre-wide adhesive bandage. The adhesive sticks to the hair and stops the dog tearing the bandage off. Most other varieties of bandage are useless. To remove these bandages, push a blunt instrument, such as a spoon handle, inside the bandage and use a razor blade to cut the bandage against the instrument. The bandage can then be removed from the hair by dabbing the margin with methylated spirits or ether, so dissolving the adhesive.

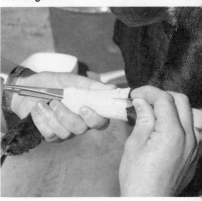

Remove an adhesive bandage with a blunt instrument.

Whenever dogs have bandages, plaster casts or any other restrictive material placed on the limbs, it is important to ensure that circulation is reaching the toes. This can be tested by feeling the toes to make sure they are warm rather than cold. Sensation can be determined by pinching the toes to make the dog withdraw the foot.

Restraint

Wherever possible, try to handle the dog by peaceful means. Where this fails, the following methods may have to be employed. When treating a savage or difficult dog, place medication inside something the dog enjoys, such as sweets, meat or chicken cubes. If this fails, starve the dog for one or two days or as long as is necessary to get the tablets down. Administer the tablets in very small quantities of food and keep the dog's appetite keen.

To restrain the dog from biting, place a commercial leather muzzle around its nose. If you do not have a leather muzzle, use the lead attached to the collar. Pull the lead tight from the collar, wrap it two or three times around the dog's snout and hold the loose end together with the collar in one hand, with your other hand keeping the rest of the lead intact around the dog's muzzle. The dog can then be held so that a second person can do whatever is necessary.

Alternatively, use a cord or tape bandage. Make a loop as if doing the first part of a bow, put the loop around the dog's muzzle and pull tight so that the twist is on top. Take the cord or tape below the muzzle and tie, then pull tight again. Take the two ends up and tie tightly behind the dog's ears.

To catch a savage dog, make a dog catcher with a piece of hollow pipe, 2 metres long, with a noose through the pipe.

A dog can be restrained from licking at wounds and bandages by placing an Elizabethan collar around its neck. Another device is a plastic bucket—cut a hole in the bucket just big enough to fit over the head. Make six to eight small holes around the cut to allow tapes or shoelaces to be threaded through and around the collar to keep the bucket firmly attached.

Pull the lead tight and wrap it around the muzzle.

A plastic bucket will prevent a dog from licking wounds.

Dog catcher.

Steps in applying an alternative method of restraint to the muzzle of a savage dog.

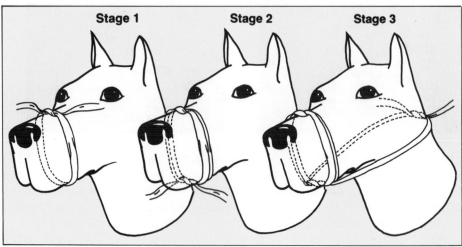

Stage 1   Stage 2   Stage 3

First aid

Artificial respiration

When a drowned dog stops breathing, hold it up by the hindlegs with the head hanging down, to allow the water to escape from the lungs. Speed is essential. As soon as the water has ceased to run out of its mouth, lie the dog on its side with the tongue out as far as possible and commence artificial respiration.

This means placing the palms of both hands over the chest surface, and rhythmically and slowly pressing and releasing so that the air is driven in and out of the lungs. This cycle should be repeated about thirty times a minute for small dogs and about twenty times a minute for large dogs. If this is going to be effective, the heart beat will resume within a few seconds. It does not always work, but is well worth a try.

Artificial respiration.

Bleeding

Major bleeding from an artery is seen as a squirting, pulsating blood stream which should be cut off by tourniquet application between the wound and the heart. Tourniquets should be gently released for a few seconds every three to four minutes if they are kept in place for any length of time. Small areas of bleeding can usually be stopped by pressure-bandaging the area.

Motor vehicle accident

Be very careful handling any dog, even your own, after a car accident. If the dog is badly injured, move it on to a blanket by approaching it from the rear, taking the scruff of the neck between the ears in one hand and the loose skin over the back in the other, and pull it on to the blanket. Take the dog to a vet.

Shock

In this condition the dog is usually in a state of collapse, and the mucous membranes (in the mouth) are very pale. Place the dog in a head down position (the head at an angle of 30 degrees). Keep the animal warm and administer warm fluids if it will drink. Take the dog to a vet immediately. See Shock, pp. 140–1.

Common ailments

Abdominal pain (Colic)

Usually the dog is reluctant to walk, and when it does it has a tucked-up appearance with an arched back. If the pain is very severe the dog may adopt a praying attitude—that is, with the chest on the ground and the hindquarters raised. The animal usually objects to the abdomen being touched. The causes of abdominal pain are many, and because treatment is dependent on the cause, it is important that a correct diagnosis is made. Always consult a vet. In some cases the dog's condition may be very serious, and its life may be in peril—for example, from torsion (twisting) of the stomach or a twisted bowel. In these cases, the animal usually exhibits excruciating pain, and rolls and may vomit constantly.

Abdominal pain often causes the dog to 'hunch up'.

Abortion

Abortion or miscarriage does not often occur in the bitch. Its causes are gross fatigue, injury or infection. Sometimes it can be caused by hormonal dysfunction. Rare chronic infections cause repeated abortions, and it is inadvisable to continue breeding from the bitch—a hysterectomy may be recommended. (See also Foetal Death, p. 107.)

Abrasions

Abrasions are sore areas of skin resulting from injury to the surface layers. Usually this kind of injury does not penetrate the skin. (If an injury does penetrate the skin layers and reveal the flesh, it should be sutured by a vet.) Ordinary abrasions can be treated at home. Remove the surface debris and any discharge by washing the wound gently with water from a garden hose. If the dog will allow it, clean the wound with cotton-wool dipped in warm water, and disinfect with 50 per cent peroxide and water. Once the wound is clean, apply an astringent agent such as gentian violet, mercurochrome or triple dye twice daily. If necessary, cut the surrounding hair away so that medications can be applied for 1 centimetre beyond the edge of the wound. Alternatively, antibiotic powders may be applied to the surface. Abrasions recover better if left open to the air, so don't try to bandage them. Don't worry if the dog licks the wound.

Abscesses

An abscess is a localised collection of pus and may occur in any part of the body as a result of infection by a pus-producing organism. It usually results from a penetrating wound such as those caused by the teeth of another dog or by a foreign body such as a stick, thorn or grass seed.

Characteristic symptoms are pain, heat and swelling of the infected area. The dog may have a high temperature.

The abscess should be brought to a head by using hot fomentations or poultices. This is done by bathing the area using a rag soaked in warm water to which has been added a tablespoon of epsom salts per litre. When the abscess is ripe the centre feels soft; it will often burst of its own accord. Lancing may be necessary to evacuate the contents, however. The condition is usually painful. Once the contents have been evacuated, the opening should be enlarged so that the abscess doesn't heal over too quickly, and it should be irrigated with a 50 per cent peroxide and water solution three times daily for three days. After three days, irrigate with clean water from a hose. If at any stage the edges cannot be separated easily it may be necessary to re-open the site. The abscess must heal from the inside outwards. If the skin closes too quickly, pockets of infection may remain and the abscess grow to a head again.

Where the abscess is small and only one is present, antibiotic treatment is often not necessary; but where a number of abscesses occur, veterinary advice and treatment is essential. Before treatment is started, ensure that the abscess is not in fact a prolapse, a hernia or a haematoma.

Accidents

See pp. 116–7.

Allergic reactions

Allergic reactions can be divided into two categories: anaphylactic shock, and urticaria.

Anaphylactic shock is an immediate hypersensitive reaction, in which death may rapidly occur following respiratory and circulatory collapse. The condition usually develops from human interference, although it may also result from a bee or wasp sting. The condition is often attributed to the effect of histamines on the body. Signs are restlessness, diarrhoea, vomiting, collapse, sometimes convulsions, followed by a period of calm, then death. The agents that may cause anaphylactic shock include penicillin and other antibiotics, vaccines (though rarely), tranquillisers, vitamins and sometimes certain foods. Treatment involves the intravenous administration of an antihistamine, so the dog should be taken to a vet immediately. On the way, ensure its air passages are clear by extending the dog's neck, putting a peg on its tongue and pulling the tongue forward. Bee or wasp stings rarely cause death.

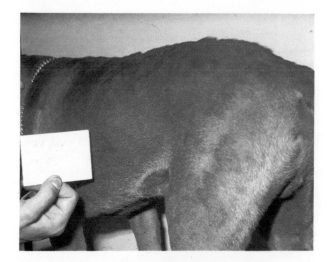

Urticaria — allergic reaction after eating orchids.

Urticaria is characterised by a swelling of the soft tissues of the head and body. It nearly always affects the eyes, mouth and ears. A discharge may develop from the eyes, and the animal frequently rubs its mouth and eyes with its paws or on the ground. The animal takes on a very old appearance. This type of allergic reaction may develop within fifteen to twenty minutes after contact with the causative agent. It very rarely causes serious damage to the animal and is usually the result of food allergies, ingestion of spoiled protein material, insect bites or contact with certain chemicals. Insect bites are probably the most common cause.

Any skin allergy may, however, become an emergency situation because of selfmutilation from excessive itching and scratching. In such a case the dog requires antihistamine injections from the vet. If possible, find out what food, place or substance seems to induce the attack.

See also SKIN DISORDERS: ECZEMA.

All-meat syndrome
See BONE PROBLEMS OF GROWING DOGS.

Alopecia
See SKIN DISORDERS.

Anaemia
Anaemia is a condition in which the blood's ability to carry oxygen is reduced. It can be caused by blood loss from a haemorrhage or by blood-sucking parasites—for example, hookworms in young puppies. A reduction in the number of blood cells able to carry oxygen is also caused by disease, parasites or nutritional deficiencies. Anaemia due to blood loss is normally quickly corrected by the body as long as the haemorrhage is controlled. The addition of iron and vitamin B to the diet will assist this process. Where anaemia is due to infection, the condition must be corrected and treated before the anaemia can be rectified, but again, supplements of vitamin B and iron assist recovery. Parasitic conditions should be treated with worming preparations and the resultant anaemia corrected by supplementation. Nutritional deficiencies resulting in anaemia are usually related to lack of iron, cobalt or vitamin B12.

Raw liver or liver extracts are very good for correcting anaemic situations. The diet should be well-balanced, nourishing and contain red meat.

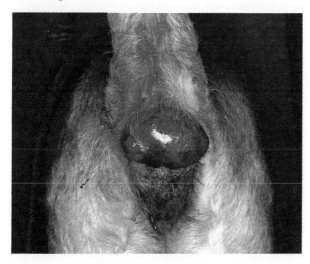

Advanced anal adenoma.

Anal adenoma
This is a small tumour that appears at the anus in both male dogs and bitches. It is a condition of old age, usually brought to the owner's attention by the dog constantly licking the anal area. Treatment is either surgical to remove the tumour, or cryosurgical, to freeze it out. Alternatively, hormone therapy will reduce the growth.

Anal fissure
Anal fissure is an infected ulcerating wound, usually caused by the passing of sharp pieces of bone. The symptoms are often identical to those in an anal abscess. When the dog squats to pass a motion it may howl in agony. Surgery is the only way to rectify the condition.

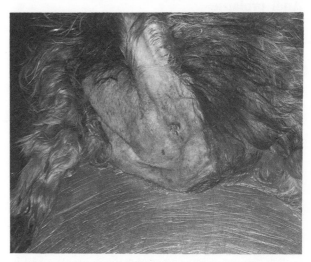

Swelling to the side of the anus indicates anal gland problems — in this case the left side.

Anal glands, infected
On either side of the dog's anus are glands called anal glands, which secrete a foul-smelling lubricating fluid intended to be emptied into the anus each time the dog passes a motion. In many dogs the anal glands have outlived their usefulness, as modern feeding patterns result in motions too soft to require the special fluid. Unfortunately, changing the diet to help the glands may make the dog constipated. The result is that the glands fill and become impacted. The impaction can become infected, forming an abscess which can recur constantly. The first sign of trouble comes with the dog dragging its hindquarters over the grass or the carpet ('scooting'). In other cases, the dog may be lying quietly when it suddenly squeals and rushes forward. Sometimes the dog may lick the anal area, suddenly looking at the tail base and putting the tail between its legs as though stung. In a simple case of impaction, all that is required is to squeeze the glands by pressing them upwards and forwards, to evacuate the contents. In some dogs the glands may require attention every three or four weeks. If the condition persists and causes the dog continual trouble, the glands can be removed surgically.

If an abscess forms in a gland, the dog shows signs of acute pain, especially when attempting to pass a motion. It may squeal or bite when its tail or hindquarters are handled. If the tail is elevated, a large, painful-looking swelling can be seen on one side of the anus. Sometimes the dog's temperature is elevated to about 40°C. In these cases the inflammation is so painful that any attempt to empty the glands by pressing them will be unsuccessful. The abscess will either have to be treated by antibiotics for a few days or lanced surgically. This is a job for the vet.

Anal irritation
Treatment depends on the case, which may be worms, enlarged prostate glands, anal gland conditions, anal fissure, chronic diarrhoea or even a foreign body, usually a bone lodged in the rectum.

Anal occlusion
Occlusion of the anus is a condition usually seen in long-haired breeds. The anal opening is completely blocked by a mass of dried faeces attached to the hairs around the anus. The dog suffers great discomfort and the smell is unmistakable. The best method of removal is to use

curved, blunt-ended scissors to cut off the hair at skin level. Care must be taken not to cut the skin. Sometimes soaking the mass in warm water before attempting its removal makes it easier for the dog.

Anal prolapse

Prolapse of the anus is seen mostly in young puppies, being caused by persistent diarrhoea which in turn is often caused by heavy roundworm infestation. Sometimes it may be caused by constipation or overfeeding. One sign of a prolapsed anus is a finger-like projection of mucous membrane from the anus. The pup is usually in considerable distress and licks the protrusion incessantly. Treatment of this condition, by replacing the prolapse and suturing it into position, is best left to the vet.

Appetite, decreased

If your dog's appetite appears to have decreased, it is important to distinguish between an actual loss of appetite and the inability to eat. The latter may be because of some painful condition in the mouth or throat—for example, bad teeth, inflammation of the gums, ulceration of the mouth, a bone caught between the teeth, a cracked tooth or inflamed and sore lips. Old age, injury and ill health often produce a decreased appetite. In old age, a lack of appetite is often because of some other underlying problem and if allowed to continue it will frequently result in a loss of weight and condition. Toy breeds invariably eat very little.

Sometimes the dog has been fed a selective diet from weaning and will not touch anything else placed before it. In addition, urban dogs are usually overfed and underexercised, so it is quite feasible for them to go a day or two without eating anything. Ill health, particularly where fever is involved, invariably produces a decreased appetite. This is very common in disease situations such as SEPTICAEMIA, TOXAEMIA, and SHOCK.

Appetite, depraved

With a depraved appetite the dog may eat stones, coal, manure or dirt. Possible causes include teething, worms, indigestion and deficiencies in salt, minerals or vitamins. Sometimes it can be because of actual hunger. Puppies exhibit this symptom more than adult dogs, and frequently they have a history of an all-meat diet. When this symptom occurs, treat the animal for worms and ensure that its diet contains a balanced vitamin and mineral supplement, particularly calcium. It is common and normal for dogs to eat grass, which is said to provide a fresh source of vitamins. Other authorities claim that grass-eating induces vomiting to rid the stomach of old, stale food. Dogs frequently bury food and then eat it when it is rotten. The eating of 'aged' meat is quite normal for the dog—though it sometimes causes vomiting—so don't be alarmed.

Appetite, increased

Increased appetite has three forms: (a) A normal situation where the increase is because of lactation, cold, increased work, food of poor biological value, or growth. The animal maintains its condition and weight. (b) Increased appetite coupled with loss of weight—as in pancreatic disease, sugar diabetes or internal parasites. (c) Increased appetite coupled with weight gain—this can be caused by hormonal imbalance, tumours or overindulgent owners who expect the dog to eat three meals a day just because they do (see OBESITY).

Arthritis

Arthritis is an inflammatory condition of a joint or a disease involving a joint. It may be caused by the effects of injury, infection or malfunction of the joint. It can be classified as acute or chronic. The joint is usually swollen and painful and the dog avoids using it. There are many different types of arthritis, the most common in the dog being hip dysplasia—an inflammatory condition of the hip joints (see BONE PROBLEMS OF GROWING DOGS). Relief from arthritis is best achieved by rest and warmth. Pain-relieving drugs and anti-inflammatory agents are often used. If infection exists, antibiotic treatment is necessary. Temporary relief can be given by administering a quarter of a 300-milligram tablet of soluble aspirin every four hours. In many cases the arthritic condition is exacerbated by obesity, and dieting may help.

Avascular necrosis of the hip

See BONE PROBLEMS OF GROWING DOGS.

Babesiosis

Babesiosis is a disease caused by a blood parasite from the bite of an infected tick. It is widespread in all parts of the world. The dog usually suffers from a high temperature, depression, rapid breathing, loss of appetite, weakness and staggering. Anaemia develops and jaundice may be present. A blood sample is needed to confirm the diagnosis. Veterinary advice is essential. The disease is present in northern Australia.

Backache

The dog with a backache is unwilling to move or to turn round, climb stairs or jump in and out of cars. The condition usually occurs in long-backed dogs such as Corgis and Dachshunds. The dog may cry out in pain without being touched. Sometimes the dog will remain on the ground, unwilling to get up; when it does, it moves stiffly. The causes may be actual physical injury, a disc protrusion, infection or, in some cases, abdominal pain. Various tests, including X-rays, are needed to pin-point the condition. Where back conditions are suspected, particularly in long-backed dogs, it is advisable to keep the dog on a flat surface for at least three weeks, otherwise the condition may progress to paralysis of the back legs.

Bad breath

See MOUTH DISORDERS.

Balance

Loss of balance is caused by conditions affecting the central nervous system, such as distemper, encephalitis, meningitis, space-occupying lesions (such as tumours), tick bite or snake bite. It can also be caused by middle ear infections. This is a problem for the vet.

Bald patches

See SKIN DISORDERS.

Barking

See BEHAVIOURAL PROBLEMS.

Bed sores

See p. 114.

Behavioural problems

Many of the behavioural abnormalities exhibited by dogs are the result of neuroses induced by urban dwelling. The most serious problem facing the urban dog is severe territorial restriction—particularly upsetting to the larger breeds. Almost invariably it is the large male dog who becomes involved in wandering, biting, fighting other dogs, chasing cars, barking excessively and destroying furniture. It is rare to see female dogs or dogs of small breeds wandering far from their homes, as their territorial requirements are more easily satisfied. Overcrowding in urban areas results in dogfights over territory, particularly between males. Exercise your dog daily. If your male dog is still a nuisance, castration is recommended. Hormone therapy using progesterone has recently proven successful in correcting abnormal behavioural traits.

Bitch on heat (Oestrus)

See pp. 83, 105.

Bites

See ABSCESSES, SNAKE BITES, SPIDER BITES.

Biting

See BEHAVIOURAL PROBLEMS.

Bleeding internally

Internal loss of blood usually follows a car accident or other injury. It can be detected by signs of bodily weakness, pallor of the mucous membranes (the eye membranes and mouth appear pale), a weak pulse and coldness of the extremities (the limbs and ears). Place the dog in a head-down position at an angle of about 30 degrees. Keep it warm and take it to a vet as soon as possible.

Bleeding from the mouth

Bleeding in the mouth is usually due to cuts or other physical injuries. Usually the dog has pierced one of the major veins under the tongue with a bone or a piece of wood. Other causes of bleeding from the mouth include inflamed gums, cut or ulcerated tongue, or a cut on the inside of the cheek. Take the dog to the vet.

Bleeding nose

Nose bleeds may result from injury, violent sneezing, a growth, ulcers or parasites in the nasal cavities. Ice placed over the nose will often help reduce bleeding. Ensure that any bleeding does not interrupt the dog's respiration and ascertain the cause of bleeding, taking the dog to the vet if necessary. Reduce excitement and exercise for a day or two after the bleeding stops.

Bleeding from the rectum

Rectal bleeding is usually the result of an inflammatory condition in the intestines caused by either bacteria or parasites. Bleeding of this nature is very serious and the dog should be taken to a veterinary surgeon urgently. (See also DIARRHOEA.)

Bleeding from the surface of the body

Surface bleeding can in many cases be stopped by bandaging a pad of cotton-wool into position over the area. Pressure bandaging is the most important thing to do to reduce haemorrhage. Where bleeding is heavy, it can be controlled by applying direct pressure over the injured vessel or to the spot where the blood is escaping. This can be done with the fingers or by applying a tourniquet. Where sizeable vessels, particularly arteries, are spurting blood, a tourniquet is essential. This should be slackened for a few seconds every three or four minutes. A tourniquet can be left in place for up to three-quarters of an hour without consequent problems. If the dog has lost a lot of blood it should be taken to a veterinary surgeon for treatment to overcome shock and loss of blood, and to restore normal blood pressure.

Bleeding tail

Injuries to the tip of the tail often cause bleeding that is difficult to control because the dog wags its tail and knocks it on various objects. Pressure bandaging with an adhesive tape is advised or cautery of the blood vessel.

Blindness

See EYE DISORDERS.

Blood in urine

Bleeding can originate from the urinary system—that is, from the kidney or the bladder—or from the reproductive system. If the bleeding is not the normal discharge that occurs when a bitch is in season, take the dog to the vet. See URINE DISORDERS.

Blue-eye (Keratitis)

See EYE DISORDERS.

Bone problems of growing dogs

The following conditions affect dogs during their growing period, most frequently the larger breeds. Before discussing the various problems it is necessary to understand the basic anatomy of the growing bone as it will be frequently referred to. Limb bones basically grow from their ends at special sites known as growth plates. Most bones have growth plates at either end, though some have them at only one end. Although one might expect the bones to grow equally from both ends, this is not necessarily so. The difference between the growth of the two ends is of little significance except in the forelimbs where the radius and ulna must grow as a pair for the forelimbs to remain straight. Many of the deformities of the forelimbs of larger breeds are due to a disproportionate growth of the radius and ulna. (See also RICKETS.)

All-meat syndrome (Nutritional secondary hyperparathyroidism. N.S.H.)

This is still an important problem, although it is becoming less common as meat prices rise and more dog owners switch to commercial foods which are properly balanced in calcium and phosphorus. It is more frequently seen in puppies of the larger breeds. N.S.H. is caused by feeding a mainly meat diet with incorrect calcium supplementation. Meat not only contains very little calcium (approximately 10 milligrams per 100 grams) but has a marked imbalance of calcium and phosphorus. In meat the ratio of calcium to phosphorus is 1 : 20 —in a normal diet it should be approximately 1 : 1. The abnormal diet leads to altered levels of calcium and phosphorus in the blood, which stimulate the parathyroid gland. The hormone released leads to correction of the blood levels, by resorbing calcium from the bones. Fractures may develop. These appear more frequently in the hind-limbs, and pelvic fractures are commonly seen. They often result in narrowing of the pelvis, problems with constipation and an extra problem in whelping. Sometimes the vertebral column may show deformities resulting in pressure on the spinal cord, giving rise to neurological disturbances. Treatment is to correct the diet by using a calcium supplement. Half a

Sources of Supplementary Calcium		
	% Calcium	% Phosphorus
Cow's milk	0.13	0.094
Dicalcium phosphate (D.C.P.)	22	18
Tricalcium phosphate	39	20
Bone meal	30	15
Calcium carbonate	40	—
Calcium lactate	13	—
Calcium gluconate	9	—

Sources of Supplementary Calcium.

Supplementing a Meat Diet.

Supplementing a Meat Diet			
	Calcium	Phosphorus	Ca:P
100 g meat	10 mg	200 mg	1:20
100 g meat + 600 ml milk	772 mg	764 mg	1:1
100 g meat + 4.8 g D.C.P. (2½ tsp)	1.1 g	1.1 g	1:1
100 g meat + 2.25 g Calcium gluconate	212 mg	200 mg	1:1
100 g meat + 1.5 g Calcium lactate	205 mg	200 mg	1:1
100 g meat + 0.5 g Calcium CO3 (½ tsp)	210 mg	200 mg	1:1
100 g meat + 1.0 g Calcium CO3 (1 tsp)	410 mg	200 mg	2:1

teaspoon of calcium carbonate should be given with each 100 grams of meat fed. Other calcium supplements can be given but the quantities need to be increased to provide a balance.

Calciostelein injections are an unsatisfactory and inadequate method of treatment. N.S.H. can be prevented by feeding young puppies one of the complete, prepared foods that make supplementation unnecessary.

The following conditions occur as a result of overfeeding together with inherited components.

Avascular necrosis of the hip

Avascular necrosis of the hip is well recognised in breeds such as Yorkshire, Highland, Cairn and Jack Russell Terriers, Miniature Poodles, Chihuahuas and Shih Tzu. It causes hind-limb lameness in dogs four to nine months, on one or both sides. Pain is localised in the hip joint; associated muscle deterioration is well recognised. Surgical treatment appears to provide a more rapid return to normal than conservative treatment.

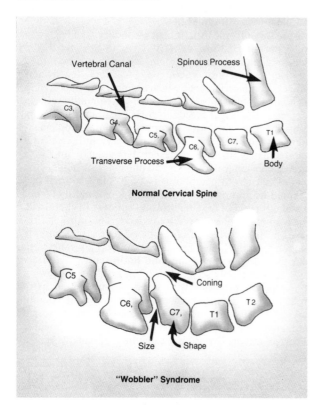

Normal Cervical Spine

"Wobbler" Syndrome

Hip dysplasia

Hip dysplasia is an inherited condition in which the ball and socket joint of the hip does not fit properly, the resultant irritation causing arthritis. It can be difficult to diagnose, as dogs that are clinically normal can be found to have hip dysplasia on radiographic examination. Puppies bred from parents and grandparents that are radiographically free from hip dysplasia may still develop the condition, although the chances of it occurring are greatly reduced. It is most common in breeds that grow to more than 15 kilograms at three months of age. Breeds most likely to be affected are Golden Labradors, Retrievers, Boxers, German Shepherds, German Short-haired Pointers, Dobermans, Great Danes and St Bernards. The condition is very rarely seen in greyhounds, however, as selective breeding has operated to eliminate affected dogs (which race poorly) from breeding programmes.

The symptoms of hip dysplasia include reluctance to rise from the sitting position. The affected dog usually takes two or three awkward steps before the hip joint warms up allowing the dog to walk normally. Affected dogs exhibit a 'roly-poly' action when viewed from the rear. The condition may prevent a dog from walking as early as six to seven months or as late as old age. Most Labradors have some degree of hip dysplasia; by the time they are nine or ten years old, it is rare to find a Labrador who can stand up quickly and walk without hesitation.

Dogs cannot be certified free of hip dysplasia by X-ray until twelve months of age. Treatment is by surgery. This involves cutting the muscles inside the legs or removing the hip joints. Alternatively, anti-inflammatory tablets and pain-killers may be used. The best prevention is not to breed from affected dogs.

Osteochondrosis

Osteochondrosis is an arthritic condition due to an abnormality in bone development which causes a delay in the conversion of cartilage to bone. Sites commonly affected are the shoulder, elbow, wrist and hock joint. Osteochondrosis has a breed and familial tendency, and is more common in overweight males. Breeds affected include Labradors, Rottweilers, German Shepherds, St Bernards, Retrievers, Irish Wolfhounds and English Setters.

Clinical signs include a low-grade progressive lameness at four to eight months. There is usually pain on manipulation of the elbow and there may be reduced flexion of the joint. Surgical treatment appears to be helpful and prevents further progression of the osteoarthritis.

Patella luxation (Knee-cap dislocation)

Most cases of luxated patella in small breeds are due to displacement of the knee-cap towards the inside. The problem affects many small breeds, generally appearing at four to eight months. Initially the lameness is intermittent, but eventually the patella dislocates permanently and the lameness becomes persistent. Surgical correction is best.

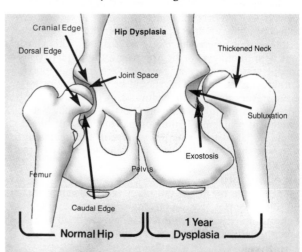

Wobbler syndrome

Wobbler syndrome is associated with an abnormality of the spine in conjunction with compression of the spinal cord. It is a problem in Bassets, Dobermans and Great Danes. The breed incidence suggests that the problem may be inherited.

The dogs usually have inco-ordination of the hind-limbs. They may knuckle the foot and fall over when turning sharply. All four limbs may be affected. Most cases occur at five to nine years of age. Treatment is not particularly successful, although various methods have been tried.

Calcium imbalance

See BONE PROBLEMS OF GROWING DOGS.

Canine parvoviral enteritis
See INFECTIOUS DISEASES.

Canker
See EAR DISORDERS.

Car sickness
The car-sick dog will first salivate profusely and then vomit if it has food in its stomach. For most dogs the problem can be overcome by taking them on short trips on an empty stomach to accustom them to car travel. Put the dog on the floor of the car rather than on the seat where it can see. Medication for car sickness includes tranquillisation and specific anti-sickness tablets available from your vet.

Cataracts
See EYE DISORDERS.

Cauliflower ear
See EAR DISORDERS—HAEMATOMA.

Chasing cars
See BEHAVIOURAL PROBLEMS.

Chorea
See NERVOUS CONDITIONS.

Coat conditions
A glossy coat indicates a healthy dog. Poor coat condition—dry and dull—can indicate illness or dietary deficiency. Diet supplementation with butter or margarine at the rate of a tablespoon per day, or the addition of a vitamin or fatty acid supplement, will often bring out the gloss in the coat.

Colic
Colic simply means pain in the abdomen and can have numerous causes, such as indigestion, flatulence, constipation, a swallowed foreign body causing pain, gastric torsion, twisting of the bowel, distension of the stomach, enteritis (inflammation of the bowel wall), kidney disease, hepatitis, and so on. If the cause is not obvious, consult your vet. (See also ABDOMINAL PAIN.)

Coma
Coma is a complete loss of consciousness often accompanied by heavy breathing and dilated pupils. Coma may be caused by injuries to the head, a stroke, heart attack, circulatory failure, poisoning, drug intoxication, kidney or liver disease, diabetes, lack of calcium in the blood, septicaemia, shock or epilepsy. It may sometimes be caused by very low or very high temperatures, brain haemorrhage, abscesses, bruising or tumours. In many illnesses it is also the last stage before death. Ensure that the dog is lying comfortably without restriction to the throat, chest or abdomen. Extend the head, pull the tongue out as far as possible and ensure a good supply of fresh air. Keep the animal still and warm, using blankets and hot-water bottles. Turn the dog over every three to four hours to aid circulation. Provide subdued light and quiet surroundings to reduce disturbance. Veterinary assistance is essential.

Conjunctivitis
See EYE DISORDERS.

Constipation
The dog has difficulty passing the hard droppings and may eventually get to the point where it strains without passing a stool. Sometimes the abdomen may appear swollen. The causes:

Nervous system Dogs with a history of slipped discs, paralysis of the back legs or weakness in the back legs are prone to constipation.

Mechanical obstruction The obstruction can be caused by enlargement of the prostate gland in male dogs, diverticulitis in the bowel walls, a fractured pelvis healing to leave a narrow outlet, perineal hernias, bowel tumours and high bone content in the diet. When bones make up more than 10 per cent of the diet they can cause constipation.

Painful anal area This can be due to cuts, matted long hair, infected anal glands or other conditions of the anal sphincter.

If the dog to be treated has been on a home diet, first try a canned food, which will sometimes loosen the dog's motions. The next step is to give the dog paraffin oil orally at the rate of 5–15 millilitres twice daily, depending on the weight of the dog and the subsequent consistency of the droppings. Faecal softener medications or warm soapy enemas may be helpful. Prevention is best instituted by correcting the diet. Increase the vegetable fibre content of the diet. Add liver and decrease the bones. Dogs which continue to strain need veterinary attention.

Contraception
See Breeding, pp. 105-6.

Convulsion
See FITS, POISONING.

Cough
A cough is an important indication of disease. Excessive coughing is physically exhausting and harmful. Coughs can be caused by:

Infectious agents—such as bacteria or viruses which cause tonsillitis or laryngitis. The most common virus is 'kennel cough' which is a contagious disease usually contracted when a dog has been kept in close proximity to other dogs. Symptoms are a dry, loud, harsh cough, with the dog sometimes bringing up phlegm. The dog may be depressed and slightly off its food. The condition can last for five to seven days, during which period the dog will produce an immunity to the virus. Although 'kennel cough' in itself is rarely serious, the dog should be put on a course of antibiotics to stop any secondary infection producing pneumonia. For home treatment, a child's cough medicine given as for a child is often helpful. A mixture of equal parts of raw egg white, honey and water can be given every half hour at the rate of 5–15 millilitres (1–3 teaspoons). Affected dogs should be protected from cold and damp and not be overexercised. (see Vaccinations p. 96.)

Parasites—such as roundworms or hookworms, which may cause bronchitis and pneumonia in young puppies (see Worming, pp. 97-104).

Chemical irritants—such as smoke, spray, gases and fine dust.

Obstructions—such as tight collars, tumours, and congestion from chronic heart failure (which is particularly common in Poodles), from tonsillitis and from pharyngitis. In these cases coughing occurs whenever the dog becomes excited or takes exercise.

Heartworm—causes coughing from a mechanical blockage of the heart.

Cysts
See FEET DISORDERS, SKIN DISORDERS.

Deafness
See EAR DISORDERS.

Debarking
Debarking is an operation in which the vocal cords are cut to reduce the amount of noise produced by the dog. The operation is illegal in many countries, including Australia and the United Kingdom.

Dehydration
In dehydration the body tissues contain insufficient fluid to carry out their normal function. It can be caused by fever, high environmental temperatures, chronic vomiting, increased urinary output because of disease, diarrhoea or decreased drinking in severe illnesses. Dehydration develops very quickly in smaller animals. The symptoms are tacky mucous membranes, a dry harsh coat, slow return of

the skin when it is lifted, and glazed eyes. Treatment is to correct the underlying cause of the condition and institute fluid therapy with electrolytes. Prolonged dehydration is fatal. Always take the dog to the vet to determine the underlying cause.

Depression
Few dogs have mental hang-ups, so depression is usually due to an underlying infectious process or disease condition. If it is the only obvious symptom the dog should be examined by a veterinary surgeon.

Dermatitis
See SKIN DISORDERS. (See also FEET DISORDERS, MALE DISORDERS.)

Dewclaws
See pp. 93, 113.

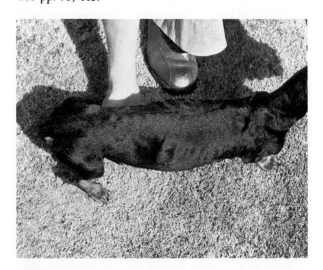

Sugar diabetes is common in Dachshunds: Note *loss of weight.*

Diabetes mellitus (Sugar diabetes)
Sugar diabetes occurs more commonly in obese bitches and also in certain breeds of dogs, particularly Dachshunds and Poodles. A diabetic animal is constantly hungry and despite an increased food intake loses weight. The other common manifestation of sugar diabetes is excessive thirst. Left untreated, the continued rapid breakdown of the animal's fat reserves results in the accumulation of toxic products in the blood, and the animal becomes depressed, loses its appetite and vomits frequently. Because it is still losing vast amounts of water in the urine, it rapidly becomes dehydrated. This combination is fatal unless treated promptly by insulin injection. The animal's daily food and exercise routine must be adjusted so that the maximum insulin effect coincides with the periods of high glucose concentration. The type of food should be kept constant. If a regular amount is given at a regular time, the control of this illness is more easily achieved. Carbohydrates should be kept to a minimum, and vitamin C should be supplied in large quantities. The insulin must be continued daily for the rest of the dog's life. Diabetes may cause cataracts.

Diarrhoea
Diarrhoea has many causes including bacterial and viral infections, worms, gut tumours, hepatitis, distemper, leptospirosis, poisoning, coccidiosis, overeating, food allergies, bad foods, sudden dietary changes, abnormal pancreatic secretions, chronic liver disease and nervousness. Diarrhoea may take several forms: it may be acute or chronic; it may affect the dog generally by causing a raised temperature and depression, or the dog may be healthy in

every other respect. Acute diarrhoea is seen as a watery, sometimes bloody stool in a previously healthy animal. If this is accompanied by elevated temperature, depression and failure to eat, the gastrointestinal tract is inflamed and bleeding. The dog should be taken to a vet immediately. Even in mild cases of diarrhoea where the dog is clinically normal, it is wise not to let the condition proceed for more than twenty-four hours without seeking veterinary advice.

Apparently normal diets can cause diarrhoea; the constituents of milk may be at fault, or canned foods, too much vegetable matter, liver or oils. Diarrhoea in young pups can be caused by cow's milk. Replace the milk with water for three or four days and give the animal Kaomagma at the rate of 1 millilitre for every kilogram body-weight (to a maximum of 10 millilitres) every six hours. After a few days reintroduce cows milk to the pup's diet but dilute it with water, 50 per cent milk : 50 per cent water, for three to four weeks. Gradually increase the concentration of the milk each three weeks by 10 per cent. Alternatively, enquire from your pharmacist about a human baby milk product that is lactose free. Worms, particularly roundworms, may cause diarrhoea in young pups. Changes of diet should always be introduced slowly—sudden switches of food, particularly if they require minimal digestion, encourage diarrhoea. In acute cases of vomiting and diarrhoea, withhold food and water for twenty-four hours to give the gut a rest. Feed the dog for a short time on the following mixture (the quantities given are for a 12-kg dog for one day). Boil one cup of dried rice in two cups of water, then add either 115 grams of cottage cheese or the same quantity of cooked lean meat. Potatoes may replace the rice and cooked eggs may replace the cottage cheese. Feed small amounts every four hours for two to three days. Where home treatment does not cure the problem within twelve hours, veterinary advice should be sought.

When taking a dog suffering from diarrhoea to the vet, be prepared to tell the vet about its diet and appetite, duration of any current and previous illnesses, environmental changes, vaccination history, past treatments for diarrhoea, worming history and daily number of bowel movements. It is advisable to take a sample of the diarrhoea (about one tablespoon) to the vet in a clean container. If this is impossible, examine the faeces to determine the consistency, colour, odour and any presence of blood or mucus. Diarrhoea is one of the principal causes of dehydration in young animals and must be rectified early.

Distemper
See INFECTIOUS DISEASES.

Drinking, increased
See DEHYDRATION, DIABETES MELLITUS, PYOMETRON, URINE DISORDERS, DIARRHOEA, FEVER, KIDNEY DISEASE, HEART DISEASE.

Dystocia (Difficult birth)
See Complications of pregnancy, p. 110.

Ear disorders
Cropping
Cropping is the procedure of reshaping the ear flap by surgical amputation. It is prohibited in many countries including Australia and the United Kingdom. It is allowed in most States of America.

Deafness
This can be a congenital abnormality (White Bull Terriers and Poodles) but is common in aged dogs. There is no treatment, although the dog's ears should be checked by your vet to ensure that debris is not causing the problem. Deaf dogs are at risk with traffic, particularly if they like to lie on the road.

Fly bite
Fly bite from blood-sucking flies can cause the tips of the

ears to become ulcerated. The dog will shake its head constantly, which may lead to a HAEMATOMA on the ear flap. The best treatment is to apply ointment containing fly repellant to the ears twice daily. If possible, keep the dog in a fly-proof area during daylight hours. To prevent further fly bites, use ordinary insect repellant sprayed on a piece of cloth.

Blood-sucking flies attack the ears causing dermatitis.

Foreign bodies in the ear
Foreign bodies in the ear include grass seeds, pieces of twig or even insects, all of which cause the dog extreme distress. If a dog holds its head on one side or paws wildly at the ear, see if you can remove the offending object. If not, see your vet.

A swollen ear-flap indicates haematoma.

Haematoma
A soft swelling on the ear flap could be a haematoma (caused by blood that has effused from a broken blood vessel). It is usually brought on by violent head shaking. The shaking whiplashes a blood vessel which bursts and allows blood to seep between the cartilage and the skin of the ear. The condition should be treated as soon as possible as the weight of the blood in the ear irritates the dog and leads to further head shaking—this allows enlargement of the haematoma which can quickly involve the whole ear flap. The haematoma can be drained but is very likely to fill up again. A more permanent cure is achieved by suturing the ear flap.

Otitis (Canker)
Otitis (or canker) is an infection of the ear canal. It is more common in dogs with long, floppy, hairy ears which do not allow proper air circulation into the ear canal and hence provide a moist environment suited to the growth of organisms. The signs of ear infection are usually a discharge, a foul smell or head shaking. Sometimes the dog will hold its head on one side. Quite frequently the initiating cause is ear mites which can lie dormant in the pup from birth, at a later stage multiplying to the point where they inflame the ear canal and allow secondary infections to move in. Infections of the ear canal can also be caused by bacteria or fungi. Treatment involves cleaning the ear with a 50 per cent peroxide and water solution, plucking out any hair in the ear canal to increase air circulation, and treating with ear drops. As most ear drops contain a local anaesthetic to dull the pain, it is important to complete the course of medication and not stop after a few days when the dog appears comfortable, as this may just be the local anaesthetic working. Where possible, try to remove any debris from the ear canal daily with cotton buds before applying medication. It is safe to gently work down the ear canal, as the dog's ear takes a right-angled bend at the bottom before the ear drum. In chronic cases of ear infections, surgery to open the ear canal further to the air can give good results.

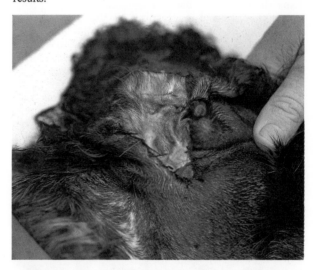

An ear-resection operation to expose the ear canal and dry it out.

Wounds
Dogs often receive injuries to the edges of their ear flaps. These may bleed profusely, and although not serious they can be very difficult to heal, as the dog scratches and shakes its head. The best home treatment is to apply cotton-wool packs to the top of the head, lay the ear flap back on to this and bandage it. Apply acriflavin or a healing ointment to the bleeding area. The bandage holding the flap to the head should be left on for a week to ten days until the wound has completely healed. Failing this, cautery will stop the bleeding.

Eczema
See SKIN DISORDERS.

Elizabethan collar
A device to prevent the dog licking/biting wounds on the body. It also stops the dog scratching the head and ears.

Euthanasia
This means putting your pet to death painlessly. There are several reasons why people ask a vet to perform euthanasia on their pet. Unacceptable reasons, in my opinion, include going on holidays or going overseas, getting married, moving from a ground-floor home to a unit or flat, grooming becoming too time-consuming, or the breed becoming 'un-

fashionable'. Legitimate reasons include old age, severe disease, accident victims with severe injuries, prolonged injury and disposing of strays. The best and most common method of euthanasia used by vets is an intravenous overdose of anaesthetic. This is a painless procedure and the pet dies within six to seven seconds. It is the only method that I can recommend. When the condition of a sick pet is grave, it is important to control emotional attachment to the animal and listen to the vet's advice. The vet knows how much sickness and pain an animal can take and how it should recover; if the advice is euthanasia, consider it seriously and do not let emotional involvement with the pet affect your decision. I believe pets have an advantage over humans at this point in their lives—the availability of euthanasia—so do not be selfish.

Eye disorders

Blindness

Blindness can occur from not treating any of the conditions described in this section. The most common cause, however, is crystallisation of the lens in old age, which reduces or stops the light rays passing through. Senile cataracts, which develop as the dog ages, are seen as a blue haze deep in the dog's eye. The dog may also bark at known persons some distance away but will quieten when the person moves closer to and is recognised by the dog. Dogs are usually nine or ten years old when the condition begins. Very little can be done except to be extra careful with the dog in strange surroundings, particularly in traffic. Cocker Spaniels and Poodles are particularly susceptible to this condition. When crystallisation is complete, there is a white, pearly, circular centre in the eye which allows little light through to the retina. If these dogs are left in familiar surroundings they can live a happy life. It is possible, depending on eye tests, to remove the lens and return about 40-50 per cent vision.

Pearly-white eyes due to cataracts.

Cataracts

Cataracts can be congenital or can be caused by diabetes mellitus.

Conjunctivitis

Conjunctivitis is an inflammatory condition of the eye and has several causes:

An acute injury—caused by a scratch from a piece of grass or twig brushing the cornea. This condition is painful; the dog closes the eye and the eye weeps.

Infection—taking the form of pus appearing in the corners of the eyes. If the pus appears only in one eye, the inflammation is usually caused by a local infection in that eye. (If both eyes are affected, it may indicate distemper or some other general disease.)

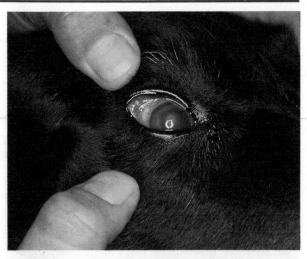

Conjunctivitis indicated by red mucous membranes.

A blockage of the tear duct—the tear duct usually drains tears from the eye to the inside of the nose.

The abscessed root of a molar tooth—in this case the conjunctivitis is usually accompanied by a lump just below the eye on the dog's face; sometimes the lump has a discharge.

Conjunctivitis is a painful condition for which it is wise to seek veterinary advice. Normal eye-washes are usually not strong enough to be an effective cure.

Corneal dermoid

Corneal dermoid—a plate of epithelial tissue on the surface of the cornea—is an island of skin that usually grows hairs from its surface which grow toward and irritate the cornea. It can be removed surgically.

Dry eye

Dry eye refers to the absence of the normal tear film covering the corneal surface. It gives the cornea a dry and lustreless appearance. It is seen in all breeds but particularly Yorkshire Terriers, Chihuahuas and Cocker Spaniels. It may be caused by severe conjunctivitis, distemper, old age or accidental damage to the tear gland. Once an eye becomes dry, the tear film must be replaced by artificial tears immediately or permanent damage can occur. A surgical technique in which a salivary duct is moved from the mouth to the eye gives satisfactory results.

Ectropion

Ectropion is eversion or sagging of the lower eyelid. Breeds commonly affected are Bloodhounds, Basset Hounds, St Bernards, Great Danes and Cocker Spaniels. Ectropion can predispose the eye to excessive drying and the easy entrance of foreign material into the conjunctival sac, which results in conjunctivitis or corneal infection. Rectification is by surgery.

Entropion

Entropion is inversion of the eyelid margin. The inherited form of this condition is seen most commonly in King Charles Spaniels, St Bernards, Cocker Spaniels, Golden and Labrador Retrievers, Irish Setters and English Bulldogs. It may be noticed when the puppies are born but usually doesn't cause any outward signs of disease until the dog is a few months old. In the mild form, the disease may correct itself as the dog ages. Mechanical damage is caused by the eyelashes rubbing on the eyeball. Treatment of entropion is by surgically excising an elliptical piece of skin from the eyelid to evert the eyelid margin. This plastic surgery is usually successful.

Glaucoma

Glaucoma is an increase in the normal pressure of the fluid within the eye. The usual signs are blueness of the lens, and conjunctivitis. Medications can control it.

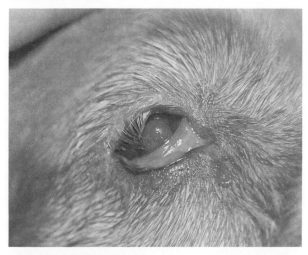

Upper eyelid entropion.

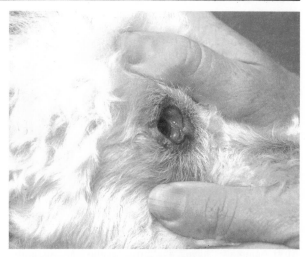

Infected Harderian gland, third eyelid.

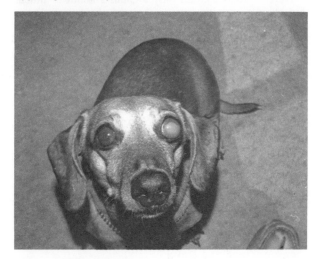

Advanced glaucoma.

Blue-eye due to live hepatitis vaccination.

Pup's eyelids glued together

Puppies should open their eyes at the ninth or tenth day of life, but a local infection may cause the eyelids to stay glued together. Never force the eyelids apart. This problem can be overcome by bathing the eyes with warm, salty water at the rate of a teaspoon of salt per half litre.

Harderian gland infections

The Harderian gland is a small gland attached to the inside of the third eyelid. Infections are indicated by the presence of a small meaty lump in the corner of the dog's eye. Treatment is usually by surgical removal of the gland.

Keratitis (Blue-eye)

Keratitis—an inflammatory condition of the glassy part of the eye—usually takes the form of a blue–grey haze over the eye accompanied by redness around the eye. There may be ulceration of the corneal surface. It should not be confused with the early stages of cataract formation, where the blue haze in the eye is deeper. Keratitis must be treated or the blue may remain and blindness results.

The causes of keratitis are: live hepatitis vaccination; swelling of the third eyelid; traumatic damage to the cornea (the glassy part of the eye) by a foreign body, such as a scratch from a cat's claw or a stick. Dogs with excessive nasal folds, such as Pekinese and Pugs, are very susceptible.

(See also entries in this section on conjunctivitis, corneal dermoid, ectropion, entropion, trichiasis.)

Micro-ophthalmia

Micro-ophthalmia—abnormally small eye—is not uncom-mon and may be seen in conjunction with other eye abnormalities such as 'Collie Eye' syndrome. Vision may be affected if the eyes are extremely small. Nothing can be done for this condition.

Nasal fold trichiasis

The nasal fold may be so excessive in the Pekinese and Pug as to be a severe cause of corneal irritation—trichiasis occurs when the hairs of the skin irritate the cornea

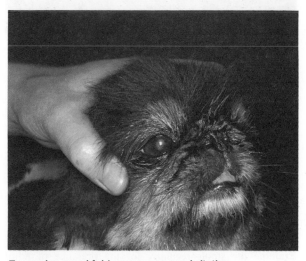

Excessive nasal fold may cause eye irritation.

—especially in animals with unusually prominent eyes. Surgical removal of the facial fold reduces the mechanical damage of the hairs to the eye.

Progressive retinal atrophy

Progressive retinal atrophy is a condition where the retina or receptive part of the eye degenerates, causing blindness.

Pupil constriction

Constriction of the pupils occurs normally in bright light; it may also occur when the dog has ingested a toxin or poison.

Pupil dilation

Pupil dilation occurs normally in dull light, but it also occurs in tick poisoning and sickness.

Strabismus

Strabismus—in-turning or out-turning of the eye—is usually seen in the broad-headed or short-headed breeds such as the Pekinese or Pug.

Third eyelid deformities

Most animals have a 'third eyelid'—a nictitating membrane—in the inner corner of the eye, controlled by an involuntary muscle. It acts to lubricate the eye, particularly in dry, dusty conditions. However, when the dog is ill, or under the influence of a tranquillising agent, the muscle controlling the lid may relax, allowing the membrane to cover one-third of the eye. Pet owners often refer to this as a 'skin growing over the eye'.

Deformities of the third eyelid—an inwards-to-outwards rolling of third eyelid margin—is usually seen in large breeds of dogs, having its highest incidence in Great Danes, German Shepherds, St Bernards, Old English Sheepdogs and Afghans. The condition usually appears before the animal is one year old and causes a mild form of corneal irritation. It can be corrected surgically.

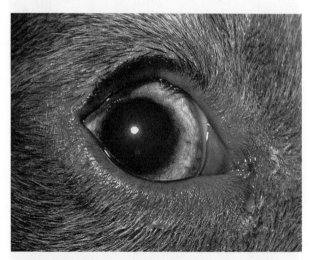

Trichiasis — an extra row of eyelashes.

Trichiasis

Trichiasis—an extra row of eyelashes—causes irritation of the cornea. It occurs most frequently in Pekinese, French Poodles, Boxers, English Bulldogs and Cocker Spaniels. The eyelashes can be removed by depilation.

Tumours

Tumours—for example, wart-like growths—can occur on the margin of the eyelid and can develop to a point where they physically and mechanically damage the cornea. They should be removed surgically.

Facial paralysis

See NERVOUS CONDITIONS.

Faeces

Examine the stools regularly for the presence of adult worms or segments of adult parasites. The most common is tapeworm segments which are the size of cucumber seeds, a greyish–pink colour, and active. They are usually on the outside of the stool. Roundworms are very common in puppies' stools—they are white, coiled, 5–8 centimetres long, the thickness of a pencil-lead, and pointed at both ends.

The presence of blood, undigested meat or fat globules in the stool indicates illness. Note the odour from the stool. The colour may also be of great clinical significance. The usual colour is brown because of pigments excreted in the faeces from the liver. A dark brown to black stool may indicate either that the animal is on a high meat diet or that blood pigments are present. Greyish–white or clay-coloured stools may indicate bile obstruction. Light brown or tan-coloured stools are frequently seen in nursing puppies and dogs on a diet high in milk. A green stool containing undigested material indicates a liver problem. A red stool may indicate a recent bleeding attack in the lower bowel or rectum.

Normal stools contain only a small amount of mucus, but chronic enteritis, chronic irritants, malabsorption or high doses of oral antibiotics over long periods may lead to excessive mucus. For further examination of the stool microscopically, a sample of about one dessertspoonful (5 millilitres) should be taken in a clean, labelled container to your veterinary surgeon.

Feet disorders

The dog's feet are often presented with problems—unclad, they come into contact with broken glass, sharp tins, nails, tar, acids, detergents and other harmful materials.

Cut pads or webbing

Cuts in the pads or in the webbing between the toes bleed profusely as this area is very vascular. Bleeding can be stopped initially by the application of a tourniquet and/or a firm bandage around the foot. Where the cut has gone right through the pad or skin, it is best to have the wound sutured, as sensitive tissues underneath the pad's surface would otherwise cause the dog prolonged irritation when they touch sand and gravel.

Fish hooks

Fish hooks are commonly found in the feet (and also in the lips after fish bait has been eaten). Do not try to pull a hook back against the barb. Instead, the shank of the hook should be cut and the passage of the barb continued through the skin. This may require a general anaesthetic.

Foreign bodies between the toes

Foreign bodies between the toes are usually grass seeds, thorns or pieces of stick. Sometimes the skin may heal over the site of the wound and days later an abscess will form. A chronically draining sinus may be the first symptom. Often a general anaesthetic has to be given while a probe is used to find the foreign body. If possible, where there is a hole in the skin, irrigate with 50 per cent peroxide and water for several days. The foreign body may wash out.

Interdigital cysts

These are swellings that appear between the toes and are caused by a blockage of the sweat glands in the feet. Soak the foot in a bowl of warm water with salt, at the rate of one tablespoon per litre. This will bring the cyst to a head. When it ruptures, clean the area with warm water and salt (1 tablespoon salt per litre) three or four times a day. Occasionally the swelling may have to be lanced by a vet. Sometimes a foreign body (for example, a grass seed or splinter) causes the problem.

Interdigital dermatitis

Interdigital dermatitis is an inflammatory, irritating dermatitis between the toes. It is usually precipitated by an allergic reaction to a grass which causes the dog to lick between the toes. The licking combined with the allergic reaction allows bacteria to multiply between the claws. Ap-

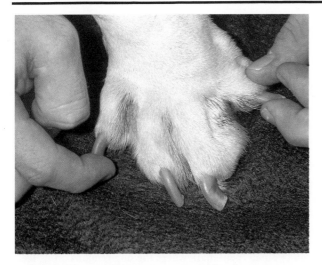

Interdigital dermatitis is a common problem in summer.

plications of astringent agents such as mercurochrome, triple dye or gentian violet will dry out the areas. The dog should be prevented from licking the areas by use of an Elizabethan collar or a bucket. Sometimes antibiotics and antihistamine injections may be necessary. (See also SKIN DISORDERS.)

Nails

See Grooming, p. 93.

Female disorders

By far the highest incidence of the female disorders listed below occur in undesexed mature bitches not being used for breeding. The incidence of these disorders in bitches desexed before they have a litter and under one year of age is practically zero.

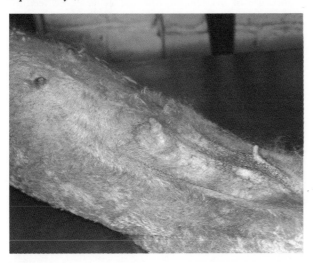

Mammary tumour: Note the hard lump surrounding the nipple.

Mammary tumours

Mammary tumours are one of the problems of older bitches, usually undesexed bitches which have not had a litter and which suffer from pseudopregnancy. There are two distinct types of tumours, both usually malignant. Mammary tumours, even the small circumscribed type, should always be removed surgically as soon as they are detected. The longer the tumour is allowed to remain, the greater the danger of secondary growths appearing, not only in the mammary gland, but also in the lymphatic glands within the abdomen. It is important to take the bitch to a vet as soon as any mammary lump is detected.

Mastitis — hot, swollen mammary glands — is caused by bacterial infection.

Mastitis

Mastitis means inflammation of the mammary gland. It is caused by bacterial infection, the bacteria usually gaining entry through scratches or wounds in the teats. These wounds are caused by hungry pups, most often when the bitch is short of milk because of an inadequate diet. The first signs are restlessness, possibly an elevated temperature, and loss of appetite. Examination will show a hot, painful and markedly swollen gland. If the condition is not brought under control quickly, all the milk will disappear and her entire litter may die. Fortunately, mastitis in the bitch responds rapidly to modern antibiotic therapy and prompt treatment is invariably successful. Hot fomentation together with manual stripping of the gland will help the condition resolve quickly.

Metritis/pyometron: pus discharging from the vulva.

Metritis

Metritis is an inflammation of the womb which most often occurs after whelping. It can be caused by the presence of dead pups, unexpelled afterbirth, injury during whelping, hormone imbalances in pseudopregnancies, or the administration of hormones to prevent oestrus. The first signs are usually a purulent discharge from the vulva, loss of appetite and a high temperature. This condition is very serious and requires immediate veterinary attention and antibiotic treatment. Treatment is usually successful, but occasionally a pyometron (womb full of pus) may develop. In these cases, a hysterectomy is needed.

Polyps

Polyps are wart-like growths on long stalks which form in the uterus. Hard lumps can be felt in the uterus. There may be a bloody discharge, but the bitch is otherwise completely normal. The only effective treatment is a complete hysterectomy.

Prolapse

Prolapse describes the condition where the cervix and the vagina fold back on themselves and protrude from the vagina. Sometimes the bladder is included in the prolapse and very occasionally the uterus as well. It appears as a red inflamed mass protruding from the vulva which the bitch licks incessantly. Treatment is to replace the prolapse surgically under general anaesthetic and suture the organs in place.

Vaginitis

Vaginitis means an inflammation of the lining of the vagina. It is usually caused by bacteria infecting an injury caused by mating or a difficult whelping. The bitch shows considerable discomfort and may repeatedly strain as though in labour. There may be a red or yellow discharge. Treatment involves a course of antibiotics together with daily insertion of a pessary.

Fever

Normal body temperature of a dog is 38.5°C. Body temperatures higher than 41°C for prolonged periods can cause permanent brain damage. Temperatures above 43°C are associated with high mortality.

The pet with a fever is usually depressed, off its food and lethargic; some will appear to be cold and shivery. Feverish dogs usually seek out a cool place such as a lino or tile floor. The dog's nose may be wet or dry. The causes are:

Overexertion from excitement or an overactive thyroid gland.

Obstructions to the panting or heat-loss mechanisms.

Obstructions in the air passages of the short-faced breeds—Pugs, for example.

Paralysis—for example, because of ticks.

Confinement in a hot, humid, poorly ventilated area.

Septicaemia and infectious diseases.

Where the animal has a high temperature, it is important to reduce the temperature or at least stop it getting higher. Place wet towels over the dog, keep it in a cool place, place it before a fan, administer half a tablet of aspirin, and seek veterinary advice as soon as possible.

Fights

Whatever you do, don't try to stop a dog fight with your bare hands. Use water, or hoses or garbage cans. If you are quick and have presence of mind, grab a tail and fling the dog away. (See also BEHAVIOURAL PROBLEMS.)

Fits

When the dog starts to have a fit, leave it in a dark room and keep it quiet. If possible, place a peg or other wooden object between the dog's teeth and pull out the tongue. The fit usually lasts only two or three minutes. Afterwards the dog will be exhausted.

If the fit continues longer than three minutes, causes other than epilepsy, such as POISONING, should be suspected. Among the most common causes of poisoning are snail bait and strychnine. Other common causes are insecticidal rinses used on dogs to control fleas and ticks. If this is the case, wash the dog immediately, use copious amounts of water and soap to prevent further absorption of the toxic material. In the case of snail bait and strychnine, take the dog to a vet immediately so that an injection can be given to make it vomit. If you are a long way from a vet, try to induce vomiting by administering a tablespoon of bicarbonate of soda to a quarter cup of water. These poisons can quickly be fatal.

Fits can be caused by epilepsy, poisoning by insecticides, insecticidal chemicals used in washing dogs, strychnine, snail bait, distemper, rabies, meningitis or low glucose levels in the blood to the brain.

Epilepsy in pups usually occurs when they are cutting teeth, from two to six months, particularly if they are heavily infested with roundworms. A roundworm-infested pup is typically pot-bellied. The actual cause in these cases is not understood.

Toy breeds are particularly susceptible to fits, but often medication will help them to grow out of the fits by six or seven months of age. In young puppies the exact causes of the fits are not understood, but it may be due to pressure on the developing brain from the cranial cavity. It is rare for this type of fit to continue through to middle age.

When it occurs in older dogs, the cause can be shock, fear, injury, sexual excitement, pain or stress. Sometimes a sudden change of temperature can bring on attacks. The fit can be small (petit mal), where the dog remains on its feet, chomps its jaws and froths at the mouth, or it can be a major fit (grand mal), where the dog collapses to its side, partly unconscious, with its legs extended rigidly from its body. The head is usually turned back and the dog may urinate or defecate.

In older dogs, fits may also be due to brain tumours or other pathological space-occupying lesions within the cranial cavity.

Pregnant or whelping bitches may suffer from fits, shaking or twitching because of low sugar or calcium levels. In these cases, stop the pups suckling, administer calcium tablets, give the bitch milk to drink, and take her immediately to the vet.

Flatulence

Flatulence occurring in bottle-fed pups is serious. It may be because of overfeeding, the use of unsterile feeding equipment, or feeding a formula that is too high in carbohydrate. The signs are an acute stress condition and a distended stomach. Prompt attention by a veterinary surgeon is vital.

Chronic intestinal flatulence and anal release is common in adult dogs, particularly the large breeds, though it can be embarrassing to owners. Flatulence is an indication of excessive bacterial fermentation in the bowel and is usually caused by feeding a high carbohydrate diet—potatoes, other root vegetables, beans, cauliflowers, cabbage and onions may be at fault. Cereals, milk and sweets can cause upsets. Some of the commercial rations with a high carbohydrate content may cause the problem. Dogs that tend to eat their food too fast and gulp air may also suffer from the problem. Change the dog's diet to a protein-type ration, ensure it is not constipated and have it treated with a wide-spectrum intestinal antibiotic to reduce the population of fermenting bacteria in the bowel.

Fleas

See SKIN DISORDERS.

Flystrike

This is a common condition in warmer countries during the summer months and is caused by flies biting the dog. It particularly affects dogs that are chained or have restricted access to sheltered areas. The flies bite prominent spots such as the tips of the ears or the highest fold in the ear. Long-haired dogs can also be flyblown around the crutch area and wherever there are sores protected by matted long hair.

Long hair should be cut away and any maggots physically removed. Douse the area with an insecticidal rinse. Where the animal cannot be placed in a fly-proofed area, use insecticidal ointments or sprays for protection. If the dog does not like the sound of the pressure pack, spray the insecticide on to a cloth and wipe it over the ears. This should be done at least twice a day. (See also SKIN DISORDERS.)

Foreign bodies
See ANAL IRRITATION, EAR DISORDERS, FEET DISORDERS, VOMITING.

Frostbite
Frostbite is uncommon in dogs, but it can affect the ears and the feet. Treat quickly with warmth and massage. Sudden heat should not be applied. The area should be wrapped in cotton-wool after being dressed with an astringent agent such as acriflavin. The dog should be offered warm milk, and all parts of its body should be rubbed and massaged. Veterinary attention is essential if the part of the body is to be saved.

Gangrene
Gangrene is the death of body tissues following degeneration of the tissues involved. Restricted circulation in an area because of tight bandages or plaster casts can sometimes result in gangrene. Fortunately these days, with modern antibiotics, gangrene is rarely seen.

Glandular enlargement
The dog has a large number of lymph nodes situated throughout the body. These have several functions, the most important being to filter the blood to remove infection from local areas as well as certain other unwanted matter. When infection is present, the glands may swell.

Glaucoma
See EYE DISORDERS.

Grass eating
Grass eating is common in dogs. It is generally used as a mechanism to stimulate vomiting to rid the stomach of stale food and may also be a symptom of gastritis, digestive discomfort or worm infestation. Another theory is that dogs eat grass as a source of vitamins.

Gums
See MOUTH DISORDERS.

Hair loss
See SKIN DISORDERS.

Harderian gland infections
See EYE DISORDERS.

Head shaking
See EAR DISORDERS.

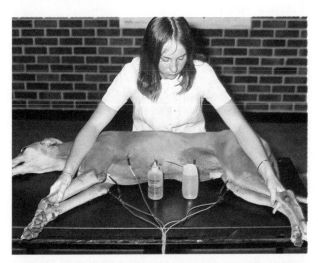

A Greyhound having an electrocardiograph to detect heart abnormalities.

Heart disease
The heart can be considered as a four-chambered pump with valves between the chambers. Disease may affect any one of the chambers, the valves, the muscles that make the heart function or the nerve centres that control the heart movement and beat.

For any heart disease, veterinary attention is essential. For first aid when the dog has a heart attack, it should be kept as quiet as possible in a darkened room, and stimuli of any type should be avoided. Where the dog suffers from a continuous cough, and veterinary advice is not immediately obtainable, a small amount (1 to 5 millilitres, or up to a teaspoon) of brandy or whisky may be given in milk, depending on the size of the dog, and a quarter to one codeine tablet as additional treatment while waiting for veterinary advice.

The most common heart condition in dogs is congestive heart failure. It is particularly common in Poodles. The initial clinical sign of this condition is a cough, sometimes referred to as a cardiac cough, which is stimulated by exercise or excitement. This is due to the congestive nature of the heart failure. Subsequent signs include difficulty in breathing, reduced tolerance to physical exercise, enlargement of the liver and a filling of the abdomen with fluid (this gives the dog a pregnant look). Treatment is aimed at eliminating the fluid accumulation by decreasing the work of the heart, reducing salt intake in the food and encouraging cardiac compensation by means of drugs.

Cardiovascular disease in dogs is not closely associated with diet problems, except for the consideration of salt in congested heart failure. A low salt diet should be considered only as an adjunct to other medical therapy and only when clinical signs of congestive heart failure are present.

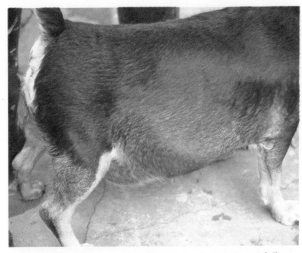

A fluid-filled abdomen, usually due to chronic heart failure.

A dog with a circulatory condition requires food with a low sodium content and a fairly high level of protein and carbohydrate. Such a dog usually cannot excrete sodium, which encourages the fluid within the body to stay in the tissues, which in turn impedes the circulation. A low salt diet can be formulated from boiled beef or chicken (discard the water used for boiling), together with rice, oatmeal or macaroni, and low-salt, bulk-forming vegetables such as corn, squash, beans or peas. Vegetable oils and honey are low in salt and seasoning agents such as garlic or onion powder may tempt the dog's appetite. Avoid the standard commercial pet foods, canned or prepared meat, dairy products, cheese and pastries and 'treat' titbits such as crackers, chips and salted nuts. It is difficult to create a palatable low salt diet.

Heartworm is also a common cause of mechanical congestive heart failure.

Heartworm

See Worming, pp. 103–4.

Heatstroke

Heatstroke is a problem in Pekinese, Pugs and Boxers, those breeds with pushed-in faces; as well as in the readily excitable breeds such as Poodles and Terriers. In the former group, it is a problem of deficient respiration, whereas in the latter group it is a result of physical activity in hot or humid environments. All dogs, irrespective of breed, are susceptible to heatstroke if confined in hot conditions—for example, in a closed car.

Heatstroke is relatively rapid in onset. The patient pants incessantly and drools saliva, yelps with distress, and champs the saliva into large bubbles which adhere to the face and forelegs as a froth or foam. There is a staring expression of apprehension and concern. The patient becomes excited with the discomfort and moves constantly to change position. This excessive muscular activity generates an increase in body temperature which further worsens the condition. Muscular weakness with distinct tremors and later spasms will be evident from the onset of distress. The heatstroke patient in a collapsed condition with muscular spasms will invariably die. Vomiting is a frequent symptom, and persistent vomiting increases the risk of death. A body temperature of 42–43°C is usually fatal, even when present for less than one hour.

First aid for heatstroke Since excess body temperature and reduced ability to lose body heat are the primary problems, any first aid measures should be directed at resolving these problems quickly. Remove the patient from any confined space to facilitate an airflow in the general vicinity. Spray the dog with cold water from a hose or iced water and place it in front of a large electric fan. Ice packs may be applied to the head and neck. Cold-water enemas are also of value in lowering internal body temperature. Massage the legs to aid general circulation and heat loss from the skin. Do not give sedatives to an overexcited dog, as they have an adverse effect on its blood pressure. When the patient's temperature has fallen to the normal level, about 38.5°C, it is usually safe to dispense with first aid temporarily and seek veterinary assistance. This will involve intravenous infusions, therapy against secondary infection and monitoring the kidneys for damage.

Preventing heatstroke Ensure that whenever dogs must be confined in a restricted space, they are protected from the direct rays of the sun. Adequate ventilation and plenty of cold drinking water are essential. Feeding times should be changed to early morning or late evening in hot weather, as the digestion of food results in a higher body temperature. Clipping the coat, contrary to popular belief, is not necessary, since the coat provides an insulation against the rays of the sun in a normal, healthy outdoor dog.

Hepatitis

See INFECTIOUS DISEASES.

Hernia

Hernia is the protrusion of an organ or part of an organ outside the space it normally occupies, while it is still enclosed in the membrane lining the cavity in which the organ is normally contained—that is, the protruding part is enclosed in a sac of lining membrane when it enters the incorrect position. The commonest forms of hernias are diaphragmatic, inguinal, perineal and umbilical.

Diaphragmatic hernia

Although the name hernia is used, this condition is strictly speaking a rupture. It is seen in dogs that have suffered from a severe accident or fall. The diaphragm is torn and parts of the abdominal organs enter the chest cavity. Respiration is restricted as the lungs become squashed, especially if the dog has its hindlegs higher than its forelegs. Surgical repair is necessary.

Inguinal hernia

Inguinal hernias are seen most commonly in adult dogs of either sex. A swelling occurs in the groin, usually on one side only, as part of the intestines press down through the weakened muscle wall. In the male, the hernia may involve the scrotum, in which case it is often termed as scrotal hernia. Surgical repair is necessary.

Perineal hernia

Perineal hernia, seen mainly in elderly dogs, is a soft swelling on one side of the anus. This type of hernia is not easy to repair, but surgery is often attempted.

Umbilical hernia

An umbilical hernia is usually seen in puppies, where the umbilical ring does not close or is damaged. A small bubble of fat forms in the opening—it may be pressed back into the abdomen but will reappear. An umbilical hernia can sometimes be caused by premature or careless tearing of the umbilical cord at birth. These hernias should be repaired where possible to prevent a piece of an organ strangulating in the hernia and causing the death of the dog.

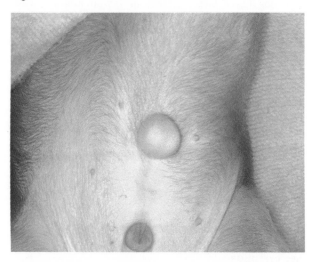

Umbilical hernia; a lump in the mid-line of the abdomen.

Herpes virus

See INFECTIOUS DISEASES.

Hip dysplasia

See BONE PROBLEMS OF GROWING DOGS.

Hookworm

See Worming, pp. 97–9.

Hormonal problems

See BEHAVIOURAL PROBLEMS, INCONTINENCE, SKIN DISORDERS.

Hysteria

See NERVOUS CONDITIONS.

Incontinence

Incontinence is the unexpected passing of urine. In puppies this is usually because of nervousness and wears off in time. In older dogs the causes are quite varied, including kidney disease, bladder disease, paralysis of the nerve supplying the bladder, bladder stones, tumours, enlarged prostate glands in the male and hormonal deficiencies in desexed females. Because the condition has a number of causes, it is best to take a 30-millilitre sample of urine along to the vet, together with an exact history of when and where the dog passes the urine. Where the incontinence is caused by the bladder becoming overfull and the excess dripping out, it is essential to ensure that the bladder is emptied twice a day using gentle pressure on the flanks if this is possible. Long-backed dogs that have had a back problem are often incontinent. Hormone therapy is useful for desexed females. (See also URINE DISORDERS.)

Inco-ordination

Inco-ordination can be the result of tick paralysis, central nervous system diseases, back problems, conditions of the middle ear, meningitis and encephalitis.

Infection

Infection is caused by micro-organisms such as bacteria, viruses, fungi or protozoa. The infection can be generalised (for example, septicaemia) or localised (for example, an abscess).

Infectious diseases

Diseases may be caused by many different viruses, and a single virus may produce many different manifestations of disease, for example, distemper. Viral diseases cannot be cured because few antibiotics or other drugs will kill the virus. However, they may often be prevented by quarantine, good hygiene and management and by vaccination.

Canine parvoviral enteritis

The signs of the parvovirus are vomiting and diarrhoea of short duration. It may occur in an isolated dog or appear in an outbreak form in a kennel, affecting both puppies and adults simultaneously. Some dogs will cease eating and vomit for twenty-four to forty-eight hours and recover without treatment. Other dogs may have prolonged vomiting and diarrhoea, and if treatment is not instituted they may die of the combined effects of dehydration and electrolyte imbalance. A third variation is the dog with prolonged vomiting and diarrhoea with a severe bloody diarrhoea developing. The dog will die within twenty-four hours.

The cause of this disease is a virus. There is no specific cure, but correction of the dehydration and electrolyte imbalance quickly and vigorously by the use of intravenous fluids is important. Veterinary attention is essential. Prevention is by vaccination.

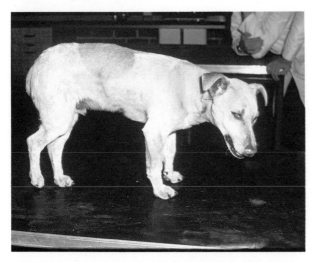

Distemper is a miserable disease and is usually fatal.

Distemper

Distemper is a highly contagious viral disease which is universal in dog populations and is transmitted through contaminated objects or by close contact. The incubation period is about nine days, the first signs being a high temperature for one to three days; the temperature may fluctuate from high to normal for a week. Pus accumulates in the corners of the eyes, which squint. Sometimes there is a nasal discharge. The dog is usually depressed, off its food and develops diarrhoea. Coughing may precede fatal pneumonia. A dog may recover from these symptoms and then succumb to further complications about four weeks later. These include nervous signs involving convulsive seizures, inability to stand, jerking movements of the head and jaws and paddling motions of the legs. Sometimes there is a trembling of the muscles in the temple, just in front of the ear. The dog may wander aimlessly, unaware of its surroundings. Attacks of distemper vary from an apparently mild infection to obviously serious disease. The disease can last as little as ten days but more often will be prolonged for several weeks or months, with intervening periods of apparent improvement followed by regression.

A typical distemper case is not difficult to diagnose, although many cases do not present the signs until the condition has advanced. Distemper should be suspected in all sick puppies, particularly if fever is present and there is no other apparent cause. Distemper is often confused with canine hepatitis and leptospirosis.

Prevention is best achieved by immunising the pregnant bitch halfway through the pregnancy to give the puppies an increased immunity at birth. All puppies should be immunised at six weeks and again at sixteen weeks. Because the condition is caused by a viral agent, treatment is not always effective. It is, however, always preferable to treat the dog because even the most serious cases can sometimes show a remarkable improvement.

Hepatitis

Hepatitis is a contagious viral disease characterised by a slight temperature, congestion of the mucous membranes and severe depression. Dogs of all ages are susceptible. The disease is transmitted through urine and droppings. The incubation period is six to nine days, with the virus localising in the liver and kidneys. The degree of severity varies from a slight fever to fatal illness. The first sign is an increased temperature, lasting for one to six days and usually fluctuating between quite high and near normal. General signs are apathy, loss of appetite, thirst and conjunctivitis, accompanied by discharge from the eyes, mouth and nose. The mucous membranes and tonsils become congested and there will be signs of abdominal pain and sometimes vomiting. After the period of general illness ends, the animal eats well but regains weight slowly. Some 25 per cent of sufferers develop a redness in the eyes seven to ten days after the disappearance of the acute stage of the illness. Although the disease can be fatal, there is a fair recovery rate. Vaccination, combined with distemper immunisation, is very effective in preventing the disease. The mother should be vaccinated halfway through her pregnancy and the pups at six and sixteen weeks. Live hepatitis vaccines may cause keratitis (see EYE DISORDERS).

Herpes virus

Herpes virus is a newly recognised, yet fairly common, fatal viral disease which occurs in pups under a month old. The virus kills the tissues in the liver and kidneys and causes pneumonia. The pups usually die within twenty-four hours. There is no vaccine.

Kennel cough

See COUGH.

Leptospirosis

Leptospirosis is caused by an organism called a spirochaete, which can be transmitted to humans. Nearly half the rat population carries it, and dogs become infected after eating food contaminated by rat urine or by eating infected rats. Dogs of all ages are affected, males being more susceptible than females.

After an incubation period of five to fifteen days, the disease may have a sudden onset characterised by slight weakness, refusal to eat, vomiting, high temperature and often mild congestion in the eye. Within two days the temperature drops sharply, depression is more pronounced, breathing becomes laboured and thirst develops. Muscular soreness and stiffness develop, particularly in the hindlegs. The mucous membranes of the mouth first show patches like a graze or burn, which later dry out and drop off in sections. In some cases the tongue may show dead patches of skin and the entire tip may drop off.

Prevention is by vaccination. Always keep your dog on a leash when in an area frequented by other dogs. A constant supply of fresh water should be available to discourage random drinking. Garbage, pools and fishponds are often contaminated and are prime sources of infection. It is essential in all cases to administer an antibiotic combination for at least ten days. Dehydration and acidosis can be treated with fluid therapy at the vet's surgery.

Myocarditis

The usual sign of myocarditis is that puppies three to seven weeks of age are found dead or dying following a brief period of difficult breathing. Those affected are usually vigorous, healthy puppies with no prior indication of any illness. The mortality rate within a litter may vary from 30 to 100 per cent with deaths occurring over a period of two to three weeks and in some cases up to six weeks. The cause is at present unknown but it is strongly suspected that it is caused by a virus. Treatment is non-specific.

Rabies

Rabies is a virus disease of all mammals, including humans, which is spread by the saliva of an infected animal entering the bloodstream of another animal, usually by a bite. The period of incubation varies from two weeks to six months, and depends on the site of infection. The virus has to travel to the brain from the point where it entered the body; therefore the further from the head the bite occurred, the longer the incubation period. Symptoms are basically a change of temperament followed by a period of great excitement. Finally, if the dog survives long enough, a period of paralysis follows. The excitement stage is characterised by the dog attacking, without fear, anything that moves or makes a noise. The dog may run for miles. In the paralytic stage the dog shows symptoms of paralysis of the lower jaw and limbs. Collapse quickly follows, then death.

Any person bitten by such a dog should report to their doctor as soon as possible. The dog suspected of suffering from rabies should not be killed but should be confined in a safe area from which escape is impossible. This is necessary for correct diagnosis of the disease. As rabies is fatal and can infect humans, it is essential that all control

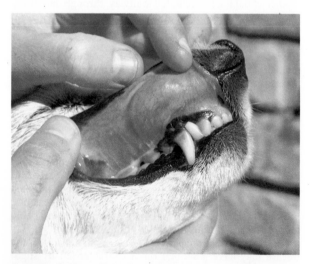

Jaundice/icterus: Note *the yellow mucous membranes of the mouth.*

measures be rigidly enforced and that suspected cases be reported immediately. Check with your veterinarian if vaccination is necessary in your area.

Jaundice

A jaundiced condition develops where there is an increase in the concentration of bile pigment in the blood, producing yellowish staining of the white of the eye, the mucous membrane of the mouth and, in severe cases, the skin itself. It may be caused by: leptospirosis; the after-effects of a blood transfusion; sclerosis and liver tumours; hepatitis; or bile duct obstruction. If your dog appears jaundiced, it is best to consult a vet.

Jaundice/icterus: Note *the yellow mucous membranes of the eye.*

Kennel cough
See COUGH.
Keratitis
See EYE DISORDERS.

Kidney disease (Nephritis)

Nephritis simply means inflammation of the kidneys. It is a common and serious disease in ageing dogs, and can be difficult to treat. It always requires the attention of a vet.

The first sign is an increased thirst and the passing of excess urine. While the dog's appetite may be good, it will lose weight. Some dogs will have foul breath. The dog may vomit, particularly in the morning, and especially after drinking water. In advanced cases the dog may collapse.

The cause is usually an infection of the kidney tissue, and veterinary attention should be sought immediately to avoid irreversible damage to the delicate and complex structure of the kidney. A 30-millilitre sample of urine should accompany the dog to the vet. This is best collected by confining the dog overnight with water, then taking the dog on a lead into the garden and quietly collecting the urine in a clean shallow vessel. Once the dog has received appropriate treatment, it should be fed a special diet.

A dog with severe kidney trouble often excretes a lot of protein in its urine, so extra protein should be supplied, preferably white meat (rabbit or chicken) or fish. Other suitable foods include cereal, milk, egg custard, cheese (in small quantities), hard-boiled eggs, vegetables, boiled rice and rice pudding. Extra vitamin B should be supplied—a yeast tablet two or three times a week is ideal. (See also URINE DISORDERS.)

Lameness

Lameness can be mild or severe, constant or intermittent. Mild cases in adult dogs are often due to an arthritic condition but may be the result of some bone development

Lameness in a puppy: Note *reluctance to bear weight on left hind leg.*

disorder. Hip dysplasia is one of the most common causes. Acutely lame dogs may be suffering from ruptured cruciate ligaments in the stifle joint, dislocated hips after a car accident, or fractures of main bones. The foot pads and webbing should be searched for foreign bodies such as thorns and glass. (See also BONE PROBLEMS OF GROWING DOGS.)

Leptospirosis
See INFECTIOUS DISEASES.

Lice
See SKIN DISORDERS.

Male disorders

Balanitis
Balanitis is an inflammatory condition of the foreskin (the prepuce). It is a normal condition in most dogs, is commonly seen as a pus-filled discharge from the eye of the penis, and is very difficult to clear up. The prepucial cavity (the fleshy housing of the penis) is warm and moist, an ideal environment for bacteria. Sexual frustration is a contributing factor; the dog continually licks himself as a form of masturbation, so reinfecting the area. Treatment can be instituted by syringing out the cavity and squirting an antibiotic cream into it two or three times a day for a five-day period. However, once medication ceases, reinfection is likely. As balanitis causes the dog so little trouble, it is regarded as an almost-normal condition and should only lead to a visit to the vet if the discharge becomes bloody, signifying an injury or inflammation of the sexual glands.

Dermatitis of the scrotum
Dermatitis of the scrotum is particularly common in Old English Sheepdogs and Chows and is extremely irritating. Treatment is by astringent agents such as mercurochrome, triple dye or any other antibacterial dermatological agent. Apply to the scrotal surface three times daily for about five days. Try to stop the dog licking the area by using an Elizabethan collar. In cases that continually recur or don't clear up, castration is the only solution.

Fracture of the os penis
The male dog has a small bone in his penis. Occasionally this bone is fractured (usually during attempted mating). Clinical signs are a severe swelling and acute pain. Diagnosis is by X-ray.

Orchitis
Orchitis is an inflammatory condition of the testicles, usually caused by an injury, a kick or bruise; very occasionally it may be due to an infection by bacteria. The testicles are hot and painful, and the dog resents them being examined. If an abscess has formed, the dog's temperature may be elevated to about 40°C. As a first aid measure, the testicles may be fomented with epsom salts and warm water at the rate of a tablespoon to 6 litres. It is best to have the condition treated by a veterinary surgeon—usually with long-acting antibiotics and an anti-inflammatory agent.

Prostatitis
The prostate gland is an accessory sexual gland in male dogs. When this becomes inflamed and enlarged, the condition is known as prostatitis. The dog, usually middle aged or older, has difficulty in passing motions; he squats for prolonged periods without success and often strains. He may be 'off' his food and tend to vomit. The vet can confirm the diagnosis by rectal examination and institute treatment with injections of female hormones. Sometimes the enlargement is caused by a cancerous growth triggered off by ageing male hormones. Large doses of the female hormone reverse the process in the majority of cases. To avoid recurrences it is advisable to have the dog castrated.

Tumours of the testes
Tumours of the testes are not uncommon, though as a rule only one testicle is involved. The testicle is hard and solid, yet not painful. It usually occurs in older dogs and is much more frequent in undescended testicles. The only effective treatment is castration.

A rather obvious testicular tumour.

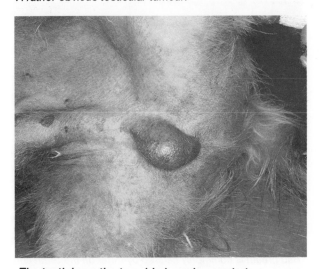

The testicle on the top side is undescended.

Undescended testicles
Undescended testicles are fairly common, particularly in the toy breeds. An owner should not worry about this condition until the dog is nine months old. Then the testicles

135

become prone to tumour formation and should be removed. This condition is hereditary.

Mange
See SKIN DISORDERS.

Mastitis
See FEMALE DISORDERS.

Metritis
See FEMALE DISORDERS.

Milk fever
See Breeding, p. 111.

Miscarriage
See ABORTION.

Mites
See SKIN DISORDERS.

Mouth disorders
Dogs do not sweat through the skin. They exchange most of their heat through the mouth, and can extend the tongue to increase the surface exposed to the air.

Most young puppies up to six months of age bite and chew a lot in the process of cutting their teeth. Some exercise on sticks, others on shoes, slippers, socks and even furniture if they get the chance. One method of satisfying a pup's requirements is to give it several 'chews', which are pieces of rolled-up, dehydrated cattle hide. Use these with caution, as small pieces may rehydrate in the intestine and cause a blockage. Another solution is to give the pup large ox shank bones from the butcher. These shanks have sheaths of meat and tissue which are good for the dog to chew and tear. Make sure that the bone is not one that can fracture into sharp pieces.

Bad breath
Foul breath can be caused by eating raw meat, or meat buried too long, by tartar build-up on the teeth, or inflammation of the gums (gingivitis). This causes the gums to fall away from the teeth, allowing food to be trapped and then decay. Ulcers, viral attacks and bacterial infection can all cause bad breath. Bacterial infections of tonsils or lymph glands of the mouth can lead to tonsillitis, pharyngitis or laryngitis, all of which give bad breath. Other causes may be gastrointestinal upsets or kidney trouble. In sugar diabetes there is a distinct smell of acetone.

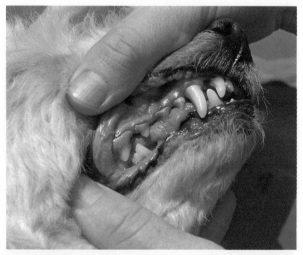

Bad breath is commonly caused by tartar on the teeth and infected gums.

Spaniels often suffer from an extremely unpleasant mouth odour which arises from ulceration of the outer surface of the lower lip. This occurs in the deep creases seen in this breed which fill with saliva and then become in-

fected. Creases so affected should be cleaned, washed with Phisohex soap, or a 50 per cent hydrogen peroxide/water solution, dried and powdered with a wound dressing powder, or one of the astringent dyes.

Bleeding
Bleeding can occur in small quantities from ulcerated or inflamed gums, or from the sockets of bad teeth. The mouth can also bleed from trauma and from cuts received from sticks or from car accidents. As the mouth contains many blood vessels, with a particularly large pair under the tongue, dogs playing with sharp sticks or bones can easily lacerate a vein. Bleeding from the mouth is difficult to treat without an anaesthetic. Dogs rarely suffer a fatal bleed, so don't panic—but do see the vet.

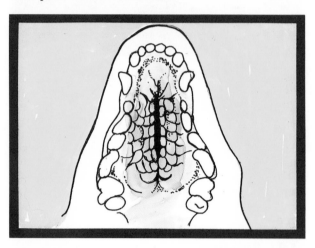

Typical gap in the roof of the mouth formation of cleft palate.

Cleft palate
This is a congenital abnormality in which the roof of the mouth fails to join down the centre, leaving a gap through which food can pass into the respiratory sinuses, subsequently causing pneumonia. Puppies with this abnormality rarely reach maturity because of pneumonia. It can be corrected surgically in some cases.

Gums
The normal colour of a dog's gums is pink.

Pale gums are a symptom of anaemia or shock. If the dog suffers from anaemia, the cause should be identified. If the anaemia could be caused by shock after an accident, have the dog examined by a vet to make sure it is not bleeding internally. Then offer warm milk and keep the animal in a head-down position. Keep the animal warm.

Red gums, particularly around the margins between the gums and the teeth, indicate gingivitis, caused by excess tartar which should be scraped off while the dog is under anaesthetic.

A generalised redness of the gums indicates a toxic condition of the blood.

Tumours of the gum, not usually malignant, need only be removed by the vet if they appear to give the dog mechanical discomfort. They are particularly common in Boxers.

Salivation
The most common cause of excessive salivation is car sickness. Anti-sickness tablets are available. Salivation can also be caused by poisons such as Baysol, Defender and Malathion. (See also FITS, POISONING.)

Teeth
Normally the dog has forty-two teeth, twenty in the upper jaw and twenty-two in the lower. The six front teeth in the upper and lower jaws are called incisors. Behind these are the single-pointed canines. The premolars and molars are

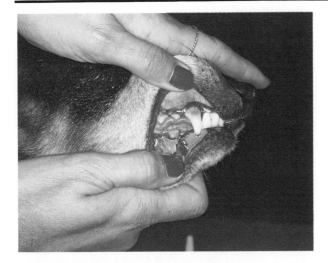

Tumour of the gum and early tartar on the teeth.

the big grinding teeth at the back of the jaw.

At birth the puppy has no teeth; later temporary (milk teeth) appear. From three to four weeks after birth the incisors erupt, the temporary canines appearing at about the same time. The three temporary premolars appear at about six to nine weeks. During the eruption period, the dog's teeth should be examined once a week, to check whether there is space for the erupting teeth and whether the adult teeth are appearing before the temporary teeth are shed. Overcrowding of the mouth is particularly common in the pushed-in face breeds such as Maltese Terriers, Chihuahuas, Pekinese, Pugs and Boxers. In the toy breeds, supernumerary or retained deciduous teeth, especially the canines, may be seen at about six months of age. Supernumerary or retained teeth should be extracted.

The retained temporary canine is immediately behind the whiter, shorter less pointed permanent tooth.

Dental decay is on the increase, as more and more owners feed soft prepared foods to their pets. Large bones or hard biscuits help to reduce tartar accumulation. Some breeds, such as Poodles, are particularly susceptible to bad teeth. Once tartar has formed in the margins of the teeth, tooth decay and bad breath quickly follow. If your dog is docile, it is possible to clean the tartar from the teeth with a metallic object or hard plastic, or even to brush the teeth with a hard toothbrush. If the tartar persists or the dog won't co-operate, it will need its teeth descaled while under a general anaesthetic.

Tongue

The natural colour of a dog's tongue is pink—except the Chow's, which is purple. The tongue is very vascular (that is, it contains many blood vessels) because it is the point of exchange of heat for dogs. Dogs that play with sharp objects can easily lacerate some of the large vessels in the tongue. If this happens, the dog should be taken immediately to the vet.

Myocarditis

See INFECTIOUS DISEASES.

Nephritis

See URINE DISORDERS and KIDNEY DISEASE.

Nervous conditions

Chorea

In dogs chorea is usually a legacy of the distemper virus (see INFECTIOUS DISEASES). Viral and bacterial infections affect the central nervous system, leaving the dog with a persistent and uncontrollable twitch. This can be in the temporal muscles between the eye and the ears, over the forehead, or it may affect a leg or the whole body. Because the central nervous system does not regenerate, the best that can be hoped for is that the twitch will not get worse. If the dog begins to have fits or becomes paralysed, the future is hopeless. Where only a limb is involved, the animal can sometimes live a reasonable life.

Convulsions

See FITS.

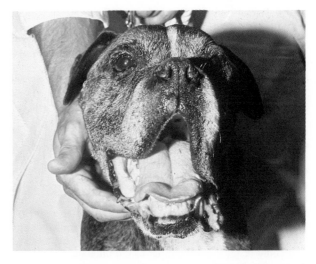

Right-sided facial paralysis: Note dropped right upper and lower lips.

Facial paralysis

This is usually due to a traumatic knock to the head which injures the facial nerve. The mouth becomes twisted and the tongue lolls to one side. Usually the nerve repairs and the dog's future is good—with patience and time the only cure.

Hysteria

An hysterical dog appears to go mad, racing around blindly, howling, oblivious of all attempts to calm it. An attack is usually triggered by excitement or sudden noise. It may last for several minutes or half an hour. At the end, the animal may fall down in a fit or convulsion. The condition is common in toy breeds and in some instances is due to a dietary deficiency of vitamin B1. Treat the dog as for FITS.

Paralysis

The most common form of paralysis (apart from radial paralysis—see below) is paralysis of the hindlegs. This can be caused by ticks, severance of the spinal cord in motor vehicle accidents, or disc protrusion in long-backed dogs such as Corgis and Dachshunds. It is important to seek veterinary advice. (See also STAGGERING.)

Radial paralysis

The radial nerve provides both motor and sensory functions to the forelimbs. It is particularly susceptible to mechanical damage as it lies just under the skin on top of the bone in the front leg. Traumatic damage to this nerve results in radial paralysis and prevents the dog elevating its foot from the ground. Consequently, the elbow drops and there is a slight curling of the leg from the wrist down. The dog has no feeling in the toes and drags its leg along the ground. In many cases the tops of the toes will be abraided to the point where the bone may show. Treatment and recovery depend on whether the nerve is bruised or actually severed. If the nerve is bruised, there is a possibility of recovery over a three-week period and the toes should be bandaged to prevent further damage. If there is no improvement after three or four weeks, it can be assumed that the nerve is permanently damaged and amputation is advised. Dogs can exist very happily on three legs.

Stroke

A stroke is caused by the rupture of one of the smaller blood vessels in the brain, generally in older dogs. The dog is usually brought to the vet with a history of staggering; the head rolls from side to side. Treatment depends on the part of the body that is affected but invariably requires a long convalescence and much loving care from the owner. If the legs are involved, they should be massaged to prevent muscle atrophy or wasting.

Nose troubles

A normal, healthy dog has a cold, moist nose. This may become dry and warm from stress, ill health or merely from excessive exercise.

Bleeding

Bleeding from the nose may occur after an accident, from a tumour, poisoning, constant sneezing from sinusitis or after violent exercise.

Changes in colour

Changes in the colour of pigmentation of the nose are common but do not seem to indicate disease.

Crusting

Crusting on top of the nose can be due to distemper or a fungal dermatitis.

Discharges

A yellow discharge from both nostrils usually indicates an infection lower in the respiratory tract, such as pneumonia. This could result from distemper or the inhalation of medication into the lung.

Pus in both nostrils could also indicate a generalised infection of the sinus cavities of the head. Pus coming from one nostril indicates a local infection of the sinus on that side of the head, a decaying tumour in one of the sinuses or even a decaying tooth root. Offensive discharges often indicate that bony tissues are involved.

Nutritional secondary hyperparathyroidism (N.S.H.)

See BONE PROBLEMS OF GROWING DOGS.

Obesity

Many urban dogs suffer from overweight problems. This is the result of the excellent diets provided by the pet food industry coupled with the small territorial space allowed for most dogs. A vicious cycle is established once the dog begins to get fat. The overweight dog is lethargic, and later develops other health problems (see p. 87). These further discourage the exercise which would normally keep the dog slim by burning up energy.

In the wild, overweight animals would not survive as they would not be fast enough to catch their prey.

As with human dieting, a rapid reduction in weight is

dangerous. Record the weight of the dog by carrying it onto the bathroom scales and then subtracting your own weight. Establish the correct weight for your dog by contacting a breed society or your vet. Do not try to reduce the dog's weight by more than half a kilogram per week. The following routine should be successful:

Give the dog access to plenty of water.

Seek out a balanced, good quality commercial dog food that your dog *does not* find very palatable. Remember, the more moisture it has the more palatable it is. Dry dog foods (unmoistened) may therefore be your answer.

Feed one meal per day of this food, and nothing else.

If the dog continues to overeat on the dry food diet, keep changing brands until you find a less palatable food, or keep the dog's intake restricted.

Be sure the dog is not 'eating out' at the neighbour's place.

Increase the dog's exercise—but slowly.

Keep the dog away from kitchens at meal-times and don't give any 'treats'. (See also How much food? on pp. 90–1.)

If all this fails, see your vet for further advice.

Oestrus

See Breeding, p. 105.

Old age

A dog's lifespan varies with the breed and weight of the dog. Larger breeds live shorter lives, usually eight to twelve years. Smaller breeds live between fifteen and twenty years, although toy dogs are relatively short-lived. There is no accurate method for determining the age of a dog after six months, when it has acquired a full set of teeth.

Diet

In old age the number of calories required by the dog is reduced, but the preparation of the food becomes more important. The amount of calcium and phosphorus may need to be increased to maintain the health of the dog's bones. Protein is essential. Carbohydrates should be cooked to break down the starch granules to help digestion, while vitamin supplements should be increased. For the older dog you could prepare a diet of cooked cereal (oatmeal, wheat or rice), plus cooked meat, cottage cheese or boiled egg for added vitamins, but there is no need to change a dog to this diet unless it is not eating its normal food. If the dog is ageing, losing its appetite and becoming thinner, it is important to upgrade the appeal of the diet. This can be done by adding more fresh meat. If the dog is fed on commercial rations, convert the dog to a tinned food rather than a dried food. Fats should be supplied only in very small quantities. Good foods for old dogs include meat (especially white meat), fish, cottage cheese, poultry, cooked eggs and cooked cereals. These should be given as small, frequent meals, rather than one daily feed. In the same way, clean water should be offered frequently.

Geriatric medicines

There are several medications available from your veterinary surgeon which will give the dog a lift in older age. They are particularly helpful for dogs suffering from geriatric conditions such as arthritis, rheumatism, and cardiac and kidney troubles.

Illness in old age

Large breeds in old age are often affected by arthritis and kidney troubles, more noticeably in cold climates. The dog may initially have difficulty rising, but after a few strides the gait becomes normal. In the early stages of illness the dog can be made more comfortable by keeping it in warm surroundings and possibly by the judicious use of analgesic or anti-inflammatory agents. Speak to your vet.

Many of the small toy breeds, such as Poodles and Cocker Spaniels, develop severe eye troubles in later life. Providing the dog is in its own familiar surroundings, it is usually able to lead a normal life. Care should be taken where the dog may be able to venture on to the road. Some eye conditions can be treated to return a little eyesight.

Heart conditions are particularly common in Poodles and Cocker Spaniels, and usually involve congestive heart failure. The signs exhibited by the dog are a cardiac cough brought on by excitement or exercise. Sometimes the dog may have an increased thirst and its abdomen appears to swell.

Signs of a kidney complaint are an increased thirst with frequent urination. (See also INCONTINENCE.) The dog may also be lethargic.

(See also ANAL ADENOMA and PROSTATITIS.)

Osteochondrosis
See BONE PROBLEMS OF GROWING DOGS.

Otitis
See EAR DISORDERS.

Pain
Pain is one of the earliest signs of disease. The pet may become restless, move constantly, refuse to stay in one place, roam and whimper. It may have a frightened expression, resent handling or forced movement of painful parts. (See also ABDOMINAL PAIN.)

Acute pain
Sharp pain is usually associated with fractures, ruptures or torsion twisting of internal organs.

Slowly developing pain
Gradually developing pain is associated with arthritis, tumours and inflammation, and here your observations may help the vet to make a diagnosis.

Although a dog may 'nurse' one part of the body—for example, a leg—it does not necessarily mean that the dog is in severe pain. Dogs can get along quite well on three legs, and sometimes even a minor complaint will make a dog carry its leg. However, it is always best to have a vet look at the dog to determine whether anything can be done for the injury or whether it is best left to rest. In some conditions, particularly after surgery, it is best that the dog does not use the affected part and therefore pain-killing drugs will not be used.

Paralysis
See NERVOUS CONDITIONS, and STAGGERING.

Parvovirus
See INFECTIOUS DISEASES.

Patella luxation
See BONE PROBLEMS OF GROWING DOGS.

Paws, inflamed/swollen
See SKIN DISORDERS.

Peritonitis
Peritonitis is an inflammatory and sometimes infectious disease problem of the lining of organs and the internal abdominal wall. It is usually caused by septic penetration from either the gastrointestinal tract or the outside abdominal wall. The animal will resent palpation of the abdomen, arch its back, be reluctant to move, have a fever and be off its food. In all cases the dog should be taken to the vet.

Pleurisy
Pleurisy is an inflammatory and infectious condition of the lining of the lungs and the wall of the thorax. The inflamed linings rub together during respiration and cause extreme pain. The problem requires veterinary attention.

Pneumonia
Pneumonia is an inflammation of the lungs caused by infection, injury or by migration of parasites, especially in young animals. Signs of pneumonia include shivering, high temperature, loss of appetite, difficulty in breathing and a grunting sound with each breath. It is often possible to hear a 'grating' sound if you listen closely to the chest. Veterinary attention is essential.

Poisoning
First aid
Poisons may be absorbed internally or through the skin or via the respiratory tract. If the animal was in physical contact with toxic or corrosive material, wash its skin clean with large quantities of water.

If the dog has eaten a poison, induce vomiting by administering orally a tablespoon of bicarbonate of soda to a quarter of a cup of water, or 5 millilitres of hydrogen peroxide. If the dog is excited or convulsing, try to protect it from injuring itself.

In all cases, after the first aid measures (given above) have been carried out, take the dog immediately to a vet.

Don't forget to take a sample of the suspected poison and its container along to the vet with the animal. This is important because the medications the vet must use will depend on the type of poison the dog has ingested. The vet will also be able to give the dog any necessary supportive treatment using medications and treatment which you will not have available at home.

Should a vet not be handy, try to induce vomiting (see above). Remember, these solutions should only be given in an emergency when there is no vet available, as neither solution is particularly efficient in making the animal vomit. It is also possible that such fluids given orally will pass through the stomach and wash the poison into the small intestines where it will be absorbed more rapidly.

Most poisons produce early gastrointestinal signs, such as vomiting, and progress rapidly to fits and weakness in the legs. Others will cause neurological signs such as fainting or trembling. Urine colour can sometimes help in the diagnosis: the carbamate in one snail bait produces a bright blue urine; the metaldehyde in another snail bait produces a light green urine.

There are so many potentially toxic substances now on the market that it is impossible to mention them all. Only the most common problems will be covered here. For additional information about poisons, contact the poisons control centre at a hospital.

Anti-coagulants
Anti-coagulants, such as warfarin, are commonly used in modern rodenticides (rat poisons). Symptoms of poisoning include anaemia from blood loss, persistent nose bleeding, bloody urine, laboured breathing, bloody diarrhoea and increased redness of the skin and the conjunctiva (eye membranes). It is unusual for a dog to suffer any problem from eating one poisoned rat—usually the dog must eat several poisoned rats over a number of days before an anti-coagulant will have any detrimental effect on the dog. It is advisable to have the dog checked by a vet.

Insecticidal rinses
Organo-phosphate compounds are the common active ingredient in many flea collars, liquid dog washes, aerosols and flea powders. Poisoning with insecticidal rinses is usually due to incorrect concentration. Sometimes the correct concentration of solution will have a detrimental effect in very young, aged or debilitated animals. Poisoning is by absorption through the skin or by licking. The symptoms vary depending on the drug, dose received and individual sensitivity, but the usual symptoms are salivation, muscle tremor, shivering, weakness in the hindlegs, convulsions, vomiting, diarrhoea and constriction of the pupils followed by dilation. Immediately this form of poisoning is recognised, wash the dog in copious quantities of fresh water to prevent further absorption of insecticides, then take it to the vet.

Snail bait
Two common generic compounds are carbamate and metaldehyde. Symptoms of poisoning are lack of co-

A poison bait — bread laced with blue snail bait.

ordination, anxiety and muscle tremors which sometimes become severe muscle spasms. These symptoms are similar to strychnine poisoning but spasms are not accentuated by auditory or physical stimulation.

Strychnine

Some rat poisons and some of the older patent medicines contain this substance, although strychnine poisoning in urban areas is usually the work of a dog hater. When this happens, several dogs in one area are usually poisoned at the same time. This form of poisoning should be suspected when a mature, healthy dog suffers from shortness of breath, blue mucous membranes, stiffness of the limbs and throwing back of the head. The animal can be stimulated into a fit by sudden loud noises near the ears or by slapping the body. Spasms increase in intensity until respiratory paralysis and death occur. Take the dog immediately to a vet; this is an emergency.

Strychnine poisoning: Note *the extended forelegs, head and neck.*

Pregnancy
See Breeding, pp. 106–8.

Prolapse
See FEMALE DISORDERS.

Prostatitis
See MALE DISORDERS.

Pyometron
Inflammation of a bitch's womb can result in a more serious disorder, pyometron, in which the womb is filled with pus. If this occurs, a hysterectomy is needed. (See FEMALE DISORDERS.)

Rabies
See INFECTIOUS DISEASES.

Respiration rate increase
An increase in the respiratory rate occurs during fever, increased environmental temperature, pneumonia, pleurisy, congestion of the lungs caused by ticks or chronic heart failure, space-occupying lesions such as tumours or diaphragmatic hernia, where some of the abdominal contents may be in the thorax.

Rickets
Rickets is a very rare disease, yet the term is frequently, but incorrectly, used to describe bone problems in larger breeds. Rickets is due to a deficiency of vitamin D and calcium and/or phosphorus. Provided an affected dog is given correct quantities of calcium and phosphorus, the condition can be somewhat alleviated. It is rare in countries with plenty of sunlight, more prevalent in the northern hemisphere. Dogs with rickets develop abnormalities of their limbs, with the growth plates becoming enlarged and prominent. Affected dogs are inactive. (See also BONE PROBLEMS OF GROWING DOGS, pp. 121–2.)

Ringworm
See SKIN DISORDERS.

Salivation
Excessive salivation can be caused by poisons, fits, car sickness or medications taken orally which can stimulate saliva production. (See also FITS, POISONING.)

Scabies
See SKIN DISORDERS.

Scooting
'Scooting' is the term used to describe the action of a dog as it pulls itself along the ground in a sitting position to relieve an irritation in the anal area. The irritation is caused by tapeworm fragments (see Worming section), compacted anal glands or itchiness around the anal sphincter. The contents of infected anal glands may be forced out by holding the dog's tail in the left hand and, with the thumb and forefinger of the right hand held at eight o'clock and four o'clock positions over a pad of cotton-wool, squeezing inwards and upwards. (See also ANAL GLANDS.) Anal itchiness can be treated with calamine lotion, gentian violet, mercurochrome or triple dye.

Scratching
See SKIN DISORDERS.

Septicaemia
Septicaemia is a condition where bacteria entering the bloodstream, sometimes from the gut or another infected source in the body, cause a generalised infection of the body. Localisation of the infection occurs in the joints, lungs, liver and kidneys. This is a very serious disease. The dog is obviously unwell, will have a fever, tends to lie in a cool place and will not eat or drink. Veterinary treatment must be given at once. Antibiotics are normally given intravenously initially to obtain a quick response to suppress the organisms circulating in the body.

Shivering
Shivering is an involuntary movement of the muscles. It can be caused by cold, fever, eclampsia (milk fever), the initial stages of poisoning or fright.

Shock
Shock is a failure of the circulatory system resulting from injury or illness. It is commonly seen after motor vehicle accidents where there is severe internal or external bleeding. It is a serious condition from which the animal rarely recovers without intensive veterinary care.

Symptoms are weakness, loss of body temperature, respiratory difficulty or failure, and pale mucous membranes (particularly of the gums and eyes). Act immediately.

Keep the animal warm and comfortable.

Stop external bleeding.

Place the animal in a head-down position at 30 degrees to the horizontal.

Call the vet immediately.

Skin disorders

Skin problems in dogs are among the most common and yet most difficult areas of veterinary practice.

Cysts

Sebaceous cysts are formed in the skin when the gland that supplies grease to a hair becomes blocked. The contents of these cysts often appear 'cheesy'. This kind of cyst can be expressed or removed surgically, but provided they do not worry the dog, there is no reason to treat them. (See also FEET DISORDERS: INTERDIGITAL CYSTS.)

Eczema

Eczema is a general term used to describe inflammation of the skin. There are five common types: acute moist eczema, allergic eczema, digital eczema, dry eczema and scrotal eczema.

Acute moist eczema (hot spots) occurs in hot, humid summer weather. The dog begins to scratch in a particular area because of fleas or mites or, in some cases, a high carbohydrate diet (bread, potatoes, porridge). If it can, it will lick and bite at the area. Finally the skin is broken and surface bacteria are able to establish a moist dermatitis. Examination reveals an acute and painful circular moist patch. This can occur within twenty-four hours. Usually the area is devoid of hair, but sometimes there may be a scab, intermingled with hair. These so-called 'hot spots' spread rapidly; light-coloured dogs such as Golden Labradors, Golden Retrievers, Corgis and golden-coloured Pugs are particularly susceptible. Common sites are those where the dog can scratch or lick—for example, the base of the ears, around the jaw and on the hindquarters. Treatment is to alter the diet to eliminate any possible allergies to a high-carbohydrate content, and to eliminate any irritating causative agents such as fleas, infections of the ears or anal gland irritation. The affected area should be washed thoroughly with an antibacterial shampoo or soap several times. Each time, keep the shampoo on the affected area for about fifteen minutes to kill the staphylococcal germs. Clip the surrounding hair so that an astringent dye such as gentian violet, mercurochrome or triple dye can be applied to the area. Sometimes the lesions can be very large and can irritate the dog severely. In these cases a veterinary examination is warranted. Anti-inflammatory injections, together with antibiotics, may be necessary.

Allergic eczema is one of the most common skin problems in warm countries. The allergic reaction may be because of fleas, mites, environmental vegetation such as grasses, or diet. Allergies to plants are the most troublesome; they may flare 'up every time the pet roams in the garden or only at certain times of the year. The types of vegetation most likely to cause allergies are wandering jew, paspalum, kikuyu and buffalo grass. Lesser irritations can result from allergies to straw, wool or nylon. Low-slung breeds such as Dachshunds, Corgis and Cocker Spaniels are more susceptible. An acute red rash will appear suddenly on the undercarriage, sometimes with angry pimples or larger infected areas. The dog scratches the affected area incessantly, setting up a self-inflicted cycle of injury. Treatment has two aims: to eliminate the allergic cause, and to break the self-inflicting cycle of events by the administration of antihistamine injections or tablets and the topical application of ointments or astringents.

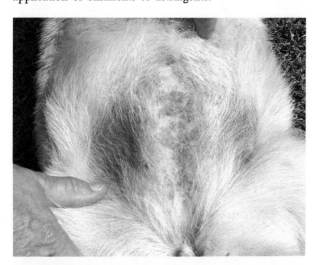

Staphylococcal dermatitis of the abdomen.

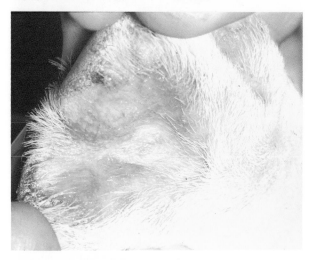

White-coloured dogs such as this Bull Terrier are prone to skin allergies.

Digital eczema This frequently occurs between the toes, where the dog licks because of some initiating cause, usually a grass allergy. The moisture and natural bacteria from the dog's tongue set up an inflammatory process. Sometimes the inflammation may be transferred to the muzzle. Frequently the pads become swollen, sore and painful. Treatment is the same as for allergic eczema.

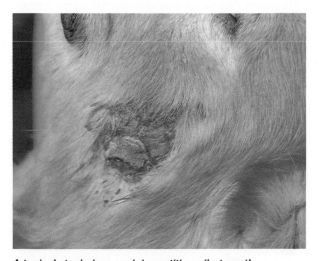

A typical staphylococcal dermatitis or 'hot spot'.

Dry eczema This is one of the most difficult skin conditions to diagnose. The causes are often obscure and it seems to be more common in pedigreed dogs. Sometimes a diet high in starch or carbohydrate can be at fault. Symptoms are persistent scratching producing a dry, scaly area. Veterinary examination will be required to eliminate other possible causes such as mange mites, fleas and lice. Treatment is usually by anti-inflammatory injections and ointments, plus any other remedial measures prescribed by the veterinarian.

Scrotal eczema This is a moist dermatitis of the skin of the scrotum, seen particularly in Old English Sheepdogs and Chows. The large pendulous testicles in these breeds cause the overlying skin to stretch to a point where circulation is impaired, allowing dermatitis to become established. Treatment is the same as for acute moist eczema. If this is not effective castration is recommended.

Fleas

Flea bite allergy is one of the main causes of skin problems in small animals. Fleas are wingless insects with legs adapted for jumping. They are not host-specific and go from one animal to another. Fleas are also the intermediate host for the flea tapeworm. The eggs are laid on the host animal from where they soon fall to the ground and infest the dog's environment. Depending on weather conditions, the egg can hatch in a few days to a few weeks. Vibration is needed for hatching, which explains why houses that have been empty for some time often suffer massive flea problems when they are reoccupied. The adult female flea can lay up to 500 eggs during her lifetime, which is usually two years. All dogs can play host to fleas, but ungroomed animals, particularly long-haired dogs, provide the ideal environment for fleas to congregate. The most common site for fleas is the base of the tail and forward along the back line, but in severe cases fleas will be seen all over the body.

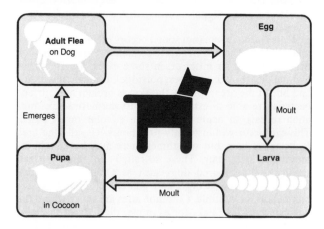

Chronic flea dermatitis: Note *the extensive inflammation of the skin and hair loss.*

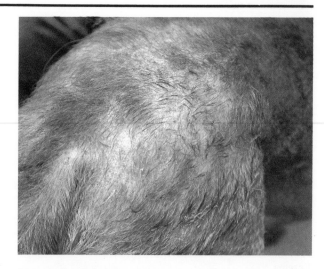

A flea chart.

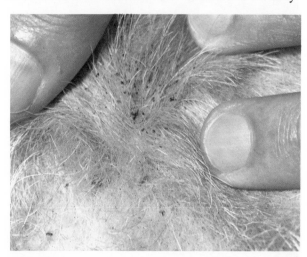

Flea bite allergic dermatitis: Note *the black spots which are flea faeces.*

Many animals become hypersensitive to the irritating bites. Symptoms of flea bite dermatitis include partial hair loss, red skin, flaky scaling and intense irritation, and in the later stages the hair becomes bristly around the tail area rather than soft. In severe cases the dog may be partially bald over the tail and back area with few hairs, and the skin becomes elephant-like. Large numbers of fleas and their droppings (little black spots) will be found if you 'back-comb' the hair over the tail area. The dog also has an unpleasant smell.

Fleas breed in dust, debris and bedding material. It is essential for control to treat both the host and its surroundings. Other hosts such as rats and mice should be erad-

icated. Dogs should be clipped prior to treatment. Flea powders containing carbaryl, amitraz or Malathion should be used—the powder should be brushed into the dog's coat twice a week and any debris burnt. Alternatively, flea rinses may be used on a weekly basis. Flea collars are 95 per cent effective for periods of up to five months but they are rendered ineffective by immersion in water. Oral insecticides given in the form of tablets or liquids are also available—these are administered every third or fourth day. Use only one of the above treatments at any one time.

In general fleas spend only short periods on the host and therefore it is extremely important to treat the environment of the affected animals. In some cases it may be necessary to employ professional fumigators. Fleas can be controlled indoors by thorough vacuum cleaning to remove all debris and thorough spraying with an insecticide of all places offering shelter for adult fleas and larvae. This can be achieved by using a residual insecticidal spray around the skirting boards and under furniture. Fumigation may be carried out by placing flaked naphthalene on the floor at the rate of 2 kilograms per 10 square metres and leaving treated areas sealed for forty-eight hours.

Stables, kennels and the ground underneath the house should be treated for fleas. Treat all animals and eradicate rats and mice, clean up dust and burn surface litter. Sprinkle coarse salt on the soil and keep damp for two to three weeks. Spray lower walls and places that would provide shelter for fleas with insecticidal preparations.

Flies

Several species of flies will attack dogs, the most troublesome being the stable-fly' which is a particular nuisance during summer and autumn. It is a blood sucker, has a painful bite and is fond of ear tips. The usual signs are black, crusty sores on the tips and folds of the ear, with loss of hair over the affected areas. Fly-repellant ointments and lotions should be applied twice daily. Where possible keep your dog in a fly-proofed area during daylight hours. The ears should be cleaned and mercurochrome or triple dye applied to the ears twice daily

Once the initiating cause is eliminated the ears will heal. Long-haired dogs sometimes harbour maggots around the anal area or around infected wounds. Hair should be clipped away and the area cleaned. Visible maggots should be removed and the area dusted with insecticidal powder.

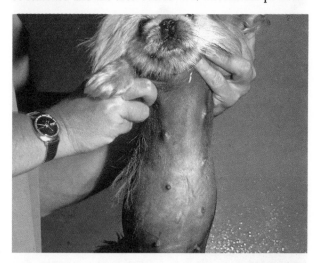

Sertoli cell testicular tumour causing extensive hair loss in this terrier.

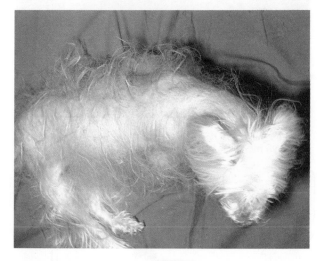

Hair loss due to Cushing's Disease.

Hormonal baldness
Hormonal baldness can occur in young pups at birth, often as the result of thyroid deficiency through lack of iodine in the mother's food. Supplementation of the pup's food with thyroid extract tablets, combined with small doses of iodine, is often effective.

The same condition can occur in females and is due to failure of the thyroid gland to produce sufficient thyroxin. The animal seems dull, the coat harsh, and bare patches appear under the throat, on the flanks and behind the thighs. Various tablets are available to rectify this problem. In whelping bitches a hormonal deficiency may cause the coat to fall out in patches especially around the rear. There

is no itching. Hormonal injections may be used, but multi-hormone tablets give a good result.

In middle-aged to old-aged male dogs the hair may fall out along the back and sides, and the dog may become attracted to others of its own sex. This may be due to a sertoli cell tumour of the testicle. Sometimes all of the hair will fall out. The best cure is castration. A completely new coat often grows in twelve to fourteen weeks.

In Cushing's disease, too much cortisone is produced by the body and the animal loses hair.

Lice
Lice are small wingless insects (1–3 millimetres long) which live as permanent dwellers on the skin of the dog. They spread from dog to dog mainly by contact and are very host-specific. The females glue their eggs to hair fibres. Lice can be found on all parts of the body but prefer areas where the skin is folded, so the pendent ears of Spaniels and similar breeds are often infested. Usual signs are itchiness, redness of the skin, hair loss and trauma caused by the dog scratching. Biting lice are most common in puppies and in dogs that cannot groom themselves, while sucking lice are more prevalent in long-haired dogs.

Eradication of lice is easy because the complete life cycle is spent on the host. In a long-haired breed, clip the dog's coat back to the skin all over and wash the dog once a week with an insecticidal rinse, such as Malathion, Seven or Diazinon, for four weeks.

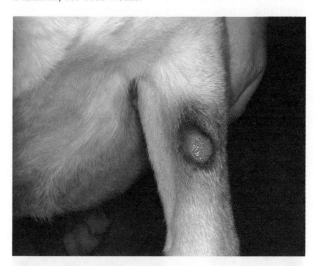

Lick granuloma always occurs on the limbs in a convenient position for licking.

Lick granuloma
This condition is brought on by the dog constantly licking a particular part of the body and causing ulceration. The most common sites are the forelegs and the outside of the hock region of the hindlegs. These are the areas which can be licked at leisure when the dog is lying down. The irritation can start from a small scratch or abrasion. Certain breeds such as Labradors, Boxers, Great Danes and Fox Terriers are particularly susceptible to this condition. As licking starts and perpetuates the problem, the first step is to prevent the dog licking the area. This can be done by bandaging, or by using an Elizabethan collar or a bucket over the dog's head. Treatment includes corticosteroid ointments, corticosteroid injections into the lesion, and in some cases cryotherapy, where the skin over the affected area is deep frozen for several minutes. Sometimes surgical excision or radiation of the lesion is successful. Frequently these conditions are the result of boredom.

Lumps under the skin
All lumps under the skin should be checked by a vet, particularly if they are increasing in size. Sometimes they are

due to tumour formation but in many cases a fatty lump may appear in an obese dog. The latter are usually not harmful and in some cases can even fluctuate in size.

Mites

These are found on or just below the skin surface. The most common are demodectic mange mites and sarcoptic mange mites (or scabies).

Demodectic mange mites These are microscopic mites which complete their life cycle deep in the sweat glands and hair follicles of the skin. Demodectic mange usually occurs in dogs under a year old, usually in short-haired breeds. Infection is by direct contact, so a bitch can transfer the mites to her pups during suckling. The most common lesion occurs around the eyes. The dog loses hair around the eyelids giving a bespectacled appearance. Other lesions can occur around the muzzle and back of the legs. There are two forms of demodectic mange: squamous, and pustular.

In the squamous form the hair falls out in patches and dry lesions appear which become inflamed and swollen. These patches appear as local areas around the eyes, muzzle folds, elbows, feet and neck. There is little evidence of irritation and the condition may remain static for several years. However, it may become generalised, with widespread hair loss accompanied by thickening of the skin.

The pustular form of demodectic mange results from a secondary bacterial infection. The skin becomes thickened, wrinkled and inflamed, and is obviously itchy.

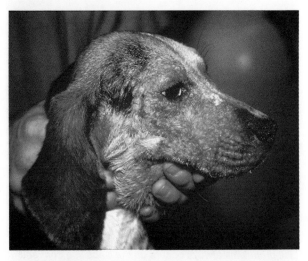

Severe demodectic mange.

Treatment for demodectic mange is complicated and requires veterinary attention.

Demodectic mange is hard to treat, and always requires veterinary attention. You should first clip the dog, then cleanse its skin with an agent such as Seleen, generally available from pet shops, chemists and vets. Treatment is complicated; always take the advice of your vet.

Sarcoptic mange (scabies).

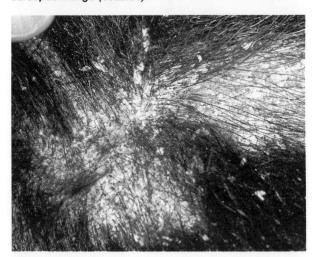

Scabies: Note *the flaking skin, and redness due to intensive mite irritation.*

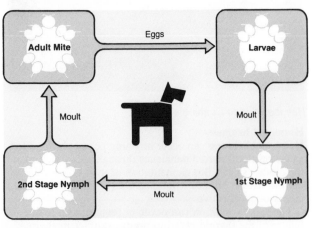

Life cycle of the mange mite.

Scabies With sarcoptic mange mites (scabies) the dermatitis is characterised by intense itching, scaling and loss of hair. The lesions usually occur on the muzzle and edges of the ears, extending backwards on to the whole body. The

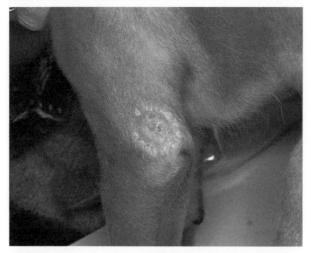

A classic ringworm lesion — a round patch of crusty skin or 'ring'.

A benign skin tumour, a common problem on older dogs.

lesions may not be sharply defined, and the coat has a moth-eaten appearance. There is also a dry form of scabies which occurs in young pups. Instead of the usual irritation accompanied by pustule formation, the skin becomes covered with large bran-like scales and the hair may lift off in large tufts. Although the diagnosis of the disease is difficult, treatment is quite simple. Insecticidal treatment with washes is highly effective. Scabies infection has become less common in urban areas as insecticides are in general use.

Ringworm

Ringworm is fairly common in young puppies. The term 'ringworm' is a misnomer in that the infecting organism is not a worm, but one of four types of fungus. The fungi live either on the skin surface or in the hairs of the affected area, and spread rapidly between puppies, particularly where there is poor feeding or overcrowding. The first signs of ringworm are scratching and biting of the skin. Examination reveals a round patch of crusty skin with the hairs falling out. Laboratory analysis of skin scrapings confirms the diagnosis. Because ringworm spreads rapidly, infected dogs should be quarantined from others. Children should be forbidden to handle the pet since all forms of dog ringworm can infect humans. The best treatment is to use antifungal tablets and washes..Ointments alone are inadequate because the fungus will spread through the hair.

Urticaria

Urticaria is a very common allergic condition. It affects pups and adult dogs of all ages and is usually the result of a bee or wasp sting. Fly bites, chemical toxins from some plants, or food preservatives can also cause the problem. The dog's head and the skin of the eyelids bulge and swell, making the dog look 'old'. Sometimes patches of skin become covered in lumps. In severe cases the dog has difficulty in breathing. The dog should be taken to the vet for an injection of antihistamine. Some relief at home is given by the application of household ammonia products.

Warts

Warts are extremely common in dogs. In young animals they appear around the mouth and lips. In old dogs they can grow anywhere. Because warts are caused by a virus, they are usually self-limiting and finally fall off. Sometimes warts may cause mechanical interference in some parts of the body and may bleed. In these cases surgery is the answer.

Snake bite

Whether the dog survives a snake bite depends on the type of snake and the amount of venom the snake was able to inject into the animal. The dog's tough skin and hair make it difficult for the snake's fangs to penetrate, particularly if the dog is moving around. Symptoms are trembling, vomiting, salivation, diarrhoea, weakness in the back legs, dilated pupils, slow or absent light reflexes of the pupils, respiratory distress, bloody urine, continuous bleeding from the wound where the snake has bitten and a flaccid paralysis progressing to coma or to respiratory failure. Reaction to the bite can be sudden. Sometimes the animal will collapse soon after being bitten, recover almost completely within half-an-hour, then begin to show other symptoms. In other cases the symptoms may not develop for some time. The key signs are weakness or paralysis in the back legs and dilated pupils. Blood takes a long time to clot. Sometimes snake bite may be confused with tick bite, poisoning by organo-phosphorus insecticides, or an acute infectious disease such as canine hepatitis or leptospirosis.

In treating snake bite it is helpful to know the type of snake responsible so that the correct antivenene can be administered—but don't put your own life at risk. The principles of treatment are:

Neutralise the venom with antivenene.

Treat locally: wash the wound and apply a firm wide bandage if the bite is on a limb, but do not cut the site of the bite. Keep the dog calm and take it to the vet as soon as possible.

Provide general supportive measures for shock, paralysis and loss of blood. Keep the dog warm on the way to the veterinarian.

Sores

See SKIN DISORDERS.

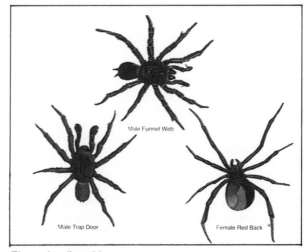

Male Funnel Web

Male Trap Door

Female Red Back

Three deadly spiders.

Spider bite

Spider bite should be treated in the same way as SNAKE BITE. The symptoms can be similar.

Staggering

Staggering can be due to a number of different causes: concussion or trauma caused by motor vehicle accident; disc lesion or disc protrusion, which may affect the nerves to the back legs; severe constipation; spondylosis, which usually occurs in the aged dog and particularly in large breeds—it is caused by calcified joints in the back impinging on the nerves to the back legs; tick paralysis; tranquillisation from drugs; or weakness caused by other disease.

Stings

See ALLERGIC REACTIONS, and SKIN DISORDERS: URTICARIA.

Strabismus

See EYE DISORDERS.

Straining

Straining can be due to: constipation; blocked anal glands; diverticulum; faecal matting in long-haired dogs (see ANAL OCCLUSION); prostatitis; or urinary blockage.

Stroke

See NERVOUS CONDITIONS.

Sunburn

This is rarely seen in dogs. (See Cat section.)

Swelling

See ALLERGIC REACTIONS.

Tail injuries

Injuries to the tip of the tail are usually caused by a young dog chasing its tail and biting it, or a dog catching its tail in a door. The happy dog wags its tail, bumping it on tables, doorposts and other objects, thus continually re-opening the wound and stopping healing. Bandage the tail with adhesive bandage until it heals or, if this fails, take the dog to the vet to have the tail cauterised.

Tail kinks

This usually occurs in puppies as the result of a dislocated joint in the tail. The joint can be reset and splinted under anaesthetic, but if left untreated will cause the dog no problem. The only reason for treating a kinked tail is cosmetic.

Tail limp

Sometimes a dog that normally carries its tail elevated will have a limp tail. This can be because of bruising or fractures at the base of the tail, or infected anal glands.

Tail removal

See Tails and dewclaws, p. 113.

Teeth

See MOUTH DISORDERS.

Third eyelid

See EYE DISORDERS.

Thirst

See DRINKING, INCREASED.

Ticks

There are several species of ticks; but the most important to dog owners is the paralysis tick, which lives on warm-blooded fauna such as bandicoots, possums and other scrub-dwelling animals. Domestic animals and humans are accidental hosts, dogs and cats being the most susceptible.

A fully engorged female can produce a single batch of between 2000 to 3000 eggs within seven to fourteen days of falling from a host. After hatching, the larvae become active within seven days and attach to a host. At this stage they are very small. After four to six days they drop off and go into a second growth stage and finally into adulthood. Infestations can occur at any time of the year if conditions are suitable, but usually they are confined to the spring and

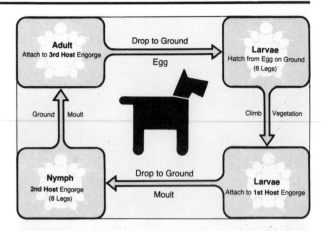

Life cycle of the tick.

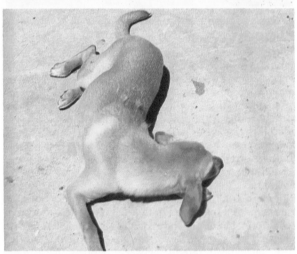

Spastic behaviour of a dog affected by tick poisoning.

summer. The tick population in any year is usually governed by the previous year's rainfall and temperature variations. The main sign of a dog suffering from tick bite is paralysis, beginning at the hindlegs, moving to the front legs and then to the respiratory system.

Progressive signs to be watched for are: the dog is reluctant to walk up a flight of stairs or jump into a car; the dog may have a slight wobbliness or weakness in the hindlegs; vomiting; depression; pupil dilation; loss of control of the hindlegs, with partial loss of foreleg co-ordination; salivation; respiration becomes laboured and more frequent; as paralysis becomes advanced, barking ceases; increased blood pressure in conjunction with decreasing and irregular heartbeat.

The cause of these reactions is not yet fully understood, as the chemical structure of the toxin has not yet been identified, but it is strong enough to paralyse cats, calves, sheep, foals and even humans. The interval between the attachment of the tick and the onset of weakness in the hindquarters is up to four days, although in some cases clinical signs may not be seen until all the ticks have engorged and dropped off. If partly engorged ticks are removed, paralysis may still occur one or two days later, depending on the amount of toxin that has already been injected. In these cases the attachment site is seen as a raised crater-like swelling.

Removal of engorged ticks from an otherwise normal dog does not mean that the dog is out of danger. Enough toxin may already have been injected into the dog to cause its death. Tick toxin is as dangerous as snake bite. A dog bitten by a paralysis tick can die if not taken to a vet for full

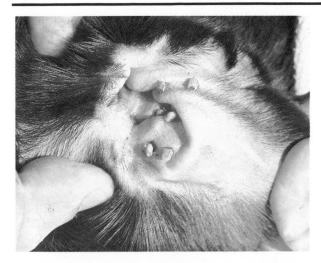

Adult 5-day-old ticks in the ear-lobe.

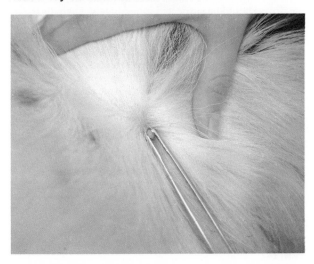

Grasp the tick as close to the skin as possible and pull it off the dog.

assessment immediately. Even if a tick is removed as soon as the first symptoms are noticed, the dog has only a 50 per cent chance of recovery without further treatment. The toxin can take up to two days to have its full effect. The longer the delay between the appearance of the symptoms and the giving of anti-toxin injections, the greater the risk to the dog's life. Therefore, take the dog to the vet for anti-toxin immediately.

Ticks can be found on any part of the body, but 80 per cent are found between the nose and the shoulders. Areas such as the toes, the external ear canal and inside the anus and mouth should be thoroughly searched. Once the tick has been found, place a pair of tweezers as close to the skin as possible and gently pull the tick out. If the mouth parts are left in the skin, do not worry; they will fester out. Another tick cannot grow from them. Do not place methylated spirits on the tick or cut the tick's body, as these methods allow a very angry tick to continue to inject toxin in its saliva into the dog's body. When searching for ticks always remove collars or leads. Dogs in tick danger areas may need to be clipped all over every summer and an anti-tick wash applied weekly. Dogs affected by ticks should be bathed in an insecticidal wash to help kill any ticks. But don't rely on this method—hand searching is the only effective means.

To control tick infestation certain steps should be taken regularly to protect your pet.

Bathe the dog weekly in an anti-tick wash and use a flea collar. These two methods will help reduce tick infestation but they are not foolproof.

Search your dog every day, particularly around the head and shoulders, remembering to remove collars and leads before you start.

Eliminate any thick undergrowth from around your home and discourage fauna such as possums and bandicoots which are major intermediate hosts for the tick.

(See also BABESIOSIS.)

Tongue
See MOUTH DISORDERS.

Tonsillitis
Tonsillitis occurs most frequently in toy breeds such as Poodles and Maltese Terriers. The symptoms are lethargy, fever, loss of appetite and a slight cough. The condition can be alleviated by antibiotics, but repeated bouts will require removal of the tonsil tissue by surgery. Once the tonsils have been removed in dogs where they are causing a problem, the difference is remarkable.

Toxaemia
Toxaemia is any condition in which the blood contains toxic products. These can be produced by the body cells or caused by the growth of organisms. The clinical signs of toxaemia vary widely and depend on the type of toxin involved.

Generally, the dog will be lethargic, off its food, and the mucous membranes of the eyes and gums may be red rather than pink.

Toxic conditions are usually dangerous and any dog suspected of having toxaemia should be given urgent veterinary attention.

Trichiasis
See EYE DISORDERS.

Tumours
Tumours are the result of an abnormal development of cells within the body, whose growth does not conform with the laws of tissue differentiation. Tumours may be classified as benign or malignant. Benign tumours usually grow slowly and are restricted to the point where they first develop. They may cause damage to surrounding tissues but usually don't invade the neighbouring areas. Surgical removal is usually satisfactory. Malignant tumours usually grow rapidly and spread to neighbouring tissues; they can develop in other parts of the body after being carried by the circulation. Surgical removal of malignant tumours rarely completely removes the cancerous development. Sometimes malignant tumours, if near the surface of the

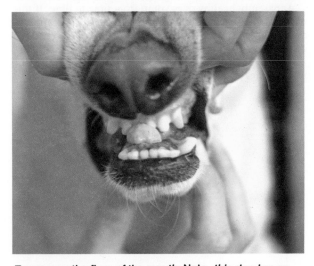

Tumour on the floor of the mouth: Note *this dog has an undershot jaw.*

body (for example, in the mammary glands), may ulcerate through the skin. Some tumours respond to radiation therapy, others to drugs. Most require surgical removal. Veterinary treatment is essential and should be started as early as possible. There is a tendency on the part of owners to delay the first veterinary consultation as they are afraid of being told that the condition is incurable.

Twitching
See SHIVERING.

Urine disorders
The urine is often a good indication of the condition of the animal. Normal urine is a light clear yellow.

Dark or bloody urine can indicate infection of the bladder (cystitis).

Bladder stones can cut the inside of the bladder wall, releasing blood into the urine. Cloudy urine means there is an abnormality.

Increased frequency is usually accompanied by thirst. The causes include DIABETES, DIARRHOEA, FEVER, HEART DISEASE and KIDNEY DISEASE. If an animal is showing signs of urinary disease, a 30-millilitre specimen should be collected in a clean vessel for veterinary inspection. This is best done by locking the dog up overnight and walking it on a lead the next morning with container at the ready. Take the sample to the vet within four hours.

INCONTINENCE usually occurs in desexed females. They unconsciously urinate while lying down. This can be because of a bladder infection or a hormone deficiency.

Urinary tract blockage
Blockage should be suspected when the dog strains to urinate but passes only a few drops. Sometimes the urine is discoloured. Usually the cause is stones in the bladder. In the male dog these may enter the urethra and pass through to block the urethral tract in the penis. The condition is extremely painful and the dog should be taken to the vet.

Urticaria
See ALLERGIC REACTIONS, SKIN DISORDERS.

Vaccination
See INFECTIOUS DISEASES and pp. 96–7.

Vomiting
The history of the vomiting attack is important to your vet when making a diagnosis and treating the animal. Is the vomiting related to eating? How many times a day does the dog vomit? Is the vomited food digested or not? What colour is the vomited matter? If possible, take a sample of the vomit to the vet when you take your dog.

Apparently healthy dogs vomit from time to time. If this happens once every fourth or fifth day and the dog appears completely normal in every other way, there is no need for concern. Dogs will sometimes eat grass for medicinal purposes and then vomit. This may be the dog's method of internal cleansing.

In the dog, vomiting is a symptom common to many diseases. Vomiting is controlled by a centre in the brain which can be stimulated by disagreeable tastes or smells, toxins, drugs, infections and poisons. Prolonged vomiting is very weakening for the dog and it is important to diagnose and treat the cause as quickly as possible. In young puppies vomiting can be caused by dilation of the food tract between the throat and the stomach. This condition can be controlled by making the dog stand on its hind legs to eat and giving it small quantities at a time, several times a day. The puppy will eventually grow out of it.

Vomiting can also be caused by: an acute abdominal condition caused by pancreatitis or peritonitis; swallowing a bone or other object which causes a blockage in the intestinal tract; a deep internal wound or ruptured organ, possibly after a car accident.

Diseases such as distemper, hepatitis, infected womb (pyometra), septicaemia, or kidney disease can also cause vomiting.

Drugs—when a dog commences to vomit while on drugs, the drugs should be suspected immediately. Digitalis (heart tablets), for example, given to excess cause vomiting. Stop the tablets for a day and then commence with half the recommended dosage. To prevent the build-up of the drug in the dog's system, only give the tablets six days a week. Certain antibiotics and morphine can cause vomiting. In any such case it is always best to consult your veterinarian about the problem.

Dry retching or coughing as if the dog has a bone caught in its throat is typical of the virus 'kennel cough'.

Indigestion, overeating, bad food (particularly if a dog is likely to dig up old bones or meat) and poison.

Nervous problems such as car or motion sickness or lesions within the brain.

Ticks—one of the initial signs of tick poisoning is vomiting and salivation.

Wandering
See BEHAVIOURAL PROBLEMS.

Warts
See SKIN DISORDERS.

Weight changes
See APPETITE, DECREASED AND INCREASED.

Small dogs can be weighed on ordinary household kitchen scales. Put a towel on the scales first.

Larger dogs can be weighed on bathroom scales. The simplest method is to carry the dog on to the scales and then subtract your own weight.

Whelping problems
See Breeding, p. 110.

Wobbler syndrome
See BONE PROBLEMS OF GROWING DOGS.

Worms
See pp. 97–104.

FIRST AID BOX

The number of things that could be kept in an emergency first aid box is limitless. The following is a basic list.

A roll of 5-centimetre wide adhesive bandage, such as Elastoplast
Two rolls of conforming gauze bandage or clean white cloth
Cotton-wool
Antiseptic wash (e.g. chlorhexidine)
Hydrogen peroxide 3%
A tape to muzzle the dog
Scissors
Guillotine-type nail cutters
50 millilitres liquid paraffin
Tweezers
Thermometer
Acriflavin, mercurochrome, triple dye, zinc cream
Wound dressing powder (preferably one containing an antibiotic)
Soluble aspirin
Bicarbonate of soda
Antibiotic/cortisone skin ointment
Antibiotic dispenser
Antibiotic eye ointment
Eye wash
Flea powder
Flea rinse

FISH

Selecting aquarium fish

There are three categories of fish suitable for the home aquarium: tropical, coldwater and marine. The marine fish require varying temperatures, from very cold to warm, depending on their natural geographical origin; because of the problems of keeping fish in saline water, they are not as popular as other fish. Tropical and coldwater fish are equally popular.

It is important for those unfamiliar with the keeping of fish to read the whole of this chapter before purchasing. Fish are very sensitive and even a few hours in the wrong environment will be courting danger.

Tropical fish

The tropical fish are kept in temperatures of about 25°C. They tend to be more expensive to buy than coldwater fish and are therefore usually kept in better aquariums (which have such equipment as aerators) and often by enthusiasts prepared to give that extra attention that ensures survival.

Some of the colourful tropical fish available

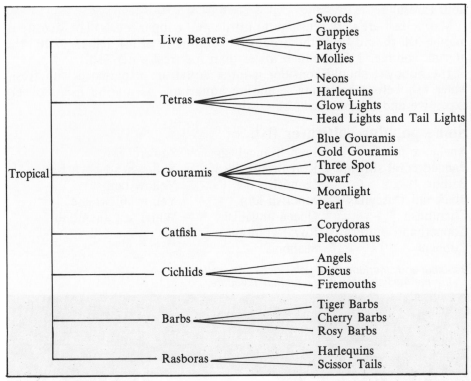

Tropical	Live Bearers	Swords
		Guppies
		Platys
		Mollies
	Tetras	Neons
		Harlequins
		Glow Lights
		Head Lights and Tail Lights
	Gouramis	Blue Gouramis
		Gold Gouramis
		Three Spot
		Dwarf
		Moonlight
		Pearl
	Catfish	Corydoras
		Plecostomus
	Cichlids	Angels
		Discus
		Firemouths
	Barbs	Tiger Barbs
		Cherry Barbs
		Rosy Barbs
	Rasboras	Harlequins
		Scissor Tails

Dwarf Gouramis — tropical fish.

Gold Sail-Fin Mollie — tropical fish.

Silver Angel — tropical fish.

If a problem begins in the aquarium, the Tetras will be first to show signs. Tropical fish tend generally to be less susceptible to build up of ammonia and nitrites—but this could be that they tend to live in better aquariums.

Coldwater fish

Coldwater fish for the home are virtually confined to the Goldfish, which like a temperature of about 22°C. They should be kept in either neutral or slightly alkaline water.

Goldfish are not very tolerant to build up of nitrites or acidity in their water. They tend to have short lives in many homes because of this. A contributing factor is that Goldfish are cheap and tend to be acquired by newcomers to aquarium-keeping (particularly children) who place them in an unfurnished bowl without aerators, heaters and so on. These people often neglect to change the water regularly, and overfeed, and leave tops off the aquarium—all things that test the livelihood of any self-respecting fish.

Gold Fantail is a common freshwater goldfish.

Comet — a freshwater goldfish.

Threadfin Butterfly fish; this coral fish is a marine fish.

Fire Clown — a marine fish.

Types of Goldfish

Goldfish
- Comet
- Fan Tail
- Blackmoor
- Calico
- Shubunkin

Marine fish

Marine fish are kept at varying temperatures depending on their origin. Some marine fish are from tropical areas of the world, while others are from temperate zones and will be kept at lower temperatures. It is safest to ask the dealer for the most suitable temperature for specific fish.

The seawater that the fish are kept in can be natural or synthetic. For those who live close to the ocean and want to use it, collect where the water is clear. Always use a non-toxic, non-corrosive vessel and store the water for six weeks in the dark before using. Always have a reserve of water in case of emergency.

Artificial seawater mixes are available commercially—follow the instructions carefully.

Marine fish are very sensitive to nitrite and copper levels. The density of marine fish should be of the order of 1 centimetre of fish length to 10 litres of tank volume. This is much lower than for freshwater fish.

The hobbyist should consider gaining aquarium experience with freshwater fish before acquiring a marine aquarium, as marine fish are very expensive and mistakes will be costly.

Some popular saltwater fish

Anemone fish
Banded coral shrimp
Batfish
Black tail Dascyllas
Cherubfish
Copperband butterfly
Cubbyu

French angelfish
Korean angelfish
Lionfish
Moorish idol
Queen angelfish
Royal gramma
Seahorse

Squirrel fish
Yellowhead jawfish
Yellow tang
Yellowtail wrasse
White sea anemone

Beautiful body markings and rich overall colouration on this marine fish make it an aquarium favourite.

The aquarium

Selecting the site of the aquarium

There are several factors that influence the choice of site for an aquarium.

Water is heavy

4.5 litres of water weighs more than 4.5 kilograms and when you add the weight of the tank and the gravel, the average weight of the aquarium is more than 4.5 kilograms per 4.5 litres. A 45-litre aquarium, for example, will weigh about 60 kilograms. Its support should therefore be sturdy.

Avoid direct sunlight

Most aquarists prefer to avoid exposing their aquariums to direct sunlight. Although it does not affect the health of the fish directly, it tends to promote the rapid growth of algae which is undesirable because it creates unnecessary maintenance problems.

Temperature control is important

Direct sunlight may overheat the aquarium. Overheating can also be caused by closeness to room heaters. Do not place the aquarium close to air conditioning units, open windows or outside doors either. Changes in water temperature greater than 2°C above or 1°C below the optimum temperature for the type of fish you are keeping can cause shock and illness.

Will the tank be accessible?

The final consideration in assessing the site for your aquarium is whether you can easily reach your heat controls and air valves.

Selecting the aquarium

When you have decided on the type of fish you want to keep, your next question is how many? These two factors will determine the minimum aquarium size. The rule of thumb for small freshwater fish is to allow 2 litres of water for every centimetre of fish; for marine fish, 10 litres per centimetre. Your first tank should be at least 45 litres, preferably larger. This allows a greater choice of fish and plants and requires less maintenance.

A tropical fish tank: Note *the healthy appearance of the tank in general.*

The capacity of an aquarium can be measured by multiplying the length, height and width in centimetres and dividing by 1000. This gives the contents in litres. Allow for any rocks or ornaments in the aquarium; these usually occupy about 10 per cent of the volume.

The height of your tank should be no more than 20 per cent greater than the width, otherwise the surface of the tank will be too small to allow the water to absorb sufficient amounts of oxygen. A rule of thumb is 65 square centimetres of water surface for every 2.5 centimetres of fish length.

Other necessary equipment

Cover and lighting

Covering the aquarium is necessary for several reasons. It saves money by reducing heat loss. By keeping the air temperature above the water the same as the water temperature, the water will stay warmer and will not overwork the heater. The cover also slows down the rate of water loss by evaporation. A cover prevents your fish from jumping out or friendly pets from jumping in. It also stops aerosol insecticides entering the water. A cover also serves as a holder for your lighting.

Thermostatic heater

Unless you plan to keep only coldwater fish, the aquarium will require a thermostatically controlled heater to maintain the water at a tropical temperature. Heaters vary in cost, accuracy and reliability, but always purchase the best you can afford.

Filtration and aeration equipment

The major objective of all filtration systems is clear water plus aeration. If the water circulates from the water surface throughout the aquarium, you will have good aeration. One device used to encourage water circulation is an air stone. Placed on or near the aquarium floor, the porous air stone releases bubbles which push bottom water to the surface and create a circular flow. Because the water will circulate debris from the bottom as well, the air stone should be placed 5 centimetres above the gravel.

The force of air rushing to the surface is often coupled to a filter by means of an airlift. The airlift is a tube that confines the air bubbles and uses them to force water through the filter. Filter systems vary in cost and complexity, and it is best to consult the pet shop dealer for advice on the one most suited to your needs.

Sand or gravel

Whether you choose natural or coloured sand it is best to obtain it from your pet store. If the gravel is artificially coloured, make sure that it is non-toxic and colourfast. As a general rule you will need approximately 1 kilogram of sand for each 4.5 litres of water in the aquarium.

Ornaments, rocks and plants

Driftwood, petrified wood, bamboo cane and non-metallic rocks are generally safe in an aquarium. Metals other than stainless steel can poison your fish. Some objects (coral, limestone and marble, for example) will dissolve in fresh water and thereby change the water chemistry.

Plants add colour and beauty to an aquarium and, very importantly, they offer areas of retreat for the fish. You can use living plants, artificial plants or both. Live plants have advantages and disadvantages. The advantages: Besides being more natural, they compete with algae for nutrients. Their very presence will help reduce or eliminate algae problems. Along with this, they absorb nitrates and slow down the nitrate build-up. Nitrates are waste products and in large quantities are toxic to fish. Plants are also a food source for a number of fish. The disadvantages: Plants are often difficult to grow, requiring specific water conditions and lighting. Decaying plants increase pollution in the aquarium, so any that turn brown or start to disintegrate should be removed quickly. Plastic plants can relieve that barren time when live plants are establishing themselves.

Setting up the aquarium

Thoroughly wash the aquarium, the sand, the rocks, and the ornaments with large quantities of fresh water. Do not use soap or detergents as they are highly toxic to fish.

To wash the gravel, put it in a plastic bag or bucket and add water. Stir the gravel, then drain off the water. When the water stays clear after stirring it is free of debris and the gravel is clean. This will usually take several changes of water. The gravel can then go into the aquarium.

How to fill a tank.

Fill the aquarium approximately half to three-quarters full. Pour the water slowly over a plate (or into the cup of your hand) so that it does not disturb the gravel.

Connect tubing from the air pump to any outlets located inside the aquarium, such as under-gravel filters, air stones or canister filters. The canister should be loaded with filter materials and placed in the aquarium before the air line is connected. Install the air pump above the level of the water so that back-flowing water cannot destroy it, or empty the tank, if the pump fails.

Decorations and plants should now be added and arranged in such a way that the equipment is concealed or at least does not detract from the appearance of the aquarium. Live plants should be kept moist from the time you buy them till they are planted.

How to place air pump correctly.

Add the balance of the water by pouring it slowly into your hand or a cup so that you do not disturb the gravel and plants. Fill the aquarium to near the top, leaving some air space between the water and the cover.

Install the outside filter, thermostatic heater and thermometer according to manufacturers' instructions, and plug in your air pump, power filter and heater. It will take some time for the temperature to stabilise and you may have to adjust your setting. Do not switch on the heater thermostat when it is not immersed in the water.

Water in new aquariums will often turn milky for a day or two. This is caused by a harmless bacterial growth and should disappear naturally. Check the pH and hardness of the water. After your aquarium is operating check the functioning of your equipment and the water conditions again.

The temperature of the water for Goldfish should be 22°C. For tropical fish, the temperature should range between 24 and 27°C. Higher temperatures result in a higher metabolic rate in the fish; lower temperatures tend to increase the risk of the disease white spot (or 'ich'). If everything is working well, purchase your first few fish.

Transferring the fish

There are two methods commonly used to introduce fish into the aquarium. One way is to transfer the fish into separate glass jars, and float the jars in the aquarium for fifteen to twenty minutes. Make certain the jars do not have so much water in them that they sink. Every few minutes add small amounts of aquarium water to each jar. After the water temperature in the jar is the same as that in the aquarium, tip the fish into a net and release it into the aquarium. Do not pour water from other tanks into your aquarium as it may introduce unwanted organisms.

The second method uses the plastic bags in which the fish are usually transported. Use the same floating technique, making sure that there is plenty of air in the bag so that the fish do not suffocate. Do not allow the bags to collapse. These methods are tedious, but they will reduce the initial shock to your fish in their new environment.

The reason for introducing only a few fish at first is to initiate the nitrogen cycle, which takes at least twenty to twenty-five days to stabilise. More fish should not be added until the nitrite level has dropped to a safe level, otherwise the fish will die. Nitrite test kits are available from pet shops.

Feeding and control

It is advisable not to feed the fish until they have adapted to their new environment. Watch them closely; if they are hiding in corners, not moving about or looking pale, something is out of order. Recheck your establishment procedure. Is the temperature correct? Was the water too fresh? Is the lighting level in part of the tank too high? Are there sufficient plants to provide hiding for the fish? Are the fish healthy?

Feeding

Tropical and Goldfish tend to be good eaters, while marine fish can be a little fussy. Generally, tropical fish, Goldfish and marine fish can all be fed a similar diet, and there is a wide range of adequate economical commercial fish foods available. The following is a list of some foods of particular delight to each group.

Tropical and coldwater

Food for tropical fish should be high in protein, low in fat and oil. Tropical and Goldfish will all eat kangaroo meat, horse meat, earthworms, mosquito larvae, slaters, house flies (without insecticide), rolled oats, lettuce, spinach, crushed peas and broad beans. Do *not* feed mutton or mince meat.

Marine

Marine fish are particularly partial to dry flake food, shrimps, tubiflex, strips of fresh meat, ground beef, heart, prawns and Pacific plankton. Marine fish are fussy and may prefer chunks, strips, mashed or ground food. When all else fails, offer live food. They love fresh, live, adult brine shrimps.

There are three basic rules about feeding fish: (1) Feed sparingly but often. If all the food is not eaten within five minutes of feeding, you are providing too much and the residue will pollute the aquarium. (2) Change the kind and shape of the food if the fish are not eating it. (3) Be patient with fussy eaters and resort to live foods if necessary.

Avoid continually modifying the aquarium conditions. A stable environment develops a necessary sense of security. Avoid overcrowding. Calculate how much your aquarium can safely keep—remember, for small tropical fish, 2 litres of water for every centimetre of fish—and always have fewer fish than that.

There is a wide range of adequate economical commercial foods available for feeding fish.

Controlling snails

Sooner or later water-snails, the uninvited guests, will appear in the aquarium. They find their way into the tank with plants or with live foods. It is not necessary to use snails for cleaning up excess food and algae. In fact, hungry snails will eat your aquarium plants. A rapid increase in the snail population is a sure sign of overfeeding.

If snails should breed beyond control, do not use chemicals to get rid of them, as dead snails will only foul the water. It is better to feed sparingly for the next few weeks and effect a natural control. Alternatively snails may be picked out with a long pair of clean tongs. Another method is to limit feeding for a few days, then place a saucer on the bottom of the aquarium upside down with some food underneath; the snails adhere to the saucer and can be removed with the saucer.

Aquarium algae

Several types of algae commonly grow in aquariums. One, blue algae, is a sign of an unhealthy aquarium. It grows on the tank floor and the plant leaves, usually an indication of water which is too alkaline or which contains excessive amounts of decayed food.

Green algae is not harmful. Regular cleaning with an aquarium scraper will keep the front glass of your tank free of it. Green algae on the side or back glass where it does not hamper visibility is harmless and does not need to be scraped away—in fact, green algae in the tank is a sign of healthy water and many types of fish nibble on it for a special treat.

Excessive green algae often results from too much light in the aquarium, while brown algae indicates not enough light. In many brightly lit aquariums a green clouding of the water will occur in spring or summer. This is due to microscopic floating algae, and is an indication that too much light is getting to the tank. Another possible cause of clouding is excessive feeding.

Signs of trouble

As you come to know your fish, there are several signs that may indicate physical problems requiring attention. If the fish stay very close to the surface of the water, it can mean that the tank is not getting enough oxygen. This may be due to inefficient or clogged filters, water pollution (due to excess particles of decomposed food), poor aeration or overcrowding. This is serious and requires immediate action. Change at least one-fifth of the water in the tank, replacing it with water of the same temperature. Clean and replenish the filter, siphoning off excess food. Increase aeration and reduce the number of fish.

Another danger sign is cloudy water. This usually results from excess feeding.

Never tap on the glass side of the aquarium, as this is like a sonic boom to the fish and can cause them to go into shock.

Water conditions

The pH level (acidity/alkalinity)

The pH level is particularly important for maintaining and breeding fish. Some fish species prefer alkaline water while others prefer acid. pH levels can be altered by chemicals: use sodium biphosphate for increasing acidity/lowering alkalinity, and sodium bicarbonate for reducing acidity/increasing alkalinity. Excessive alkalinity or acidity for freshwater fish can also be reduced by the use of bottled water. It is best, however, to adapt the fish to the tap water in your community.

A pH level between 6.8 and 7 suits most tropical fish; 7 to 7.2 suits Goldfish; and 8 to 8.3 suits most marine fish.

TABLE OF WATER CONDITIONS

Variables	Tropical	Coldwater	Marine
Temperature	24-27°C	22°C	Varies with origin
pH	6.8–7	7–7.2	8–8.3
Hardness of water	soft	medium	saltwater
Density of fish	1 cm/2 litres	1 cm/2 litres	1 cm/10 litres
Specific gravity	1.00	1.00	1.025

Hardness

Tap water, like natural water, varies in hardness from area to area. 'Hardness' refers to the dissolved salts in the water, mainly those of calcium, sometimes also magnesium. Many tropical fish prefer a relatively soft water. White deposits at the water line are a clear sign of high hardness. Hardness can be reduced by regularly replacing part of the water with aged tap water—the water is aged by allowing it to stand exposed to the atmosphere for one week. This does not decrease hardness if the tap water itself is hard. Then the water needs to be filtered through peat or Zeocarb 225.

An occasional hardness test is a good idea, as sometimes a rock or the gravel in the tank can cause a problem. The hardness level should ideally be below 100 parts per million, except for the few fish species that thrive in hard, alkaline waters. Water can be softened by using an ion exchange resin such as Zeocarb 225. The most logical approach is to remove the hardening factor—that is, the rock, gravel or whatever, from the tank. There is no place for coral or seashells in freshwater tanks because of their hardness factor.

Pollutants

The amount of dissolved nitrites and nitrates in the water is a direct indication of the level of water pollution. High pollution levels impair the health of fish and can be lethal.

Chemical kits for testing the pH, hardness and pollution levels of nitrites and nitrates in your aquarium are available. They should be used regularly. To maintain a low nitrite/nitrate level it is essential to change part of the water regularly.

Regular water changes

A weekly water change of approximately 20 per cent with water of the same temperature is advised. For freshwater fish do not use water from the hot water system as it may be contaminated with copper. The water to be changed should be siphoned from the bottom, making sure that the gravel is gently agitated and that any algae that has accumulated is removed with the water. If the water is very soft, the addition of half a teaspoon of common salt with a pinch of both magnesium sulphate and potassium sulphate is recommended to each 5 litres of replaced water. Temperature and pH should be checked and adjusted if necessary.

Brackish water

Most Catfish will tolerate slightly brackish water such as that containing half a teaspoon of salt, a pinch of potassium sulphate and one of magnesium sulphate per 5 litres of water, as recommended. Most of the common aquarium Catfish (and the Discus) are derived from high up the Amazon River where the water is very soft, very low in salt and very acid. These fish are bred in water containing these quantities of salts at a pH of 6.8 and a temperature of 24–26°C—although the purists may prefer a pH of 6.2 and a temperature of 29–31°C in water containing no salt. Live bearers such as Mollies, Swords and Platys appear to suffer more from lack of salt than do Corydoras and Discus, from the addition of the above quantities.

New fish

Ideally new fish should be quarantined for up to six weeks in a tank reserved for this purpose. Use the transfer methods already described when introducing them to the main tank.

Breeding fish

There are two types of breeding fish: live bearers and egg layers. Goldfish and marine fish are all egg layers only, while tropical fish have both live bearers and egg layers. Live bearers are by far the easiest to breed and are ideal for the beginner.

Live bearers

The most popular live bearers are the large, active tropical fish, which include Swordtails, Platys and Mollies. These all require plenty of space. Live bearers are highly inbred and although inbreeding is necessary to fix the beautiful strains, it also has undesirable effects. Live bearers, if not properly cared for, may suffer from diseases such as ich, shimmy, and various skin diseases. Should the tank temperature fall, the live bearers are usually first affected. They are active fish, both sexually and in growth potential.

Live bearers usually come from harder, more alkaline waters than egg layers. Poorly managed tanks tend to become more acid and hence cause live bearers problems. Live bearers can be kept at lower temperatures (22°C). Those raised at slightly higher temperatures mature more quickly, but their lifespan tends to be shorter. .

pH for live bearers should be 7.0–7.2. Hardness is tolerated by live bearers but it should be kept at approximately 200 p.p.m. General aquarium maintenance as discussed elsewhere in this chapter is most important.

The sex of live bearers is easily distinguished by the presence in the male of the gonopodium. All young live bearers have a fan-like anal fin, but as they mature the male's begins to change shape to the typical narrow 'stick-like' fin (gonopodium). This is usually carried close to the body, while the female anal fin is spread out. By means of a series of specialised muscles, the gonopodium can be moved and inserted into the female for fertilisation. Live bearers' eggs are not discharged from the ovary until long after fertilisation has taken place, and just before the fry are fully developed and ready to be born.

Guppies, Swords and Platys have a regular brood production and will drop young at intervals of twenty-five to thirty-five days, depending on temperature and lighting conditions.

Mollies have irregular brood production and are greatly affected by seasonal or artificial changes in temperature or light. However, since most aquariums provide constant conditions they usually deliver at constant intervals.

The number of young delivered at one time is variable and depends on the age of the mother as well as on her size. The young are about 5 millimetres in length and may number from six to 200 or more. Mollies usually number between twenty and forty, while Swords and Platys number sixty to eighty. Guppies average twenty-five to thirty.

Live bearers have the ability to store the sperm in the female oviduct for up to six months, which means that five or six broods at monthly intervals can be produced without further contact with the male.

Fish selected for breeding should be placed in their own quarters and fed well. Since there is no need for the male after fertilisation, he should be removed as delivery time approaches, because he will eat the young.

In all but dark coloured live bearers, a dark area can appear on the female's body near the vent as she fills with eggs. This is known as the 'gravid spot'. It should not be used as a reliable indication of the fish's sex.

Protection of newborn fry

Since newborn fry are often eaten by adult fish in the aquarium, it is important to provide some form of protection for them. It can be provided mechanically or naturally.

The mechanical method involves the use of devices known as breeding traps which are usually small containers, partially submerged in an aquarium, and which have small openings or slots at the bottom. The female is placed in the containers and the young, which do not swim immediately after delivery, fall through the openings to safety. Obviously, the aquarium containing the trap should be free of other fish likely to eat the fry. Care should also be taken that food does not escape through the bottom of the trap and pollute the water.

The natural method of protection is to provide dense, fine-leaved plants at one end of the aquarium and make sure that that end is more brightly lit than the other. The young will move towards the light and the protection.

Some hobbyists prefer to use this natural method and to overfeed the female so that she will be less tempted to pursue the fry as food.

Food for new fry should include newly hatched brine shrimp, small worms, and powdered dry food, all of which are fed in small amounts four or five times daily.

Egg layers

Egg layers breed in a multitude of ways. Some scatter the eggs carelessly, while others place them carefully; some protect them by carrying them in their mouths, while others will eat the freshly laid eggs.

The most common egg layers are Tetras, Cichlids, Gouramis and Goldfish.The specific breeding requirements of each fish are beyond the scope of this book but the following is a summary of how to breed the popular Goldfish.

Goldfish, if well fed and cared for, will be ready to spawn in their second year. The normal season for spawning is the spring. The eggs are usually round, jelly-like and about 1.5 millimetres in diameter. There may be any number between one hundred and thousands per spawn.

Sexing the Goldfish is very difficult and should be left to the experts. However, during the mating season, males can be recognised by small, white, raised spots on their gill covers and along the first ray of the pectoral fin. Females during spawning become round and swollen.

At this time, the tank conditions should be kept ideal and food can be increased. The tank temperature should be raised a few degrees.

During the mating process, the male relentlessly pursues the female, butting his head against the female's abdomen until she finally releases the eggs. As they fall the male ejects milt, and each egg is fertilised by a single sperm.

Immediately the egg leaves the mother, it absorbs water and doubles in size within seconds. The sticky eggs attach to any object they touch and stay there until the young emerge.

Goldfish will eat eggs and fry, so fish and eggs should be separated once spawning is complete. Alternatively, provide a shallow area well stocked with thick plants as protection for the eggs and fry.

If the pond is outdoors, very few young will survive the onslaught of frogs, predatory insects and birds unless a cover is placed over the pond. It is best to take eggs or fry inside where they can be given adequate food and constant temperatures until they reach a length of 4 or 5 centimetres.

Sickness in fish

The commonest causes of outbreaks of disease in a hobbyist's tank are the absence of quarantine, overcrowding and overfeeding. A large number of proprietary remedies are available in pet shops for treating fish diseases, but many of them are useless, and the composition of practically all of them is not stated. Under these circumstances, it seems best not to recommend any of them, even though a few seem worthwhile.

Because of the sensitivity of even a healthy fish to transfer from its usual aquarium environment, consultation with a vet to identify and treat sick fish can be difficult. The home aquarist may therefore need to spend a little more time in observing the appearance of the sick fish and in reading through the Common Ailments listing that follows before taking steps to rectify a problem.

Non-infectious conditions

Various aquarium conditions can give rise to symptoms resembling those of the common diseases. If no obvious disease can be diagnosed, it should be remembered that chilling, over-heating or poisoning of some kind may well have occurred. A sudden fall in temperature or continued exposure to a temperature lower than that to which the fish is accustomed will typically result in a condition known as 'shimmies', characterised by a slow, swinging movement which doesn't get the fish anywhere. Temperatures should be raised to 27–30°C and kept high for a few days. In contrast a sudden rise or a chronic high temperature can cause trouble, usually manifested by the fish gasping at the surface of the water or dashing around the tank.

Poisoning by exposure to excess of metals, chlorine in raw tap water, insecticidal sprays or even extreme pH may cause patchy discoloration of the fish, variations in behaviour, or even blood streaks or ulceration of the skin or fins. When no other signs can be detected and poisoning is suspected, progressive half-changes of water should be made day after day in the hope of a cure. A complete change of water is usually too dangerous and may shock the fish even though they are being poisoned by the current contents of the tank.

The source of trouble should of course be searched out. It may lie in exposed metals, new copper house piping, too-fresh tap water, tobacco under your finger nails, or the aerator sucking in fly spray and pumping it into the water. Always suspect trouble if your water supply has been tampered with recently or copper piping has been laid down. Water from such a source should be used only after it has been allowed to flow for several minutes before being introduced to the tank.

Marine fish

Many diseases similar to those described in the following sections occur in marine (or salt water) aquariums, but the treatment is sometimes quite different. Where applicable, treatment is described separately.

Common ailments

Anchor worm

The first really visible sign of anchor worm infestation is the presence of small, wormlike creatures about 20 millimetres long, hanging from the body of the fish. After a while they drop off, leaving behind a rather large hole which readily becomes infected. Anchor worm infests large coldwater species such as Goldfish, and rarely develops in tropical fish. Treatment is by using DFD (difluoro-diphenyltrichlormethylmethane) in a bath at 0.1 millilitres per litre of aquarium water for two to three minutes.

Red spots on the body surface of this Angel fish indicate Anchor worm infestation.

Bacterial infections
(Fin rot, tail rot, red pest)

Bacterial infections often have internal effects as well as external ones. Treatment via tank water is liable to be less successful unless it is with a substance that will rapidly be absorbed by the tissues of the fish.

Symptoms of some of the commoner bacterial infections of aquarium fish are clamping of the fins and tail with blood streaks or ragged areas visible. In extreme instances pieces of fin or tail drop off. This condition is also known as fin rot or tail rot.

Blood streaks or ulcerated patches on the surface of the body may be seen also; this is a condition frequently referred to as 'red pest'. The scales may be raised with or without reddening of the skin beneath them. Sometimes

Fin and tail rot.

the disease may spread to give an appearance similar to that of DROPSY. Patchy discoloration of the skin accompanied by emaciation is usually termed tuberculosis.

Treatment may be applied to the tank as a whole, with monacrine or acriflavin (as for velvet disease) or with wide-spectrum antibiotics such as Chloromycetin, Erythromycin or Ampicillin at 100 milligrams per 5 litres of tank water, but it does tend to irritate the fish. A very effective method of treatment is to mix antibiotics (0.1–1 per cent) with the food.

Marine fish

As with freshwater fish, bacterial infections in marine fish are frequent and of multitudinous origin. Chloromycetin again appears to be the most useful antibiotic in the marine aquarium. Antibiotics, for reasons unknown, are less effective in salt water than in fresh water. The dose rates may be increased by five times.

Blood streaks on the body

See BACTERIAL INFECTIONS.

Discoloration of the skin

See BACTERIAL INFECTIONS.

Dropsy

Dropsy is a rather non-specific condition which has at least two different types. Symptoms of true dropsy are swelling of the body and abdomen without scale protrusion except in extreme cases. Excessive internal pressure may cause this to occur. No external signs of the infection are usually seen. The cause of true dropsy is usually a bacterial infection of the kidney causing upsets in fluid balance, and increased internal pressure. False dropsy, 'red pest', (see BACTERIAL INFECTIONS) is accompanied by scale protrusion, and in fact this may be all that is occurring.

The only worthwhile treatment appears to be Chloromycetin, administered in the food as described for treatment of FUNGAL INFECTIONS: ICHTHYOPHONUS.

'Dust' covering the body

See VELVET DISEASE.

Exophthalmos

See POPEYE.

Fin rot

See BACTERIAL INFECTIONS.

Flukes

The term 'fluke' is usually employed to describe infestations of creatures smaller than fish lice or anchor worms. Fish infested with the flukes look pale and have droopy fins. If the gills are infested there is rapid respiration, irritation and wasting. It mainly occurs in the coldwater fish. Tropical fish are, however, infested from time to time. Look for greyish minute worms on the gills or skin. It may require careful observation to differentiate this infestation from white spot.

Treatment is best achieved with trichlorofon 0.25–0.4 p.p.m of aquarium water. Alternatively formalin may be used as a bath, but not in the tank. A forty-five minute bath in 0.2 millilitres of 40 per cent formalin solution per litre of water is recommended.

Marine fish

Parasitic infestations occur similar to those observed in freshwater fish. The treatment of choice is a formalin bath as described for freshwater flukes, but of course the bath must be of seawater.

Fungal infections

Fungal infections are seen in freshwater fish, particularly coldwater fish. Usually only weakened or damaged fish are susceptible, so the problem tends to be individual rather than a whole aquarium infestation. If only one or two fish are infected and it is possible to net them out without too much trouble, this is the best method of dealing with the condition. They should then be treated with a fungicidal bath.

The symptoms are a grey or whitish growth in the skin of the fish, often associated with visible damage from poor handling, wounds from other fish or severe attacks of white spot or other infestations. The growth may occur anywhere on the body or fins and will eventually assume cotton-wool-like appearance protruding from the surface of the fish. The fish do not usually show great distress from the fungal infestation, but if left untreated they will eventually be killed by it. The fish therefore do not normally show the distress typical of velvet disease or white spot unless the fungus is subsequent to these particular diseases. (See also ICHTHYOPHONUS.)

If fungal infections are not treated the fish will eventually die.

Treatment consists of zinc-free malachite green or brilliant green (dyes) in an isolated bath (a cup or jam jar or whatever is suitable according to the size of the fish) at a strength of 60 milligrams per litre. Immerse the fish in the solution for 30 seconds and return to the tank immediately after treatment. The cotton-wool-like tufts will eventually fall off in a few hours. Repeated treatments may be given but a single one is usually effective.

If a tankful of fish has the fungus, a different treatment is required. Phenoxethol at a strength of 1 per cent in distilled water is used here; 10 millilitres of this solution per litre of aquarium water is adequate. Repeat (once only) if absolutely necessary after two or three days.

Ichthyophonus
This is a common fungal disease, characterised by the fish's slow, sluggish movements with loss of equilibrium, possibly a hollow belly, and the appearance of yellow to black cysts or sores virtually anywhere on the surface of the fish. The fungal attack is essentially internal, and usually becomes apparent only when it is widespread and generally past curing. It is a disease of tropical rather than coldwater fish.

Treatment of infected fish is frequently unsuccessful. It is best to destroy individual infected fish in the hope that the disease will not spread to the others. A big problem is that infected fish may live for months before showing signs of the disease. Two treatments are recommended, both given in the food: Chloromycetin at a dose rate of 1 per cent of the fish's food mixed in with the food for three days, or 1 per cent phenoxethol solution at the rate of 10 millilitres per litre of tank water, once only.

Mouth fungus
The signs of mouth fungus are similar to the fungal infections mentioned above, but are usually confined to the mouth, starting with a white line around the lips and pro-

ceeding to the production of filaments of cotton-wool appearance. It is a highly contagious disease with tropical fish rather than coldwater fish and is a rapid killer. Treatment must be given to the tank and its inhabitants or further infection will occur. The disease is so toxic and rapid-spreading that an antibiotic should be used. The most effective treatment is Chloromycetin or Erythromycin at 20 milligrams per litre. This is administered to the tank water.

Marine fish
Fungal infections resembling ICHTHYOPHONUS cause similar conditions in marine fish to those already described. Feeding antibiotics offers the best chance of limiting the spread of the disease.

The fungus on this Angel fish looks like cotton-wool.

Mouth fungus starts as a white line around the mouth.

Gas bubble disease
See POPEYE.

Ich
See WHITE SPOT.

Ichthyophonus
See FUNGAL INFECTIONS.

Lice
Fish are prone to attack by a tremendous variety of so-called lice and flukes of various kinds, which are often quite difficult to eradicate. Removing the affected fish from the aquarium to treat it individually can be a nuisance because of the difficulty of trying to get it out of a large tank. Irritation is obvious, with the affected fish scratching itself against rocks or aquarium decorations. The parasite is often quite visible.

The fish louse may be introduced by live feeding, such

as with Daphnia, or if fish have been taken from ponds. The louse is a flattened, rather spiderlike animal, about 5 millimetres in diameter, which attaches itself by two large suckers to the exterior of its host and feeds on its blood.

The lice may be physically removed using forceps. If there is a heavy infestation or if the fish are rather delicate and should not be disturbed by handling, it may be better to use Trichlorofon at 0.25–0.4 p.p.m. of aquarium water.

Parasites attached to the body
See ANCHOR WORM, FLUKES, LICE.

Poisoning by chlorinated water
This can occur where city water supplies are chlorinated. Ridding the water of chlorine can be achieved by letting it stand for a couple of days—the chlorine passes into the air, and the water is safe to use. Alternatively, the addition of a few drops of sodium thiosulphate will instantly negate any chlorine present.

Poisoning by insecticides and other pesticides
This is common. Dichlorvos, a constituent of pest strips, is particularly toxic to fish and pest strips should not be placed in the same room as the aquarium. Avoid using aerosol insecticide sprays in the aquarium room. If it becomes necessary to do so, make sure the aquarium is well covered first.

Popeye (Exophthalmos, gas bubble disease)
Popeye is a protrusion of one or both eyes, which may subside or may progress, leading to the loss of one or both eyes. It may occur in association with infectious disease, and treatment for the disease in question may cure the condition.

The eye or eyes affected should be carefully inspected to make sure that the cause is not so-called gas bubble disease. If the condition is not caused by an existing infection, true gas bubble disease due to the deposition of gas, usually nitrogen, in the tissues in the eye should be suspected. In this case, popeye resembles 'the bends' and if the eyes are showing these symptoms then it must be realised that similar bubbles may be forming elsewhere in the body and be the cause of severe trouble.

When gas bubbles are seen in the eyes, the water temperature in the aquarium should be lowered as far as is tolerable to the fish species concerned to increase the solubility of the gas. Any brisk aeration should be cut down as far as feasible. It is possible if small bubbles in the eye coalesce to form a visible large bubble, to extract this with a fine hypodermic needle. This is a job for a veterinarian.

Red pest
See BACTERIAL INFECTIONS.

Scale protrusion
See BACTERIAL INFECTIONS.

'Shimmies'
It is not only diseases that may cause symptoms of illness in fish. Sometimes chilling, over-heating or poisoning may be the cause. Either a sudden fall in temperature or continued exposure to a temperature lower than that to which the fish are accustomed will result in a condition called 'Shimmies'. In this condition the fish adopt a slow swimming movement which is non-progressive. The temperature of the aquarium should be raised to 27–30°C and kept high for a few days.

Care should be taken to avoid a sudden rise in temperature or chronic high temperatures as this can cause trouble. The usual signs are gasping at the water surface or darting around the aquarium. However, this usually occurs at 30–33°C. While it is feasible to raise the temperature to 30°C reasonably quickly, it is dangerous to lower the temperature quickly. Overheated fish should have maximum

aeration instead. 'Shimmies' may also be a sign of velvet disease in marine fish.

Sores and cysts
See FUNGAL INFECTIONS: ICHTHYOPHONUS.

Swelling of the body
See DROPSY.

Tail rot
See BACTERIAL INFECTIONS.

Tuberculosis
Patchy discoloration of the skin accompanied by emaciation is usually termed tuberculosis. (See also BACTERIAL INFECTIONS.)

Velvet disease
Velvet disease is caused by a flagellated parasitic organism called *Oodinium*. Irritation, rapid respiration (gill movement) and clamping of the fins are symptoms common to a number of diseases and any fish showing them should be examined carefully. In velvet disease a very fine golden or brownish dust covers the surface of part or all of the body and fins. If looked at very closely it can be seen to move rather like corn in a breeze.

Velvet disease is highly infectious and kills most of the specimens it attacks, particularly fry (the young, recently spawned fish). Immediate steps should be taken to eradicate the condition. The preferred treatment is a solution of blue crystalline copper sulphate in distilled water at the concentration of 1 per cent. This solution should be used at 1 millilitre per 10 litres of aquarium water. The alternative treatment is with 0.2 per cent stock solutions of monacrin or acriflavin, adding 1 millilitre per litre of aquarium water.

The addition of a teaspoonful of common salt (approximately 5 grams) per 5 litres of aquarium water helps the action of the drug. Monacrin is the preferred treatment as it forms a weak blueish solution in the aquarium and looks attractive rather than otherwise—acriflavin gives a darker, yellowish appearance. It is not necessary to change the aquarium water to a greater extent than normal after the use of these preparations, although acriflavin has been said to sterilise fish. If the fish are intended for breeding, all the water should be changed gradually after the cure has been effected.

Marine fish
Velvet disease in marine fish is related to the well-known freshwater pest, the usual active agent in the marine tank being a close relative. It also infests the gills and outer surface of the fish but usually is white in colour and often quite difficult to see unless carefully sought out under a stronger light. It is easiest to detect on the dark surfaces of the fish. It is more predominantly a gill disease in the marine fish.

The usual signs are increased respiration, scratching against rocks and coral, and quite often 'shimmies'. The copper sulphate treatment of velvet disease for freshwater fish can be used successfully in the marine tank. Marine fish can take a higher dosage than recommended for freshwater treatment, and can stand up to about 0.4 parts per million of metallic copper. Biological filters and other types of filter that may extract copper should be turned down or off during copper treatment and brisk aeration supplied by other means.

White spot, or ich (pronounced 'ick')
White spot used to be the most common disease in freshwater tanks, but has been displaced by velvet disease. The symptoms of infestation by the parasite are irritation and glancing (bumping against) rocks and plants, usually with

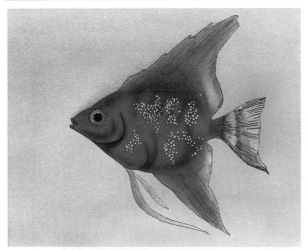

Angel fish with white spot — raised white blisters on the body surface about the size of a grain of salt.

severe gill irritation since the parasites are filtered off by the gills (as with velvet disease). This causes the fish to rub the nose and head region against the plants or rocks. White spots up to 1 millimetre across appear. The gills are often severely infected and respiration impeded before many spots are visible on any other parts of the fish. Eventually body, fins and tail may be covered by the spots in untreated fish.

The drug of choice is quinine hydrochloride at 30 milligrams per litre of aquarium water, or quinine sulphate which is less soluble but may be used. Quinine is not effective against velvet disease, just as copper, monacrin and acriflavin are not effective against white spot. The best method of treatment is to dissolve the total dose required in about 1 litre of water and add it to the tank a third at a time at twelve-hourly intervals. Aeration should be as brisk as possible, and the water may cloud. It is not necessary to change the water afterwards. As with velvet disease the cure is not sudden. The higher the water temperature, the quicker the result. The treatment should not need repeating because the drug acts on the free swimming larval stage of the parasite. If there is a renewed outbreak, it should be treated with quinine again. More than one additional dose of quinine is not advisable as quinine starts to become toxic if administered for too long.

(See also FLUKES, as their appearance can seem quite similar.)

Marine fish
White spot disease in marine fish is similar to the white spot found in freshwater fish. The best treatment is with copper sulphate exactly as described for marine fish for velvet disease. Copper treatment is effective in the marine tank—not in the freshwater tank.

GUINEA PIGS

Guinea pigs as pets

The guinea pig's name belies both its geographical origins and its ancestry. It comes neither from the Guinea coast of West Africa nor from Papua-New Guinea, nor is it a pig. The domestic guinea pig was developed from the wild guinea pigs (called agouti) of South America, which the Indians used as food and as sacrifices in religious ceremonies. The guinea pig is a rodent belonging to the same group of animals as the squirrels, mice, hamsters, beavers and rats. It probably acquired the name 'pig' in reference to the grunting pig-like sounds it makes. Or perhaps, because it was used for food, it was referred to as a little pig.

There are several varieties of guinea pigs. Unlike the domestic guinea pig, the wild guinea pig has short hair and generally comes in only one colour, 'agouti', which gives it a grey, grizzled appearance.

The domestic guinea pig, or 'cavy' as it is often called, comes in three basic fur types. The short-haired or English variety has a short, smooth coat like its wild ancestors. The rough-haired or Abyssinian variety has its coat formed into a number of distinct whorls or rosettes. The long-haired or Peruvian variety has a long, full coat. A wide assortment of colours is seen in the domestic guinea pig.

The short-haired English guinea pig.

Housing

Temperature requirements

Housing the guinea pig is quite simple as long as its exacting temperature requirements are met. A location where the temperature will not drop below 21°C is essential. At lower temperatures, especially below 18°C, guinea pigs develop colds and other respiratory diseases, and the young are either born dead or die soon after birth. Draughts and damp are not tolerated well by guinea pigs. Although they cannot tolerate cold, neither can they tolerate temperatures above 32°C. It is particularly important in very cold and very hot weather to make sure that the guinea pig is comfortable.

Cage construction

Ideally the cage should be made of metal so it cannot be chewed, but suitable cages can also be made of wood and netting. At least three sides of the cage (the two ends and the back) should be solid, to block out

The rough-haired or Abyssinian guinea pig with its distinct rosettes.

A movable wire-bottomed cage with shelter at one end makes an ideal home for guinea pigs.

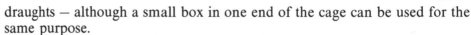

Wood shavings are used for bedding in this deep litter accommodation.

Hay is a good combination of bedding and food supply.

draughts — although a small box in one end of the cage can be used for the same purpose.

The floor of the cage is best made solid, although a bare wire or mesh base may be convenient for keeping the cage clean, since urine will pass through it. A wire-floored cage can also be moved around the lawn, allowing the guinea pig to graze different areas. This kind of cage must be kept properly cleaned, as droppings get squashed around the intersections of the wire mesh and are difficult to remove. Bare mesh presents a hazard; guinea pigs may injure their legs or feet, particularly if disturbed by a sudden movement or loud noise. A solid floor may be covered with six to ten sheets of newspaper or with wood shavings, which allow a good degree of drainage for urine.

Where guinea pigs are raised in large numbers, deep litter systems are successful. Hay also makes a good combination of bedding and food supply. Hay is not particularly absorbent, but it does form a thick layer which keeps the guinea pigs above the wet cage bottom. If you do use hay, check that it is free from poisonous insecticides which may be eaten by your pet. Pelletised, absorbent, commercial litters are available from pet shops.

Cage size

Guinea pigs are sociable animals and a number of females (sows) and one male (boar) can be kept together without fear of fighting. Two boars, however, will generally fight, particularly if there are sows present. The size and quality of the cages depend on the number of guinea pigs you plan to keep.

Ideally, the guinea pigs should be kept in a cage no smaller than 1 metre in length, by 50 centimetres in width, by 30 centimetres in height. A cage this size is also suitable for breeding, where the ratio is usually one boar to two to four sows, or will accommodate a sow with a litter of young.

Nest boxes

Some breeders recommend that each cage be provided with a nesting box. A small box 30 centimetres square with a door through which the guinea pig can enter the main cage area is suitable. It can be made of wood or cardboard, but the top should be removable for easy cleaning.

Cage cleaning

Each week all old bedding should be removed and replaced with fresh material. One of the advantages of an open mesh bottom is that less frequent cleaning is necessary.

Lysol is a satisfactory cleaning solution, though it can cause damage to the feet of guinea pigs if not properly rinsed off.

Feeding

Successful breeding and rearing depend on correct feeding, as guinea pigs are very susceptible to vitamin C deficiency (scurvy). Guinea pigs should be fed the following foods:

Green food

This must be of good quality and can include lucerne, lettuce, carrots, apples, cabbages, clover and corn. Green feed should be fed in racks, leafy greens should be given once a day, even when a pelletised diet is fed. Kikuyu grass is not recommended, as it can cause sudden death.

Lucerne hay

Kikuyu grass is not recommended as it can cause sudden death.

Good-quality lucerne hay reduces the amount of green food required to provide roughage and bulk in the diet. It also reduces boredom and prevents barbering (stripping of hair). Supply the hay in a rack also—this prevents the food being trampled over and thus wasted.

Pellets

Rabbit and guinea pig pellets should be available all the time and are best kept in pellet dispensers to prevent soiling and spoilage. Good pellets contain various grains, such as oats and wheat, minerals (particularly calcium) and vitamins (especially vitamin C). Pellets should be fed to guinea pigs even if they are getting green feed.

Cereal straw or hay (oaten or wheaten)

This is fed to breeding sows and is essential to prevent teeth problems in lactating sows.

Watering

Supplying water to guinea pigs using water dishes is not satisfactory because of the labour involved in cleaning and filling the dishes, contamination by feed, faeces, litter and urine, and the frequency with which the dishes get tipped over. The best system in a small pen is the tube-and-bottle arrangement used for mice, rats and other rodents. Clean, fresh water should always be available.

Clean fresh water is best served in a tube and bottle arrangement.

General care

Grooming

Guinea pigs can be groomed just like a dog or cat. Brush the short-haired English variety with a soft hairbrush and smooth the hair afterwards to add extra lustre. A toothbrush makes an ideal grooming tool for the rough-haired Abyssinian, while the long-haired Peruvian requires a long-bristled brush. Unless you are going to show the long-haired Peruvian guinea pig, it is best to clip the hair away from its eyes to allow the animal to see without difficulty. If long-haired guinea pigs develop knots in their coats use scissors to cut the knots into strips in the direction of the hair and then pull out as much of the matting as you can.

Bathing

Guinea pigs usually don't require bathing and it is best not to do it. If a bath becomes essential, do it on a warm day with warm water. Wash all soap off thoroughly and towel the animal down. Keep the animal warm and out of draughts until it is completely dry.

Handling

Guinea pigs very rarely bite, although some may nibble curiously at a finger nail. Handling the guinea pig is the best way to make it familiar with people and one of the tamest of all pets.

To pick up a guinea pig, hold it firmly behind its shoulders with one hand, while allowing it to rest on the palm of your other hand.

Pick up a guinea pig by holding it behind its shoulders with one hand, and letting it rest on the palm of your other hand.

Breeding

The sex of the mature guinea pig can be determined by observing the area of the lower body openings while pressing down gently on the animal's abdomen just above the lower body openings. In the male, the genitals will appear. In the female only the body openings will be visible.

Each boar can be placed with from one to six sows; three or four sows is the optimum number for most males.

No special preparations are needed other than that the guinea pigs should be in good health and have a good diet, particularly of greens. Lack of greens and vitamin C will cause infertility, early abortion, reduced litter sizes and stunted growth. The cages should be of sizes discussed earlier.

Long-haired guinea pigs should be kept clipped, especially around the hindquarters; otherwise the coat will interfere with the nursing of the young.

Sexual maturity is reached at about five or six weeks of age, though sows should not be bred until they are about five or six months old. Breeding at this later age is less of a strain on the sow and the litters are usually stronger and more robust.

The female guinea pig's oestrus cycle runs from fourteen to seventeen days, with an average of about sixteen days and is repeated continually until pregnancy occurs. There may be some pauses in the cycle during the late winter months. The sow is willing to mate for one day during each cycle. This mating time, called oestrus (or heat), occurs early in the cycle, on about the second day.

Pregnancy or gestation runs from fifty-nine to seventy-two days with an average of sixty-three.

Problems associated with pregnancy

Pregnancy toxaemia

Fat sows in late pregnancy are especially susceptible to toxaemia. The animals become lethargic, refuse food and usually die within twenty-four hours. This disease is nutritional in origin and better-quality food will prevent deaths.

Dystocia (Difficulty giving birth)

This is not a common cause of mortality in guinea pigs, though it does occur, particularly with large single foetuses. It has been suggested that it is more common in sows that are first mated at six to eight months of age.

Abortion

This occurs in varying stages of pregnancy. Examination of foetuses has not revealed a common cause though several bacteria have been incriminated. If abortion becomes a common problem it is best to cull the sow.

Smothering

The most important cause of mortality in the peri-natal period in many colonies is smothering, common in large litters when the sow fails to clean the newborn, and the baby's nostrils are blocked by the foetal membranes. Prevention can only be by supervision at the time of birth.

Smothering can occur at any age if sudden loud noises occur and they all rush to the far corner of the cage and huddle up to five deep until the threat has passed.

Losses from injuries in suckers

Injuries to suckers (baby guinea pigs) are usually caused by adults disturbed by overcrowding. The injuries most frequently are seen as subcutaneous abscesses, often in the thoracic region. Remove some of the adults from the pen to prevent recurrences.

Malformations

These are rare except where there is gross inbreeding.

Small weak suckers

Runts are seen on odd occasions in litters of all sizes and are associated with feeding poor-quality green food to the sow some two to three weeks before birth. Control is by paying more attention to the diet of the sow.

Farrowing

Farrowing (giving birth) seems to be one of the more common worries by owners, yet it rarely causes problems. Internal palpation is readily done, as the pelvic size is relatively large. Manual delivery can be successful due to the large size of the pelvis.

A good indicator of viability for the mother is that one or more live babies are already out. Where all previous have been dead, manual delivery does not always save the mother. The membranes of the newborn look like small kidneys when passed.

The average litter is three or four young, but depending upon the strain of guinea pigs the litters may vary in number between one to ten. The first litter of a young female is usually quite small.

The sow at the prime of her reproductive life—from six months of age to four years—can have as many as four or even five litters per year, but if you want strong young you should not allow the sow to bear more than three litters in the year.

Post-partum heat

Sows come into heat very soon after giving birth—between ten to twelve hours later. Some commercial breeders leave the boar with the pregnant sows so that they can mate during the post-partum heat, but for the home breeder it is best to remove the pregnant sow to her own cage and prevent this post-partum heat mating. This allows her to rest between litters.

From the time the young begin to nurse until they are weaned, the sow will not have other heat periods. Except for the post-partum heat it is usually safe to leave the suckling sow with the boar.

Only in the rarest instances will the boar bother or injure the young. Males have been known to eat the young.

Young guinea pigs (suckers) are born fully haired, toothed and with their eyes open. They begin walking and running within an hour after they are born. In two or three days they begin to eat solid food in addition to nursing from the mother. The guinea pig is communal in its rearing of the young. The sow will allow any sucker in her pen to suckle. However, groups of more than twelve sows (with thirty-five to forty-five suckers) can suffer from over-crowding, with losses due to fighting and starvation. Smaller groups of four to five sows are best. Where a number of sows are having litters it is best to keep the sows with similarly aged litters together.

Growth after weaning

Suckers should be weaned at eighteen to twenty-one days of age. If they are left any longer, some of the young sows will be mated by the adult boar.

At weaning time the young should weigh about 250 grams. Growth continues until about eighteen months of age, when the boars will average 25

Sow with litter, usually three young will be born.

Children can be encouraged to keep an eye on their pet's condition.

centimetres in length and about 1 kilogram in weight. The sows, unless pregnant, average slightly less.

Guinea pigs will generally breed up to their fifth year, but after the third or fourth year breeding becomes irregular and litters are smaller. Very few guinea pigs live beyond seven years of age. Five or six years are considered a very full life.

Caring for the sick guinea pig

Guinea pigs are generally subject to few ailments but almost all of these should be treated by a veterinarian rather than at home. A sick guinea pig will refuse food or eat very little. Sometimes it may drink excessively and seem listless and lethargic. It may cough, have watery eyes and nose and its respiration may be laboured. It may have diarrhoea, a bloated appearance or a dry rough coat.

Diarrhoea can be caused by overeating greens, in which case the guinea pig should have its diet reduced for a few days. Most other conditions will require veterinary treatment.

Nursing care

Guinea pigs are difficult patients because many medications cause more problems than the original disease. Putting medication in their food, for instance, is not recommended as it causes alteration of the gut flora, leading to interference with the digestion and absorption of food. Many of the common antibiotics are toxic to guinea pigs. Oral or injectable penicillin usually causes death within seven days.Always leave veterinary treatment to a qualified veterinarian.

The sick guinea pig should be provided with a warm, dry and draught-free cage. It is best to keep it indoors to prevent sudden changes in temperature. The ideal environmental temperature is in the range 23–27°C. Because they have such a small body they are affected by sudden environmental temperature changes. Isolate the guinea pig if possible.

The bedding should be changed daily and the sick guinea pig should always have available fresh food and water. Plenty of tempting greens are important. Regular grooming (daily) is a good pick-me-up.

The healthy guinea pig

Rectal temperature: 39–40°C
Respiration rate: 110–150 per minute
Pulse rate: 115–160 per minute

Short-haired guinea pigs are normally smooth-coated. Sick animals can be detected by their rough coat, hunched appearance or poor condition.

Common ailments

Abscesses

Abscesses are most commonly found around the jaw, neck and feet. They usually need to be lanced and hence require veterinary treatment. Abscesses are generally the result of fights, so the best method of prevention is to ensure no overcrowding, and to segregate boars.

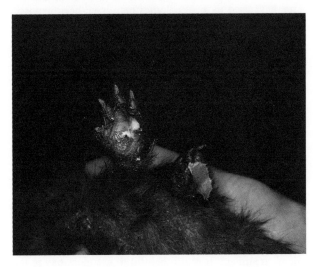

This type of abscess on the foot usually needs to be lanced.

Dietary diseases

Vitamin C deficiency (Scurvy)

Guinea pigs, unlike other animals, cannot make their own vitamin C. They are rapidly affected by vitamin C deficiencies, and will survive for only twenty-five to thirty days on a diet of pellets alone (vitamin C has a short life in prepared foods). Death is preceded by loss of condition, dermatitis, scouring, slobbering and bone fragility. On other diets low in vitamin C, the same symptoms will develop, but not so rapidly. The problem can be readily cured by the provision of good green food.

Dermatitis associated with scurvy.

Slobbers

Slobbers is a disease of lactating sows, usually when they are having their first or second litter. The first sign, often unobserved, is a loss of condition associated with enlargement of the jaw bones. Overgrowth or malocclusion of the teeth occurs at this stage and is followed by slobbering.

Examination of the animal at the slobbering stage will reveal overgrown incisor or molar teeth. In severe cases the bottom molar teeth may meet over the top of the tongue. Symptoms can occur any time after the sow farrows. There is no treatment. The condition can be prevented by providing cereal straw or hay to the sows. This is thought to allow even wear of the teeth. Any guinea pig in poor condition should be checked to ensure there is no malocclusion. Affected guinea pigs should be destroyed before they starve to death.

Fluoride slobbers

Slobbers due to excess fluoride in the diet has been observed in several colonies of guinea pigs. This differs from slobbers in lactating sows in that it also affects animals other than lactating sows. The upper incisor teeth tend to be overgrown with a backward curvature and there is often tartar and abnormal wear. There is no treatment and affected guinea pigs should be destroyed before they starve to death.

Starvation

This is associated with a sudden change in diet when the guinea pig refuses to eat the new food. It can be prevented by always ensuring the animals are given a diet to which they are accustomed when they are moved to a different environment. Any dietary change should be gradual.

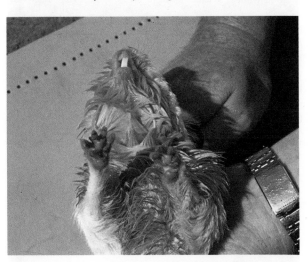

Overgrowth of teeth causes slobbers: Note the wet hair.

Ear disorders

Otitis (ear infection) is seen occasionally in guinea pigs. It is usually caused by bacterial infections, rather than mite infestations. Suitable ear drops can be obtained from the veterinary surgeon. It is important to continue treatment of the ear for two to three weeks, as the quick relief afforded by the drops may deceive you into thinking that the infection has cleared. Ensure that any debris or discharge is cleaned from the ear using a 50 per cent methylated spirits/water mixture before administering the medication to the ear. Ensure that the drops go into the ear canal and the guinea pig does not shake its head immediately after administration.

Eye disorders

Guinea pigs can be affected by any of the eye disorders suffered by dogs and cats. However, the most common conditions in guinea pigs are corneal ulcers and keratitis. (These disorders are described in the section Common Ailments of Dogs: EYE DISORDERS.)

Feet disorders

The most common foot problem in guinea pigs is peeling of the skin and thickening of the hock, with or without ulceration. It seems to be associated with unsuitable bedding and the presence of moisture. Hard damp straw will cause the problem. Mercurochrome or triple dye should be applied to the affected area of the foot three times daily until it clears, and old clean towelling should be placed on the floor during treatment. To prevent the condition recurring, switch to a different type of bedding and change it regularly.

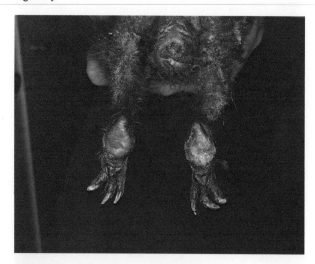

Bed sores resulting from unsuitable bedding.

Fighting

Fighting between boars will occur where there are three or four boars with a group of sows. The boar at the bottom of the social order is savaged and may develop abscesses on its back. The answer here is to remove one or two of the boars. If fighting occurs in a pen of boars, check the sex of these animals again to ensure that there are no sows present. If not, reduce the overcrowding in the pen.

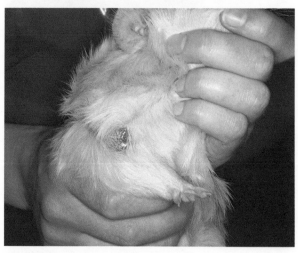

Bite wound due to overcrowding in the pen.

Fractures

Fractures of the legs most frequently occur in guinea pigs kept in cages with wire bottoms. If the guinea pig's legs are protruding and the cage is pulled across the lawn rather than being lifted, damage is inevitable. Minor fractures at the ends of the limbs may be repaired by splinting, but breaks in major bones require major surgery, which is not always an economic possibility.

Infectious diseases

Salmonellosis

The salmonella bacteria can cause heavy losses in guinea

pig colonies, usually attacking suckers from five to fifteen days of age. In bad outbreaks losses have also occurred in adult sows and growing stock. Infection is by ingestion of contaminated feed, litter or milk. The disease can be controlled by weaning all animals in the infected pen, including suckers even though they may be only seven to fourteen days old. In the subsequent two to three days, up to 10 per cent of the young in that pen may be lost.

Prevention may be difficult because the cereal and lucerne hays used in most colonies may have been exposed to germ-carrying rodents. Losses in an outbreak in large establishments can be controlled by using a killed vaccine. This vaccine is made during the outbreak from affected guinea pigs and used on healthy ones, particularly pregnant sows. The sucker is able to absorb antibodies in the sow's colostrum for two to three weeks after birth so that suckers can be protected against the infection.

Mastitis

In large colonies, sows suffering from mastitis (inflammation of the mammary glands) should be culled. In smaller groups, individual treatment with antibiotics can be administered under veterinary supervision.

Lip disorders

Scabbing and ulceration in the nasal fold are common, possibly caused by mechanical damage due to the diet. Try mercurochrome or triple dye in the nasal fold three times daily for four days. If there is no improvement, seek veterinary treatment. It is also helpful to use more hay in the diet and take the guinea pigs off pellets for seven to ten days.

Dermatitis: Note *loss of hair and inflamed skin.*

Skin diseases

Dermatitis

Dermatitis is an inflammation of the skin and in guinea pigs can be caused by scurvy (vitamin C deficiency), bacterial infections, parasites or ringworm. (See the section on SKIN DISEASES in Dogs.)

External parasites

Guinea pigs may be attacked by various external parasites such as fleas, ticks, lice and mites, which feed on their blood or skin products. Guinea pigs can be treated in the same way as are dogs or cats, but it is preferable to try an insecticidal powder first.

The infested animals' cage and food utensils should be disinfected using an insecticidal wash. Be sure that the utensils and cage are thoroughly rinsed and dry. When the cage is dry, dust the cracks and corners with an insecticidal powder. Leave this for half a day, and then shake out or remove the excess powder. Place clean fresh bedding inside and only then return the guinea pigs to their cage.

Ringworm

The signs of ringworm include loss of hair and scaling of the skin. Usually there is mild to severe itching, often leading to secondary scabbing and bleeding. It may affect only one guinea pig in a group or all of them. The treatment is by bathing the guinea pig all over twice weekly in an iodine-based scrub or solution. The animal can be dunked up to its neck in water and then rinsed in the same manner in fresh water. Most cases improve dramatically within seven to ten days. If there is not sufficient improvement, use griseofulvin tablets, available from your vet.

Stripping (Barbering)

Stripping of hair occurs in some colonies, especially in animals reared on wire. It is thought to be due mainly to boredom and can be prevented by allowing access to hay. It can be self-inflicted or mutually inflicted.

Teeth disorders

Broken incisors are common. There is no need for treatment, as guinea pigs' teeth (in common with those of other rodents) keep on growing. Keep roughage and chewing wood available. In young cavies malocclusions due to jaw deformities are quite common. Old cavies have malocclusions due to a failure to wear down the teeth correctly. Be careful when trimming teeth not to cut back long incisors unless you are sure the molars are not meeting. If you cut the incisors too short, the guinea pig cannot close them to bite and will starve.

Urinary problems

The most common urinary problem is cystitis, evidenced by pus and blood passed when the animal's bladder is pressed. The guinea pig is slightly lethargic and may be off its food and be drinking more water than usual. (This should not be confused with the slightly thicker urine that is occasionally passed and which is quite normal.) The cystitis does not seem to cause pain and responds well to veterinary treatment.

Worms

Worms do not seem to cause any problems in guinea pigs and are not health hazards to humans.

Wounds

Minor cuts and scratches may be treated by applying mercurochrome or triple dye to the affected area. Boils can be treated by cutting away the hair around the infected area and hot-poulticing with a warm cloth three times daily until the abscess is ripe. Wash with a mild antiseptic such as 50 per cent peroxide and water, then lance the boil with a razor blade that has been sterilised in a flame. Use a pad of gauze to pick up the material that oozes out of the infected area when you gently press the sides of the boil. Irrigation with the 50 per cent peroxide solution should continue three times daily for three or four days. Veterinary attention is frequently necessary.

HAMSTERS

Like the guinea pig, the hamster is a small rodent. Their care and problems are similar but here are some differences.

The hamster is a nocturnal and solitary animal with a life-span of 1–2 years. Two or more will always fight, regardless of sex. The most common is the golden hamster originating in Syria.

The young begin eating solid food when 7–9 days old and drinking at 10 days. Coprophagia in the adult is normal.

Oestrus occurs every four days. Mating occurs at night and male and female should only be together when the female is in heat or they will fight. The gestation period is only 15–18 days. Litter size 4–7. The young are naked and develop hair by 7 days and are weaned at 20–25 days. Eyes are open at 5 days.

Cannibalism

A female hamster with newborn young may conceal an entire litter in her cheek pouches when disturbed. If sufficiently upset she may eat her young. They should not therefore be handled for the first 10 days. Fostering of orphan litters is rarely successful and both the adopted and natural litters may be cannibalised. Hand rearing is usually unsuccessful.

Constipation

Usually occurs at 10–15 days of age in hamsters still suckling. Affected hamsters have a large swollen abdomen with a bulging anus. Prompt veterinary attention is required.

Hibernation

Below 5° (40°F) body temperature drops to 1° to 2°C above the ambient temperature and pulse and respiration fall.

Sleeper disease

If the environmental temperature reaches 22°–25°C the hamster may become stiff and lifeless and if disturbed moves the head from side to side. It will return to normal after 5 minutes. 'Apparently dead' hamsters should be warmed and stimulated prior to disposal.

Impacted cheek pouches

Empty and flush with water.

Overgrown teeth

Teeth grow continuously and clipping is necessary if the diet provides insufficient wear.

'Wet tail' (Diarrhoea)

There is severe diarrhoea with moistening and inflammation of the anal area leading to death in 2–7 days. Usually occurs in recently weaned animals of 3–5 weeks of age. Prompt veterinary attention requiring electrolytes, antibiotics, and antispasmolytics is necessary.

Worms

Tapeworm and pinworm are the most common and respond to appropriate veterinary treatment.

HORSES

Selecting a horse

Why do you want a horse? For a particular purpose, or do you think it would make a nice pet? The most important difference between horses and all the other animals mentioned in this book is that a horse is not meant to be a pet—it is too big, too time consuming and too expensive to keep to be classed as a pet. A horse is meant to be used—to be loved and cherished, certainly, but not just to admire and keep.

Before you actually purchase a horse, decide how much you really want one. Unlike other hobbies, horses cannot be put to one side and forgotten. They are costly to purchase and they go on costing money once you have got them home. In fact, horses are amongst the most expensive animals you can own. In addition they require a reasonably large tract of land. In many cases they are very time consuming, as they need to be fed twice a day, groomed and regularly exercised.

In order to put the idea in perspective, it is sometimes best to attend a riding school and have some lessons. In this way you will be introduced to the whole concept of horse ownership. If you decide you still want to own a horse, ask the person who runs the riding school if they know of any horses for sale.

There are many things to consider when choosing your ideal horse. How well can you ride? Are you bold or a bit nervous? Will you soon want to enter competitions such as gymkhanas, shows or endurance rides? Or are you happy just riding around the countryside? How big a horse do you want—a 120-centimetre pony, or a 160-centimetre thoroughbred? Are you fully grown or will you outgrow the horse? What is your rate of progress in your riding lessons?

If you are progressing quickly, you will soon become bored with a quiet horse which seldom gets out of a trot. An amateur or a child should always have a quiet, gentle, well-broken horse that is neither headstrong nor unmanageable. Old horses are often ideal for beginners. The horse should never be too spirited for the rider's skill. Only very experienced riders should contemplate an ex-racehorse, whether thoroughbred or standardbred.

Where to buy

Having decided that you can justify owning a horse—or pony—the next step is to find the animal that best suits your purpose. It may be a particular breed (for example, Arabian, quarter horse, thoroughbred, Welsh mountain pony) or a type (that is, beginner's pony, sporting horse, show hack or pleasure horse).

This sturdy riding hack is suitable as a good all-rounder.

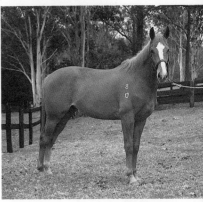

A thoroughbred is usually bred for racing and may not have a suitable temperament for a beginner.

Take particular care when selecting a child's first pony. Many small ponies are bad tempered and not quiet.

A good type of show hack. Good training and presentation will make him ready for the show ring.

Walk

Trot

Canter

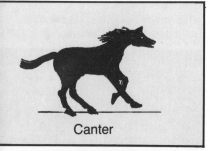

Gallop

Natural gaits are the walk, trot, canter and gallop. Refinements include the jog (slow trot) and the lope (slow gallop). Some horses also amble and when speeded up the action is called pacing.

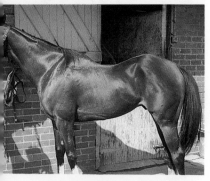

Poor conformation: Note the dip in the horse's back, called 'swayback'.

Horse trading is one of the oldest arts. Nowhere else is the phrase 'buyer beware' more applicable. For this reason it is best to avoid auction sales, or any other form of purchase where a rush decision has to be made. It is best to purchase the horse after a long-term association. Where this is not possible, many owners will allow you to spend a few days riding the horse, getting to know it and being satisfied that it is in good shape. Never buy a horse without having it thoroughly examined by an experienced equine veterinarian. Many problems, both current and potential, may be avoided by thorough veterinary examination.

What to look for

Before you get the equine veterinary surgeon to examine the horse, you should examine it yourself. This will save you unnecessary expense if there is something obviously wrong with the animal. You will, however, need to know the main things to look for. (These are shown in the illustrations on page 179.)

Temperament is a very important factor when choosing a new horse. Horses, even the smallest ones, can be very dangerous. It is most important for your safety that you assess the temperament of the horse very carefully. A horse should have kind eyes and should appear friendly with its ears forward. If the owner claims that the horse is quiet ask him to thoroughly handle it (for example, rub his hands all over the back and body of the horse, rub down its legs, and pick up the feet). Once the owner has done this, repeat the process yourself. *Never stand immediately in front of or behind the horse.* Unfriendly horses will have their ears back. They may attempt to bite or kick, and will not face you when you enter their box or yard.

It is important that you have complete confidence in the horse before you buy it. You may need to visit the animal several times to gain this confidence. Watch carefully as the owner bridles and saddles the horse, and assess whether the animal remains stationary or whether for example it is head-shy (resents having its head touched). Once the horse has been saddled, ask the owner to ride it at a trot and canter. You may then feel confident to ride the horse yourself. This will give you an opportunity to get the feel of the horse.

Assess whether it has the confidence to suit you, and generally appraise the horse's ability. If you are happy with the horse, then call in a vet to give the animal a thorough examination before you commit yourself to the purchase.

Terms applied to horses

At birth: a foal. A colt is a male foal; a filly is a female foal. The term yearling is used in the year after a horse is born. The next year the horse is called a two-year-old. Up to three years of age a young male horse is called a colt; a young female horse is called a filly. An entire or stallion is an uncastrated male horse over three years of age. A gelding is a castrated horse of any age. A mare is a female horse over three years of age.

The height of a horse used to be given in *hands* with one hand being four inches in measurement. Today horses are measured in centimetres and normally a *horse* measures over 142 centimetres and a *pony* is under 142 centimetres in height. A horse or pony is measured with a special measuring stick placed at the highest point of the withers.

Conformation

The conformation of a horse is the key to its progression. Conformation is basically the way the horse has been put together. The body should be in pleasing balance with the limbs and should be well-proportioned. The horse is a working animal and its working ability is determined by the condition of its limbs and feet. Poor conformation of limbs may contribute to lame-

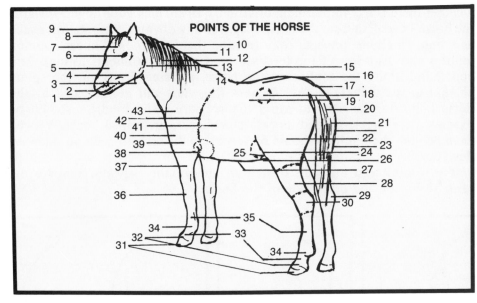

POINTS OF THE HORSE

Points of the horse.

1. Muzzle
2. Nostril
3. Jaw
4. Cheek
5. Face
6. Eye
7. Forehead
8. Poll
9. Ear
10. Mane
11. Crest
12. Neck
13. Throatlatch
14. Wither
15. Back
16. Loin
17. Croup
18. Hip
19. Coupling
20. Tail
21. Point of buttocks
22. Thigh
23. Quarter
24. Stifle
25. Rear flank
26. Sheath
27. Underline
28. Gaskin
29. Point of hock
30. Hock
31. Foot
32. Coronet
33. Pastern
34. Fetlock
35. Cannon
36. Knee
37. Forearm
38. Point of elbow
39. Arm
40. Point of shoulder
41. Ribs
42. Heart girth
43. Shoulder

ness, and can actually be the cause of lameness in some cases. The proportions of the body conformation as compared with the limb conformation may determine whether the horse is safe and comfortable to ride. Conformation is a major factor in the soundness of the limbs and it often determines the useful lifetime of the horse.

Very few horses have perfect conformation. Conformation of the body varies from breed to breed and this factor must be considered in the evaluation of your horse. For example, an Arabian has a short back compared to a thoroughbred. A quarter horse of certain blood lines has a shorter, heavier body and shorter legs than a thoroughbred.

The horse should be examined from a distance of about 15 metres. You should have a mental image of the type of horse you are selecting. The head should be in proportion to the rest of the body. The legs should be the correct length, thickness and shape; viewed from the front, they should not turn inwards or outwards. The neck should be the right thickness and shape compared to the rest of the body. The withers should not be narrow, and the backline should be more straight than hollowed. The rump should look strong, and the hindlegs appear in proportion to the body.

After examining the animal from a distance, make a closer examination, starting at the head. Check that the horse is not 'parrot-mouthed'. To test

Blemishes and unsoundness.

1. Undershot jaw
2. Parrot mouth
3. Blindness
4. Moon blindness
5. Poll evil
6. Fistulous withers
7. Thoroughpin
8. Capped hock
9. Stringhalt
10. Curb
11. Bone spavin
    or jack
12. Bog spavin
13. Bowed tendons
14. Sidebones
15. Quittor
16. Ring bone
17. Windgalls
18. Splints
19. Calf kneed
20. Capped elbow
21. Sweeney
22. Contracted heels,
    corns, founder
    thrush, quarter
    or sand crack,
    scratches or
    greasy heel
General: Heaves,
    hernia, roaring,
    thick wind.

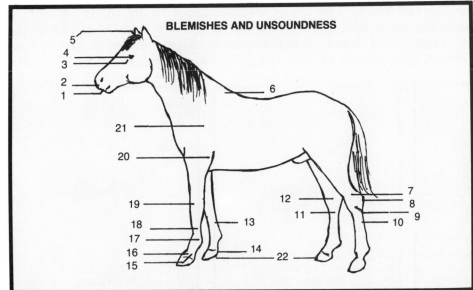

BLEMISHES AND UNSOUNDNESS

When selecting a horse the obvious points to avoid are faults connected with his conformation. Some common bad points of conformation to avoid in the hind-legs are illustrated here.
(a) Base narrow behind, usually accompanied by bow legs.
(b) Sickle hocks and camped behind.
(c) Cow hocks with base wide feet.
(d) Standing under behind. Too straight behind.

whether there is any impairment of vision, quickly flick your fingers towards the horse's eye. Examine the horse's legs for any obvious abnormalities such as splints, ringbone, unusual conformation (bent or crooked knees), tendon injuries and disorders of the feet (see the Common Ailments listing). Run your hand along the topline of the horse, pressing firmly on the spinal column to see if there is any soreness. (Soreness will be indicated by the horse hollowing its back to avoid the pressure.) The hindlegs should be examined for 'sickle-shaped' hocks, 'cow' hocks, or capped hocks. Viewed from behind, the hindlegs should be vertical to the ground, with no sideways deviations.

If you think you have discovered an abnormality, always compare the same region on the other side of the horse.

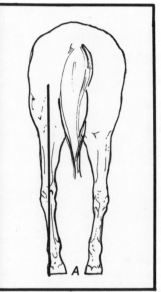
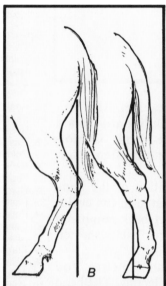
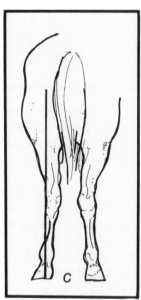
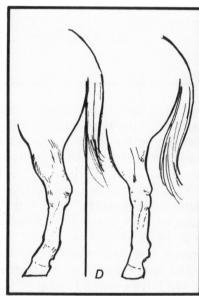

A   B   C   D

Determining age

The life span of horses is twenty to twenty-five years, about one-third that of human beings. Horses are generally in their prime between the ages of three and twelve years—this may vary because of individual differences in animals or because of the different kind of work they do.

The approximate age of the horse can be determined by noting the shape and degree of wear of temporary and permanent teeth. Temporary or milk teeth are easily distinguishable from permanent ones because they are smaller and whiter. The age of a horse cannot be determined accurately when it is more than twelve years old. At that age the cross-section of the teeth is changing from oval to triangular in shape, and they project or slant forward more and more as the horse becomes older.

The age of a horse is determined by looking at the 6 incisor teeth in each jaw. But you must be able to recognise the shape, marks and degree of wear which appear on the teeth at varying ages.

Corner temporary incisors are erupting at six months. The corner permanent incisors begin to wear at 5 years. At 7 years note the notch or hook on incisor.

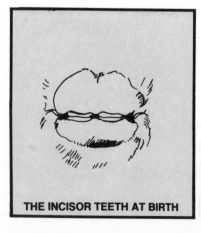

THE INCISOR TEETH AT BIRTH

SIX MONTHS

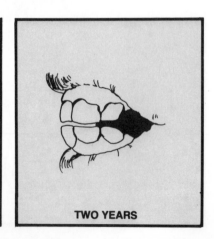

TWO YEARS

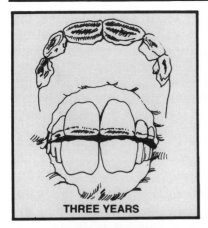

THREE YEARS

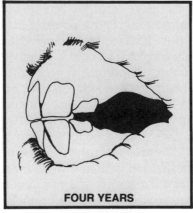

FOUR YEARS

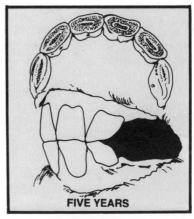

FIVE YEARS

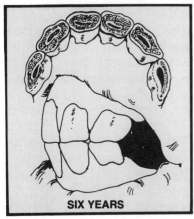

SIX YEARS

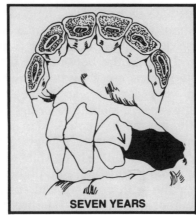

SEVEN YEARS

TEN YEARS

Veterinary examination

Once you have completed your examination of the horse and it has passed all your tests with flying colours, the next step is to engage an equine veterinarian to examine the horse on your behalf. Make sure the vet is a recommended equine practitioner. Such a person is examining horses all day long and will be able to give you both a professional opinion and a practical opinion as to the horse's suitability for your purpose.

With the advent of modern drugs it is easy for a dishonest vendor to mask lameness and other abnormalities—by sedating an hysterical (highly strung) horse, for example. Even experienced equine veterinarians may overlook a problem under these circumstances, so it is best to take the horse on a ten-day trial basis. Most drugs are out of the system after five days and any lameness or mental quirks begin to show.

Be sure to take special care of any horse lent to you on this basis. It is, after all, not yours. Always insure the animal in case of any fatal accident and make sure you are covered against any damage the horse may cause.

Housing and paddocks

Stables

The minimum dimensions of a stable (stall/box) should be 4 × 4 metres, with a clear headspace of at least 5 metres. The stable should have a pleasant outlook, as horses confined to small areas can become bored and develop the vices of crib-biting, wind-sucking and weaving. It helps to have chickens, dogs or other animals roaming about the yard. Preferably face the stable towards the yard where there is human activity.

In the northern hemisphere the box should face south; in the southern hemisphere the box should face north. This will ensure that it catches as much sun as possible.

The box should be well ventilated, have a high ceiling and be well

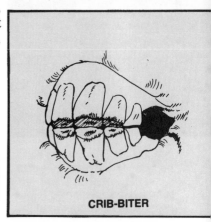

FOURTEEN YEARS

Crib-biting is a vice or bad habit usually caused by boredom (see page 217). These teeth show the typical signs of wear.

CRIB-BITER

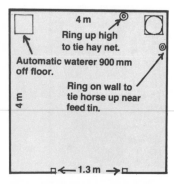

4 m
Ring up high
to tie hay net.
Automatic waterer 900 mm
off floor.
Ring on wall to
tie horse up near
feed tin.
4 m
←— 1.3 m —→

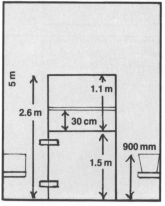

5 m
2.6 m
1.1 m
30 cm
900 mm
1.5 m

Suggested plan for a stable. The feed tin should be at least 350 mm diameter. The floor must slope slightly to allow drainage towards the door. Stable doors should be in two halves, top portion overlapping bottom. Floors must be non-slippery, resistant to moisture and long-wearing. Walls must be solid and have smooth surfaces.

drained. The drainage from the box should run towards the door rather than towards a drain in the centre. Drainage from each box can then be collected in one long drain. Enclosed drains should be avoided where possible because they are easily blocked. In colder climates, stables should be well insulated.

One of the most important aspects of stables is their safety. It is essential that the wall surfaces are smooth, and preferably made of a solid material such as brick or boards that are tongue and grooved. Fibro asbestos or corrugated iron sheets are dangerous.

The stable door should be in two halves, with the bottom half at least 1.5 metres high. This provides safety for the horse, and prevents it from jumping out. At the same time, it is low enough for the horse to look over. Provision should be made for inserting a bar about 30 centimetres above the bottom door. This will inhibit horses who may still have thoughts of jumping over the door, and can also be used to restrict the activities of 'weavers'. (A weaver stands with its head over the door, rocking from one foreleg to the other and exhausting itself.) The door should be at least 1.3 metres wide so that the horse does not knock its hips as it passes through. Two bolts, one at the top and one at the bottom, are essential. This will ensure that the efforts of bolt-openers are frustrated, and will also discourage the persistent 'door banger' who likes to hear the door rattle each time it is kicked.

Stable fittings should include two rings, one for tying up the horse and the other for fastening the hay net. A manger and a self-filling waterer should be secured in a corner at breast height. All light fittings, plastic pipes and anything chewable should be kept well away from the horse. To deter wood-chewers, and avoid maintenance on timber fittings, use metal cover strips on the edges or paint with creosote and sump-oil (50/50).

The stable floor may have a waterproof base such as concrete or bricks, or be of a porous substance such as ashes or sand. The former are the most hygienic and provide the basis for a clean-smelling, fresh stable. Bedding for the horse (in decreasing order of preference) is straw, wood shavings, saw-dust, sand or soil. Stabled horses should be groomed daily and their stables mucked out three times a day. This involves removal of manure and urine and any contaminated bedding.

In good climates stables should be open so the horse does not suffer claustrophobia and can view what is happening in its immediate neighbourhood.

Some racehorse stables include such amenities as a spa and a swimming pool to ease horse's weary muscles.

Fencing

Fences should be constructed of hardwood rails and posts. The rails can be round, about 10 centimetres in diameter, or flat, 15 × 4 centimetres. Paddocks for horses can have either two or three rails. Two rails are suitable for large paddocks where horses graze—but where they are small and the horses hand fed, it is best to have three rails. The horses in the latter group tend to have little grass in their paddocks; they get bored and are likely to spend more time against the fence getting into mischief.

The hardwood posts should be at least 20 centimetres in diameter and can be left whole or split into halves. The posts should be at least 75 centimetres into the ground, leaving 1.5 metres out of the ground. They should be spaced 2.5 metres apart. The rails can be wired or bolted to the posts—but there must be no protrusions to cut a horse.

Fences can be painted. But to prevent chewing (crib-biting) and to preserve the wood, it is best to paint with a 50/50 sump-oil and creosote mixture. The sump-oil should be at least three months old.

An alternative fence is one made of 7.5 centimetre pipe.

Keeping horses in paddocks with steel posts and wire is very dangerous and invariably leads to injury, sometimes of a serious nature.

Yards containing hand-fed horses should be separated from adjacent yards by a gap of at least 2 metres to prevent fighting.

All rubbish should be removed from yards and paddocks to avoid injury.

Pipe gates are best—but avoid mesh sizes that can trap a horse's hoof. Wooden gates are less suitable because they sag and horses chew them. Gate latches must be hard for horses to open.

Horse yards should be of solid construction to avoid injury.

Fences should be constructed of solid posts and rails. A gap of at least 2 metres between each yard prevents fighting and biting.

Releasing horses

If the horse is entering a new paddock for the first time, always take it to the watering point, unless there are other horses already in the paddock.

Always release a horse into a new paddock in daylight so that it can orientate obstacles before dark.

Making the horse miss its previous meal will encourage it to graze rather than dash about.

Check the paddock before releasing the horse for obstacles such as wire, tin sheets or glass.

Try to avoid releasing with strange horses.

After releasing the horse, wait for 15 minutes while the horse settles.

Feeding

It is most important to feed a horse a balanced diet adjusted to its exercise level. A balanced diet must include the following seven elements: proteins, fats, starches, water, fibrous roughage, salts and vitamins.

Proteins replace muscular wastage and form muscle fibre. Fats and starches produce heat and energy. Water is essential so that body functions and the digestive system can work. Fibrous roughage is the agency by which concentrated foods are broken up and absorbed, and it is necessary for proper functioning of the intestine. Roughage includes chaff and fresh grass. Hay provides the main source of fibrous roughage for the stabled horse and can contain high percentages of protein. Oats, barley, peas, beans and maize—in fact most of the grains are good energy foods. Additional foods include bran, linseed, and fresh foods such as apples and root vegetables. All tend to have a laxative effect on the horse.

How much food?

The quantity of food required depends on the individual horse and the work it is doing. As a general guide the total daily intake for horses between 150 and 160 centimetres is 11 to 12 kilograms and for animals over 160 centimetres, 12 to 13 kilograms.

Artificially fed horses need more dental care than those living in a more natural state in paddocks. Special instruments are needed to care for a horse's teeth.

A mouth gag is used to hold the mouth open while the horse's teeth are filed.

For a horse exercised daily and worked solidly one day per week, the proportion should be 50 per cent bulk to a corresponding weight of concentrate. Horses in fast, hard work would require an increase in concentrate but the proportion of bulk in the diet cannot be below one-third of the weight of the total intake or the concentrates will cause trouble in the digestive system. The horse is unable to cope with large quantities of concentrate foods at the one time. The golden rule is: feed little and often. Bulk foods such as hay may be given in larger quantities because they are eaten more slowly. Concentrates, however, should be given in small quantities not more than 2 kilograms in any one feed. The amount of concentrates fed to the horse will depend on the type and the amount of work it is doing.

Horses should never be worked immediately after feeding, as most of their blood will be concentrated around the stomach and intestines helping to absorb the food. Exercise at this time will cause indigestion and possibly severe colic (see the Common ailments listing). Fresh, clean water must always be freely available to the horse except immediately after hard exercise.

If the horse becomes too 'frisky' the solution is either to cut the grain back until the animal is more manageable, or to increase the exercise period.

A horse receiving 13 kilograms of food should have 6.5 kilograms of concentrates and the same amount of hay. The concentrates might comprise 4.5 kilograms of oats, 1 kilogram of bran and 1 kilogram of a mixture of cracked corn, sunflower seeds and milo. A racehorse eating this type of ration would be working regularly and hard. It would be exercised from forty-five minutes to one hour daily.

Suggested Diet for Horse in Hard Work

Morning Feed
1.5 kilograms oats
200 grams cracked corn
500 grams oaten chaff
500 grams wheaten chaff
1 kilogram lucerne

Noon Feed
1.5 kilograms oats
500 grams oaten chaff
500 grams wheaten chaff
1 kilogram lucerne
500 grams carrots—3 days per week

Evening Feed
1.5 kilograms oats
500 grams wheaten chaff
500 grams oaten chaff
1 kilogram lucerne
500 grams cracked corn, sunflower,
  milo mixture
225 grams powdered milk
  (spray dried)

225 grams cotton-seed meal
  (de-gossipoled)
33 grams calcium
55 grams salt mixture
A prescribed iron tonic (in honey
  if possible)
250 grams vitamin and mineral
  pellets (including vitamin E)

1 kilogram of mixture of boiled barley, corn, milo and linseed* **OR**
1 kilogram of bran and molasses*
*The last two should be given on alternate nights.
1. At 6.30–7.00 p.m., when closing for the night, give sheafs of oats to good doers.
2. Provide rock salt permanently, either in food bin or on wall.
3. If possible, give long green feed in mid-afternoon.

Some horses may not eat the whole lot—if this is too much, reduce everything in quantity rather than upset the balance of the diet. Some horses may consume this quantity by being fed four meals per day rather than three.

Any change to a horse's feeding programme must be introduced slowly, as their stomachs are very sensitive to change.

Complete commercial rations

It will be more convenient for the average horse owner or those with small numbers to purchase a complete ration. A good quality mix from a reputable supplier will have been formulated by a nutritionist. These are available as a pellet or a loose feed. Some pellets may require the addition of hay or chaff. They can be purchased by the bag, and one bag lasts about a week. This avoids the need for a large feed-room with several different bags or bins. Complete rations can be used on their own, or concentrates may be added if necessary if the horse is in hard work.

No matter what ration you are feeding, it is important to regulate the ration according to the appearance of the horse's droppings. There should be a reasonable quantity of manure, and the bulk of droppings should just form upon hitting the ground. If the droppings appear small in total quantity, and have small firm units, then the horse is becoming constipated. If this is not rectified, the horse can develop an impaction colic. At the next feeding the horse should be given 2 litres of warm bran mash mixed with molasses or linseed oil instead of its normal meal. This should be continued at each meal until the droppings loosen. It may be necessary to give this laxative meal as a twice-weekly routine. Impaction colic is one of the most common forms of colic, and if it is not rectified the horse may roll and develop a twisted bowel which can be fatal. Finally, remember that it is not economical to feed good food if the horse has not been wormed or had its teeth attended to.

Twenty minutes of lungeing is a good exercise alternative to a hard ride. Always give equal time in each direction.

General care

Exercise

A stabled horse must be exercised each day, whatever the weather. To keep the horse alert and interested, the exercise must be varied and carried out intelligently. It should be the equivalent of walking for ten minutes, trotting for five minutes and cantering for five minutes, with a walk of about twenty minutes in the afternoon. If the horse is receiving a high-grain diet, it should be given at least this amount of exercise each day of the week, otherwise it is likely to become 'tied-up' when exercised the day after a rest. ('Tied-up' is the common term for azoturia, a condition in which the stored-up energy in the muscles breaks down into an acid which causes the muscles to cramp and stiffen painfully. It can be very dangerous.) The horse may get its daily exercise by riding or lungeing.

A walking machine can be employed where large numbers of horses need to be exercised.

Lungeing should always be done in an enclosed paddock or round yard, so that if the horse escapes it will not run on to the road. Lungeing gives the horse an opportunity to develop its muscles without carrying the weight of a rider. Twenty minutes of lungeing is a good alternative to a hard ride. It calms down very fresh horses, and if a horse has a sore back or can't be ridden for some other reason, it is the ideal way to exercise it. Horses in large yards or paddocks do not require daily forced exercise.

If a horse has raised a sweat after exercise, it should be washed down with warm water (in winter) or cold water (in summer). Excess water should be removed with a scraper. In cold weather, the horse should be towelled down until it is dry and warm. If the horse cannot be washed all over, at least use a sponge or wet cloth to rub over the saddle, girth and bridle marks, particularly behind the ears. The areas between the hindlegs and under the tail, the sheath, and around the elbows must also be washed thoroughly. Once the horse has been washed, the legs should be inspected for cuts and thorns, and the feet picked out.

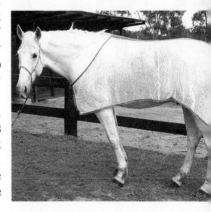

A mesh 'sweat' rug is used after exercise to prevent rapid evaporation which could cause chilling and often colic.

To avoid colic, always allow a horse to cool down completely before offering it even a small amount of water. Do not feed for at least one and a half hours after severe exercise.

Grooming tools l. to r. metal curry comb, scraper, hoof-pick and soft body brush.

The scraper is used to remove excess water after the horse has been washed down.

The correct way to use a rubber curry comb.

All parts of the body must be brushed; horses appreciate gentle grooming of the head.

Grooming

Grooming is an important part of the horse's hygiene, particularly where horses are stabled and hand fed. To keep your horse healthy and clean, you will need at least the following basic gear:

Brushing the coat

The dandy brush is used especially in winter on dirty, muddy horses with long coats. It has long stiff bristles and removes dried, caked mud from the horse's coat. Take care not to brush too vigorously in tender areas. Do not use it on the flanks or the legs.

In summer when the hair is shorter, it should not be necessary to use the dandy brush at all. A body brush is generally quite adequate, and much more comfortable for the horse. Hold the brush in the hand nearest to the horse's head. In other words, use your left hand when you are grooming the near-side (left side) and your right hand when you are grooming the off-side (right side). Use the brush in long, sweeping, slightly circular movements in the direction of the hair. Every few strokes the brush can be cleaned by pushing it across the teeth of a metal curry comb. (A rubber curry comb can be used lightly on the horse to remove caked sweat, but the metal curry comb should never be used in this way.) The whole of the horse's coat, except for the mane and tail, can be brushed with the body brush. Make sure you also clean the awkward places such as the inside of the legs, under the belly, the neck, and under the mane. Clean the horse's eyes and wipe its nostrils with a damp cloth. Use a second cloth to wipe out its sheath and under its tail.

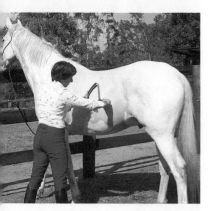
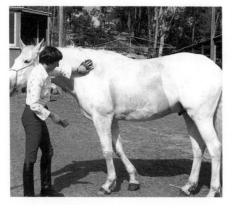

In more temperate climates, where the winter is not severe and where horses are stabled and rugged, owners often prefer to clip the body hair. This is done for better hygiene and for appearance, especially in show horses. The horse generally dislikes the noise and vibration of the clippers and hence the clipping should be done by a professional. The horse can be clipped all over or longer hair left over the ribs or flanks to provide some extra protection against the cold.

Cleaning the feet

The horse's feet are the most important part (hence the old saying, 'no feet, no horse'). If they are neglected, the horse will be ruined. The feet should be picked out every day; the shoes should be removed every four weeks and the feet trimmed by a blacksmith. The horse's hoof is equivalent to your fingernail and does not feel pain.

To pick up the horse's foot, lean gently against its shoulder and push its weight on to the other foot. At the same time, lift the leg just above the fetlock, while giving the order 'Up', or 'Lift'. If the horse fails to obey, put one hand behind and below its knee and push forward while the other hand lifts the fetlock. Hold the horse's foot up by placing one hand under the

A Horse's Hoof

Heel

Bulb of heel

Central sulcus of frog

Bars

collateral sulcus

Quarter

white line

Apex of frog

Wall

Toe

Sole

fetlock. Using the other hand, clean out the foot with the hoof pick. Make sure that all dirt and stones are picked out, particularly in the grooves beside the frog. (The frog is the triangular area in the centre of the sole. It is slightly rubbery and acts as a shock absorber to help prevent the leg from being jarred. It also helps return blood from the ends of the horse's leg to the heart. The frog should be kept trimmed so that it does not provide a crevice for infection such as thrush to grow.) Always clean out your horse's feet before and after it is ridden. If the horse is kept in a stable, its feet should be picked out every day. Once the feet have been thoroughly cleaned inside and out, a hoof dressing can be applied.

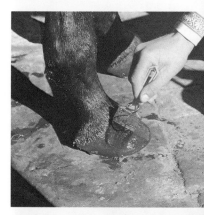

The correct position to hold a horse's foot to avoid being kicked.

Using a hoof-pick to clean the frog area.

Apply a hoof dressing daily to walls, soles and heels to keep them supple and to prevent cracking.

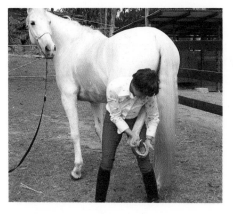

Grooming mane and tail

The mane and tail should be carefully combed to remove tangles, and then brushed out using a dandy brush. The mane should lie flat against the horse's neck. Many manes fall naturally to the off-side, but a thick mane may fall to either side. It is a good idea to brush all the mane over to the wrong side, and then over to the other side. This allows you to get to the underneath hairs of the mane. So that the head collar and bridle will lie flat across the poll, many people trim away a few centimetres of mane just behind the horse's ears. This can be done with scissors or special mane clippers (much easier to get a good result).

To brush a horse's tail, stand well to one side of the horse, hold the end of the tail in one hand and the brush in the other. Many people like to cut the tail horizontally about 10 centimetres or so below the point of the hock. This ensures that when the horse is moving the tail is level with the hock.

Teeth

The horse's teeth should be inspected twice a year. Young horses up to the age of five should have their teeth checked more frequently. Teeth can become sharp or worn, or there may be retention of caps. All these problems will prevent proper mastication and may contribute to biting and riding problems. (See earlier section Determining age.)

Handling

The major reflex in the horse is one of flight not fight. When handling a horse it is of the utmost importance to show that you are not going to hurt it. Speak to the horse before approaching it and always move slowly. In many instances, because they are inquisitive animals, the horse will approach the quietly spoken person. When catching a horse in a paddock, carry some feed and talk softly as you approach. Avoid chasing the horse and do not make loud noises. Always let the horse know what you are doing.

The approach should be to the shoulder of the near-side, whether the horse is in a paddock, yard or box. Once you are close enough, pat or stroke the lower neck or shoulder. To touch an area such as the fetlock, start at the shoulder and run your hand down the horse's leg.

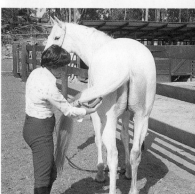

Stand well to one side when grooming the tail.

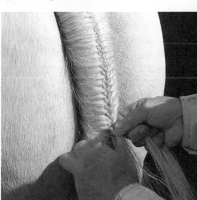

A plaited tail adds a touch of class for the show ring.

Correctly fitted headgear is essential when handling horses.

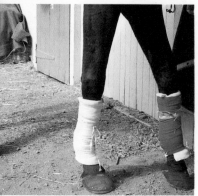

Horse's legs are bandaged for protection in the stable and during travelling, or for slow work.

A difficult horse can be loaded using a rope around its hind-quarters.

Head gear

Properly fitting head gear is essential. Rope halters should have a knot to prevent the noseband from becoming too loose or too tight. Bridles should be comfortable with the bit just touching the corner of the lips. Lead-ropes should be thick and soft; thin nylon can burn the handler's fingers.

Transport

Whenever transporting a horse ensure that all gear is in first-class condition. Use strong, well-fitting headstalls and lead-ropes. Protective knee-caps, hock boots, tail guards and leg bandages can be used if desired to further protect the horse when floating.

If a horse is difficult to load:
Allow plenty of time for the horse to be loaded.
Leave the float in the yard for the week and gradually move the feed tin into the float, until the horse is walking right inside.
Tie a rope to one side of the float and place it around the horse's buttocks. Blindfold if necessary.
Place the front legs, one after the other, on to the tailboard or ramp.
Coax with feed, apples, sugar, etc.
Use a fence and gate to form a shute with sides.
Avoid a steep ramp, or a ramp with no sides.
Walk another horse on just in front of the difficult horse.
Leave the front door open so the horse can see daylight.
Use a broom on the horse's rump.
Avoid violent punishment.

Horses tend to travel best on large floats, but the small two-horse float is equally adequate and so much more convenient. Ensure that the float has a clean, solid floor with a good gripping surface; rubber matting is ideal. When pulling a float drive carefully and avoid sudden changes of direction or speed.

Vaccination

Three diseases that can be prevented by immunisation are equine influenza, strangles and tetanus. For information about vaccinations against these and other diseases in your area, contact your veterinary surgeon. Horses can be vaccinated at a very early age and usually require annual boosters. Every horse should be vaccinated against tetanus, at the very least.

Worming

Horses are host to a number of internal parasites or worms. Many owners erroneously think that if a horse is fat and performs well there is no need to treat it for worms. Even in small numbers, some worms can cause severe and permanent damage to the internal organs of the horse, particularly in young horses and aged horses. A regular preventative worming programme is essential.

Worms have adapted to survive and spread rapidly in horse populations. They do not multiply within a horse's body, but through eggs passed in the manure. These eggs are passed in huge numbers and contaminate the horse's surroundings. Because horses graze close to the ground they are prone to rapid reinfestation in short pastures. Under damp conditions worm eggs and larvae can survive for extended periods on pastures and stable beddings. Immature developing stages of the worm cause severe damage to the internal organs of the horse's body. Unfortunately, these immature migrating stages are not affected by worming compounds. As young horses have little resistance to worms, they are prone to heavy infestation during their developmental period. The state of pregnancy in mares allows resting, immature stages of the worm to activate, thus ensuring that the foal is guaranteed early worm infestation. Some worm species have built up resistance

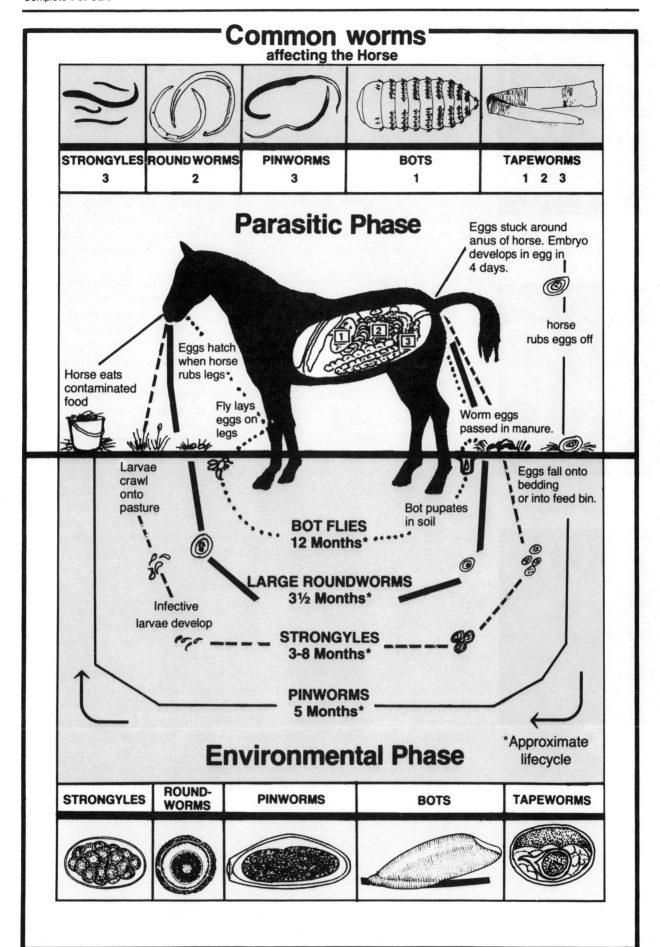

Common worms
affecting the Horse

STRONGYLES	ROUNDWORMS	PINWORMS	BOTS	TAPEWORMS
3	2	3	1	1 2 3

Parasitic Phase

Eggs stuck around anus of horse. Embryo develops in egg in 4 days.

horse rubs eggs off

Horse eats contaminated food

Eggs hatch when horse rubs legs

Fly lays eggs on legs

Worm eggs passed in manure.

Larvae crawl onto pasture

Eggs fall onto bedding or into feed bin.

Bot pupates in soil

BOT FLIES
12 Months*

Infective larvae develop

LARGE ROUNDWORMS
3½ Months*

STRONGYLES
3-8 Months*

PINWORMS
5 Months*

Environmental Phase

*Approximate lifecycle

STRONGYLES	ROUND-WORMS	PINWORMS	BOTS	TAPEWORMS

189

A large strongyle worm — commonly called large redworm (S. vulgaris).

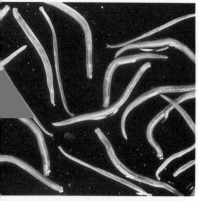

Another variety of the large strongyle worm (S. edentatus).

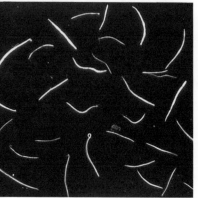

Although small strongyle worms are not as destructive as large strongyles they still cause many problems (Trichonema spp.).

against certain worming compounds. Those that survive the treatments rapidly pass resistance to new generations. As a result, worms may persist although regular worming has been carried out, making it necessary to change worming compounds regularly.

Large strongyle worms

Large strongyle worms grow to 5 centimetres long and are about as thick as the lead in a pencil. They are commonly called large redworms. Another worm in this group, the bloodworm, is about half the size.

Despite its smaller size, the immature wandering bloodworm is considered one of the most damaging of all internal worms in the horse. The adult female can lay as many as 5000 to 6000 eggs a day. These are passed out in the manure and then hatch to contaminate the horse's environment. The horse eats the larvae when grazing, eating hay or food from the ground, or picking at stable bedding. The larvae then travel to the intestine and burrow into the bowel wall.

The bloodworm larvae migrate along and within the walls of the major arteries that supply blood to the gut and the hindlimbs, and can cause aneurisms. These occur when the wall of the blood vessel becomes thin and forms a bulge, thus inhibiting blood flow to the gut and hindlimbs. When they have completed this damage, the fully developed larvae migrate back to the bowel, develop into adult bloodworms, and commence production of eggs. This whole phase takes up to six months.

Large redworm larvae migrate through the organs in the gut cavity. They burrow into the lining of these organs and grow to almost mature size, leaving huge scars as they burrow. After several months of migration through these organs, they then return to the large bowel for the development phase to the adult.

Clinical signs of large strongyle infestation   Large strongyle adults attach themselves to the lining of the large bowel. They feed on the lining and reduce nutrients available to the horse. They also take blood from the horse as they feed. In large numbers they can cause anaemia and symptoms of illness such as poor coat, lack of stamina, poor condition, colic, lameness and 'tying up' because of restricted blood flow to hindlimb muscles. At this stage very little can be done in the way of treatment except to adopt a stringent worming programme and hope the horse can compensate the blood flow caused by the aneurism.

Small strongyle worms

Small strongyle worms have a life cycle similar to large strongyles. Once they enter the bowel, however, the larvae burrow into the lining of the bowel wall to produce small lumps and ulcers. They can remain in a resting stage in the lumps in the bowel wall for extended periods. The development phase can last up to six months. They then re-enter the bowel and mature to adults.

Clinical signs of small strongyle infestation   The small strongyles may be attached to the gut wall or free in the gut contents. The ones attached to the gut wall feed on the bowel lining and ingest blood. The free stages digest part of the food. In large numbers, the combination of the two can cause symptoms of illness, anaemia, diarrhoea, and constipation. Horses with heavy infestations may also pass large numbers when eating laxative foods such as lush pasture, bran mashes, molasses or linseed meal or after being dosed with paraffin oil.

Again, the adult small strongyles have been shown to have developed resistance to certain worming compounds. This means that some adult worms will not be removed at drenching time and will pass the resistance on to subsequent generations. This results in a rapid build-up of resistant adult worms, especially if the same worming compounds are used continuously. Despite a worming programme, periodical faecal tests should be done to determine if the worming preparation is effective—if not, change it.

Large roundworms

Large roundworms are round white worms up to 40 centimetres long and about as thick as a pencil. The adult females can produce up to 30 000 eggs per day which are passed in the manure. The eggs are resistant to the effects of weather and can remain in the manure or in moist, shady conditions for long periods. The horse becomes infested by ingesting the eggs. Once inside the horse the eggs hatch, the larvae penetrate the gut wall, enter the bloodstream and travel through to the liver and lungs within a few days. Here they break into the airways and cause the horse to cough. They are coughed up from the lungs into the mouth and are then reswallowed to develop into large adult worms which begin passing eggs. This development phase takes up to twelve weeks.

Clinical signs of large roundworm infestation   Severe roundworm infestations can be found in foals as young as three to twelve weeks. Heavy infestations rob the foal of nutrients, and toxic substances produced by the worm may cause colic, diarrhoea, poor appetite, poor growth, loss of vitality and listlessness. The foal may also develop a pot-bellied appearance. Severe infestations may block the bowel completely, leading to constipation, colic and death. Much damage is also done during the migratory phase through the lungs and liver, with damage to the lungs leading to pneumonia ('rattles'), abscess formation, coughing and at times a nasal discharge. The development of 'rattles' in young foals may be partly associated with heavy burdens of immature migrating roundworms which take organisms from the gut through to the lungs to cause abscesses. Treatment in these cases not only involves a worming programme, but also antibiotic cover.

Pinworms

Pinworms come in two sizes, male and female being greatly differentiated. The male pinworm is 1 centimetre long and the female 12 centimetres. The female migrates to the anus of the horse where she deposits her eggs, up to 60 000 at a time, around the area under the tail in a mass of yellowish sticky jelly. After laying the eggs she dies. This process causes the horse to be intensely itchy in the tail area and is responsible for tail-rubbing. The intense rubbing causes eggs to fall off on to the ground or into feed utensils and water troughs, so that the horse recontaminates itself.

Typical signs of pinworm infestation   Heavy infestation of adult pinworms causes a loss of condition or general ill-health, mild diarrhoea, and excessive rubbing of hindquarters to relieve the itchiness caused by the eggs. Infected horses continuously rub their tail on fences, posts, trees and feed bins, not only pushing over fences and stretching wires, but also denuding the base of the tail of hair. Horses that spend a lot of time trying to relieve the irritation may not feed. Pinworms are effectively eradicated by most worming treatments (described later). In addition mercurial ointments can be deposited inside the anus to kill the adults.

Bots

Bots are the larval stages of the horse bot-fly. They attach themselves to the horse's stomach wall during one period of their life cycle. The bot-fly lays its yellow eggs on the hairs on the front legs and flanks of the horse in autumn. (The life cycle can be broken by shaving off the eggs or by wiping over with kerosene.) These eggs are licked off by the horse, and hatch in the moist conditions of the gastrointestinal tract. In early spring the larvae detach from the stomach wall and pass out into the manure. They burrow into the soil and after a few months, depending on the temperature, emerge as adult bot-flies.

Typical signs of adult bot-fly infestation   Adult bot-flies annoy horses as they dart around their legs to deposit the eggs. Young horses may be panic-stricken and gallop off and run into fences. Sometimes horses in groups will

Roundworms (Parascaris equi) are very common and cause much tissue damage during the migratory phase.

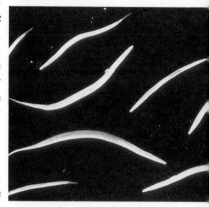

Pinworms (Oxyuris equi) are a common cause of tail rubbing.

A post mortem stomach showing bot-fly larvae attached to the wall.

bunch up for protection. Migrating stages of bot-fly larvae may burrow into the tongue, causing irritation and interference with feeding. At times they may cause pockets of pus to form between the teeth, resulting in bad breath and difficulty in feeding. They may also cause the horse to resent the pressure of the bit in the mouth. Large numbers of bot larvae in the stomach can interfere with digestion, lead to colic or signs of unthriftiness, and in some cases rupture of the stomach may result; this is usually fatal.

Large stomach worms

Large stomach worms (habronema) live in large nodules or growths in the stomach wall. The adult worm is about 2 centimetres long, white, and as fine as a pin. The females lay very small eggs which are passed in the manure, and then swallowed by fly maggots. When the maggot pupates it hatches as a fly, still carrying the larval stage of the large stomach worm in its mouth parts. The common small black housefly and the stable fly are common carriers. As the fly feeds, it deposits larvae around the horse's mouth and eyes, and on cuts and sores. Horses may also eat whole flies that crowd feed bins. The larvae gather in the stomach and invade the gastric lining.

Clinical signs of habronema infestation Typical disorders include runny eyes, pussy conjunctivitis, lumps of proud-flesh-type tissue on the eyelids, irritation to cuts and sores (commonly called summer sores or cutaneous habronemiasis). These worms can affect skin on the shoulders, belly, sheath and penis, causing itchy lesions which the horse rubs vigorously. Adult worms live in the gastric lining, and heavy infestations may cause inflammation and ulceration of the stomach wall, interfering with digestion. Large numbers may cause colic and unthriftiness. Again, most worming preparations are effective.

Tapeworms

Tapeworms are not very common in horses. Adult horses are not greatly affected, though young foals can become infested when grazing contaminated pastures. This can lead to poor growth, diarrhoea and at times colic.

The general symptoms of worms are failure to thrive, poor appetite, poor condition, rough coat and lack of vigour.

How to diagnose a wormy horse

Most horses have worms, but it is normally a question of how many and what type. A combination of clinical signs, combined with a check for worm eggs in the manure, is the most practical method of diagnosis. Sometimes clinical signs of worm infestation may not be obvious, and a dramatic response to worming might be the only indication that worms were present. The general symptoms indicating the presence of worms are failure to thrive, poor appetite, poor condition, rough coat, reduced performance, lack of stamina, pale gums, anaemia, poor recovery from work, impaired digestion, bouts of colic or constipation, lack of vigour, pot-bellied appearance in foals, poor growth rates, diarrhoea, coughing, nervousness, persistent scours (diarrhoea) in foals, without a rise in temperature (and not associated with foal heat in mares), tail rubbing, skin irritation or discharge from the eyes.

Manure examination is the best way to diagnose which worm is present and to what extent it is causing the problem. Collect a fresh sample of still-warm droppings. One ball of manure is required. If there is diarrhoea, collect about 20 millilitres (3 tablespoons). Place the sample in a small glass jar or other container, label it with the name of the horse, date of collection, date of last worming, and the wormer used. Store it in a refrigerator and take it to your vet as soon as possible. If long-distance travel is involved, cool the sample in ice. Under refrigerated conditions worm eggs will delay hatching for seventy-two hours. Samples of diarrhoea, however, must be examined within twenty-four hours. Results from manure worm egg counts and cultures will enable your vet to give you the best advice on the method of treating and controlling worm infestation in your horse.

Control of worms

Do not graze horses on very short pastures. Confinement on heavily grazed areas increases the intake of worm eggs.

Rotate grazing with other forms of livestock.

Regularly harrow pastures.

Small paddocks should be cleaned weekly and manure piled so that it heats up and destroys worm eggs.

Ensure adequate drainage. Wet, marshy areas should be avoided.

Collect and dispose of manure left around feeding areas.

Provide water troughs if possible. Horses drinking from dams or puddles can increase their intake of worm eggs.

Provide feed tins. Do not feed horses directly from the ground. Food eaten from the ground increases worm intake.

Provide an above-ground hay rack.

Avoid making hay for horses from their grazing areas.

Control flies in the stable.

Avoid grooming horses in their stable.

Reduce contamination of the horse by regular grooming and hosing down after work.

Remove bot eggs with a bot knife or bathe the hairs with warm water to stimulate hatching of the larvae. Alternatively, wash with an insecticidal compound such as diluted Malathion at 10 millilitres per litre.

Use worming compounds regularly. Modern wormers are very efficient in removing adult worms. They are reliable, have a wide safety margin and do not usually affect the horse's performance or health. Check for the best current wormer with your vet.

Before using any wormer read the directions carefully.

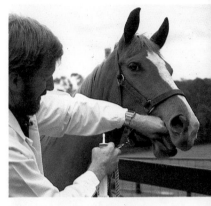

Giving a worm paste.
Step 1 Pass the hand into the mouth and grasp the tongue.

Step 2 Pull the tongue out and deposit the paste as far back on the tongue as possible.

Worming programme

Worm pregnant mares every three weeks until a month before foaling. Do not use organophosphates in late pregnancy.

Worm lactating mares every four weeks until foals are weaned.

Worm foals when they are two weeks old, again at eight weeks, and then every six weeks until weaning.

Worm foals every eight weeks from weaning onwards.

Worm adult horses every four weeks while the worm burden is present, and extend the period to eight weeks once control has been achieved.

All horses over the age of six months should be wormed every eight weeks. Change the type of wormer every six to twelve months.

Worm all horses in a group at the same time.

All new horses, introduced horses (including foals over six weeks of age), and horses returning from agistment should be wormed on arrival.

Oral pastes are just as effective as drenches by stomach-tube, provided the horse gets the full dose.

If a resistance problem develops, the vet may need to make up a special mixture, unavailable as a commercial paste—and this will need to be given by stomach-tube.

Step 3 Hold the head up to prevent dribbling of the medication.

To give a worm paste

Slide your flattened left hand into the left side of the horse's mouth where there are no teeth. Take hold of the tongue with your whole fist and turn the tongue back on itself—so that your clenched fist with tongue inside is forcing the jaws apart. Pull the tongue out of the left side of the mouth through the toothless area as far as possible. Holding the paste in your right hand, enter it via the right side of the mouth and deposit the contents as far back on the tongue as possible. Then let the tongue go, and elevate the horse's chin until the paste has been swallowed.

Worming compounds

Most modern worming compounds are very efficient in removing adult worms. They are formulated into injections, suspensions, powders, granules, pastes and pellets. Worming preparations come and go according to their efficacy against the different species and the build-up of resistance. It is advisable to regularly check with your veterinarian as to which product should be used currently.

Breeding

The mare will show oestrus (be on heat, come into season) several times during the breeding season (spring into summer). When the mare is in season she will elevate her tail and stand with the back legs slightly apart. The clitoris will move in and out (winking) and she will urinate frequently. At the beginning of the breeding period oestrus may last for a considerable length of time, up to two weeks. As the season advances oestrus becomes shorter so that at the height of the season it lasts only three to five days. Ovulation occurs about forty-eight hours before the mare goes off oestrus; therefore mating in summer during the short oestrus periods is more likely to succeed.

Breeding in the mare can take the form of 'paddock mating' where the stallion is allowed to run free with the mares and mate naturally, or it can take the form of 'hand-mating'. Many studs employ a veterinarian to follicle-test in-season mares to determine when ovulation is about to occur. This ensures that the mare is bred at the optimum time and prevents overuse of the stallions. It also eliminates some risk of injury, as many mares will lash out at a stallion, despite showing interest to the teaser, if the follicle is not quite ripe.

When it is determined to mate the mare, a tail bandage is applied which extends down the tail about 30 centimetres. The mare's genitals are then washed down thoroughly with an antiseptic solution. When the stallion has an erect penis, it too should be washed in antiseptic solution. Both horses should be re-washed after mating. The stallion should be led up to the side of the mare to test her reaction. If she is receptive lead the stallion to the rear of the mare and allow him to mount. Sometimes the penis may need to be directed into the vulva of the mare.

If the mare is difficult to mate, check that she is on season and, if so, restraints such as hobbles or a twitch may be applied. The hand-mating of mares is a skilled job for the horseman and should only be attempted after considerable experience is gained working on a stud under a stud groom.

Maiden mares

There is usually a difference in the general condition of maiden mares entering the stud. Frequently they are turned out of racing just prior to or during the breeding season. Because it takes time to relax and become accustomed to the stud procedures, these mares are often very nervous. Also, mares turned out to pasture after being hand fed most of their lives will take at least eight weeks to adapt to a whole grass diet, in which time weight loss can be expected. It is particularly desirable to obtain maiden mares as early as possible to get them settled in before the season begins.

Breeders generally believe that examination of a maiden mare for breeding soundness is unnecessary, and this may be true in most cases. However, there are a few specific conditions encountered in maiden mares which, if not found and corrected before breeding, may result in injury. These include an infantile genital tract, imperforate hymen, vaginal septum and sutured vulva as a result of a Caslick's operation.

Special attention should be given to the teasing and breeding of maiden mares. Teasing is the act of using a stallion (or gelding treated with hormones) of negligible value to test the mares each day to see if they are in

A mare on heat showing interest to a teaser.

Tail elevation and clitoris winking indicate that the mare is in season.

A tail bandage is used for transporting a horse or when a mare is being served. Take care that the bandage is not too tight.

season. This horse is called a 'teaser'. His job can be hazardous because mares not in season can be vicious. Often a very small stallion is used—because he can mount without fear of penetration, to fully test the mare's response. Once it is determined that the mare is receptive, the valuable stud stallion is introduced. There is often a degree of roughness in the teasing procedure, and this is especially undesirable when handling young, inexperienced mares. Early mistreatment can result in the development of surly or vicious behaviour in the presence of the teaser which makes it difficult to determine the right time for breeding. Maiden mares should not be teased too vigorously. Observe them after the teaser has gone, and when they are with the mares in their group. Each mare tends to develop a relatively consistent oestrus cycle and characteristic behaviour at the different stages. An experienced, competent observer is able to predict the proper breeding time.

Maiden mares can be very unpredictable in the early spring. At this time they can go into a 'spring oestrus' and exhibit signs of heat practically every day for extended periods especially if the weather is mild. Some will accept the stallion, others will not. An occasional mare might be showing true oestrus, but the majority will not. Breeding at this stage is a waste of time and semen (particularly where a stallion has a heavy booking of mares). Patience is the best approach with these mares as they eventually settle into a normal cycle.

The 'jumping' procedure is recommended for young, nervous or timid maiden mares. 'Jumping' is simply a precaution to protect the stallion and, indirectly, to avoid any excitement that might cause the mare to injure herself. She is restrained as for breeding (twitch, leg strap or hobbles) and then a quiet, gentle teaser is allowed to mount the mare. Actual intercourse is prevented by directing the penis to one side. This procedure can be repeated several times to accustom the maiden mare to stud procedure. At the same time it gives the attendants an idea of how she reacts.

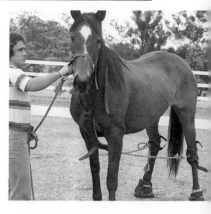
A mare with boots and hobbles on, is ready to be served.

Washing the stallion's penis with a mild antiseptic before service.

Pregnancy determination

The period of pregnancy in the mare is about eleven months. Determination of pregnancy can be made in three ways:

Manual testing

This is done by a veterinarian who examines the mare internally via the rectum. This requires considerable experience and dexterity if it is to be carried out with any degree of accuracy. An early indication can be given at twenty-one days, although a final legal decision is not possible till six weeks into the pregnancy. This is called a 42-day pregnancy test, on which a certificate may be issued.

Laboratory testing

There are two types of tests: blood tests which are done between sixty and ninety days after service, and a urine test which is done between two hundred and two hundred and seventy-five days after service.

Hand-serving a mare to prevent injury to either the mare or the stallion.

Ultra-sound scanning

This is a non-invasive technique which is harmless to the operator and the mare. An electronic probe sweeps the area under examination. Echoes, produced as the beam scans the various organs, provide a clear, moving image on a display screen. Accurate diagnosis of pregnancy can be made as early as 14 days after ovulation.

Manual and ultra-sound testing gives a much quicker result and allows time for rebreeding if the mare is not in foal; the other tests are used if there is any danger to the vet, the mare or the foetus in manual testing (for example, very highly strung mares, or mares that abort easily).

Barren mares and empty mares

'Barren' usually means chronically unable to go in foal and 'empty' means mares that have had foals but have not been rebred. Occasionally, a mare may produce ten or twelve foals in as many consecutive years, but on average this cannot be expected. A certain percentage of mares fail to conceive each year because of natural causes, accidents, infections and human errors. The breeder who breeds only one or two mares each year should make a particular effort to get the mare in good breeding condition well ahead of the season. The mare should have a pre-breeding check-up to assess her physical condition. Age will be a factor, as mares over the age of fifteen tend to go in foal less regularly. Teeth should be attended to, and if they are beyond repair a special ration is advisable. In addition, a vitamin or vitamin–mineral supplement is often beneficial to older mares.

Many older mares may be chronically lame or sore. Mares retired from racing often have arthritic conditions which plague them in later life. In these cases consideration may be given to special shoeing.

Sometimes a blood sample from a mare in poor physical condition will reveal an anaemia or even an infection. If a mare is barren, the possibility of a parasitic infection should never be overlooked, particularly in studs where horses are often yarded for periods. Proper worming programmes should be in force on all horse-raising establishments.

On the other hand some mares stay fat on little or no grain, appear sluggish and do not have a glossy or thrifty appearance. Often these mares have a history of erratic heat periods and fail to conceive despite repeated matings. Some of these mares respond well to thyroid extract, while others do better on a restricted diet together with exercise.

A veterinarian should be consulted to examine mares that do not go in foal. The vet will look for evidence of discharge from the vagina, or matting on the buttocks and tail. Special attention should be paid to the conformation in the region of the anus and vulva. The anus and vulva should form a nearly vertical line. If the line falls forward to any great extent from vulva to anus, there may be trouble from so-called 'wind-sucking'. This refers to the movement of air into the vagina, sometimes carrying with it faecal debris which has dropped on to the edges of the vulva. Further examination of the mare is made internally by the vet to examine the ovaries and womb.

This pregnant mare is due to foal and has been brought to the foaling paddock for 24-hour-a-day observation.

Infections can be introduced by contaminated hands or instruments at a previous foaling, during breeding or as a result of 'wind-sucking'. Mares that become wind-suckers should have a 'Caslick's operation', in which the lips of the vulva are stitched together except for a small opening at the lower end for urination. At breeding time the stitches are removed to allow service, and then replaced to prevent entry of infection during pregnancy. The stitches must be removed again a week or two before foaling.

Most breeders commence teasing their empty mares in early spring. Though all mares cannot be expected to have a regular oestrus cycle at this time of the year, most will cycle within a short time. When an empty mare sheds her winter coat, it is a good sign that she is ready to begin breeding. However, while it is important to get mares in foal as early as possible (so that the foals are bigger at yearling sales), most mares cycle best and are most fertile in mid-summer. A complete and accurate teasing chart is valuable for recording changes in heat periods, as mares tend to follow fairly consistent patterns from year to year.

'Foaling heat'

According to most data, the average gestation period for thoroughbreds is about 340 days. Data indicate that colts are generally carried longer than fillies. Disease can influence the length of gestation.

Normally, the mare has a 'foaling heat' soon after the birth of the foal, usually on or about the ninth day. This is usually a short oestrus, but the mare will accept the stallion and, under favourable conditions, will conceive. If the mare has had a rough foaling with evidence of bruising and haematomas of the birth canal, it is advisable not to breed at this time, nor should a mare that has foaled for the first time be rebred at foal heat, as she is more likely to have suffered damage.

Some breeders hesitate to breed on the ninth day for several reasons:
The mare showing signs of oestrus may not be near ovulation.
There is a possibility of uterine infection.
Traumatic injury to the birth canal often goes unnoticed.
The womb of a mare kept in a box for nine days after foaling has rarely contracted properly, and while there may not be infection the presence of secretions and retained debris is unfavourable for conception.

For these reasons, routine genital examinations at the seventh or eighth day after foaling are indicated. If the mare is not mated on foal heat she will normally cycle again eighteen to twenty-one days later. Failing this, it will be fifty to sixty days.

Broodmare management at foaling

Ideally, the mare should arrive at the stud at least six to eight weeks before the foaling date. This allows her time to recover from travelling stress and allows her system time to develop antibodies against local germs.

On the mare's arrival, the stud groom should be furnished with her medical record containing the following:
Anticipated foaling date and date of last service.
Type and date of any recent hormonal therapy.
Caslick's operation.
Vaccination status.
Date of last thorough worming.
Behavioural idiosyncrasies (for example, resists a stallion, can't be tied up, cycles irregularly, or doesn't exhibit oestrus).

After successful mating the mares will usually be grouped into early, mid-season and late foaling groups, and dry mares (those not in foal). About seven to ten days before foaling, the mare should be moved to a home paddock—a grassed individual paddock close to the house which can be illuminated to dusk level. Valuable mares should be observed every hour.

This mare is about to foal. Note the wax on the teat and the engorged udder.

First stage of labour—the mare is uneasy catching her breath and yawning.

Both forelegs should appear with soles facing the mare's hooves.

Next follows the foal's head between the knees.

The udder of the mare will have begun to increase in size and become quite swollen. At this stage it should be gently handled each day, particularly in a maiden mare, so that if her foal is awkward when feeding she will not resent it. In older mares at this stage, particularly if they have poor circulation, an oedematous swelling (soft, puffy swelling) may appear forward of the udder along the belly. It will disappear once the foal begins to suckle.

The hours before the birth

Between six and forty-eight hours before foaling, a small amount of clear, thick, serum-like material oozes from each teat canal (there are two canals per teat in the mare). This serum hardens to a wax-like material, and once this appears most mares will foal within the following twelve to twenty-four hours. But some mares show little or no wax. A particular mare will usually be constant in her foaling procedure and any unusual behaviour should be recorded, especially where the mare is not seen to wax at all.

Vulvas of sutured mares should be cut at least a week before the foal is due, to prevent tearing.

In most mares the pelvic ligaments show slackening twelve to eighteen hours before foaling. A hollow appears on either side of the root of the tail, and the tail loses its power to hug down over the perineal region. Unfortunately, however, mares do not always follow rules. A mare can appear days off foaling when examined at midnight, and yet have a foal several hours old at her side at dawn.

Foaling

During the first stage of labour the mare may paw the ground, look at her flank, kick at her belly, crouch, catch her breath or wander uneasily around—and then resume feeding. This may be repeated in ten to fifteen minutes. From this point on, the mare should be kept under supervision. It is preferable to keep out of sight and not to interfere unless there is an obvious emergency.

There are no fixed rules for the act of foaling. Most mares lie on their side to foal, raising the upper hindleg at each contraction. At this stage the labour pains, which have been intermittent and of short duration, become intensified and succeed each other at shorter intervals.

When the cervix has relaxed sufficiently, the contractions will force the fluid-filled membranes through the vulval lips of the mare. About five minutes after the appearance of the water bag, the first leg appears and the bag bursts, discharging about 4 litres of placental fluid. After a short rest the second leg appears 8–10 centimetres behind the first. Never pull on the less-advanced leg in an attempt to level it with the first, as this invariably results in fractured ribs for the foal. Both feet should appear with the soles facing the mare's hooves, and the foal's muzzle between the knees. Any other combination of the above, such as head only, or soles up, requires a vet immediately, as the foal is probably presenting abnormally.

One of the most important conditions to prevent is the recto-vaginal fistula, where the foal's foot ruptures the roof of the vagina and tears it longitudinally as the mare strains. This will be evidenced by a leg being caught in the roof of the vagina, and possibly even the appearance of a hoof through the anus. In this case a sterilised, lubricated hand should be placed in the vagina around the offending leg and the leg pushed towards the mare's head and redirected into the vaginal cavity. This should be done immediately the problem is noticed. This condition is most common in young mares foaling for the first time but may also occur in older brood mares with deep bellies. Repair of the tear is a complicated surgical procedure requiring skilled veterinary attention.

Occasionally the mare will expel her foal until its hips become wedged in her pelvis. In this event she needs help, and delivery must be made quickly or the foal will be lost. If reasonable added traction does not help, wiggle the foal slowly from side to side. If this is not successful, the attendant should pass a sterilised, lubricated hand into the birth canal, over the rump of the foal and grasp the tail. A hard pull on it as the mare strains almost always brings the foal.

Allow the umbilical cord to tear of its own accord about 3–5 centimetres from the navel.

If the mare has not passed her entire afterbirth within three hours of foaling it should be considered retained placental membrane. A vet can apply medication to help the mare pass all of the membrane and contract the uterus.

Once the head and neck are delivered the membrane must be away from the nose.

Do's and don'ts

Don't hurry the mare or hover over her.

Don't touch the mare or foal while the labour is progressing normally—that is, let the mare foal as decreed by nature.

Don't hesitate to call your vet if the mare is in trouble. Trouble is indicated by the mare straining for more than one hour without the appearance of the foal; the appearance of the head and no feet, or the head and one foot, or the feet and no head. Once normal foaling begins the foal is born within 15 minutes of the appearance of the feet. If waiting for help, keep the mare walking, provided the foal is not hanging out.

Be sure the membranes over the foal's nostrils are torn; if this does not happen by the time the head is out, quickly tear them away with your fingers.

After foaling

Always spread the membranes out on the ground and make sure both uterine horn tips are present. Many mares who retain the afterbirth for more than three hours will have difficulty conceiving at the next foaling heat. Never pull the membranes out manually, unless under veterinary supervision. Keep the membranes for your veterinary surgeon to examine.

The membranes of the mare should be spread out to ensure that the tips of each uterine horn are intact.

The following should be carried out after foaling:
Enema for foal (100 millilitres of warm soapy water).
Navel swab of tincture of iodine.

Foals should suckle frequently. Pay particular attention to the foal who is sleepy all the time as it may be an indication of disease.

Shot of wide-range antibiotic to both mare and foal, especially if there is a history of infection.

Tetanus anti-toxin or toxoid, to both mare and foal.

Drench of 4.5 litres of mineral oil for the mare to prevent post-partum colic.

Repair of episiotomy (cut vulva) or tears.

Wash mare's hindquarters with disinfectant.

If the mare fails to lick the foal and show it affection, a little table salt rubbed on the foal's neck and shoulders may help. A little of the dam's milk rubbed on the foal's muzzle and face may overcome resentment. A mare should be supervised until she thoroughly accepts the foal and allows it to suckle. On rare occasions this may take as long as a week, in which case tranquillisation may be used to allow the foal to suckle. Very rarely a mare may reject the foal so savagely that it is best to bring the foal up by hand, if a suitable foster-mare cannot be found. Consideration should be given to culling such a mare from the breeding programme.

A contented mare and foal. In the first week after they are born foals tend to rest frequently.

Weaning can take place between four and seven months. The guiding factor is the condition of the mare.

Care of the foal

Colostrum

The first milk (colostrum) is thick, yellowish and sticky. The foal should get this at all costs. It contains essential vitamins, minerals and proteins, as well as antibodies which give the foal protection against disease. It also has a laxative effect on the meconium (faeces). The necessity for the foal to get this colostrum cannot be overemphasised. The haemolytic foal is the only exception. In this case your veterinary surgeon should be consulted and the foal muzzled and kept from sucking.

Foals deprived of colostrum, which include orphaned foals and haemolytic foals, together with foals whose dams have run milk profusely just prior to foaling, need artificial protection for a few days with a wide-spectrum antibiotic, together with colostrum from another mare.

Orphan foal

The rearing of orphan foals is nearly always difficult, since in addition to the loss of natural food (mare's milk), loneliness and fretting must be overcome. The best method is to rear the foal on another mare. If possible select a mare that has just lost her own foal, although sometimes an older, quiet, heavy milking mare that has a foal the same age will accept the orphan. The introduction of the orphan foal to the foster mother must be gradual and very closely supervised.

The first difficulty is to overcome the recognition of the change by sight and smell. It is best to wet the head, neck and back of the orphan foal with water and then rub a little dry salt into the coat. Rub a little salt around the mare's muzzle also. Milk a pint or two of the mare's milk by hand and sprinkle some of it over the foal's head.

At the first introduction make sure that the foal is hungry and the mare is full and slightly uncomfortable. Give the mare a sedative, restrain her, and allow the foal to suckle. It may need a deal of encouragement, particularly if some time has elapsed since its mother died and it has been fed by other means. The mare and foal should not be unattended until there is obviously no risk of rejection.

Where no foster mother is available, three other methods can be tried. One is to select a very quiet, healthy goat and try to teach the foal to suckle; the goat may have to be elevated so that the foal can gain access to the udder. Where only cows are available, give the foal about half a litre of warm water containing 30 grams of sugar or glucose by bottle immediately before each feed; this increases the sugar intake and helps break up the curd of the cow's milk. There are other more complex formulas for bottle-feeding foals with cow's milk. The third method is to rear the foal entirely on artificial milk. Many commercially available artificial foods for feeding foals can be used. Contact your veterinarian for advice and assistance.

Illnesses of foals

You should be aware of several diseases that may affect the foal in the first few days of life.

Straining

Straining can indicate constipation (retained meconium). The meconium is tissue debris that has accumulated in the intestinal tract of the foal during pregnancy. It often becomes hard and difficult to pass. This can be relieved by using 30 millilitres of warm soapy water enema each four hours until normal faeces are passed. Vaseline your index finger and insert. Try to remove hard faecal matter. This condition usually appears as a problem in the first twelve to forty-eight hours, but may not manifest itself in extreme cases until two to five days after birth. Close supervision of the foal is absolutely necessary until normal bowel movements are established. If the foal shows signs of colic, straining or is not suckling call the vet.

Young foals can be taught to handle at a few days old.

Ruptured bladder

Ruptured bladder occurs in the first thirty-six to seventy-two hours, with the foal initially straining and then its abdomen beginning to swell. The foal fails to urinate. The mucous membranes become pale and the foal is unwilling to nurse. Some foals may show signs of blindness, while others convulse. A vet should be called immediately to perform surgery to save the foal.

Haemolytic disease

Rapid breathing can indicate haemolytic disease; it occurs in the first twelve to forty-eight hours and is indicated by an increased heart rate and yellow mucous membranes. This is a condition of foals caused by incompatible blood groupings between sire and dam. The colostrum antibodies of the mare cause blood destruction, anaemia and icterus in the foal. Generally the foal is healthy for about twelve hours after birth but then becomes weak, anaemic and jaundiced. Death will occur within hours unless corrective action is taken. This involves blood transfusions for the foal from a suitable donor and action to prevent its access to the mare's udder for at least twenty-four hours. Milk the mare out for that period and feed the foal artificially with colostrum from another mare. Once colostrum ceases to be secreted by the mare the foal may be allowed to suckle. Repeat matings to the same sire should be avoided. Tests can be done before mating or during pregnancy to foreshadow this disease.

Sleepy foal disease

Sleepy foal disease can occur from a few hours to a few days. It can indicate a number of different diseases including meningitis, several bacterial infections, the beginning of diarrhoea or joint-ill. Usually the foal will have a temperature. (See also Joint-ill, p. 202, and Convulsive Syndrome of Newborn Foals, pp. 203–204.)

Diarrhoea

Diarrhoea in the foal may start after a float trip by the mare and is due to the excitement of travel, a change of grazing, water or environment. The trouble will usually clear up within twenty-four to thirty-six hours. Sometimes a foal may have diarrhoea that is loose and yellow and yet the foal still seems to be actively normal, does not stop suckling, and has no temperature. This may be the first motion after the meconium has passed. It also may indicate that the mare is coming into season. The mare's milk will change and this is what is causing the foal to have the diarrhoea. The diarrhoea will last during the heat period of the mare but will disappear when she is out of season.

If the foal stops suckling and the diarrhoea continues, the vet should be called at once. The vet should also be called if the scour becomes thin, watery and evil-smelling or if the foal is really ill and is not suckling. Speed of treatment is very important. Protracted diarrhoea has a burning affect. The buttocks should be washed down, dried and coated with vaseline. It is also best to wash the diarrhoea from the walls of the box as it may be contagious. (See also Joint-ill described below.)

Pussy nose

If a foal develops a runny nose, however slight, the foal must be inspected night and morning and its temperature taken. The normal reading for a healthy foal is 38.3°C but when it has a cold, a fever will develop raising the temperature to approximately 40–41°C. The glands between the jaw bones and in the arch of the neck should be checked for swelling. If the glands are not enlarged and the temperature is normal, there is no cause for concern. However, the foal should continue to be checked. If the temperature rises above 40°C, the discharge stays pussy and the foal stops suckling or eating, the vet should be called immediately. The foal should be separated from other animals to prevent the disease spreading. (See also Joint-ill described below.)

Joint-ill

Joint-ill (or bacterial arthritis) occurs as a generalised body infection with localisation in joints or tendon sheaths. It mainly affects foals of either sex up to forty days of age.

The disease can take two courses: generalised infection of the whole body (septicaemia); or localisation in various organs (that is, joint-ill, diarrhoea or respiratory disease).

The infection gains entry before (intra-uterine) or after (extra-uterine) birth of the foal.

In intra-uterine infection, the disease gains entry to the foal via the placenta (foetal membranes) and is usually due to an existing disease of the womb of the mare. There is usually a 100 per cent correlation between a sick neonatal foal and post-foaling disease in the dam. The converse is not true.

In extra-uterine infection, the disease gains entry via the navel or mouth, by skin penetration or by inhalation. In all of these cases, the environment is the source of infection. Many cases of joint-ill occur after such disorders as scouring or sleepy foal disease. The paddock is an important source of infection in joint-ill.

The signs in young foals (0–10 days) are acute septicaemia, temperature above 38°C, depression, disinclination to suckle, scours, lameness or stiffness in one or more joints. Sometimes it is difficult to determine which joint or even which leg is affected.

The only sign in older foals (older than 10 days) may be lameness. Invariably the temperature will be elevated, even though the foal appears quite well. 'Propiness' or 'stiffness' are an indication. Diagnosis is based on lameness, stiffness, 'propiness', temperature rise, heat, pain or swelling of joints, blood count results, and examination of joint fluid.

Joint-ill can be confused with many other problems including being 'kicked' or 'trodden on', foot lameness due to abscess, fractured pedal bone, fractured ribs, fractured limbs, contracted tendons, rickets, bone growth problems, muscle degeneration, hip dislocation, high limb fractures and epiphysitis.

Early diagnosis and veterinary attention is absolutely essential if successful treatment and remission of symptoms is to be achieved. Immediately confine the foal and dam to a box or yard with a healthy environment. Comfort, warmth, good nutrition and good nursing are essential. Restrict exercise, wash hindlegs of dam and investigate post-foaling disease in mare. Treat if necessary. Call the vet.

To prevent this important disease:

Wash stallion in disinfectant before and after service.

Wash mare thoroughly after foaling to prevent soiling of udder and teats.

Examine foetal membranes for disease and treat mare if necessary. Bury or burn all foetal membranes.

Alternate foaling paddocks every two to three years.

Carry out worm control.

Dress the navel of newborn foals (tincture of iodine) but do not ligate.

Other neonatal limb problems

Other limb problems of the neonatal period (up to 30 days) are as follows:

Forelimb conditions include 'buckled knees', 'contracted tendons', 'knock knees', 'back at the knees', 'weak knees', rotation of fetlocks outwards associated with 'knock knees' and bowed legs.

Hindlimb conditions include hock deviation outwards and hind fetlock deviation inwards.

Treating limb abnormalities in foals

The incidence of limb abnormalities in thoroughbreds is estimated at 10 per cent. Some mares tend to produce a series of foals with neonatal limb problems. And malpositioning of the foetus in the dam is undoubtedly one of the major causes (for example the maiden mare with little room for the foetus). The incidence of abnormality inherited from the sire is doubtful, although some stallions have been incriminated as 'getting bad legged foals'. The environment of and nutrition available to the mare during pregnancy are important—

In one instance recorded, in one year approximately 50 per cent of pregnant mares on 'highly improved' pastures produced foals with limb abnormalities. Trauma is also a cause of growth plate defects and consequent angular limbs.

Treatment of limb abnormalities takes three forms: *Management* is by far the most important, and the majority (90 per cent) of foals with neonatal limb problems will respond simply by being confined in a small yard or box. The period of confinement varies, but badly deviated knees, for example, have responded after eight weeks in a box. Adequate rest even without other treatment is the most beneficial.

Local limb treatment includes such things as casts and splints. A simple aid to correction of limb problems is hoof paring or rasping (for the hoof rotated out, rasp the outside; for the hoof rotated in, rasp the inside). The third form of treatment is *surgical*—'stapling' of knees can help in really obstinate cases.

The *contracted foal* has its legs in a flexed position—that is, the leg or legs are not completely extended. This condition can be caused by rupture of extensor tendons (repair by surgery); by overweight unweaned foals (exercise and reduce feed intake); by malposition of the foetus in the uterus; or by nutritional deficiencies of vitamins or minerals. An equine veterinary surgeon should be consulted on the best course of treatment, which is invariably successful if nursing and handling facilities are adequate.

Convulsive syndrome of newborn foals

Also known as 'sleepy foal disease', and the sufferers as 'barkers', 'dummies' and 'wanderers', this is a nervous disorder of newborn foals, characterised by convulsions and/or blindness, usually only in thoroughbreds and usually only in those born under human supervision. The terms 'barker', 'dummy'

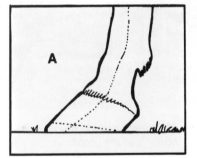

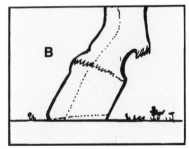

Correcting common posture faults in the feet. As a general rule a horse's hooves should be trimmed every 4 weeks whether the horse is shod or unshod. Incorrect postures can be caused by hooves grown too long either at the toe or heel. In Illustration A the toe is too long and the hoof should be trimmed along the horizontal dotted line to restore the correct stance. The heel is too long in Illustration B but trimming along the horizontal dotted line will correct this problem. (See Feet disorders p. 220 for care of a horse's feet.)

or 'wanderer' are descriptive of this disease, which is caused by lack of oxygen to the brain. Signs occur within a few minutes to hours after birth, and generally consist of jerking the head up and down, aimless leg movements, and spasms of the limbs, neck, head and body.

The 'barker' syndrome is followed by convulsions, during which the foal makes a barking noise. The 'dummy' moves about aimlessly showing no fear of man or animal. If a barker survives the convulsion, it passes into the 'dummy' or 'wanderer' stage. Affected foals will not nurse, but with force feeding many make complete recovery.

When a mare is allowed to foal unattended, both mare and foal rest after parturition. During this period all of the blood from the placenta (membranes) enters the foal. But when an attendant is present, unwarranted assistance hurries the events and may cause premature rupture of the umbilical cord with subsequent loss of blood to the foal. This can amount to 30 per cent of the foal's blood. Bacterial infections can cause similar symptoms.

The barker syndrome may require sedation to control convulsions. Most foals will need force feeding by stomach tube.

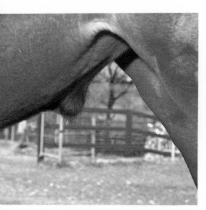

The most common hernia in the horse is at the umbilicus.

Hernias

A hernia is the protrusion of a loop or portion of an organ or tissue through an abdominal opening. The skin and the internal membrane of the abdomen (peritoneum) remain intact over the protruded contents. Nearly all hernias in the horse are located in the region of the abdomen: umbilical hernias, inguinal hernias, scrotal hernias and ventral hernias. A ventral hernia occurs in the midline at various points other than the umbilicus or inguinal openings. Umbilical and scrotal hernias appearing at birth or shortly afterwards are usually congenital and some are considered to be inherited.

Any defect in the abdominal wall can predispose an acquired abdominal hernia. Such defects are caused mainly by trauma and abscesses. Straining may be a cause of herniation, as may any external force or trauma.

Umbilical and ventral hernias commonly appear as spherical enlargements ranging in size from that of a golf ball to that of a tennis ball. They usually have a definite ring or opening which is palpable.

Hernias are either reducible (meaning the contents can easily be pushed back into the cavity) or irreducible (meaning the contents are caught). If the contents are caught, it may mean there are adhesions or that the contents are swelling.

If strangulation occurs there is evidence of acute inflammation. The enlargement becomes firm and painful. The strangulated tissue becomes darkened and necrotic. When signs of digestive disorder and intestinal obstruction occur, death follows rapidly.

Most scrotal hernias in foals will correct themselves in time. Rarely is surgery indicated except in cases of strangulation.

Umbilical hernias may be present at birth or develop within three to seven days. Most of these will undergo spontaneous reduction by the time the animal reaches twelve to fourteen months of age.

In all cases of hernia get the vet to check.

Navel urine (Pervious urachus)

Within the umbilical cord there is a small ureter-like structure that connects the bladder of the foetus with the placenta. Its outlet is usually closed at the time the umbilical cord is severed, but in some foals it does remain patent and urine will continue to drip from this opening. This is obvious, especially when the foal urinates. It is not a serious condition but it does keep the umbilical stump moist and soiled. Most cases correct themselves within a few days. The navel cord should not be tied off in this condition. The area should be cleaned and cauterised daily, with tincture of iodine.

Worms

Worm infestation can cause severe problems in foals. Treatment and prevention are therefore essential. (See section on Worming, pp. 188–94.)

The foal's diet

A suckling foal has no problem regarding nourishment provided it is getting an adequate supply of mare's milk from a well-fed mare and is also able to feed from her feed tin. The weaned foal should continue to be fed the same diet it shared with its mother before weaning. It should have an extra meal a day, if possible late in the evening.

Suggested ration

Pasture   Daily grazing on mature dry grass.

Hay   Best-quality mixture, also some meadow hay; total 3 to 3.5 kilograms daily.

Grain and concentrate   Oats 3 to 3.5 kilograms, bone meal or white fish meal 250 grams, linseed or soya bean meal 250 grams, hay or chaff 500 grams; total grain and concentrate increasing from 4 kilograms to 7 kilograms per day depending on the age and size of the weanling. The horse should be worked up to as much as it will eat leaving a clean manger.

Many young horses find damp feeds easier to eat. There is no need to make the food wet or sloppy but simply dampen the food or bran before mixing and add a bowl of clean chaff cut from good hay for each feed. The diet can be varied by occasionally adding grated carrots or molasses. For exercise the foal should be turned out every day.

Weaning

Weaning can take place between four and seven months. The guiding factor should really be the dam's condition. For instance, a fat mare with plenty of milk can suckle her foal for six months or longer, particularly if she is empty (not in foal again) and therefore does not need to nourish a foetus as well. A day or two before separation, accustom the mare to having her udder and teats gently handled and milked.

On the morning selected for weaning, the mare should be walked to her new paddock leaving her foal behind in its usual box with both upper and

This mare is the mother of only one of these foals. Live twins are extremely rare in the horse world.

lower doors shut. It is important that the foal is strictly confined in a safe enclosure, which must have solid high walls. The mare should be placed in a sturdy yard well out of earshot of the foal's cries. The mare's udder should be inspected twice a day and she will need to be milked to relieve the pressure. Do not strip her out completely as this only stimulates further milk secretion and production.

Caring for the sick horse

Signs of sickness

Note the obvious symptoms—for example, loss of appetite, lethargy, unusual excretions, coughing, diarrhoea, lameness. Under what circumstances did the sickness begin? What was the management of the horse and feeding? Was there a previous illness or the presence of disease in other animals? These are all important aspects of determining the cause of illness.

The position and actions of the horse should be noted without disturbing it. Healthy animals usually get up when approached and horses usually remain standing during the day. Very sick animals appear very languid. The head is depressed, the ears may be drooping, the horse may rest its feet alternately. A stiff, quiet attitude may be noted in gastrointestinal disturbances of a minor nature. Unnatural attitudes are observed in brain diseases. Horses will remain constantly standing when old and stiff or in acute diseases of the chest, in severe respiratory distress, in tetanus, and in shivers. Extension of the neck and head may indicate cases of choking, severe throat infections, poll evil, tetanus, rheumatism affecting the neck or arthritis of the neck bone. Drooping of the head and neck may occur in depression or paralysis of the neck muscles due to injury of the neck. Unsteadiness of the gait indicates weakness, or infections of the brain. 'Dog-sitting' may point to impaction colic (constipation) or a gas-filled stomach. A stiff, outstretched stance may be noticed in tetanus, azoturia, spinal weakness, fractures or injuries to the back or the pelvis. Yawning frequently is a sign of pain.

An expression of anxiety is indicative of serious and exceedingly painful conditions. The coat is a good indicator of a horse's general condition. In some chronic diseases the coat may become dry and lustreless. In dehydration the skin loses its elasticity; if a pinch or fold of skin at the base of the neck in front of the shoulder takes more than three seconds to return to its normal position, dehydration is present. Excessive sweating may occur from work when an animal is unfit or excited. In painful diseases such as colic, sweating may be patchy or diffuse.

The character of the respirations and number per minute should be noted as the animal is resting. Frequency of breathing is greatly increased in exercise.

In the normal horse at rest the range of respirations is 8 to 16 per minute. An increase in number usually means a fever; decrease in number is observed in brain infections. Shallow and irregular respirations are noted in some brain infections and in complete or deep anaesthesia. Where there is severe abdominal pain, as in colic or acute peritonitis, abdominal muscle breathing movements cease and the rib cage moves. If the rib cage remains still and the respirations are controlled by abdominal muscle movement, there is usually pain in the thoracic cavity, such as from pleurisy. Respiration may be laboured in the case of bronchitis, fluid in the lungs and pneumonia. Coughing is a sign of ill-health (see COUGHING in the Common ailments listing that follows).

Nasal discharge may come from one side if it is from a nasal chamber, but when it occurs on both sides it comes from any part of the respiratory tract behind the throat. In catarrh the discharges are first clear and watery or mucoid, later becoming yellowish or yellowish-white. The nasal discharge may be dark and offensive in gangrene of the lung. This is also noted in

A chronically sick horse with dramatic weight loss due to diarrhoea.

pneumonia that results from a foreign body going the wrong way.

The mucous membranes of the conjunctiva, the mouth, the nose and (in the female) the vagina are normally moist and a light pink colour. In local inflammations and in some cases of general disease, there may be a pussy or catarrhal discharge. Changes in colour of the mucous membranes may also be noted in disease. They may be red, congested, or injected in specific fevers, in painful infections, after severe exercise, and in local inflammations. Brick-red mucous membranes are noted in fevers with a tendency to jaundice. Pale mucous membranes are indicative of anaemia or haemorrhage; yellowish membranes are due to build-up of bile, or to haemolytic disease.

A loss of appetite is noted in fevers, digestive disturbances and pain. An increase is noted in parasitism and sugar diabetes. A depraved appetite occurs in indigestion, rabies, mineral deficiency and other conditions. Where the appetite is defective but there is no evidence of disease, the mouth and teeth should be examined and the food inspected.

An abnormal desire for water is seen in fever, sugar diabetes, water diabetes, kidney disease, diarrhoea and certain forms of gastritis.

Vomiting is rare in the horse, but when it does occur the vomitus usually rushes out through the nostrils. In the horse it is found to be associated with a ruptured stomach. In the case of choke, there are repeated efforts at vomition, without producing vomitus. There is usually profuse salivation.

The amount of faeces produced in twenty-four hours varies with the quantity and nature of the food given. Faeces are normally passed 8 to 10 times a day, the daily amount passed being between 15 to 20 kilograms. The consistency depends on the nature of the food. In constipation the passage of faeces is reduced to much less than normal or completely stopped. There will usually be smaller quantities than normal in each dropping, and within each small dropping the balls will be small and hard. The colour of the droppings, from brownish-yellow to deep green, is also governed by the nature of the food.

Diarrhoea means liquid faeces; in dysentery there is usually blood in the faeces. The blood may be fluid or in spots and is derived from the blood vessels and mucous membranes of some part of the alimentary tract, as a result of a very acute enteritis or of ulceration. If the blood comes from the first part of the alimentary tract it is black, because it has been acted upon by the acids in the stomach. If it comes from the rear part of the alimentary tract it will be passed unchanged.

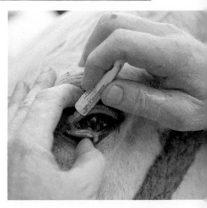

To administer eye ointment — press in and towards the horse's forehead with the thumb and forefinger to form a sac at the corner of the eye.

Nursing care

Where practical the horse should be placed by itself in a loose box which should be comfortable, clean, well-bedded, properly ventilated and free from draughts. The box should be warm, particularly in diseases of the chest and air passages. Unless the horse needs to be tied up or held in a sling, it should be kept in a loose box so that it may lie down or move about as it chooses. Sawdust or wood shavings will often be better than straw as bedding in cases of lameness, for it accommodates itself more readily to the animal's movements.

Any clothing placed on the horse should be changed regularly, beaten, brushed and dried as required. If the horse has an irritable skin a cotton sheet should be used between it and the major rug.

A sick animal should be allowed at least 85 grams of salt a day, or a lump of rock salt should be kept constantly in the feed tin. Salt is a condiment that promotes digestion and aids in the building of tissue.

Grooming is essential for the weak and the depressed horse. Horses are like people—being clean makes them feel better. The best grooming for a sick horse is vigorous and well-applied hand-rubbing or wisping to remove scurf and other debris from the skin. In all cases ensure that the eyes, nostrils and dock are clean. Other good stable routines should be strictly adhered to, to promote the animal's comfort and health.

Where possible the horse should be exercised. In the case of injury this should be gradual so as to restore the function of the part without interfering with its repair.

After any illness that has involved medical treatment the owner should be wary in permitting the horse to leave its stable until all danger of a relapse is past.

Advice on first aid and nursing of horses with specific disorders is given in the Common ailments listing that follows. See, for example, ABSCESSES, ACCIDENTS, BURNS, POISONING and WOUNDS.

Feeding the sick horse

All sick animals should be tempted with appetising food; its nature should be varied and it should be given in small quantities and often. Remove any feed that remains in the manger before the next feed.

Where horses are ill and confined, it is important to watch the droppings carefully to ensure that an impaction colic does not develop. Laxative foods are the order of the day: green grass, green oats, green barley, lucerne, carrots, parsnips, apples, turnips, gruel, bran mashes, and linseed and bran mash. The employment of laxative foods is especially indicated in the acute stages of inflammatory diseases and in cases of injury. All grain should be cooked with a minimum of water so that it is comparatively dry when taken off the fire. Salt should always be given with the boiled food. To make a bran mash take 1.5 kilograms of bran, 30 grams of salt, add 1.5 litres of boiling water, stir well, cover over and allow to stand for fifteen to twenty minutes so that it is well cooked.

For a bran and linseed mash, boil 500 grams linseed slowly for two to three hours with enough water, 2.5 litres, to make a thick fluid to which 1 kilogram of bran and 30 grams of salt should be added. The whole should be stirred up, covered over and allowed to steam as advised for the bran mash. The thicker the mash, the more readily will the horse eat it.

Linseed oil in quantities from 150 to 300 millilitres daily may be mixed through the food. It keeps the bowels in a lax condition and has a good effect on the skin and air passages.

To increase the nutritive value of the food, various additives such as milk, eggs, bread and biscuits can be used. Milk is usually given skimmed and may be rendered palatable by first mixing in it a little sugar; a horse may have 5–9 litres daily. Eggs may be given raw as a drench, or may be boiled hard and mashed up in the milk. Horses soon learn to become fond of bread and biscuits.

As a rule the sick horse as well as the healthy horse should have a constant supply of fresh drinking water. The temperature of the drinking water should never be higher than 27°C.

Administering medicines

Most modern drugs are given by injection into the body by intravenous, intramuscular or subcutaneous routes. Larger quantities of drugs can be given in drips.

In the past the oral route was used quite frequently but today it is usually only used when physical effects on the bowel contents are desired, such as in impaction, other cases of gastrointestinal colic, artificial feeding or worming. In most cases it is best to use the oral route via a stomach tube which is inserted through the nostrils. It is most important that only persons with experience attempt to pass a stomach tube in a horse, because it is very easy to insert the tube into the lungs—any preparation poured on to the lungs will cause a fatal pneumonia. In the event of an emergency, medicines such as oil can be given while the horse's head is raised by a lead strung over a roof

In an emergency, medicine can be given while the horse's head is raised, but it is essential that the horse drink the medicine slowly.

beam and allowing the horse to swallow from a bottle inserted between its lips. It should be emphasised that the horse must drink the material slowly, as any attempt to force it and flood the mouth will result in passage of the medication to the lungs.

Some modern drugs are now administered in oral pastes. These include worming mixtures, antibiotics, butazolidine, vitamins, iron tonics and diuretics. When administering pastes and other oral preparations to the horse, ensure that it gets the full dose, by pulling the tongue out as far as possible and depositing the material as far back as possible before letting the tongue go. For how to administer worm pastes see p. 193.

Administration of medication via feed or water is always risky. Most horses have a very sensitive palate and will not take food or water that has been medicated.

Inhalations are not used as frequently today as they were previously. Oil of eucalyptus, oil of turpentine and Friars Balsam are all of value in cases of respiratory disease. The usual method is to fill a stable bucket three-quarters full of boiling water, pour in the medicinal agent chosen, and then cover the top of the bucket with hay while stirring the contents with a stick. Hold the animal's head over the steam as it rises. Some recommend the use of a nose-bag or sack in which some medicated sawdust or bran is placed. The head must not be covered as this interferes with respiration and the horse resents the state of partial suffocation that it induces. Vicks VapoRub wiped in the nostrils is a good alternative.

Enemas are often used to procure evacuation of the bowels and also in some instances in the treatment of 'seat' worms or pinworms. The rectum is first cleared of its contents by hand; a length of flexible tubing up to 2 metres in length lubricated with vaseline or oil is introduced into the rectum. It is most important that no force is used. The fluid must be pumped in very slowly for, as the bowel becomes distended, the tube can be readily passed forward into the distended rectum. From 22 to 45 litres of warm soapy water can be introduced.

Other treatment

Bandaging the legs

Bandages are used for support when the horse is being worked or floated, or when a wound needs covering. Whether an adhesive bandage or a non-adhesive bandage is used depends on how active the horse is, the region of the leg requiring bandaging, and the frequency with which the bandage has to be changed. It is very difficult (in fact, almost impossible) to bandage the hock without using a self-adhesive bandage. Where dressings need to be changed daily, it is best not to use self-adhesive bandages because they are expensive, cannot be re-used and can pull out hairs quite easily.

When applying bandages to the various parts of the limbs, it is best to commence by using a wad of cotton-wool from a roll. Wind this once around the affected limb. Start the self-adhesive bandage so that there is at least 3 centimetres on the horse's skin, then wind the rest around the cotton-wool. Continue winding the bandage around the leg until the bottom of the wadding is reached, finishing off with another 3 centimetres on the skin. In the case of the fetlock and the knee, it is important to criss-cross to the opposite sides of the joint to get a firm holding. It is vitally important that the rear of the knee is not bandaged, and the bone (accessory carpal bone) left exposed. Bandaging over this bone will result in a pressure sore which takes a long time to heal.

Whenever restrictions such as bandages are applied to the limbs of a horse, they should be checked twice a day for the first few days and then daily to detect any undue swelling. If the limb begins to fill below or above the bandage, the bandage should be removed immediately. If possible, the horse should be walked for exercise to reduce the swelling.

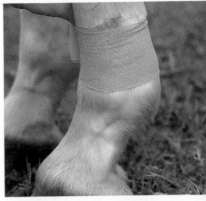
To bandage a fetlock begin by leaving a flap out to grip.

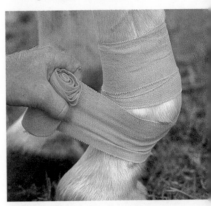
After two firm rounds above the fetlock go diagonally below the fetlock for a few rounds . . .

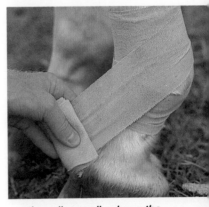
. . . then diagonally above the fetlock for a few rounds.

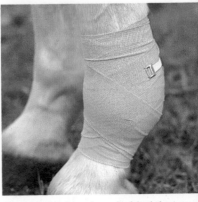
Try to finish bandage behind the leg.

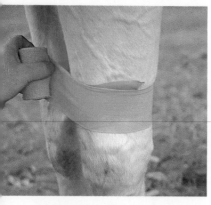

Begin bandaging the knee by leaving a flap out to grip.

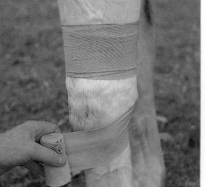

After two firm rounds above the knee, go diagonally below the knee for several rounds.

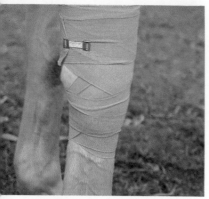

Repeat the procedure above and below the knee several times. Note: Never cover the point behind the knee.

An epsom salts bandage, applied to filled (swollen) legs, is prepared by spreading cotton-wool, sprinkling it with epsom salts, dampening with water; applying to the affected area with salt against the skin and bandaging over. This should be repeated at least twice daily for three to four days.

Blisters

Blisters are chemicals which, when rubbed into the skin surface, cause a burning sensation. Blistering is a very old remedy for 'curing' such problems as arthritic joints and sprained tendons, and the treatment is usually accompanied by a period of rest. Recent research has shown that it is the rest rather than the blister that does the good.

Blood counts

The blood count of a horse is analysed in exactly the same way as the blood count of a human. Blood count techniques have now become so sophisticated that there is hardly any abnormality of the horse which cannot be detected. Blood count figures should be interpreted by a trained person.

THE NORMAL RANGE OF VALUES FOR THE EQUINE BLOOD COUNT

TEST		NORMALS	TEST		NORMALS
P.C.V.	%	35-47	Total Protein	g/dl	6.0-7.7
H.Hb	g/dl	13-16	Albumin	g/dl	2.8-3.6
R.B.C.	x10⁶/µl	8-11	A.P.	IU/L	<200
M.C.V.	µ³	41-49	Glucose	mg/dl	60-100
M.C.H.C.	%	30-36	S.G.P.T.	IU/L	<40
W.C.C.	x10³/µl	6.5-12	Amylase	U/L	
N.R.B.C.	x10³/µl		Creatinine	mg/dl	1.2-1.9
CORR. W.C.C.	x10³/µl	6.5-12	CPK	IU/L	<100
			L.D.H.	IU/L	<250
Band Neut	/µl	0-240	S.G.O.T.	IU/L	<400
Seg. Neut.	/µl	2470-6960	Bilirubin Total	mg/dl	0.2-6.2
Lymphocytes	/µl	1625-5400	Direct	mg/dl	0-0.4
Monocytes	/µl	65-720	Indirect	mg/dl	0.2-6.2
Eosinophils	/µl	65-960	BUN.	mg/dl	10-20
Basophils	/µl	0-360	Cholesterol	mg/dl	42.2-176.9
			Chloride	mEq/L	99-108
			Calcium	mg/dl	11.2-13.8

Liniments

Liniments are liquids or ointments which are rubbed into tendon or muscle areas to increase the circulation in the area, thus bringing warmth and easing pain. They have pain-killing properties and increase the rate of healing. Various commercial preparations can be purchased from chemists or veterinary suppliers.

Physic ball

A physic ball is a gelatine capsule, approximately 5 centimetres long and 2 centimetres in diameter which contains a medicine that causes the horse to scour. It is used by horse-trainers to 'clean' the horse out. It does have some genuine use where the horse is getting 'tight' (impacted).

Pin-firing

This is a very old remedy designed to cause scar tissue formation in the region with the aim of giving it added strength. It involves local anaesthetic and then creating pin-point burn holes with a hot iron. Bar-firing does the same thing—in this case lines are burnt. As with blisters, the subsequent rest forms a large part of the treatment. It is used in cases of 'apple-joints', curb, bone spavin, shin soreness and some tendon conditions.

Poultices

Poultices work by the action of drawing fluid to the surface. They are particularly useful where there is a filling of a joint or a portion of the leg due to bruising, sprain or mild infection. Poultices tend to limit infection or non-infectious inflammatory processes. They are very good over puncture wounds.

Some poulticing agents should not be applied directly to the skin as they have a tendency to cause excessive moistening of the skin and blistering. Poultices that tend not to blister are Denver mud, magnesium sulphate (epsom salts) bandages, boric acid paste, kaolin poultice and Unna's paste. A simple home remedy is to dampen a wad of cotton-wool about 30 centimetres square and to sprinkle it with epsom salts. Apply this to the affected part and wrap with a conforming bandage. The cotton-wool should be remoistened every twelve to twenty-four hours, either by replacing the bandage or by hosing the leg with the bandage intact. If slight blistering (scaliness) occurs, change the type of poultice.

Rolling in stable (Cast)

This term is used when a horse rolls in the confines of the stable box and is unable to rise because its legs are against the wall. If the horse is not completely on its side and help is available, one person should sit on the head to immobilise the horse while the other stands beside the horse out of range of 'flaying' legs.

Loop a rope noose over the leg closest to the ground and pull the horse over, turning its head as the body rolls. If single-handed do as above but don't worry about the head. If the horse is completely on its side, use two or three people to swivel the horse by grasping the mane and head. Drag the shoulders and head to the centre of the box.

Taking a horse's temperature

The normal rectal temperature for an adult horse is 37.5–38.5°C. A stubby thick bulb ended thermometer is best. The thermometer should be shaken down to below normal temperature level, inserted along the wall of the rectum and left in place for one minute. The normal body temperature may be higher in animals during pregnancy, parturition, lactation and in the young animal.

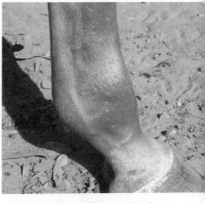

An apple-jointed horse that has been pin-fired.

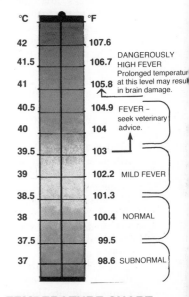

°C		°F	
42		107.6	
41.5		106.7	DANGEROUSLY HIGH FEVER
41		105.8	Prolonged temperature at this level may result in brain damage.
40.5		104.9	FEVER – seek veterinary advice.
40		104	
39.5		103	
39		102.2	MILD FEVER
38.5		101.3	
38		100.4	NORMAL
37.5		99.5	
37		98.6	SUBNORMAL

TEMPERATURE CHART

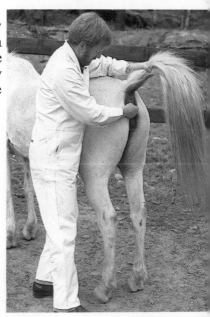

Shake the thermometer down to 37.5°C. Stand beside the horse, elevate the tail and slide thermometer in 3 cms along the rectal wall. Remove after 1 minute.

Common ailments
Abortion
The normal gestation period of a mare is between eleven and twelve months. Abortion in horses is defined as the death and expulsion of the foetus before ten months. The causes of abortion are varied but they can be grouped under general headings.

Foetal infection
The three possible routes of infection are the mother's bloodstream, through the cervix during pregnancy, or the presence of infection already in the uterus at the time of conception. Infection may be caused by fungi, bacteria, or viruses. A virus that is at present causing a great deal of concern world-wide is the rhinopneumonitis virus, or virus abortion. This causes a respiratory disease in all horses, male and female, but in the pregnant mare some six to eight weeks after the respiratory head-cold it causes abortion of the foetus. In some countries it has become the most common cause of abortion. The mare will usually conceive quite normally the following year and carry the foal. In some countries a vaccine is available against the disease.

Foetal starvation
The developing foetus depends for its supplies of vital food material in the first few weeks on the secretions of the uterus and then later on the placenta. These mechanisms may fail for one reason or another and cut the food supply from the foetus. Death results. It may be due to malnutrition of the mare, extreme changes in her management, growth of twin foetuses or from hormonal or glandular problems.

Hormonal deficiencies
Where the mare has been shown to abort because of hormonal deficiency, she can be given hormone injections throughout the term of a subsequent pregnancy. Seek veterinary advice.

In any case of abortion, no matter what you think the cause is, remove other in-contact mares to a separate, empty paddock. Then call your vet to do a postmortem and to take samples for examination. Burn or bury the remains of the foal and membranes and isolate the stall. The dead foal's membranes and the uterine fluids from the mare are highly infectious to other horses if virus abortion was the culprit. Disinfect the general area where the abortion took place. Unfortunately, if all the mares have been together for several months the damage is probably done and the other mares are also likely to abort.

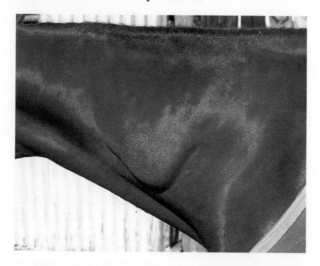

Swelling due to infection five days after an intramuscular injection with a dirty needle.

Abrasions
An abrasion is where several layers of skin have been taken off, leaving a weeping or bleeding patch. It does not go right through the hide. Abrasions occur round the back of the pastern, round the cannon bone (wire burns) and on the extensor surfaces of the legs and joints (gravel burns). The materials causing the abrasions are frequently: rope (the tethered horse gets tangled in rope or sometimes it is the result of stringent methods of breaking in, when a foal is roped up); wire (the horse gets tangled in fences); and gravel (the animal falls when on a gravel road).

The best therapy is hot and cold foments followed by the surgical removal of tags of tissue that have lost their blood supply. Apply Socatyl paste (an antibiotic/anti-inflammatory) to the area, and bandage. Change the bandage each two days. Once the lesions have stopped leaking serum, they can be allowed to dry out and a topical astringent agent such as mercurochrome or acriflavine can be applied to the areas twice daily. Do not pick scabs off wounds unless pus is accumulating. (See also WOUNDS.)

Abscesses
Abscesses can be caused by infection with strangles, dirty injections, or foreign bodies. Abscesses in the mouth are frequently caused by grain, grass seeds or a decayed tooth root. An abscess is effectively present in fistulous withers and poll evil. An abscess is really an accumulation of organisms producing pus.

Hot foment the area six times daily by holding a warm, wet cloth against the abscess site. This should be done for a few days until the abscess becomes soft and pointed. Once there is an obvious fluid accumulation under the skin surface, sterilise a razor blade or scalpel blade by holding it in a flame for thirty seconds. Nick the top of the abscess quickly with the blade and allow the pus to drain out. If possible, enlarge the opening to at least 1 centimetre in diameter; this will prevent the skin from healing too quickly. Next, wash out the abscess with 50 per cent peroxide and water, using a large syringe without a needle, four times daily. Continue to hot foment and massage the area. After four days, continue to wash out the wound three times a day with plain water until it heals from the inside out. Do not let the skin edges seal together prematurely as this leaves a cavity in which the abscess can reform. If the horse is affected generally, antibiotics should be given.

See also POLL EVIL, FISTULA.

Accidents
If a horse has had an accident, very calmly keep talking to it, as it is probably in a state of panic. If the horse is off its feet and entangled in wire or rope, hold its head to the ground to prevent the animal from standing (sit on the horse's head if necessary). Remove any obstacles from around the horse, and apply a tourniquet or pressure bandage to bleeding points. Keep the horse warm and, if necessary, contact a vet.

A first-aid box should always be kept in the stables for emergencies. (See page 241.)

Actinomycosis
Actinomycosis is a rare bacterial condition in the horse. When an animal is affected, however, areas of the jawbone become very swollen, and may burst and discharge pus. The condition can be controlled by antibiotics. The condition is caused by organisms entering via tooth sockets.

African horse sickness
African horse sickness is a fatal viral disease of horses and is confined to Africa. It can affect the heart, the lungs, or both. The condition begins with a fever, and the incubation period is from two to four weeks. Some horses show slight symptoms of illness such as loss of appetite, conjunctivitis,

laboured breathing and an accelerated pulse, but the characteristic symptom is the raised body temperature which reaches 40.5°C in about one to three days (see also FEVER). There is no treatment available.

Allergy
See SKIN DISEASES: URTICARIA.

Anaemia
Dietary deficiencies of certain amino acids, proteins, iron, copper and cobalt can all cause anaemia, but worms are probably the most common cause in horses. Equine infectious anaemia (swamp fever) and loss of blood in the gastrointestinal tract are also causes. Signs of anaemia are pale mucous membranes of the mouth and eyes, lethargy, ill-thrift, and poor coat. When treating anaemia it is essential to first eliminate the cause. Follow this up with iron supplementation, and increase the protein level in the diet. This can be done by feeding the horse milk powder at the rate of 250 grams per day or soya bean meal, or meatmeal or cottonseed meal at the rate of 500 grams per day, and giving injections of vitamin B complex and folic acid twice weekly until the horse's health is restored.

Aneurism
An aneurism is a dilation in an artery wall. In the horse this is caused by worm infestation weakening the wall of the artery and allowing it to distend and stretch. The wall may become so weakened that it ruptures, causing the animal to bleed to death internally. Alternatively, the wall may become thickened due to inflammation caused by the migrating larvae. In these cases blood supply can be interrupted to a section of intestine or to a limb. (See also COLIC and the section on Worming, pp. 188–94.)

Anthrax
Anthrax is a highly contagious, world-wide bacterial disease characterised by septicaemia. The horse develops an acute colic and fever, and hot swelling may occur in the neck, throat or chest. In other cases, the symptoms are lack of breath with fever, and bloody discharges from the rectum. Death occurs in one to two days. The carcass should not be touched by anyone apart from the vet who does the diagnostic postmortem, and must be disposed of by burning. Sudden death after a short, acute illness indicates the possibility of anthrax. In most countries the Department of Agriculture must be notified, and the property where the disease occurs put under strict quarantine. Anthrax is always fatal, and can easily infect other animals and humans.

Apple-joints
See ARTHRITIS.

Arthritis
Arthritis is the name given to inflammation of a joint. In horses it usually results from an injury, but there can be other causes. In performance horses such as racing thoroughbreds and standardbreds, jumpers and endurance horses the most common joint affected is the fetlock. Arthritis can be either septic or aseptic. When it is septic the initial symptoms are usually a sudden development of heat and pain, with the joint becoming swollen and tense. Movement is restricted and there is marked lameness. The joint appears to be filled with fluid. The horse may have a temperature and the area over the joint feels hot to the touch when compared to the joints on the other leg. In an aseptic arthritis the injury is usually due to chronic workload. In these cases the onset of soreness and lameness is much slower, perhaps developing over a period of months. One of the initial signs is decreased flexion of the joint. The joint area itself becomes enlarged (apple-jointed) and there will be a concurrent increase in size of visible joint capsules (wind-galls). (See also CARPITIS, SPAVIN.)

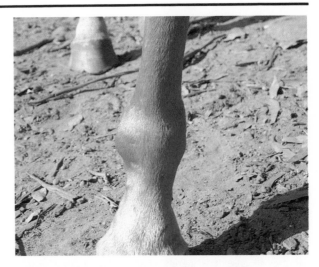

Swelling of the joint, apple-joint, due to arthritis.

Antibiotics are essential treatment for septic arthritis. For both types of arthritis complete rest is essential. Make frequent cold applications to the part involved, or irrigate with cold water several times a day. In between, drawing agents such as antiphlogistine packs, epsom salt bandages, or other commercially available packs can be placed on the joint. Systemic anti-inflammatory treatments such as butazolidine or cortisone are often helpful in reducing the degree of inflammation. In cases of open arthritis (open joint), where there is an opening from the joint to the skin, it is best to seek the advice of a veterinary surgeon. (See also FETLOCK JOINT DISORDERS. For arthritis of the backbone (spondylitis), see BACK INJURIES.)

Artificial insemination
Artificial insemination simply means the artificial introduction of male semen into the genital tract of the female, as compared with natural insemination. This technique is feasible in mares. For information contact your veterinarian. The practice is banned by many breed registries, notably in thoroughbreds, to preserve the economics of the horse-breeding industry.

Azoturia (Tying-up)
The signs of this disease vary from mild to severe. In mild cases, when the horse cools down after exercise it may 'dip' when pressed over the loins or become stiff in either the shoulders or hindquarters or both. In these mild cases the horse has a shortened stride of either the front or hind legs or both. In severe cases the horse might go only a hundred metres before all its muscles jam and the horse is unable to move.

The muscles over the loins become rock-hard and urine may be of a port wine colour. Azoturia is extremely painful. It is usually caused by a high-grain diet combined with a low exercise level. The energy from the high-grain diet is stored in the muscles, and finally breaks down to form an acid. This acts on the muscles, causing the condition. Classic cases are seen in horses fed hard-grain rations seven days a week, and exercised six days with a day off on Sunday. The disease hits them on Monday when they begin working (its name used to be 'Monday morning sickness or disease').

The horse must be stopped immediately from any work that it is doing. Do not even try to walk it back to its stall. Warmth is helpful—double-rug the affected animal, or at least use one rug with a folded blanket or feed sack over the loins. Treatment consists of neutralising the acidity with intravenous injections, and applying anti-inflammatory agents. Alkaline solutions can also be given as saline drenches by stomach tube. It is essential to rest the horse for several days after all symptoms have gone. Eliminate all grain from the diet. The horse should be brought back into work gradually, over a protracted period of several weeks. Control of the disease involves working the horse seven days a week, reducing the high-grain diet, or reducing the oat content of the diet and replacing some of it with corn. Injections of selenium and vitamin E are helpful. Add electrolyte preparations to feed or water—these contain alkaline salts to neutralise the acid in the muscles and act as a mild diuretic to flush the acid and waste products from the muscles.

A horse that has tied-up once is more likely to suffer from the problem again.

Back injuries

Back injuries are rarely serious unless the horse has reared over backwards, is steeplechasing, racing or jumping, in which case there is a possibility of fracturing the spine. If a horse comes down in a fall, let it lie quietly for several minutes in case it is merely winded. The animal should then be encouraged to rise.

If there is no sign of attempts to rise, or if the horse appears able to use only its forelegs, it can be concluded that the back is probably fractured and the horse should be destroyed. Crushing or severance of the spinal cord produces typical signs of hindquarter paralysis. The tail is completely limp and the anus relaxed and open, possibly with faeces dropping from the passage. In the male the penis will be relaxed and protruding from the sheath. Definite indications of paralysis are not always present in the case of fracture of the back. Sometimes the injury is a cracked vertebra with insufficient displacement to do any damage to the spinal cord. In these cases the horse can usually walk awkwardly and box-rest is advised—but your vet will advise on individual cases.

Muscle soreness over the loins is usually due to mild 'tying-up' (AZOTURIA). It is rare for a horse to strain these muscles. Additional supportive treatment includes ray-lamps and liniments rubbed into the affected areas.

Sacroiliac ligament strain is evidenced by wasting of the muscles on both sides of the rump. Usually there is a peaking at the backline between the points of the hip. The only satisfactory treatment is to spell the horse for at least sixteen weeks.

Saddle-rub is most commonly caused by an ill-fitting saddle and/or insufficient padding between the saddle and the horse. Rub the area of the saddle sore with methylated spirits to dry up and harden the area. If the horse must be used before the wound is treated, purchase a 5-centimetre foam rubber saddle-pad and cut a hole over the saddle sore. This will allow the horse to be ridden while the saddle sore repairs. Once the sore has healed, use an extra saddle-blanket to prevent recurrence.

Spondylitis (arthritis of the backbone) is more common in older horses that have been used for work or sport. Sometimes this condition is due to the horse being cast or even flipping right over in a float or stable. Symptoms of spondylitis include dipping when mounted or palpated along the midline of the back. Treatment includes rubbing in a muscle liniment or warming the area with a ray-lamp. However, better results are usually achieved by using anti-inflammatory analgesic agents such as butazolidine. Chiropractors and physiotherapists have been involved in treatment with varying success rates. The difficulty is the huge mass of muscle to manipulate successfully.

Bar-firing

See the section on Pin-firing, pp. 210–11.

Bee stings

If possible remove the sting. Apply ammonia, a strong solution of washing soda, or a paste of washing soda. If there are a number of stings, antihistamines can be given by a veterinary surgeon and antibiotic cover is often necessary. (See also SKIN DISEASES: URTICARIA.)

Belly-ache

See COLIC.

Bleeding

Nose-bleeding

Nose-bleeding can occur from a knock to the head. This should be suspected if the bleeding is unrelated to exercise, and particularly if it is from one nostril. Tie the horse up, so that its head is in the normal position, and apply cold towels to the forehead and nose. Horses in hard training and reaching the peak of fitness will often bleed a few drops (up to a cupful) from one or both nostrils after they have finished exercise. This is caused by either a rupture of a vessel at the top of the nose or, more dangerously, bleeding in the lungs. A veterinary surgeon should be consulted after any such bleeding attacks.

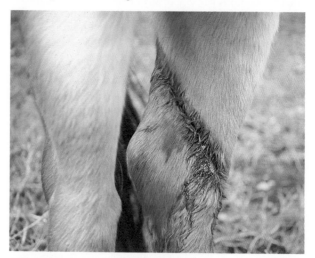

Wire cuts are a common problem. This cut is healing satisfactorily with little swelling.

Leg wounds

The horse has many large blood vessels in the limbs. When these are cut it is best to stop the bleeding by tight pressure bandages and, if necessary, a tourniquet applied above the knee or hock. (The need for a tourniquet is rare, however.) Self-adhesive bandages 7.5 centimetres wide make ideal pressure bandages.

Blindness

See EYE DISORDERS.

Blood counts

The normal blood count of the horse is given in the section Caring for the sick horse, p. 210.

Blood poisoning (Septicaemia)

Blood poisoning occurs where organisms enter the bloodstream either from the bowel or by penetrating wounds (for example, abscesses). The signs of blood poisoning are lethargy, depressed appetite, sometimes a fever, and a darkening of mucous membranes. This condition can be fatal unless the horse is treated properly, usually with antibiotics.

Blue-eye

See EYE DISORDERS, PERIODIC OPHTHALMIA.

Bog spavin

See HOCK DISORDERS.

Boil

See ABSCESSES.

Borna disease

Borna disease is an inflammatory disease of the brain.

There is fever, paralysis of the pharynx, muscle tremor and lethargy. Paralysis is seen in terminal stages and death occurs one to three weeks after signs begin. Mortality is usually 60–70 per cent. The disease has only ever been recorded in Germany.

Bots
The larval stage of the horse bot-fly. (See the section on Worming, pp. 188–94.)

Bowed tendons
See TENDONS.

Broken wind ('heaves')
Broken wind or 'heaves' is a chronic respiratory condition caused by emphysema of the lungs. Emphysema is a persistent over-distension of the air-sacs. As a result of this distension the walls separating one sac from another become thin and weak and finally rupture. In this way a number of sacs may 'run together' and form a large gap. This reduces the area available for the exchange of oxygen. In many cases it is the result of violent expiratory efforts such as coughing. It can also occur after bronchitis or pneumonia, particularly if the horse is kept in work while it has a virus. It may be due to feeding dusty food, which brings about coughing, or too bulky food, especially if the animal is habitually worked hard immediately after feeding. The animals affected are usually good feeders and are often in good condition. The two main signs of the condition are a double expiratory effort and a cough. The cough is fairly frequent and can be induced by finger pressure over the larynx. It is long, deep, and hollow and may appear in spasms. In severe cases the animal will exhibit signs when at rest. In moderate cases animals exhibit the signs only after exercise.

The movements are exaggerated during expiration. There is at first a short normal contraction of the abdominal muscles and after a slight pause a second more prolonged contraction. There may be a slight discharge from the nose. Depending on the degree of damage, some horses will be useless to the owners. There is no likelihood of recovery.

Prevention: Attend to feeding. Avoid dusty feed. Avoid bulky food before exercise. Do not give forced exercise to a horse in soft condition, after feeding or while coughing from any cause.

Bronchopneumonia
See LUNG DISORDERS.

Bucked shins
See SHIN SORENESS.

Burns
Burns and scalds are extremely painful and animals will resent anything but the most gentle handling and dressing of the affected parts. All extensive burns and scalds (covering more than 5 per cent of the body surface) should be attended to by a veterinary surgeon at the earliest possible moment. The burnt or scalded area must be covered with a clean, dry dressing (for example, gauze, a clean handkerchief or a towel) and a bandage applied to keep it in position. Never apply oil, grease, flour, soot, baking soda, spirit, tincture of iodine or lysol to the burn or scald.

Where the burn results from a flame, the burned area will be devoid of hair. Any loose, charred debris can be removed by gauze soaked in warm, normal saline—one teaspoonful of salt to 600 millilitres of warm, boiled water. If there is gross dirt or grease around the affected area, soap and warm water may be used before the normal saline swabbing. Alternatively, acriflavine (one part in one thousand) may be used in the same way, thus cleansing and disinfecting the burnt area at the same time. For first aid of trivial burns, use tannic acid, jellies, warm, strong tea or acriflavine (one part in one thousand).

If the burn is caused by corrosive acid, bathe the part with an alkaline solution which can be made by adding a dessertspoonful of baking soda (sodium bicarbonate) to 600 millilitres of boiled water. Washing soda (sodium carbonate) may be used in the same strength. If neither of these is available, wash the part gently with plenty of warm water.

If a burn is caused by a corrosive alkali such as quicklime, brush out any of its remains from the animal's coat and bathe the area with an acid solution. This can be made by mixing equal parts of vinegar and water. After acids and alkalis have been neutralised the burnt area should be treated with one of the local applications previously mentioned.

Calcium deficiency
If a complete commercial ration is being used, there is no need for the addition of calcium. When high-grain diets are fed calcium carbonate should be added because these are high in phosphorus and low in calcium. The calcium : phosphorus ratio should be 1.1:1. A horse suffering from calcium deficiency may sometimes eat manure. (See MANURE EATING.)

Calf-kneed
The knee is concave at the front like a young calf's knee. Little can be done for this conformation abnormality.

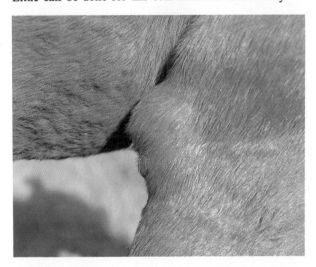

Capped elbow — a fluid swelling over the elbow joint.

Capped elbow
Capped elbow is caused by the heel of the front shoe touching the elbow when the horse is lying down with its legs tucked beneath it. The bone is bruised, and a serious (watery) discharge forms to protect the bone from further mechanical damage. This appears as a fluid swelling on the point of the elbow. As long as the heel of the shoe continues to touch the elbow, the condition will persist, despite treatment.

Either remove the shoe, or place an Elizabethan collar around the fetlock. Once remedial action has been taken to prevent contact, the elbow can be drained by a veterinary surgeon and the blemish, provided it has not been present for a long period, will disappear.

Capped hock
See HOCK CONDITIONS.

Carpitis
Carpitis is an inflammation of the knee joint. It is caused by hard performance work such as racing, endurance work or jumping, or by a horse continually knocking a knee against an object. An X-ray may reveal a chip of bone at the front of the knee. It is common when immature horses

are worked hard and long on hard tracks. The causative agent must be detected and stopped, and the condition can be controlled with cold packs, antiphlogistine, or by cold hosing. Rest for several weeks is essential. (See also AR-THRITIS, OPEN KNEES.)

Caslick's operation
Temporary stitching of the vulva to prevent faecal matter from entering the vagina and setting up infection that would threaten a pregnancy. See the section on Breeding.

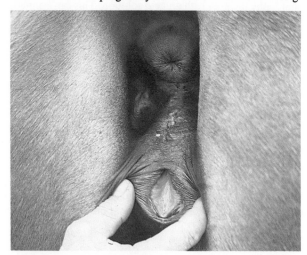

In the Caslick's operation the top two-thirds of the vulva are sutured together.

Cast
See Rolling in stable, p. 211.

Castration
A male horse can be castrated (gelded) from the age of two months, but the most common age is between eighteen months and two years. The modern method for castration usually involves a general anaesthetic. Local anaesthetic can be used, however, if the horse will stand quietly. The castration wounds are usually left open to drain, as the most common problem after castration is swelling and/or infection. To prevent swelling building up, the horse should be exercised by lungeing or riding for twenty minutes twice daily for fourteen days after the operation. The more exercise the horse gets the less possibility there is of unwanted side effects. After each exercise period the wound should be hosed for five minutes so that it does not attract flies. The horse should be carefully observed for the first three days in case there is any protrusion of bowel or fat through the wound. This is most likely to occur in the first few hours and is more common in standardbred horses. If it is detected confine the horse, use moistened clean towels on the wound and call the vet urgently. (See also CRYPTORCHIDISM.)

Cataract
See EYE DISORDERS.

Choking
Choking can be a problem with horses because the oesophagus (gullet, foodpipe) is so long—1.5 metres—and so narrow. In the heart region it narrows even further. Choking is usually caused by a piece of carrot, turnip, potato, apple, or by the administration of gelatin capsules containing medication. Dry food such as corn, cut hay or chopped chaff, swallowed rapidly by a greedy feeder, can pack up in the gullet. The usual signs are difficulty in swallowing or complete inability to swallow, profuse salivation and evidence of spasm of the food pipe. The horse suddenly ceases to feed and makes several attempts to swallow or to get rid of the obstruction. There is marked evidence of distress. A

veterinary surgeon should be called. If the obstruction is in the region of the back of the throat, the vet will attempt to remove it by using a gag. If the obstruction is further down the food pipe, a stomach tube can be used to gently push the obstruction into the stomach. Sometimes surgery is required to free the obstruction.

Coffin bone
See PEDAL BONE.

Colds
See NASAL DISCHARGES.

Colic (Belly-ache, gripes)
The term 'colic' means a set of symptoms that indicate severe or violent abdominal pain. True colic relates to those conditions arising in the stomach and intestines. False colic is caused by conditions affecting other abdominal organs, such as calculi (stones) in the bile duct, or ureter and acute infections of the bladder or genital organs. Colic is far more common in horses than in any other animal. This can be attributed to the small size of the stomach and its small digestive surface; the inability to vomit or unload the stomach; the great length of the intestines and the puckerings of the large intestine which allows food or foreign bodies to lodge there; the great range of movement allowed to the intestine within the abdomen; the great frequency with which the horse is affected with internal parasites; and the fact that the horse has to work at the direction of its owner. Colic is more common at night and is frequently connected with irregular feeding.

Dietary errors such as insufficient supply of water, neglect of regularity in feeding, and long fasts followed by the allowance of extra large feeds, or cold water are responsible for a large number of cases of colic. Preventive measures cannot be ignored in stable management. Improper food is most likely to cause harm when it is associated with sudden change of diet, imperfect mastication, greedy feeding or excessive quantity. Many foods, such as uncooked barley, corn, mouldy food, badly made mouldy hay and wheat are notoriously indigestible. Overeating, as when a horse breaks into a feed shed, is a common cause.

Foreign bodies such as bits of metal, sand or earth will also cause abdominal pain. Sand is particularly a problem where horses are confined to small areas of sandy soil. Sand colic can still occur when horses are fed in feed tins off the ground—but the condition is more frequent in horses fed on the ground.

Water may cause colic if given in large quantities and very cold to a horse still sweating. Insufficient water and drinking from shallow, sandy pools can also cause problems.

Colic can also be caused by heavy work combined with irregular feedings. Many serious cases develop during high-stress work. Working the horse hard immediately after feeding may also cause colic.

Other causes, some of which cannot be prevented even by good management of the horse, are strangulated hernias, twisted bowels, defective secretion of digestive juices, lack of muscle tone, stricture of the bowel, wind-sucking and even nervous upsets, such as a long float trip or a bad thunderstorm.

The signs of colic can be mild or severe. A horse with a mild form of colic may be on its feet, with its neck outstretched and upper lip curled back. It may look at its sides, paw the ground, yawn frequently (a common indication of pain), or just be off its food. In more severe cases the horse will lie on the ground and roll continuously from one side to the other. The horse will begin to sweat, the mucous membranes will become darker and the pulse rate/heart rate will exceed 45. Once the heart rate exceeds 70 it invariably indicates a serious form of colic which may require surgery. Because the causes of colic are so numerous and so varied, it is important to call the vet so that a full examination of the horse can commence in order to determine exactly what is causing the colic. If the horse is lying down but not rolling, leave it be. If the horse is rolling, get it to its feet and keep it walking until the vet arrives.

One of the most common types of colic is impaction colic, which occurs when the horse becomes constipated. Constipation is indicated by reduced numbers of droppings per day, and reduced quantity, with the pebbles being very small and hard. The horse should be given a warm bran mash with molasses at each feed time until the droppings become soft. Some horses require bran mashes two to three times weekly in order to keep their digestive systems flowing. (See CONSTIPATION, FLATULENCE, and the section on Caring for the sick horse.)

Some hints on preventing colic:
Have the teeth checked regularly.
Worm regularly.
Provide a regular diet and water.
Don't exercise on a full stomach.
Let the horse cool off after work before giving it food or water.
Adjust the food by consistency of the droppings; if the droppings become too hard and pebbly, introduce bran or molasses to the diet.
Don't feed green food unless the horse is used to it.
Check food (especially bales of lucerne hay) for mould.

Conjunctivitis
See EYE DISORDERS.

Constipation
Constipation in newborn foals is quite common and is called retained meconium. It can be corrected by administering 30 millilitres of warm, soapy water to the rectum as an enema, and then using a finger to manually rake out the faeces. (See Illnesses of foals, pp. 201–204.)

In older horses the condition is evidenced by hard, pebbly droppings in small quantities, and reduced frequency of defaecation. It can be corrected using warm bran mashes with molasses, linseed meal, boiled barley, increased bran content in the diet or 4.5 litres of medicinal paraffin oil. If the oil is administered by lay persons without a stomach tube, care must be taken to give the oil slowly so that it does not go into the lungs and cause pneumonia.

A manure dropping of ideal consistency.

Contracted heels
See FEET DISORDERS.

Corns
See FEET DISORDERS.

Coughing
Coughing can be caused by viruses, allergies to dust or straw (which can be associated with broken wind), growths in the larynx of the horse (usually in old age), parasites (particularly migrating roundworms) which stimulate the horse to cough as they are brought up into the larynx for reswallowing, pharyngitis caused by fungi, bacteria and viruses, and bronchopneumonia and pneumonia, both of which are caused by viruses, bacteria or foreign bodies such as medications that inadvertently go into the lungs rather than into the food pipe.

Coughing is not a disease on its own, but a symptom of many different conditions. In order to eliminate the cough it is important to determine what is causing it. If it originates from an inflammatory condition of the larynx, local cough pastes may have an effect. If the infection is bacterial, antibiotics will help, but if it is viral little can be done until the horse builds an immunity to the virus. Some countries now have vaccines against the influenza virus.

All horses with coughs should be rested for one week after the cough has gone.

Cracked heels
See GREASY HEEL.

Crib-biting
Crib-biting, like wind-sucking and weaving, can become a problem with stabled horses suffering from boredom. A horse cribs by seizing in its teeth the edge of the manger, the edges of the wall, or any projection in its stall or loose box; the horse then arches its neck and swallows a quantity of air, at the same time emitting a peculiar characteristic grunting sound. Unfortunately, as horses are great mimics, other horses in the same stables are likely to acquire the habit. Young foals have been observed using their mother's hock joints as a source of crib-biting. Chronic cribbers are usually hard to keep in condition; in bad cases this can amount to emaciation. Sometimes crib-biting can be a cause of colic. Crib-biting is classified as a vice and generally lowers the horse's value.

Painting the edges of mangers, rails and boxes with unpleasant-tasting chemicals does not usually deter the determined crib-biter for long. Muzzles (with bars across the bottom) work in some cases. They enable the horse to pick up grain and to pull at hay, but not to grasp the edge of the manger. Once the muzzle is removed, however, the horse will begin crib-biting again. It is claimed that the horse is unable to crib-bite unless it has a vacuum in its mouth, and the use of a hollow bit tends to do away with the vacuum. Crib-biting horses are sometimes kept successfully in loose boxes in racing establishments with the aid of electric wires strung 45 centimetres in from the walls of the box so that the horse cannot touch any solid object. Wide leather straps or metal chains placed tightly around the horse's throat will prevent the ingestion of air and diminish in number the horse's attempts at cribbing. Reducing the horse's boredom by putting it out to pasture will reduce the incidence of cribbing.

Cryptorchidism
Cryptorchidism, or failure of normal descent of the testicles, is a relatively common condition in horses. One testicle can be involved or both. After the age of twelve months it is rare for retained testicles to descend. The condition is hereditary. Retention of one or both testicles can cause behavioural problems and the horse may become dangerous.

In monorchidism, where one testicle descends and the other is retained, the descended testicle should never be removed without removing the retained testicle. The reason is that the horse may be sold as a gelding—yet cause serious injury by its unpredictable behaviour.

Curb
See HOCK DISORDERS.

Dandruff

See SKIN DISORDERS.

Dehydration

Dehydration occurs when there is a net deficiency of body fluids. It can occur when the horse is losing a lot of fluids because of diarrhoea, or through increased sweating in working horses. It can also occur where horses fail to drink sufficiently. (This sometimes happens when a horse is sick or working under stress.) Varying degrees of dehydration with disturbances of electrolyte metabolism are far more common than one would expect. Signs can vary from sub-optimal performance, to the clinically obvious hide-bound appearance seen in severe cases. Dehydration can be identified by analysis of blood samples.

To prevent dehydration use a commercially available electrolyte mix in the horse's food or water every day. Some horses are reluctant to take the electrolytes, so it is best to add them to the horse's water. Give the water following exercise, when the horse is thirsty. As the horse drinks the water, keep topping it up to dilute the salts. If the horse will not take the electrolytes in food or water—even after adding a sweetener such as molasses—then use a stomach tube. Many trainers of racehorses have them stomach tubed once or twice weekly with electrolytes to prevent dehydration.

To test for dehydration, pinch and lift a fold of skin on the neck directly in front of the shoulder. The skin should immediately return to its normal position. If it stays in a fold for more than three seconds, the horse is dehydrated. (See also ELECTROLYTES.)

Stomach tubing is a delicate and dangerous procedure which should be left to the veterinarian.

Diarrhoea

In the suckling foal diarrhoea will occur as a natural phenomenon when the mare comes into season.

In both foals and adult horses diarrhoea may be caused by bacteria, viruses, fungi, the protozoan giardia, nervousness, oral antibiotics, electrolyte imbalances, parasites (this is very common) and dietary changes. Dietary causes include fresh lucerne, grazing on winter oats, bran mashes, molasses and damp feeds. The diarrhoea may be apparent only four to six times daily, while the horse is apparently otherwise normal. On the other hand the diarrhoea may be more frequent and have a foul smell. This usually is due to blood and mucous membrane lining from the gut and is called dysentery. It is very serious and requires veterinary treatment urgently.

The diagnosis and treatment of diarrhoea is often very difficult. Sometimes massive wasting of body tissues can occur before treatment is effective. The diagnosis of the cause of diarrhoea is based on microscopic examination of the faeces for worm parasite eggs and giardia, and faecal cultures to locate causative bacteria. Blood counts are often helpful in determining electrolyte abnormalities. Diarrhoea in foals and horses is a condition that requires urgent veterinary attention. In young foals particularly, it can cause colic. The condition can progress to one of septicaemia with infection of joints and pneumonia (see Illnesses of foals—Joint-ill, p. 202).

The treatment of diarrhoea cases depends on the cause of the disease. The owner should not deprive the horse of water, as this will only increase the possibility of dehydration. The diet should be changed to increase the amount of pollard and chaff, creating a bland diet and eliminating lucerne. Various treatment regimes under veterinary supervision may include dosing the horse with manure (to re-establish a balanced bacterial population in the gut), electrolytes, systemic antibiotics, opium compounds or antispasmolytics such as Lomotil. Dosing with yoghurt is often very helpful.

Discharge

A discharge means that there is an area of infection draining. This can be soft tissue (for example, an abscess in a muscle), an embedded foreign body, or decay of bone or tooth. It is pointless cleaning the superficial discharge. The basic cause must be identified and treated. Examples are infections of the womb, with vulval discharge (see the section on Breeding); tooth root abscess, with discharge on the face below the eyes (see NASAL DISCHARGES); nail in the foot, with discharge at the coronet. When the cause is eliminated treat as for abscess.

Drenching

Drenching usually refers to the oral administration of liquid medications. It is done for the purpose of worming, correction of dehydration or feeding the sick horse. It can also refer to the administration of these compounds by stomach tube. Stomach tubing is the insertion of a tube through the nostril and into the stomach of the horse. This is a delicate procedure, for if the tube enters the lungs and medication is administered the horse will die. Stomach tubing of horses should be left to a veterinary surgeon (see also DEHYDRATION, and the section on Worming, p. 193.)

Dropped elbow (Radial paralysis)

In this condition, which is caused by injury to the radial nerve where it passes over the front of the shoulder, the animal stands with the knee of the affected leg bent and the fetlock semi-flexed. The horse cannot draw the leg forward. The lameness (paralysis) rapidly worsens, and if it occurs during a journey the horse may experience great difficulty in getting to a stable. The condition can also occur after the horse has been lying on its side for some period during an operation (damage can be prevented by elevating the bottom shoulder and pushing an inflated tyre-tube under it). The nerve may also be damaged by a car accident or a kick from another horse.

The animal can be put into slings for the first few weeks or until it becomes accustomed to the loss of use of the limb. Massage of the shoulder muscle for an hour or so daily is very helpful; sometimes electrical massage procedures help the muscle retain its tone. Beyond this, one can only wait for natural healing to take place. If there is no improvement after six weeks, euthanasia may be the only choice. Complete healing is a very long-term process—often up to six months.

The elbow will also drop, and the leg assume a similar picture in severe lameness of the foot. However, in this condition, the horse can draw the leg forward and place it.

Dropsy

This is a filling of the head, legs, dependent parts of the chest, the prepuce and belly with fluid. It can occur as a normal syndrome in mares in late pregnancy, but it is usually associated with a heart or circulation problem. If it occurs in one area (for example, one limb) only, the poor circulation may be due to infection or tight bandages. (See also FILLED LEGS, EQUINE INFECTIOUS ANAEMIA.)

Dysentery

See DIARRHOEA.

Ear disorders

Horses rarely have trouble with their ears. If there is an ear infection, the horse will carry its head on the side, or hold both ears in a lop-eared (horizontal) position.

Wind a wad of cotton-wool around the end of your finger and clean out the ear canal. If the infection is caused by ear-mites, these will be seen under a magnifying glass on the dirt on the cotton-wool; they are white and their legs can be seen moving. Ear-drops used for dogs and cats are suitable for use in the horse's ear and will clear out the mites. The horse's ear does not need routine cleaning out during grooming.

Eczema

See SKIN DISORDERS.

Electrolytes

The main electrolytes are sodium, potassium, chloride and bicarbonate ions. These ions are lost in such body fluids as sweat, urine, diarrhoea and saliva. Their function is to generate electrical impulses in the muscles of the body. Deficiencies lead to ineffective muscular movements and dehydration. (See also DEHYDRATION.)

Emaciation

See MALNUTRITION.

Emphysema

See BROKEN WIND.

Encephalitis

Encephalitis is an inflammation of the brain often associated with meningitis. It is caused by bacteria and viruses and can sometimes be a complication of STRANGLES. Symptoms may range from dullness to head pushing and excitement. Suspected cases should be referred to a veterinary surgeon.

Enteritis

See DIARRHOEA.

Entropion

See EYE DISORDERS.

Equine encephalomyelitis

See ENCEPHALITIS.

Equine infectious anaemia (Swamp fever)

This is an acute or chronic viral disease of horses transmitted by biting flies, mosquitoes, or by injection of minute amounts of blood. It can also be transmitted by the ingestion of contaminated material. It is characterised by intermittent fever, loss of weight, progressive weakness, marked depression, and dropsy of the lower parts of the body. The disease also may exist in a subclinical form, in which the animal appears normal.

The disease is found in Europe, Japan, North America and Australia. As the virus is present in all the organs, blood, saliva, urine and milk of the horse, contamination of shared food and water supplies is common. There is no specific treatment for the disease.

Equine piroplasmosis

This is a specific disease affecting horses, mules and donkeys, and is caused by the invasion of the red blood cells by a parasite. The symptoms are a high temperature and a yellow discoloration of the mucous membranes of the eye and mouth which after a few days become deep orange or reddish-brown in colour. There is an irregular intermittent fever reaching 40.5–41°C. The urine may be a deep orange or reddish-brown colour. The disease can be successfully treated with drugs.

Euthanasia

Sometimes a horse suffering from an incurable illness or severe injuries must be put down. Drugs now available allow a horse to be put down with more dignity than if it were shot. However, if drugs are not available and the case is urgent, the horse can be shot with a .22 calibre rifle. The bullet should be aimed 10–12 centimetres above the eyes in the centre line of the forehead—the gun so angled that the bullet passes upwards through the brain to the spinal cord.

Eye disorders
Cataracts

Cataract refers to an opacity which affects the lens of the eye. The lens becomes chalky so that light does not pass through it. The cataract may be congenital (present in the foal at birth) or it may be progressive, which means that a small congenital cataract may become more extensive. The condition may be acquired during life as an extension from an eye infection, or it may result from injury. There is not yet a successful treatment for cataract in the horse.

Cuts in the bottom lid allow tear flow down the face.

Conjunctivitis

Conjunctivitis is an inflammation of the mucous membrane of the eye, usually indicated by a flow of tears and half-closed eyes. The horse is usually disinclined to allow the eye to be examined. In the early stages the discharge is watery. Later it becomes thicker, sticky and sometimes pussy. Conjunctivitis may be caused by an infection. Often, however, it arises when the eye is irritated by flies (see the section on Worming—Habronema), dust, or mud thrown up in a race or other event. It can also be caused by getting soap in the eyes, or by allergic reactions to certain foodstuffs. General diseases such as viral influenza and strangles may also bring on conjunctivitis and it is one of the first signs of periodic ophthalmia.

As a first aid measure, wash the eye with lukewarm saline—a teaspoonful of common salt to each 600 millilitres of warm boiled water. This will help remove offending irritants. Commercial human eye-washes are also suitable. In some cases the third eyelid may partially cover the eye, but this will disappear when the inflammation subsides.

Tears falling freely down the cheeks can sometimes indicate that the tear ducts, which carry excess tears into the nostrils, are blocked. This condition can also cause conjunctivitis. A veterinary surgeon can clear the obstruction from the ducts. The treatment of conjunctivitis is always best left to a veterinary surgeon.

Entropion

Entropion is where the upper or lower eyelid may be turned inwards so that the lashes rub against the glassy part of the eye and cause an irritation. This is particularly common in newly born thoroughbred foals. It may be overcome by placing a fingertip on the lower part of the lid and drawing it back from the eye to the normal position. If this is done frequently throughout the first day of life, the lid may regain its normal position. If no improvement occurs, the vet will suture the lid in place and may remove an elliptical piece of skin at the lid margins. When this heals it will cause sufficient contraction of the skin of the eyelid to keep the lid from curling inwards. Unless the irritation is quickly relieved the cornea will become inflamed (a condition known as keratitis) and may ulcerate and cause loss of sight.

Eyelids damaged

The eyelids may become torn by barbed wire or by nails protruding from a feed bin or doorway. Never remove any hanging portions of an eyelid. Seek veterinary advice immediately, as all the fragments still adhering will be needed to bring about healing without undue contraction and distortion of the eyelid. If a section of the bottom eyelid is missing the result can be a constant overflow of tears.

Keratitis (Blueness)

Keratitis is an inflammation of the sensitive, transparent cornea (glassy part of the eye). It is sometimes an extension of conjunctivitis, but can be caused by direct injury by a foreign body, or by infection. When the cornea suffers this inflammatory change, the lids are always tightly closed and there is evidence of marked pain and discomfort. There is considerable discharge of watery fluid (mainly tears) at first, but this diminishes after the first day and the cornea

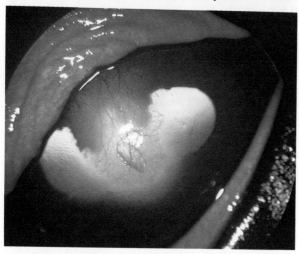

This eye has been specially stained to show the ulcer in the very centre of the eye. Note also the red conjunctivitis.

tends to become dry. The whole eye may appear to be covered by a blue haze. The lids are closed so tightly that little of the eye is visible unless a local anaesthetic is introduced between the lids to relieve the pain. Within a few days small blood vessels will creep from the white part of the eye across the cornea. Soon afterwards the cornea becomes ulcerated. If allowed to progress, the ulcer may finally rupture, allowing the fluid inside the eye to escape. (See Periodic ophthalmia, below.) Obviously this is a condition that must be referred to a veterinary surgeon for urgent treatment.

Periodic ophthalmia (Recurrent uveitis)

The symptoms of this condition are very similar to keratitis. The first symptom is photophobia (a dislike of light). The eye is closed and sticky tears accumulate on the lower lid and cheek. If the eye can be seen there is an intense keratitis (blueness) with a marked circle of blood vessels apparent on the white area of the eye surrounding the cornea. After one or two days the cornea becomes cloudy and yellowish at its margins. This condition responds very well to depot cortisone injections placed in the mucous membranes of the eye. The sooner a veterinary surgeon is contacted the better the result. The 'periodic' in the name is because the disease can return periodically.

Squamous cell carcinoma

This is a fast-growing, fleshy tumour which may appear in the corner of the eye, attached to the third eyelid. It can also occur in the eyelids themselves. In early cases where the tumour is not deeply entrenched surgical excision and radiation give good results. (See also SKIN DISORDERS.)

The near side of this horse's head is affected by facial paralysis.

Facial paralysis

Facial paralysis is caused by such things as blows to the side of the head, the use of heavy and ill-fitting bridles, or pressure on the head while the animal is held on the ground during operations. The signs are drooping of the eyelid, inability to close the eye fully and inability to erect the ear.

The chances of recovery are best when the injury is recent and paralysis is confined to the lips and nostrils. Treatment consists of removal of pressure from the part, warm fomentations, and light blisters (see Caring for the sick horse) below the root of the ear. Assessment should be made throughout the convalescence as to whether the horse should be put down. Most will show signs of recovery within six weeks. Those that don't will usually be permanently affected.

Feet disorders

It is extremely important to keep a horse's feet in good condition. 'No feet, no horse' is as true today as it ever was. In countries with a dry climate, light to sandy soil and unmetalled roads, unshod horses can do light work without causing undue wear and damage to their feet. Feet of young horses, even before they are due for shoeing, should be inspected and manicured at least every month. The shoes on horses in work should be removed or replaced at least once a month, but horses turned out for a spell, broodmares and unworked horses should never wear shoes unless they have a specific problem which requires they be shod—special shoeing may even be required.

The new horn at the coronet reaches the lower border in about eight months, the rate of growth varying with different animals and their state of general health. Dark-coloured horn is generally supposed to be of better texture and wearing property than light- or white-coloured horn.

As part of regular daily care, the horse's feet should be cleaned out with a hoof pick, particularly the grooves around the frog. This is absolutely essential in damp conditions. Hoof dressing should be applied to the hoof wall and the sole. The frog should always be kept trimmed so that there is no cavity formation allowing the development of thrush.

Brittle feet

Cracks and splits may occur in normal feet, but if the horn is very dry it loses much of its elasticity and is more likely to suffer injury. Brittle horn is generally associated with deficiencies in the diet (see the section on Feeding). Good results have been achieved by adding half a cup of gelatin daily to the feed. Hoof dressings can also help. (See also Sandcrack, pp. 222–23)

Contracted heels

A horse is said to have contracted heels when the width of the foot at the heel is less than one-quarter of the circumference of the hoof at ground level. The frog does not reach the ground, so there is no pressure from it to push the heels apart when the foot touches the ground. One of the commonest causes of contraction of the heel is lengthening of the toe.

Lack of frog pressure induced by improper shoeing may also prevent contact of the frog with the ground. Lameness in the limb from any cause can prevent the horse from pressing the foot firmly to the ground. Any of these causes prevent the slight expansion of the hoof that should occur when the weight of the animal is placed on the foot. Heel contraction is usually accompanied by a so-called dished sole. It can also have a hereditary origin. Methods of treatment are to allow the frog to grow so that it touches the ground and to rasp the side walls of the heels. Rasping the walls of the hoof allows them greater flexibility so that they can spread under pressure.

Corns and bruised sole

Corns most frequently occur in the front feet, rarely in the hind feet. This is because the front feet bear more weight than the hind feet. Corns are usually caused by ill-fitting shoes. When a shoe is left on the foot too long, the heel of the shoe is forced inside the hoof wall thus causing pressure on the sole at the angle of the wall and the bar. Corns are rare amongst horses that are used barefooted, but rocks and other objects can cause sole bruising.

Where shoeing is causing corns, removal of the offending shoe is usually all that is necessary. To prevent the problem, the heels of the shoes should always extend well back over the end of the heel and should fit full on the wall at the corners. The soreness caused by a corn can be relieved by removing some of the tissue over the corn. A solution of 5 per cent formalin can be applied to the area daily for four days to harden it.

Laminitis (Founder)

Laminitis is a very painful condition usually affecting the forefeet. It occurs when an inflammation is set up in the sensitive tissues (laminae) between the hoof wall and the pedal bone. Because the hoof structure is so unyielding the pain from the build-up of pressure in the inflamed tissues can become almost unbearable to the horse. The condition can vary from warmth in the hoof wall with no lameness, to warmth with lameness in both front feet or all four feet. In severe cases the horse is unable to stand.

In cases where the horse is just able to stand it adopts a typical posture, which gives rise to the description, 'stuck to the ground'. The horse advances its forefeet and brings its hindfeet well forward under the belly to lighten the load on the forefeet. Tapping the foot with a light hammer causes the horse pain. It is difficult to make the horse lift any of its feet because this brings more pressure to bear on other affected feet.

The causes of laminitis are:

The ingestion of large quantities of grain (including rabbit feed, chicken feed, pig feed or oats), resulting in grainfounder. Always keep a close eye on a horse that has broken into a feed shed.

The ingestion of large amounts of cold water by an overheated horse.

Roadfounder, the result of concussion to the feet from hard or fast work on a hard surface.

Post-parturient laminitis, seen shortly after foaling in mares that have retained a portion of the foetal membrane, or have developed a uterine infection without retention of the foetal membrane.

Superpurgation, following the administration of a purgative drug. Some horses may be too sensitive and react to the procedure with laminitis.

Grassfounder, common in horses that are grazed on spring and summer pastures. Pastures containing clover and alfalfa (lucerne) cause the problem, particularly when the horse has had no access to green feed for a long time. Overweight ponies are particularly susceptible.

Laminitis is a painful inflammation of the sensitive parts of the foot. In chronic cases the horse is reluctant to move.

Signs of laminitis may be acute or chronic.

In acute laminitis there is increased pulse in the vessels over the fetlock. The hoof, the sole and the coronary band are hot to the touch. Many horses show anxiety, trembling of the musculature from severe pain, increased respiration and injected mucous membranes.

The signs of grainfounder usually do not appear until twelve to eighteen hours after the horse has eaten the grain, leading the owner to believe that the horse will not be affected. Then laminitis, diarrhoea, toxaemia, muscular tremors and increased pulse and respiration appear and there is a variable rise in temperature.

In severe untreated laminitis the hoof may slough and fall off as a result of a separation of the sensitive and insensitive layers.

In chronic laminitis there is rotation of the pedal bone in the foot. This rotation may cause the pedal bone to push out through the sole of the foot. Horses suffering from chronic laminitis tend to step on the heel in an exaggerated fashion. The sole is dropped and flat, and it sheds excessive quantities of flaky material. Although corrective shoeing can be attempted, such cases are nearly always destroyed eventually. Chronic laminitis causes heavy ring formation on the hoof wall. The rings, usually present throughout the life of the horse, are caused by inflammation in the coronary band. The hoof wall grows more rapidly than normal because of the chronic inflammation and the foot may develop a long toe that curls up at the end. Horses that have suffered an attack of laminitis seem prone to get it again. Where laminitis is suspected, a veterinary surgeon should be contacted immediately and the horse's feet soaked in icy water or at least hosed with cold water. An alternative is to stand the horse in a cool running stream.

In grainfounder and grassfounder the treatment is directed at neutralising the effects of the grain. Purgatives such as mineral oil or magnesium sulphate should be used. Antihistamines are useful, as are conticosteroids and phenylbutazone. Veterinary advice should be sought regarding the treatment and prognosis of each case.

In chronic laminitis the foot should be trimmed as nearly normal as possible and more often than is necessary for a normal horse. Grooving the hoof wall by various methods, or rasping the quarters to thin the wall and provide expansion of the quarters, are often of value. Cutting the nerve (neurectomy) to alleviate pain is not recommended, as it is potentially dangerous to horse and rider.

Nail prick
Sometimes when horses are being shod, the farrier may place a nail too near to the inner part of the wall and the sensitive tissues. In such a case the nail should be withdrawn immediately and the tract disinfected with tincture of iodine. If the nail enters the inner part of the wall it can cause a painful wound which can last a long time. In most instances, however, soaking in a bucket of warm water (with four tablespoons of epsom salts added) four or five times a day for a few days relieves the pain.

Navicular disease
Not all horses affected with navicular disease are in pain and not all will go lame, but in most cases attention is drawn to the problem because the horse is lame. Usually the horse first goes lame very suddenly; the lameness may disappear or settle down to a slight lameness. The horse may be uneasy and restless, adopting a slight rocking action. As time goes on it points its forefeet; if both feet are affected the horse will point first one foot and then the other. Navicular disease rarely affects the hindfeet. If the horse is taken out and warmed up by exercise, the lameness will probably be relieved; but if the horse is left to cool off and then moved again when cold, the lameness will reappear. For the first few steps it will be more severe. Observe the action—flexion and extension of the lower pastern and the foot will be diminished, and the toe of the shoe may show wear as the horse puts its toes down first. This solid, block-like action of the foot will increase as the disease progresses. The stride becomes shorter, and as the feet are put down flat, like a block, the term 'blocking lameness' is used. Sole bruising from constant landing on the toe should be kept in mind when using hoof testers.

The first corrective shoe for the victim of the disease is one that has a roll toe. This results in the horse's foot 'breaking over' more quickly, so there tends to be a slight shortening of stride. The heel of the shoe should be thickened so that it is about one and a half times the thickness of the toe of the shoe. The outer half of the sole surface of the shoe is chamfered to three-quarters of its thickness from the last nail hole back, and the inner edge of the sole surface is fined down so that it is no longer pressing on the wall of the foot. Cutting the nerve (neurectomy) should be discussed with your vet. The prognosis in all cases of navicular disease is unfavourable.

Pedal bone fracture
This is a fracture in the lowermost bone of the leg. The bone is within the hoof. The cause can be as simple as turning quickly or landing the wrong way. Horses suffer this type of a fracture when racing. The signs are acute lameness and the sole of the foot is very sensitive to pressure. In most instances fractures of this nature will heal readily with a shoe that has a bar across the heel and four clips equally spaced around the circumference of the hoof wall. This holds the foot together and the fracture in place. Keep the horse strictly confined in a box for eight weeks. It should then be rested for six months in a soft paddock and X-rayed to determine that healing is complete. If the fracture involves the joint and the horse is very valuable, surgery can be performed by a veterinary surgeon to compress the fracture site with screws.

Pedal osteitis
Pedal osteitis is an inflammatory condition, usually caused by repeated concussion, in the last bone of the foot (which is enclosed by the hoof). It is one of the most common causes of lameness and is usually found in horses that work at a fast pace such as jumpers, racehorses and standardbreds. The inflammatory reaction in the foot begins to dissolve the bone, causing tenderness. The horse may step short, particularly if it is made to run over loose gravel so that the pain is accentuated. X-rays will confirm the diagnosis.

The most effective treatment is to turn the horse out on to soft land for six months. If the horse must continue working, it should be shod with special light, wide shoes, which sit on the wall of the hoof to eliminate any pressure on the sole. The heel should be thick, and the toe half the thickness of the heel. The toe of the shoe should be more square than round and rolled at the bottom. This produces a slight rocker effect.

Quittor
This is the term applied to a persistent, pussy sore opening at or near the coronet. The cause in most cases is direct injury such as being stepped on by another horse, thus injuring the lateral cartilage. It may also arise in an indirect way following an infection within the hoof when the outlet in the sole is obstructed and the pus moves upwards, following the line of least resistance. This may be the result of a puncture to the foot, a corn or a sandcrack.

Early cases of quittor will respond to irrigation of the tract with a 20 per cent silver nitrate solution, followed in ten minutes by saline solution to neutralise the silver nitrate. In chronic cases successful treatment depends upon removal of the dead or infected tissue; in most cases this involves surgery on the cartilage.

Ringbone
Ringbone is a new bone growth which may involve the articular surfaces of the pastern or coffin joints or may surround the articular surfaces and interfere with overlying tendons and structures causing lameness. It can be caused by wounds such as wire cuts or abrasions to the pasterns, or it may be due to a congenital abnormality. The treatment of the condition is usually unsuccessful, but it may help the horse to be given anti-inflammatory agents. Corrective shoeing consists of shortening the toe and applying a full roller motion shoe. The prognosis for ringbone involving the joints is poor. For ringbone outside the joints, prognosis is guarded.

Sandcrack
Sandcrack is a vertical crack or split in the wall of the hoof. Such cracks vary in length and depth, but true sandcrack extends from the upper border (coronet) to the lower border of the wall. It begins at or near the coronet. Some

sandcracks are so deep that they reach the sensitive tissues. These tissues may suffer direct injury, and foreign bodies such as grit or sand may gain access, causing the area to become infected. When this occurs, there is pain and the horse may be very lame.

Small shallow cracks that extend upwards from the edge of the hoof should not be ignored, but they usually cause little trouble. They arise as a direct injury and in these cases, the horn is usually dry and brittle. When a horse puts its weight on a foot affected with a sandcrack, the crack tends to open and shut, causing the split to extend. Any new horn growth continues to split. Remedies are designed to stop further splitting of the hoof and allow a sandcrack to grow out. The simplest method is to rasp across the top of the split if it begins at the bottom of the wall. If the split begins at the coronet, rasp around the bottom. Other methods include transfixing with a horizontal clenched horseshoe nail, filling with epoxy glue or plastic, and corrective shoeing using clips either side of the crack.

Sandcracks — note the dryness of the hoof and the lack of trimming.

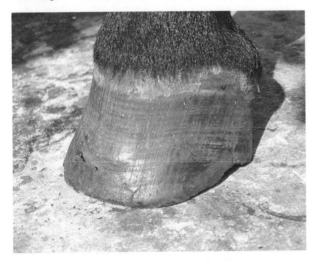

Seedy toe usually occurs around the toe area. Growth lines on the hoof wall indicate a history of foot problems.

Seedy toe

Seedy toe is the formation of cavities between the outer wall of the hoof and the inner sensitive layers. It usually occurs around the toe area, right at the edge of the sole and the white line, but may occur anywhere between the toe and the heel. To correct this condition, allow the black-

smith to trim the foot back as far as possible. The cavity of the seedy toe should then be thoroughly cleaned out, disinfected with tincture of iodine and packed with stockholm tar. The growth of good new horn can be promoted by rubbing a light blister around the coronet of the foot.

Thrush

Thrush is a disease affecting the cleft of the frog. It is seen in horses stabled in dirty conditions or horses paddocked in unclean, damp conditions. It is generally considered to be an indication of neglect and poor stable management. Bacteria and germs in the cleft of the frog thrive in such conditions. The sign of thrush is a blackish discharge which gives off a typically offensive smell. The site can become quite raw and painful and the horse may go lame. Superficial thrush can be cleared up by transferring a horse to a dry area, picking its feet out twice a day and cleaning them thoroughly with a brush and water, finally applying a 5 per cent formalin solution. This solution must not get on to the skin. If the frog has been eaten away and the horse is very lame, antibiotic therapy may also be necessary.

Fetlock joint disorders

The most common problem with the fetlocks is an arthritic condition called 'apple-joint'. This is often associated with windgalls (see ARTHRITIS) or with puffy swellings at the side of the joint. Both of these conditions are caused by strain on the joint, usually when young immature horses are used for hard work, such as endurance, racing or jumping. The swelling of the joint and the windgalls are due to arthritis caused by overextension of the joint. If work continues the joint will gradually lose flexion, the horse will become sore and consequently lame.

If the horse is young, stop any forced exercise and spell the horse until three years of age. If the horse is older, rest for four months—but the prognosis is unfavourable long term, if the same hard work is contemplated. Antiphlogistine packs, epsom salts bandages or cold hosing for ten minutes four times daily, will help to reduce the swelling and heat in acute cases. The administration of anti-inflammatory agents (for example, phenylbutazone and cortisone) also is helpful in relieving this condition.

Blistering or pin-firing have very little long-term effect. Once the joints have enlarged and are hard, nothing can be done to reduce their size. If the horse has been in work and the joints are cool and not sore on flexion, the prognosis is favourable.

Other conditions of the fetlock joint, such as fractured sesamoids, dislocation of the sesamoids, fractures of the long-bones either side of the joint and deviation of the joint should all be left to the vet for discussion.

Fever

Fever is a rise in body temperature. The fevered horse usually looks depressed and feels hot, particularly its ears. The normal rectal temperature for an adult horse is 37.5–38.5°C. A stubby thick bulb ended thermometer is best. The thermometer should be shaken down to below normal temperature level, inserted along the wall of the rectum and left in place for one minute. The normal body temperature may be higher in animals during pregnancy, parturition, lactation and in the young animal.

Fevers can be caused by various organisms, viruses, toxic products, certain chemical agents, heat or sunstroke. A fever usually has three stages: a cold stage or shivering fit, a hot stage, and the decline of the fever. As a rule fever is a protective reaction of the body against invading organisms. Providing the fever is mild and not therefore endangering the nervous system, the heart or the digestive organs, clean stabling and good food alone are satisfactory treatments. The animal should be kept in a well-ventilated, clean box and provided with a comfortable bed. If the horse is normally rugged, it should have a light-weight rug sufficient to keep it warm without sweating. If it sweats leave the rug off. There should be a plentiful supply of fresh clean drinking water and the diet should be laxative and easily assimilated. If the fever looks suspiciously like a symptom of a contagious disease, the animal must be isolated. Once temperatures get over 39.4°C veterinary attention should be sought.

Filled legs

Filled legs refers to swelling in the legs, usually from the coronet upwards around the cannon bone. It may occur in one leg or all four. Where it occurs in one leg it is usually due to a blow or injury. Greasy heel is also a cause. Close examination usually reveals a small nick or mark, perhaps where the horse has struck itself, where a small infection has developed. The horse should be lightly worked, then cold hosed and an antiphlogistine or epsom salts bandage placed on the leg. An epsom salts bandage is made by spreading out a piece of cotton-wool sufficient to cover the affected area. Lightly sprinkle epsom salts over and dampen. Place around the affected area and bandage over. This should be repeated at least twice daily for three to four days. Spray the nick with an antibiotic solution.

Sometimes the hindlegs or all four legs fill overnight, but after work in the morning the swelling subsides. This may be associated with high-grain diets or a virus. If the swelling in any leg is hot and does not improve with the above treatment, seek advice as the horse will need antibiotics.

See also DROPSY, EQUINE INFECTIOUS ANAEMIA, GREASY HEEL, WINDGALLS.

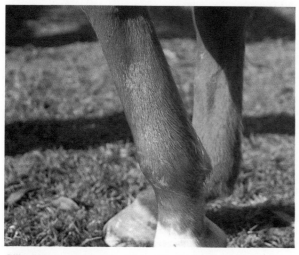

Filled legs are legs swollen with fluid due usually to infection — cellulitis.

Fistula

This is a weeping wound—such as an open abscess site. It may be due to an infected bone, the root of a tooth, or to a foreign body lodged deep in the body (bits of stick, wire, or a nail in the foot). Fistulous withers (infections of the withers), and poll evil (infections of the poll of the head), also give rise to fistulas. In the case of weeping wounds or fistulas, the source of the problem must be dissected out, for the wound will not heal with irrigation alone. Once the cause is removed, treatment is the same as for abscesses (see ABSCESSES).

Fistulous withers

See FISTULA.

Flatulence

Anal flatulence in the horse is rarely offensive and is rarely a problem. It is almost always associated with a change in diet, particularly when the horse goes on to fresh pastures. Some horses always break wind when they start to work.

Flatulent colic may arise from an obstruction of the bowel leading to a build-up of gas in the stomach. It may also occur when a hard-fed horse is given sudden access to lush green grass. New hay, especially if damp, may cause excess gas production. In these cases the animal has symptoms similar to those of spasmodic colic but the pain is continuous and the animal frequently crouches but seldom lies down. It will yawn, paw the ground and look at its sides. There are frequent attempts at urination. The respiration becomes very frequent, short and only the thoracic area moves because of pressure on the lungs from the distended abdomen. A veterinary surgeon should be called to relieve the gas by stomach tube.

Fly bites

Fly and other insect bites can cause a number of diseases in horses, particularly in Africa and South America. Horses can also become allergic to insect and fly bites. In Australia, for example, they develop the so-called Queensland itch. The bot-fly, although it does not bite the horse, irritates by its loud humming. As it circles around seeking to lay its eggs on the hair, it can annoy horses to the extent that they group together for defence, or else bolt to escape from it. Flies can annoy horses to such an extent that they may go off their food or lose weight. Methods of protection include using a fly-bait material around stables and yards, regularly picking up manure to keep yards and stables hygienic, locking the horse in a fly-proof area, using fly-proof rugs, and spraying the horse with a residual aerosol. A simple and effective method of protecting horses from the worry of flies is to provide a darkened stable with hessian bagging hanging in the doorway which the horse can push through to leave the flies outside. Bush flies and the biting flies will not normally go into a darkened area.

Flies congregating around the eyes can cause a chronic conjunctivitis (see EYE DISORDERS). Flies will also irritate wounds on a horse. (See also SKIN DISORDERS: RAIN SCALD.)

Forging (Over-reaching)

This is a defect of the gait, in which the toe of the hindfoot overtakes and strikes the bottom of the front foot of the same side at the moment the front foot is rising. It can cause severe downward cuts to the heels of the front foot, and bruising at the very least.

The front feet should be trimmed short at the toe and shod with rocker or rolled toe shoes of equal and light weight. The hindfeet should be trimmed, leaving the hoof long in the toe: and if still necessary, the shoe on the hindfoot should extend beyond the heels by 1–2 centimetres. This increases the rapidity of the breaking over of the forefeet and decreases the rapidity of the breaking over of the hindfeet.

The risk of injury can be further reduced by putting bell boots on the front feet whenever the horse is worked.

Founder

A common name for laminitis (fever of the foot). (See FEET DISORDERS: LAMINITIS.)

Fractures

The term 'fracture' is given to the breaking of a bone or cartilage. Criticism is often made in the press and by the public if a horse that breaks its leg is destroyed. In the horse, with few exceptions, these cases are incurable in the sense that the animal will, if treated, be unfit or unsafe for work. Unless it can be used for breeding purposes it cannot repay the owner the cost of the treatment incurred. One of the problems in treating fractures of major support bones in the horse is its sheer size. The horse is difficult and sometimes unwilling to be restrained during both the operation and subsequent convalescence.

Fracture is often caused by a kick from another horse. Or the animal may fall on its muzzle and fracture the lower jaw, or base of the skull or neck. Jumping may result in fracture of the legs, spine or pelvis. Spinal fracture can occur when the animal is cast for surgery. Struggling during recovery can result in fractured limbs. Horses while lungeing have fallen on their head and fractured their neck. Spontaneous fracture of the legs, vertebrae of the back, or the shoulder, can all occur even at slow work. It can occur as a result of muscular inco-ordination and is the most probable explanation of these spontaneous fractures when they occur.

Sometimes a distinct crack is heard. Great lameness is apparent immediately and there may be excessive mobility or deformity of the part. Grating or grinding may be felt on movement of the area. Inability to bear weight is strongly suggestive of fracture, but not conclusive. Muscular twitching may be present and patchy sweating may occur. Pain is usually present.

In cases involving the nose there is usually deformity and haemorrhage and breathing may be noisy because of obstruction of the nasal passages.

Fractures of the ribs may cause paralysis of a limb and, if complicated by a punctured chest wall, may allow air to pass to and fro from the chest.

In cases of fracture of the skull (sometimes caused by rearing up in a stall) haemorrhage from the ear is common. If the fracture is severe, haemorrhage may occur into the brain causing death. If fractures occur behind the mid-section of the neck, paralysis of the diaphragm may occur.

Fractures of the spine cause paralysis and inability to raise the hindquarters.

In fracture of the limbs with displacement, there will be shortening of the limb.

The diagnosis of a fracture may be quite easy or very difficult. A major fracture of a long bone is easy, but a split pastern, pelvic fracture, and fractures of minor bones are difficult. When in doubt, X-rays are advised. Fractures are always a serious affliction and it is best to consult a vet for diagnosis and available treatment, if any.

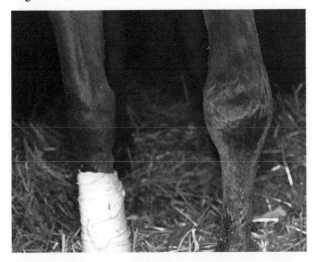

Two-year-old thoroughbred filly with race fracture of the carpal (knee) bones. The other leg is bandaged for support.

Frog troubles
See FEET DISORDERS: CONTRACTED HEELS, THRUSH.

Frostbite (Mud fever)
The action of excessive cold on the skin may produce frostbite, a condition resembling a burn. Horses are capable of withstanding very cold weather without suffering, as long as they are well fed and are allowed to grow their natural protective coat of long hair. Minor forms of frostbite can occur on the lower legs, particularly if the animal is forced to stand in mud and water in cold weather. The wet, cold conditions can cause death of the surface cells of the skin and damage to the deeper layers. As in burns, dilation of the small blood vessels of the skin occurs followed by oozing of fluid through their walls into the surrounding spaces. This results in the skin becoming swollen and painful. Sometimes the affected area may be the size of a matchbox. The condition is called mud fever.

To prevent problems, do not wash the horse's legs in wintertime but dry the legs thoroughly without delay. If winter pasturing the horse, avoid ground that easily becomes waterlogged. Always make sure that animals get sufficient food to keep them in good general condition throughout the winter.

Galls and saddle sores
Girth galls and saddle sores are eroded areas of skin which can eventually die and slough out, leaving a nasty open sore. They are caused by constant pressure from ill-fitting gear.

Predisposing causes include:
Low withers, allowing the saddle to be displaced forwards.
High withers, which are apt to be compressed by the pommel (front arch) of the saddle.
Narrow chest, making it difficult to tighten the girth, sufficiently to prevent the saddle moving.
Poor condition, causing the skin to be severely compressed between the gear and protruding bones.
Excess condition, causing saddle and girth to move about.
Faulty construction of the saddle, lumps in the stuffing or rips in the lining.
Rough dirty girths.
An awkward or tired rider, who rolls about or sits lopsidedly.
Walking in hilly country, causing movement of the saddle.
Ill-balanced pack saddles.
Sweating, or the skin being wet from rain.

Galls may sometimes be prevented by leaving the saddle on for about half an hour after the horse finishes work to allow the blood to return gradually to the squashed vessels and thus prevent their rupture (haematoma) from sudden forcible distension. Gradual return of blood without rupture of vessels will still allow fluid through the bruised vessels into the subcutaneous tissues. Galls should be treated first with cold water and astringent lotions to prevent further distension, and afterwards with moist heat and massage to promote absorption of the fluid.

Once a gall or rub does appear, the horse must not be worked until the sore is completely healed. Spray the area with acriflavine, triple dye, mercurochrome or an antibiotic solution. Commercial sprays are available. Determine the cause of the injury and if necessary adjust the gear. Thick foam saddle pads and sheepskin girth-covers are good insurance against recurrence.

Gelding
A gelding is a desexed male horse. (See CASTRATION.)

Glanders
Glanders is a highly contagious disease of the lymphatic system caused by bacteria. It causes nodule development, ulcerations and degeneration in the respiratory passages or in the skin. It is a very difficult disease to treat, and requires veterinary attention. Australia and New Zealand are free of the disease.

Infection is by inoculation (cuts, abrasions, scratches, needles), inhalation, and ingestion. The first is the common method of transmission in humans. Care should therefore be exercised in handling diseased animals, for example, at postmortems.

In horses, mules, and donkeys, infection can result from the inhalation of particles of nasal discharge floating in the atmosphere of the stables. The most frequent source is ingestion of the organism in water or food that has become contaminated with nasal discharge through the medium of mangers, nosebags, buckets and waterers. Sponges, rags and other grooming cloths also commonly convey the disease directly from nose to nose.

The incubation period can vary from a few days to months. The signs of the disease present themselves in two forms:

Glanders form (localised in the respiratory passages) Discharge from one or both nostrils of a sticky nature, snuffling breathing, ulcerations on the nasal mucous membranes, hard lumps in the glands under the jaw on the side on which nasal symptoms are apparent. Variable amount of fever. In acute cases, the whole face may become swollen, and the respirations of a characteristic wheezing, snuffling or snoring type. While the symptoms of nasal glanders are quite unmistakable, they should be differentiated from other similar disease. (See NASAL DISCHARGE.)

Farcy form (nodule formation in the lymphatics of the legs, head, neck or other parts) Nodules or 'buds' and ulcers along their course. The ulcers do not show any tendency to heal. Both glanders and farcy can occur together.

In the case of an outbreak, destroy all affected animals as the disease is to all intents and purposes incurable. Dispose of carcasses (burn or bury). Other animals on the property should be isolated, as should in-contact animals on farms either side of the diseased animals. Call the vet.

Granulation tissue
See WOUNDS.

Grass sickness
Grass sickness is a very well-known disease in Scotland where it occurs year by year in epidemic form. Sporadic cases occur in England and Sweden, but most other countries are free of the disease. In Scotland it affects all breeds and any age group except suckling foals. The disease was originally thought to come from grass, particularly in horses having access to grass in the late spring after having been housed and fed on hard feed during the winter, but more recent opinion is that it is caused by a virus. Grass sickness is almost invariably fatal, as it produces non-reversible paralysis of the entire alimentary tract. The very rare cases that do survive would generally be better off dead as suffering is extreme.

Greasy heel
Greasy heel is a dermatitis of the back of the pastern, and is particularly prevalent in damp conditions. The skin is inflamed and has a pussy discharge which forms a scab. Often horizontal cracks in the skin occur. The condition can become so painful that lameness occurs. Horses with white or pale-coloured hair in the pastern region are more susceptible, as are horses that have had the feather cut from the fetlock, allowing water to run down the back of the pastern rather than drip off the feather.

Treatment is to ensure that the pasterns are dry all the time. Wash the affected legs down with an antibacterial soap or shampoo to remove excess exudate, towel dry gently, then apply mercurochrome, acriflavine or triple dye twice daily to the area. If this fails, an antibiotic, antifungal cortisone cream should be applied three times daily after thorough washing and drying. (See also SKIN DISORDERS: RAIN SCALD.)

Gripes
See COLIC.

Guttural pouch
The guttural pouch is a blind sac on either side of the throat of the horse. It is a distension of the Eustachian tube—its function is unknown.

They are quite susceptible to infection introduced by way of the Eustachian tubes, usually being the aftermath of strangles or other respiratory disease. There is a chronic nasal discharge, which appears only during feeding or when the head is lowered to eat from the ground, or to take the bit, or during exercise. There may be interference with swallowing and respiration, and swelling at the base of the ear behind the jaw bone. Treatment is surgical. Call the veterinary surgeon.

The other problem affecting the guttural pouches is tympanitis (filled with air). It is found in foals or horses up to one year. It results from a congenital defect which forms a one-way valve resulting in the pouches inflating. Signs are obvious. The area below the ear is distended and soft like a balloon. Treatment is surgical.

Habronema (Stomach worms)
See the section on Worming, pp. 188–94.

Haematoma
A haematoma is a soft, often painless swelling filled with blood. It can be caused by a kick, or by running into an object. It is best to confine the horse to a stable for ten days, so that the ruptured vessel wall has time to repair. If it is in an area that will allow a firm bandage, this will reduce the eventual size of the haematoma.

Most haematomas will eventually disappear of their own accord without leaving a blemish. If drainage of an especially large haematoma is desired, let it settle for ten days first. Drainage may be done under surgical asepsis, otherwise the haematoma will easily become infected. (See also CAPPED ELBOW and CAPPED HOCK.)

Haemolytic disease
A blood disorder in foals resulting from incompatible blood groupings between sire and dam. See Illnesses of foals, p. 201.

Harvest mites
The larval form of the harvest mite is found in grass, hay and other fodder. When present on the skin in protected parts such as the heels and back of the fetlock, they produce marked skin irritation and often play some part in giving rise to cracked heels or the so-called heel bug. They can cause irritations of the mane and tail to form a dermatitis. This causes constant rubbing and loss of hair from the mane and the root of the tail. (See also SKIN DISORDERS: SCRUB ITCH, and section on Worming—pinworms, p. 191.)

Head shaking
This condition is sometimes met with in riding horses, making them uncontrollable and extremely dangerous to ride. It should not be confused with head shaking as an attempt to escape from the pain inflicted on the mouth by a heavy-handed rider. Irritation from ear mites, a badly fitting bit, too tight a throat latch or a sinus infection can all cause the problem.

Heat-stroke
Heat-stroke usually occurs on extremely hot, humid days in horses left to stand in the sun unprotected. Working animals may also suffer heat exhaustion, but usually less severely. Heat-stroke is usually rapid in onset. The symptoms are staggering, coma, laboured breathing, slow and irregular pulse and usually a dry skin (dehydration). Rectal temperatures may reach 41.1°C or higher. Emergency treatment includes reducing body temperature by getting the horse into the shade (an improvised shelter will do), spraying it with water, giving cold water enemas and applying cold packs to the head. Veterinary attention is essen-

tial. Further treatment to combat shock involves administering saline or electrolyte intravenous drips. To help prevent laminitis, the feet should be immersed in cold water. Full recovery will take seven days of complete rest.

Heaves
See BROKEN WIND.

Hernias
See Illnesses of foals, p. 204.

Hock disorders

Bog spavin
Bog spavin is a soft distension of the joint membrane which is filled with joint fluid. It is most common in young animals or in those with more upright or straight legs. It is also more common in animals in which great strain is thrown upon the hocks (such as entire horses, aged stallions and breeding mares).

In recent acute cases the usual symptoms are heat, pain and marked lameness. Usually, however, the swelling is cold, painless, and fluctuating on pressure, and lameness is rare. Animals affected will commonly work well throughout their life without treatment and may experience few problems. In acute cases, cold applications with astringent lotions and massage are indicated. Provided there is no lameness or heat it is best left alone.

Bone spavin
Bone spavin is the name given to a bone enlargement on the lower and inner aspect of the hock. It is regarded as a hereditary disease. Conformation (see Selecting a horse) plays a large part. Whilst it may affect any hock, it is more likely to occur in hocks which when viewed from in front appear narrower or to taper towards the shank—and less likely in square hocks. Defective conformation also includes 'small' hocks, 'tied-in' hocks, 'sickle-shaped' hocks, and 'cow' hocks. These conformations constitute weaknesses, rendering the joint liable to inflammation under the stress of work.

Lameness is always most marked on starting after rest, but diminishes with exercise and in some instances disappears. The horse takes a short stride with the affected leg, the hock is not flexed normally, and as a result the toe of the shoe is frequently worn. Turning the horse in a small circle with the lame leg outside increases the lameness and the animal has a jerky way of taking the foot off the ground, possibly through increased pain when the joint is extended. Forced flexion of the joint will increase the lameness.

Hold the affected leg up in flexion for a minute or two and then release it and move the horse off. If the horse is lame from spavin there may be great aggravation of the lameness. It should be remembered that the same result will follow from sprained tendons, or any lameness at or below the hock.

In most instances the treatment for horses under twelve years of age is favourable—but not so favourable beyond this age. The best method of treatment is to pin-fire the affected area and apply a red mercurial blister into the punctures and around the whole enlargement. Repeat the blistering in about a month. By the end of the second month the animal should be better with no apparent lameness. If not, re-apply the blister.

Capped hock
This condition is similar to capped elbow in that it is caused by a physical bruising of the bone of the hock. It is usually caused by the horse kicking its stable or float doors. This can be prevented by building a barrier in the stable or float that is about 60 centimetres wide at the height of the horse's buttocks. A wooden or pipe rail will do the job. The condition will resolve itself (if not of long standing) once physical contact stops, although the cure may be hastened by drainage of the area.

Curb
This is the name given to a swelling, as a result of a sprain, which is situated about a hand's breadth below the point of the hock towards the inner side. It is seen in all breeds, but more commonly in harness and riding horses.

A frequent cause is landing on wet and slippery ground after jumping, and sliding along. Pulling horses up quickly on to their haunches or putting young horses at jumps too early are all predisposing causes. Bad conformation such as 'sickle-shaped' hocks or 'tied-in' hocks may predispose. Lameness may be present immediately after the accident. In the stable the leg is 'favoured', with the heel raised and resting on the toe of the shoe. If made to move, the horse is inclined to go 'on its toes'.

If the horse is not lame, treatment is not advisable. If there is lameness and swelling, the treatment advocated for sprained tendons should be followed. A wedge-heeled shoe is useful in the early stages. Sometimes lungeing four or five times a week over a low wall or pole is helpful. The jump is increased by a few centimetres each day till it reaches 1.2 metres.

Occult spavin
This is the name given when there is no bony outgrowth as in bone spavin, but only an arthritis. The difference between this and bone spavin is that with occult spavin the lameness is continuous and does not diminish with exercise. In most cases the lameness becomes more pronounced with exercise.

The behaviour of the lame leg when turning, wearing of the shoe at the toe, dropping of the quarter on the lame side and all other symptoms, are present as in bone spavin. There is no appreciable enlargement.

When this cause of lameness is diagnosed, line-firing around the whole of the joint (but excluding the front of the bend of the joint) is necessary followed by rest for six to eight months. The prognosis, even with treatment, is unfavourable.

Stringhalt
In this condition one or both of the hindlegs are lifted in an exaggerated movement caused by over flexion of the hock. The cause of the disease is unknown, but it is thought that nervous diseases or degeneration of the sciatic nerve play a major role. Sometimes the condition occurs following damage to tendons as they pass over the nerves. Adhesions develop which interfere with the nerve. The condition can be variable ranging from very mild flexion at the walk to a marked jerking of the foot toward the abdomen. In most cases the condition is exaggerated when the horse is turning. Any breed may be affected. Mild cases do not hinder the horse's usefulness.

Surgery to remove a section of muscle tendon is the best that can be done and gives moderate success.

Thoroughpin
This is a swelling at the rear of the hindleg just above the point of the hock and about 5 centimetres in front of the Achilles tendon. When pressed on one side with a finger, it will bulge out on the other side.

It is often present in young horses that have not done any work. Straight hocks tend to favour distension by allowing relaxation of the sheath around the tendons. Horses that are pulled up suddenly from galloping (especially in soft soil) or those that rear or kick violently are predisposed. In recently injured cases the area is hot, tense and painful. Usually, however, as in bog spavin the area is cold and not tender to touch. As the membrane becomes distended it bulges upwards and is evident on the inner aspect.

In acute cases cooling astringent applications are best, followed by pressure bandages, which should be applied most carefully, a layer of cotton-wool being moulded evenly over the distended area.

Hoof disorders
See FEET DISORDERS.

Icterus
See JAUNDICE.

Immunisation
See the section on Vaccination.

Impaction
See COLIC, CONSTIPATION.

Incontinence
See URINE DISORDERS.

Infections
Infections in the newborn foal, usually bacterial in origin, frequently involve the joints. Such infections (navel-ill, joint-ill) are sudden in onset—the foal goes off suck, is dull and dejected and has a high temperature, 40–41°C. Often pneumonia develops, characterised by increased respiratory rate and even respiratory distress. Some cases show abdominal pain and a degree of diarrhoea. Many of these cases die very quickly unless antibiotic therapy is instituted very early. Once the foal's temperature drops below normal, treatment is rarely of any value. (See also Illnesses of foals, pp. 201–202.)

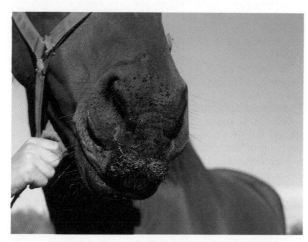

Early sign of a cold — a slight purulent (pussy) discharge from the nose.

Infections in horses can be caused by viruses, bacteria, fungi or protozoa. They can be insect-transmitted or transmitted from one horse to the other directly by droplets (by coughing or sneezing). A generalised infection is usually indicated by a rise in temperature, loss of appetite, lethargy and usually some other symptoms such as diarrhoea, pussy discharge from the nose, or coughing.

A localised infection is indicated by local swelling, heat and pain—for example, infection following a splinter under the skin or a nail in the foot. In all cases of infection it is best to consult a veterinary surgeon unless you know exactly what is causing the problem. (See also ABRASIONS, ABSCESSES, FILLED LEGS, FISTULA, SEPTICAEMIA.)

Infectious diseases
In most of the developed countries of the world, the most important infectious disease of horses are the influenza viruses which cause upper respiratory tract infections and viral abortion. Strangles is also highly contagious. There are many other infectious diseases, some of which are particularly prevalent in Third World countries. For information about these diseases, it is best to contact your veterinary surgeon.

Infertility in the mare
Infertility has a number of causes, one of the most common being failure to cycle. This may be merely that it is the wrong time of the year—most mares cycle naturally from late spring to the end of summer, with a peak at midsummer. Sometimes failure to cycle is a behavioural problem which can be solved by putting the mare with other cycling mares. Sometimes it is a hormonal problem which may be solved by the injection of artificial hormones. Some mares are silent cyclers, giving no indication that they are in season unless they are put out with a stallion to be paddock-served. The stallion can detect cycling.

If the mare is cycling but keeps returning for service, she may have an infection in the womb, the stallion may be infertile, or a hormonal problem may be causing early abortion instead of allowing implantation. Infections are probably the most common cause of infertility in cycling mares, particularly in wind-sucking mares which draw air in through the vulva when they gallop, or in older mares with retracted anuses which allow faecal matter to drop into the vulva. In both instances the mares can be treated with antibiotics and the vulva sutured (Caslick's operation). (See also BREEDING: BARREN MARES.)

Itch
See SKIN DISORDERS.

Jaundice (Icterus)
Yellowish discoloration of the conjunctiva, the mucous membranes of the mouth and in the female the vulva are the common signs of jaundice. The urine nearly always contains bile, giving it a yellow to orange colour. Jaundice is seen in cases of equine piroplasmosis, haemolytic jaundice in foals, infectious equine anaemia, protozoan and viral diseases, chronic copper poisoning, phenothiazine poisoning, pasturing on rape or other poisonous plants, and the bites of some snakes. Other symptoms such as lethargy, fever, loss of appetite and discomfort may occur depending on the disease causing the jaundice.

The treatment of jaundice is dependent on the cause, and always requires veterinary attention.

Joint-ill
See Illnesses of foals, pp. 202–203.

Keratitis
See EYE DISORDERS.

Kidney disease (Nephritis)
Kidney disease is very rare in the horse. Horse owners often mistakenly call 'tying-up' or mild azoturia, kidney disease. The muscles overlying the kidneys are some of the first to be affected with the 'tying-up' syndrome. Many trainers give the horse a diuretic ball when they think it has an inflammation of the kidneys. This tends to clear the condition and relieve the soreness in the back simply because it allows the muscles to be flushed out by the increased water intake caused by the administration of the diuretic ball.

True kidney disease is very rare but may be caused by chemical poisons such as mercury, arsenic, copper, insecticides and carbon tetrachloride. Substances toxic to the kidneys are also produced during azoturia. Treatment depends on isolating the cause. Usually the horse has sufficient functional tissue to keep it alive but secretes large volumes of poorly concentrated urine and remains a 'poor doer' for life.

'Flooding of the box', a condition in which the horse urinates frequently and drinks copious quantities of water, is called water diabetes, and is caused by a deficiency of the hormone which controls fluid retention. Injections are available to supplement this deficiency and should be given under veterinary supervision. It is not a kidney disease.

Lameness
Lameness is any condition that affects one or more limbs

during the progression of the horse. Lameness may be continuous or intermittent. It is governed a great deal by the pace of the animal, being very noticeable at one pace and not at another—for example, in splint lameness the animal may walk soundly but trot lame. Exercise may increase or decrease the symptoms. In most instances of muscle injury the lameness becomes less during exercise but returns after the animal has cooled off. In an animal lame from occult spavin the lameness is almost always continuous. Lameness arising from acute arthritis is constant. A horse lame from bone disease or a strained tendon may merely appear to be stepping carefully.

When a horse becomes lame three things have to be determined: Which leg is it, or is more than one involved? Where is the seat of lameness? What is the cause of the lameness?

Lameness in the horse is such a vast subject and requires such expert knowledge in diagnosis and treatment that it is far outside the scope of this book. In fact, there are whole books written on lameness in the horse. By all means examine the horse yourself and if you can locate a swelling in the tendon, an abscess in the foot, a nail in the sole, thrush or other infection, or swelling of the fetlock joint, or seedy toe, well and good. But beyond those common ailments it is best to seek the advice of a good equine veterinarian. (See also FEET DISORDERS and Illnesses of foals, p. 202.)

Laminitis
See FEET DISORDERS.

Lice
See SKIN DISORDERS.

Ligaments, sprained
See TENDONS.

Lockjaw
See TETANUS.

Lung conditions
The most common conditions affecting the lungs are pneumonia and bronchopneumonia, which are inflammatory conditions caused by a virus or bacteria, by fluid introduced during drenching, or by heavy infestation with large roundworms ('rattles' in foals, see Worming, p. 191). The signs are heavy breathing and sometimes a cough and nasal discharge. Pneumonia is always serious and should be treated quickly with antibiotics.

Pleurisy is another inflammatory condition involving the pleural membrane which covers the lungs and lines the chest cavity. It is very painful, again very serious, and should be treated with antibiotics. It generally occurs with, or after, pneumonia. In both of these diseases the earliest symptoms are rapid and shallow respirations, fever, loss of appetite and dullness. The animal is not inclined to move.

The horse should be kept warm, rugged and put in under shelter in a loose box and allowed plenty of fresh air. Inhalation of Friars Balsam or Vicks VapoRub are useful. A dab of such an ointment can be placed just inside the nostrils of the horse. An old remedy for relief of respiratory distress is to rub mustard paste on to the chest: add one-third of a cup of mustard to 4 cups of lard, mix, and rub the paste over the chest walls for two minutes.

Maggots
Maggots are the larval stages of flies. They sometimes invade wounds, causing fly-strike. An infested wound should be cleaned up using a hose and any maggots physically removed. If there are sinuses hiding the maggots, an insecticidal powder can be applied to the wound. Although the idea turns most people's stomachs, maggots rarely cause much damage to a wound—rather they tend to clean up any debris (that is, dead or decaying tissue). The main risk is that they may introduce bacterial infection. Prevent their appearance by the use of fly repellants.

Malnutrition
A healthy horse is one kept in a slim condition with the ribs well covered—overweight horses are always in danger of suffering laminitis (founder). Horses in poor condition are usually suffering from simple malnutrition. Horses are large and expensive to keep and many people cut corners on feeding. (Other factors contributing to poor condition may be worms, bad teeth, cold weather, or an underlying disease problem.)

Mane eczema
See SKIN DISORDERS: LICE, QUEENSLAND ITCH.

Mange
See SKIN DISORDERS.

Manure eating
This can be due to a vitamin/mineral deficiency in which case it is called 'pica' (see CALCIUM DEFICIENCY). Place a lump of rock salt in the feed tin and if necessary make clay available. Clay is a good source of calcium and is palatable to horses.

It can also be a 'vice' or due to a dietary imbalance. Make sure the diet is balanced and adequate in quantity. (See the section on Feeding, pp. 183–85.)

Melanoma (Skin cancer)
See SKIN DISORDERS.

Mites
See HARVEST MITE, SKIN DISORDERS: MANGE, and SKIN DISORDERS: SCRUB ITCH.

Mouth disorders
See also TEETH PROBLEMS.

Dry mouth
Dry mouth is a condition where the mucous membranes become very dry due to lack of saliva production. This is seen in cases of atropine poisoning (atropine is the active ingredient in Belladonna—an old remedy included in cough pastes). In other cases there is no apparent cause. In the case of steeplechasers or polo ponies which suffer dry mouth because of excitement, the administration of 225 grams of glucose in warm water in the last meal before racing or playing polo is advisable. An abnormal desire for water is seen in fever, water diabetes, and certain forms of gastritis, enteritis and kidney disease. Fever may cause horses to stand over water, just playing with it with their lips without actually drinking.

A gag locks the mouth open for examination of the mouth or teeth treatment.

Glossitis (Inflammation of the tongue)
Glossitis is fairly common in the horse. The causes include direct injuries, reaction to irritant substances (biting at blis-

ters applied to the legs, licking at chemicals), foreign bodies (grass seeds, splinters) in the tongue, irregularities of the teeth causing the horse to bite its tongue, and careless handling of the tongue during the process of rasping teeth or paste worming. Bits may also cause serious wounds.

In mild cases of glossitis apply a simple antiseptic mouth-wash, such as a 3 per cent solution of boric acid, and feed a diet of boiled porridge gruel and milk. Use a large disposable syringe without a needle to apply the mouth-wash. When the tongue is swollen, repeated cold-water irrigation will help. Some horses will tolerate irrigation with a slow-running hose.

Lampas

This is a swelling of the soft palate just behind the incisor teeth. It is usually due to an inflammation of the gums in the young horse, when shedding the temporary or milk teeth. In the majority of cases the swelling will subside without medical treatment. It is a fallacy that lampas will affect the health of the horse.

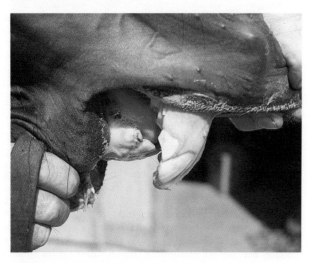

In a parrot mouth the upper incisor teeth overlap the lower incisors.

Parrot mouth and undershot jaw

These are congenital deformities. In parrot mouth the upper incisor teeth overlap the lower, and in undershot jaw the lower incisors overlap the top incisors. Such animals have difficulty in feeding. Bad cases may be unable to graze and hand feeding will be necessary.

Quidding

A horse is said to be quidding when its food is rolled and twisted about in the mouth and finally ejected into the manger as a bolus. In most cases it is due to dental irregularities and can be readily fixed by a competent person 'floating' (rasping) the teeth.

Shear mouth

Shear mouth is a condition in which the upper and lower molars overlap like the blades of shears. It is usually seen in old horses. Treatment is not satisfactory. It is usually due to irregularities in wear and age changes involving the shape of the lower jaw.

Nasal discharges

A slight watery nasal discharge can be quite normal, merely a reaction to dust, but excessive watery discharge can indicate early viral infection. This is generally accompanied by a dull eye, loss of appetite, a slight fever and a cough. Pussy discharges from the nose indicate advanced viral infections, head colds caused by influenza viruses, and bacterial infections such as glanders and strangles. Pussy discharges can also indicate pneumonia or bronchial pneumonia. A foul-smelling discharge from the nose indicates

decaying roots of teeth, or possibly a tumour in the nasal passages. If the discharge is watery, or slightly pussy, but the horse is bright, is eating and does not seem to be generally affected by the condition, there is no need for alarm.

Keep the horse warm and give plenty of fresh green feed. Wipe the nostrils out regularly, and apply some Friars Balsam or Vicks VapoRub inside the nostrils. Injections of 500 milligrams of ascorbic acid (Vitamin C) daily are also helpful. If the horse is coughing, it may be relieved by applying to the back of the tongue one of the available cough pastes.

However, if the nasal discharge becomes copious, the horse has a temperature higher than 39.4°C, or is off its feed, then the vet should be called.

Navicular disease

See FEET DISORDERS.

Neurectomy

Cutting of a nerve, as a treatment for navicular disease.

Nose bleeding

See BLEEDING.

Oestrus

See the section on Breeding, p. 197.

Old age

The first five years of a horse's life may be considered equivalent to the first twenty years of our life. At seventeen years of age, which probably represents fifteen years' work, most horses are past their physical best. Deterioration of their teeth probably prevents most horses from reaching a ripe old age. In general, ponies are much longer lived than horses. Instances are on record of animals attaining the age fifty, and one is attested to have lived to sixty-three, but the average for ponies is probably thirty-five and for horses thirty. As horses get very old it becomes more and more difficult to keep weight on them and emaciation is the usual cause of death.

The following points will help keep the aged horse in good health.

Worm every three months.

Have horse's teeth checked every six months.

Rug the horse in cold weather.

Give regular and gentle exercise.

Hand-feed as soon as there is any sign of weight loss.

Trim the feet every six weeks.

Groom and pick out feet daily.

Open knees

Open knees is the term used to describe a horizontal depression at the top of the knee in immature horses. Horses should not be given hard work until this disappears. If worked, other conditions are more likely to occur such as shin soreness, carpitis, chipped bones in the knee, and tendon problems. (See also SHIN SORENESS.)

Opening-up behind

In this condition the anal sphincter relaxes, allowing air to pass into the rectum. It usually occurs after a long training campaign and is due to fatigue. The horse should be rested. Good results are also achieved with anabolic steroid injections administered by the vet.

Over-reaching

See FEET DISORDERS.

Parasites

See the section on Worming, pp. 188–94.

Parrot mouth

See MOUTH DISORDERS.

Parturition

See Breeding.

Patella locking (Upward fixation of patella)

Locked patella is a condition usually seen in horses that are very straight in the hindlegs. It occurs more frequently in horses just out of the paddock in debility and poor condition in the initial stages of their training. The leg locks in a stiff, outstretched position. To unlock the leg, push the horse backwards or alternatively wrap a soft rope around the pastern and pull the leg forward. In less extreme cases the patella slips in and out of position as the horse moves, and a clicking noise may be heard. The horse characteristically drops its toe. Call your vet and discuss the problem, as it is likely to recur. Surgery is available.

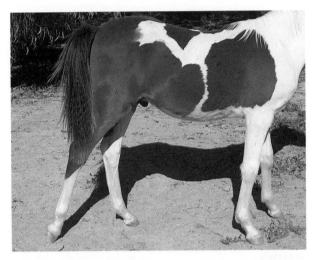

Patella (stifle joint) locking is usually seen in horses that have very straight hindlegs. Note the extended leg locked in an outstretched position.

Pedal bone fracture
See FEET DISORDERS.

Pedal osteitis
See FEET DISORDERS.

Periodic ophthalmia
See EYE DISORDERS.

Pica
See MANURE EATING.

Pimples
See SKIN DISORDERS.

Pin-firing
See the section on PIN-FIRING, pp. 210–11.

Pinworm
See the section on Worming.

Pleurisy
See LUNG CONDITIONS.

Pneumonia
See LUNG CONDITIONS.

Poisoning
Demulcents are frequently used in the treatment of poisoning. These are drugs of a viscous character which protect mucous membranes from irritation—for example, gum acacia, purified honey, glycerine and starch.

Arsenic poisoning
Chronic arsenic poisoning affects the complete body hair coat. The usual symptoms are a long-haired coat, heavy scurf development and emaciation, even though the appetite is normal. The usual cause is over-use of arsenical tonics. These tonics are used to stimulate the appetite of horses in full work. The usual method of diagnosis is ill-thrift after a time in training when arsenical tonics are known to be used. Many horses make a slow recovery if the cumulative dose is not too high. Many others die unless restored to good condition by supplementary feeding on arsenical tonic with gradual weaning off the tonic as the condition improves. Treatment with injectable organic arsenic compound gives a dramatic response. During the administration of the tonic, the horse's body becomes dependent (addicted) and a sudden withdrawal causes collapse of the horse's metabolic system.

Copper poisoning
Chronic copper poisoning can occur where low molybdenum levels enhance copper storage in pastures. Treatment is to use demulcents and iron filings which attract and fix the copper, or potassium ferrocyanide which produces a comparatively insoluble and harmless salt.

Acute cases have severe diarrhoea and colic with characteristic blue–green mucous membranes. Chronic cases have thirst, no appetite, red-coloured urine and jaundice. If detected and treated early, the prognosis is good.

Lead poisoning
Acute lead poisoning is very rare in the horse. It can result from pasturing near rifle ranges and picking up bullet spray, grazing on pastures near smelting furnaces, drinking water from lead piping recently installed and licking lead batteries and paint. Symptoms include rigors, colic, grinding of the teeth and constipation, followed by diarrhoea.

Under no circumstances should oil be given in any form as this renders the lead more soluble. Large doses of epsom salts—1 kilogram of epsom salts in 9 litres of water—should be given, thus bringing about the formation of insoluble lead sulphate. Prognosis depends on the amount ingested but is usually favourable if treated early.

Other types of poisoning include the ingestion of such things as rodenticides, insecticides, fumigants and moulds. (See also POISONOUS PLANTS.) In most cases there are no specific antidotes and treatment consists of controlling symptoms. Where the poison is known, contact your vet or the poisons centre at a hospital.

Poisonous plants
As a general rule animals will not eat poisonous plants if there is plenty of other food available. Inadvertent poisoning can happen—for example, poisoning from ragwort included in hay.

Acorn poisoning occurs in early spring when grass is scarce and the horse eats the new green leaves of the oak tree. Cases resemble impaction colic. Treatment consists of large doses of liquid paraffin.

Bracken poisoning can be caused by the green plants, and by bracken cut in the green state, then dried and stacked. The poison is an enzyme which destroys vitamin B1 and is cumulative. There is progressive loss of condition, a general unthrifty appearance and a slow pulse. The appetite remains fairly good but the horse loses its rotund belly and becomes tucked-up and hollow in the flanks. Treat with repeated injections of vitamin B1.

Autumn crocus or *meadow saffron* will poison horses if they eat the leaves in the spring. The symptoms are abdominal pain, violent purgation and straining. The only treatment is using demulcents to soothe the bowels.

Privet poisoning causes a loss of power in the hindquarters, the mucous membranes become congested, and the pupils are dilated. Death occurs in thirty-six to forty-eight hours. Symptoms of colic and unsteadiness in the gait are common. Treatment is to relieve the horse of the colic and treat the horse symptomatically. Horses usually die very quickly if they have taken a reasonable dose of privet.

Ragwort poisoning usually follows the ingestion of hay harvested with ragwort. The common symptoms are colic with subsequent death at variable periods up to a few days. In the chronic case there is a loss of condition, loss of appetite, dullness, the gait is staggering and there is constipation, or sometimes diarrhoea. Because the condition affects the liver, mucous membranes are pale and may be jaundiced. There is no satisfactory treatment.

Vetch can also induce liver damage in the horse and the horse will be sensitive to sunlight.

Yew is by far the commonest form of plant poisoning encountered in Great Britain. All parts of the tree are poisonous. The alkaloid taxine is the active principle and occurs in the leaves of all species but in only a small proportion in the berries. Horses will eat yew at any time, and cases of yew poisoning usually occur when straying from pastures or eating overhanging branches. The alkaloid is rapidly absorbed and exercises its chief effect on the heart. Symptoms—rarely observed, because the animal is usually already dead when found—are trembling, difficulty in breathing, collapse, and then death within five minutes. Treatment must of course be immediate. Purgatives and demulcents are indicated and stimulants such as large quantities of strong coffee should be given frequently. It is best if purgatives are given by injection to ensure a quick action. The heart's action should be supported by injections of adrenalin.

Walkabout disease (Kimberley horse disease) is common in north-western Australia and the Northern Territory. It is due to ingestion of certain native plants restricted to areas with low river banks and flats which are subject to periodic flooding. Cases are seen mainly in the wet season and involve a loss of weight, depression alternating with periods of excitement, and compulsive walking. There is no treatment and the prognosis is poor.

Birdsville horse disease is seen in south-western Queensland and central Australia. It is usually seen in summer in average seasons about six weeks after rain. It is due to the ingestion of *Indigophera*; the minimum toxic amount is 4 kilograms per day for at least two weeks. The symptoms are rapid and extreme loss of weight, loss of appetite, depression, sleepiness and toe dragging. There is no treatment, but an animal may recover completely if it is only mildly affected.

Coastal ataxia is seen along a 450-kilometre wide strip of the central Queensland coast in horses on overgrazed paddocks in which *Gomphrena* has become the dominant plant. This is readily eaten by horses, but large quantities have to be eaten over a month or more for symptoms to develop. Symptoms include dullness, loss of appetite, swaying of the hindquarters and dragging of the toes, and feet placed wide apart with swaying of the body from side to side. There are no known treatments; prognosis is poor.

Selenosis (also known as change-of-hoof disease, alkali disease, blind staggers). Selenium toxicity is associated with eating plants called *Morinda neptunia* and *Astragalus*, which are found in various parts of the world. If the animals are diagnosed early, treatment with sodium arsenite or arsenilic acid is useful. Selenosis usually affects the mane, tail and hooves. The horse has a stilted gait with unnatural stance. The mane and tail hairs fall out and there is a transverse separation of the wall of the hoof at the coronary band. Acute cases may slough the hooves.

The list of poisons and poison plants is never ending. Contact your vet or local Department of Agriculture for more comprehensive lists.

Poll evil

Poll evil and fistulous withers are similar conditions which affect separate regions. Both are caused by a physical injury to a bony prominence—either the poll at the top of the head or the withers. Ultimately an infection is set up which leads to a deep-seated death of tissues and the development of a constant pussy sinus. Poultices or antiphlogistine should be applied to the area. Once sinus formation is present, culture the organism and determine which antibiotic to use. Usually these conditions require surgical eradication of the dead tissue before the sinus will clear up. (See also FISTULA.)

Pot-belly
A sign indicating worm infestation in the horse. (See the section on Worming.)

Pregnancy problems
See ABORTION, and the section on Breeding, 194–99.

Proud flesh
Granulation tissue (see WOUNDS). Occurring on the eyelids, it is one of the signs of habronema (stomach worm) infestation. (See the section on Worming, p. 192.)

Quarter crack
See FEET DISORDERS: SANDCRACK.

Queensland itch
See SKIN DISORDERS.

Quidding
See MOUTH DISORDERS.

Quittor
See FEET DISORDERS.

Rabies
A viral disease. See Common ailments of dogs.

Radial paralysis
See DROPPED ELBOW.

Rain scald
See SKIN DISORDERS.

Rash
See SKIN DISORDERS.

Rattles
'Rattles' is the name given to a young foal with pneumonia—in these cases, the chest develops a 'rattle'. Rattles is common on farms where there is a roundworm problem. (See the sections on Worming, and Illnesses of foals, and see LUNG DISORDERS.)

Redworm
See the section on Worming, p. 190.

Respiratory tract diseases
See LUNG CONDITIONS, NASAL DISCHARGE.

Rickets
Signs of rickets can occur in horses up to three years of age but foals between six months and twelve months are most commonly affected. In older horses demineralisation of the bone can occur as a result of calcium or phosphorus deficiencies.

Rickets in horses is primarily a disease of the epiphysis rather than the joint itself. (The epiphysis is either side of the joint and is the growth centre for the long bone.) Arthritis of the knee, the pastern and the fetlock and hock joints may also occur. The arthritis of these joints usually follows stresses resulting from conformational changes due to rickets.

Rickets is a metabolic bone disease resulting from a deficiency of any one or a combination of calcium, phosphorus, vitamin D, vitamin C and/or vitamin A. Many rations for horses that are high in protein and composed primarily of hay may contain practically no vitamin A. Vitamin A deficiency also causes a rough and lustreless coat. It is not uncommon for both young and adult horses to have pica appetite (chewing on fences, gates and other objects) when there is a deficiency of one or more of the above elements. The clinical signs of rickets in the horse are deviation of the limbs, resulting in the knuckling forward of the fetlocks of the front and/or hindlimbs due to contraction of the flexor tendons. Phytic acid, found in oats and wheat, may interfere with the metabolism of calcium and aid in causing rickets when the horse is fed greater quantities of grain than necessary for normal growth. These conditions are particularly common in yearlings being pushed along to get them in top condition for sale. These animals are usually on high-protein, high-grain diets likely to contain an excess of phosphorus.

Ringbone
See FEET DISORDERS.

Ringworm
See SKIN DISORDERS.

Roaring
This is a condition usually seen in thoroughbreds or hunting horses and is only noticed at a very fast gait. The horse makes a roaring noise because a paralysed vocal cord acts as a reed in the passage of wind through the larynx. This may act as an obstruction to the free passage of air and make the horse breathless at speed. The condition can be corrected by surgery, but unless the animal is very valuable, surgery is not recommended. (See also BROKEN WIND.)

Rough coat
See the section on Worming, p. 192.

Roundworms
See the section on Worming, p. 191.

Runny eyes
See EYE DISORDERS. Runny eyes may indicate infestation by habronema (see the section on Worming, p. 192).

Saddle sores
See GALLS.

Salivation
Excessive production of saliva may arise from inflammation of the mouth, abnormal conditions of the teeth and the presence of foreign bodies such as a stick caught between the teeth. Paralysis of the pharynx, the oesophagus or the lips may prevent saliva being swallowed so that the horse drools. It is often seen in greedy horses anticipating feed.

Sandcrack
See FEET DISORDERS.

Sarcoid
See SKIN DISORDERS.

Selenosis
Selenium toxicity. See POISONOUS PLANTS.

Septicaemia
See BLOOD POISONING.

Sesamoid bone disorders
The sesamoids are two small bones at the rear of the fetlock joint. They can be fractured in animals that perform vigorous sports, such as racehorses or endurance horses. A more common condition is sesamoiditis which is an inflammatory process around the top of the sesamoid due to tearing of the suspensory ligament. In these cases the animal should be rested and poultices applied to the joint. In the case of fractures the horse will need a twelve months' spell; seek the advice of a veterinary surgeon.

Shin soreness
This is a condition seen in young horses, usually yearlings or two-year-olds, which are suddenly asked to perform galloping exercises. Work over excessively hard ground exacerbates the problem. The horse steps short in front, and if rubbed down the front of the cannon bone it reacts painfully. In the latter stages of shin soreness there may be a swelling about midway down the cannon bone. If the work is stopped, the condition will recede. Applications of poultices to the area will hasten a return to normal, but a spell of several months is essential. It is due to immaturity of the bones. (See also OPEN KNEES.)

Shivering
This is generally regarded as a nervous disease. When the horse lifts a hindleg, or moves backwards, the limb is sud-denly raised, semi-flexed and moved out away from the body, shaking and shivering in suspension. It occurs sometimes after diseases such as influenza, after strangles or a severe fall. It is seen frequently in horses ridden in violent sports such as polo and polocrosse, and sometimes in race-horses. Shivering is also seen in the initial stages of a fever or when the horse is cold, but this is natural, not a disease. There is no treatment for a true shiverer and the horse is regarded as unsound.

Sidebone
Forms in the external cartilages in the heel region. Flexibility of the heels is lost. The cartilages are enlarged and tender, with hardening which causes lameness.

Sinus
See DISCHARGE, FISTULA.

Skin disorders
Bacterial acne (Saddle boils, dermatitis, heat rash)
Commonly seen under the saddle-cloth, over the back, loin and rib cage or wherever harness has contact with the horse's skin. It is frequently caused by dirty harness, and it affects sweaty and ungroomed horses kept in unhygienic conditions. They are small (1–2 mm) areas of raised skin which are extremely painful and hot. The sores usually have a sticky yellow discharge and form scabs. This condition should not be confused with Queensland itch, fly bite and food allergies. Harness from affected horses should be sterilised and a fresh saddle-cloth used for each ride. The condition is not infectious. The condition can be cured by shampooing with an iodine shampoo for three consecutive days; recovery takes about seven days.

Bursattee (Leeches, kunkers, Florida horse leech, phycomycosis, swamp cancer and equine granuloma)
This condition usually appears on the legs and lower abdomen, the head, the neck and the ribs. Is is caused by a fungal-like organism. It appears as a chronic, granulated wound covered with a mucoid discharge, draining from one or several sinuses. Severe itchiness is present, and self-mutilation is common. It should be differentiated from sarcoid and wounds caused by parasitic larvae. Bursattee is best treated by surgical excision of the lesions and twice weekly intravenous sodium iodide injections for four weeks.

Cattle tick bites
Cattle tick bites are usually found on the legs and lower portions of the body but can affect the horse all over. They leave small, swollen areas with raised hair. Infestation in large numbers will cause loss of condition. The horse may bite affected parts, causing self-mutilation. Remove ticks with your fingers or with tweezers. Spray the horse with 0.025 per cent Dursban or 0.25 per cent Malathion (fortnightly) to prevent infestation.

Dandruff
Dandruff is a condition in which the skin becomes scaly, and the coat dry and dirty. In some instances the skin becomes reddened and the hair falls out. Dandruff may result from lack of exercise and grooming.

Sweating should be induced by lungeing or riding, and the animal should be thoroughly washed with a medicated soap or shampoo. It is essential to leave a medicated shampoo in contact with the skin for at least fifteen to thirty minutes. Then ensure that all of the soap is rinsed off and the animal dried thoroughly. The animal's diet (see the section on Feeding) should include a generous quantity of carrots and 60 millilitres of linseed oil daily. The animal should also be examined for worm infestation (see the section on Worming pp. 188–94). Sometimes a course of tonics is useful.

Equine coital exanthema

In equine coital exanthema (in the male horse) the penis and reflection of the prepuce or (in the female horse) the external skin and internal mucous membranes of the vulva are affected with multiple discrete sores. The lesions first appear as slight wounds or watery blisters which quickly change to a yellowish dead type of ulcer. The cause is a virus. It is usually self-limiting, running its course in fourteen to twenty-eight days. Sexual rest is essential, as the disease is highly contagious. There are no after-effects of the disease and it is not notifiable.

Irritant dermatitis

Irritant dermatitis can appear on the surface of any part of the horse's body. Usually there is severe irritation with self-mutilation caused by biting or by rubbing the body surfaces on fences. There are weeping areas. Generally the hair is roughened and the skin is hypersensitive to scratching. The cause can be contact with irritant chemicals such as Stockholm tar, kerosene or insecticides, mange and Queensland itch cures, or bacterial infection.

Shampoo the entire horse and wash all soap from the body. Apply a 2.5 per cent lime sulphur wash to all affected areas. Antibiotic corticosteroid ointments can be applied to local areas of dermatitis.

Lice infestation

Lice frequent long-haired areas—manes and tails. Heavy infestation may occur all over the body. It may occur as district outbreaks transmitted by mutual grooming, birds or unhygienic harness. Usually there is intense itching and the horse rubs the affected site vigorously. This is associated with loss of hair on the body and scrubbing of the hairs on the mane and tail. Horses will sometimes bite the infested areas. Self-trauma can make the bites look like Queensland itch, mange or stable-fly bite. Clip the mane if possible and wash the horse with 0.5 per cent dieldrin solution or 0.1 per cent DDT solution. Repeat in several days' time.

Chorioptic mange with the typical hair loss and scurfing of the skin.

Mange

Mange in a horse is usually confined to the legs below the knee and hock, but in severe cases it may extend to the belly and the inside of the front legs and groin. It is caused by a small mite. Affected areas become inflamed, the skin flakes and becomes cracked with inflammatory exudate. Horses stamp their feet, bite their legs, and rub their legs with their head.

The disease will transmit between horses on their harness or grooming implements.

All of the affected areas should be scrubbed with 0.1 per cent BHC once weekly for three weeks.

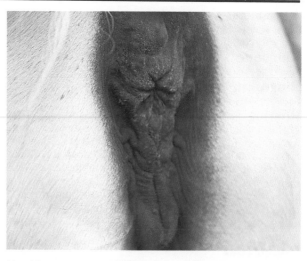

Hard lumps which develop around the anus and base of the tail indicate melanoma.

Melanoma

Melanoma (skin cancer) is usually found around the anus and (in the female) around the vulval lips, under the line of the tail, and on the underside of the tail. Isolated tumours under the skin may occur anywhere on the body. Melanoma is much more frequent in grey horses.

Surgical excision should only be performed where the tumours are isolated, and occur on general body surfaces. When the tumour occurs around the peri-anal area, surgery is not advisable because of the danger of secondaries and the inaccessibility of the tumour. The tumours are painless unless they grow inwards and create mechanical problems with the rectum. The prognosis long-term is poor.

Mosquito bites

Some horses are very sensitive to mosquito bites, which are found all over the body as small swellings with raised hair. As in humans the bites are itchy. Horses should be rugged, put in mosquito-proof stalls or sprayed with insect repellants. The treatment is similar to that for Queensland itch as described below.

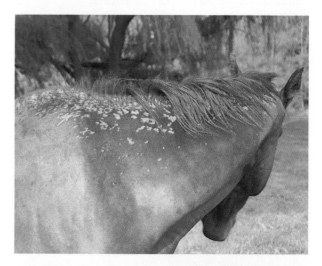

In most cases of Queensland itch the irritation usually begins on the topline of the horse between the mane and the tail.

Queensland itch

Queensland itch, an allergic dermatitis caused by the horse's sensitivity to the bites of flies, usually affects the topline of the horse, especially the ears, the mane, the withers and the tail. The most common symptom is excessive itching and rubbing of the withers and tail, which causes loss of hair and self-inflicted sores. The skin becomes thickened and wrinkled. In horses in the southern hemisphere this condition is seen most commonly between December and May. Hair regrowth on damaged areas begins in late winter.

Treatment of Queensland itch is largely symptomatic. There is no cure but time. Preventive measures include rugging the horse between 4 p.m. and 7 a.m. nightly, and keeping the horse in fly-proof stables during the summer period. Local treatment with antihistamine cream is helpful. Individual horses can also be rubbed or sprayed with insecticidal agents. A good, cheap, but oily treatment is to paint affected areas with used 'sump oil' from motor engines. The condition is very hard to control until the fly season is past.

The face is a common site of infection from rain scald.

Rain scald (Aphis, sunburn, greasy heel, swamp fever)
The usual sites are the loins, saddle, face, muzzle and lower portions of the body. Characteristic signs are the matting together of long hair of the coat. Closer examination shows lower layers of the hair firmly matted in plaques with pus at the bottom. These hair clumps can be plucked out, leaving a bleeding surface. The affected area is sore to touch. With greasy heel, horses show acute lameness because of cracking of the skin at the rear of the pastern and fetlock region. Swelling of the fetlock and lower cannon region is also common.

The condition is the result of infection with a bacterium (*Dermatophilus*) occurring in prolonged periods of wet and overcast weather conditions. Rapid spread is caused by flies, mosquitoes and birds. It usually only occurs in horses left in paddocks without rugs. Harness can be contaminated if used on affected horses.

The most successful treatment is 0.25 per cent chloramphenicol in water applied with a brush for two consecutive days. Sometimes antibiotic therapy is necessary. Ordinary washing-up detergents are also effective—but it is essential to remove all plaques so that the detergent can reach the skin. Local areas, such as greasy heel, can be treated with an ointment containing cortisone and antibiotic. (See also GREASY HEEL.)

Ringworm
Ringworm affects mainly the girth area, shoulders and loins. Sometimes generalised infections can be caused by the use of contaminated grooming gear. The symptoms usually commence with raised hair and roughened skin. Examination may irritate the horse. The hairs usually have scab encrusted around the base and may be easily plucked

out to leave a grey, moist, glistening area. The lesions lose their hair three to ten days after the infection starts; hair regrowth commences about thirty days after infection. The condition in the early stages should be distinguished from allergies; and in the latter stages from Queensland itch.

All scabs and scales should be removed from the infected sites and burned. As this condition may affect humans, wear plastic gloves when treating the horse. All the sores should be scrubbed daily with 10 per cent thiabenzole, or 2.5 per cent lime sulphur or 0.5 per cent Ectimar. Where only a small number of sores need to be treated, 10 per cent iodine can be used. All contaminated gear should be scrubbed with 0.3 per cent halomid; each horse should have its own grooming gear. Ringworm is a highly infectious fungus. Outbreaks often occur after long periods of damp weather.

Sarcoids (Skin tumours)
Sarcoids appear on the chest, head, neck and lower limbs and in multiple growths anywhere on the horse's body. They are skin tumours usually raised above the surface of the skin. They appear as nodules in and under the skin and are usually hairless and smooth. They may be pink or pigmented in colour. In advanced cases ulceration occurs. There are two forms of sarcoid, one with a pedicle (stem) and the other flattened against the skin. They are usually resistant to local treatment, but some success may be achieved with 50 per cent podophylline in alcohol applied daily for up to thirty days. Care must be taken to restrict the application to the affected area; the normal skin around the lesion should be protected with soft paraffin. Excellent results are now being achieved with radiation therapy. If left untreated, sarcoids progress in size until they cause physical problems, especially for harness.

Scars
The majority of permanent scars are found on the limbs. The head and chest are often common sites. Scars may be the result of burns or sunburn, of trauma from wire or a foreign body, or of the application of blisters. The original wound has usually healed and is quite satisfactory from a health point of view but is cosmetically undesirable. Scar tissue can be surgically removed only if the remaining skin can be closed or skin grafts applied. Otherwise, it is usually preferable to leave it untouched. Lanolin cream keeps the skin soft and prevents cracking. To prevent scar formation on a fresh wound, keep the area moist with zinc or lanolin cream while healing occurs. Where possible, bandage.

Scrub itch (Trombidiosis)
Scrub itch usually occurs on the legs and on the lower abdomen, but can be generalised. It is caused by the microscopic red grass mites which gather in clusters on the horse in spring and summer. It is more likely to occur if there are heavily grassed areas nearby. The mouth parts of the mites are buried in the horse's skin causing severe irritation. The horse bites itself and stamps its feet vigorously. Malathion spray or 1 per cent DDT should be used on stables and bedding to control the mites. Wash or spray the legs with a 5 per cent lime sulphur or Malathion solution.

Sebaceous cysts
These are unsightly but harmless lumps which appear on the midline of the horse anywhere from the withers to the tail. They do not irritate the horse, unless under harness, but are unattractive. They vary in size from a few millimetres to several centimetres in diameter. The contents are usually a grey, cheesy material, which is readily expressed when the cyst is squeezed. They are aused by a blockage within an oil gland. The lesions can be surgically excised under local anaesthetic, curetted and sutured.

Squamous cell carcinoma (Cancer)
In this condition the third eyelid is most often affected (a condition commonly referred to as 'cancer eye'). The nose

and lips are also common sites, as are the prepuce and penis of the male horse and the vulva of the mare. The lesion is usually a single, discrete, irregular-sized hairless mass protruding above the normal body skin level. It is composed of granulating tissue with ulcerative areas. The best therapy is surgical excision and cobalt radiation treatment. If the lesion is small the outcome is good. (See also EYE DISORDERS.)

Stable-fly bites

Stable-fly bites are raised swellings, 1 centimetre in diameter, with a scab in the centre. They are found all over the body but mainly on the lower body and legs. The bites cause intense itching; the horse will stamp, cow kick (with the hindlegs), 'shiver' and switch the tail violently.

Reduce fly infestation by regularly picking up manure around the stables and spraying 5 per cent DDT on stable walls. Use 2 per cent DDT on the horse. The bites cause intense irritation and can be relieved with calamine lotion, or antihistamine/analgesic creams.

Summer sores (Cutaneous habronemiasis, swamp cancer)

Summer sores are rapidly granulating masses which bleed very easily when knocked or brushed. They are commonly found on the legs and lower thorax and abdomen, the eye, the penis (in the male), the vulva (in the female). They are caused by infection of wounds with larval forms of habronema (a worm) by infected flies.

On nictitating membranes and the penis it is best to remove the growths surgically. Growths on the body and legs generally respond to treatment with 80 per cent Neguvon fluid as a 50 per cent mixture with DMSO.

(See also SARCOIDS (skin tumours), p. 235.)

Sunburn (Solar dermatitis)

This usually occurs on white or unpigmented skin areas of the body, particularly along the backline and on the muzzle. It looks like an acute dermatitis. The affected skin becomes swollen, crusty, and sensitive to the touch. Sometimes serum may leak from the area.

Keep the horse out of the sun, preferably in a darkened stable, and treat the affected area with an antibiotic steroid cream. Human 'block out' agents can be used, or zinc cream. Preferably keep the horse out of the sun.

Urticaria (Blue-nose, nettle rash, hives, feed allergy)

Urticaria usually affects the nose, eyelids, chest, prepuce, vulva, the abdomen and the thoracic wall. Wheals or blotches, appear suddenly on the skin. They are usually not sensitive to touch and disappear rapidly without treatment.

The usual cause is an allergy to insect stings, to spoiled feed, to flowers of spring grasses, or to foreign proteins such as are found in injections of serum or vaccine. The horse can be treated with intravenous antihistamines. Local areas can be dabbed with ammonia solution to relieve the swelling. Extreme allergic reactions can cause swelling within the windpipe, requiring emergency treatment of antihistamines to prevent asphyxiation.

Viral papular dermatitis

This virus causes swellings up to 5 millimetres in diameter which can occur anywhere on the body. (The swellings do not develop into pustules or fluid-filled bubbles.) A scab forms about seven days later and drops off, leaving a bare, hairless area. There is no itchiness. The disease invariably runs for three weeks and treatment is a waste of time.

Warts

Warts are frequently seen in foals and young horses under the age of three years. They are generally located on the nose, the upper and lower lips and on the side of the face. Severe infections may extend back on to the jowl and up to the eyes. Isolated warts are sometimes found on the lower front legs. Usually they disappear spontaneously after three to six months. A mixture of salicylic acid 25 per cent plus podophylline 20 per cent cream, or crude castor oil can be used on large clusters to hasten their disappearance. Warts are caused by a harmless virus.

Sleeping sickness (Encephalomyelitis)

Sleeping sickness is caused by a virus which attacks the brain. The horse is usually depressed and feverish. It may become very excited, then lapse into a coma, followed by death. It occurs in the Americas. There is no treatment.

Sleepy foal disease

See Illnesses of foals, p. 201.

Snake bite

A horse bitten by a venomous snake usually develops serious symptoms, largely because the horse has a relatively thin skin and the snake has good purchasing power, leading to the injection of large quantities of venom. Horses are usually bitten on the nose or the head area, less frequently on the legs or chest.

Nose and head bites are very serious because of the tremendous swelling that rapidly follows a bite. Later a blood-stained, frothy discharge may hang from each nostril. The eyes are swollen shut and the ears are swollen and lying flat. Breathing is difficult. Soon there is extreme depression and helplessness. The mortality rate is about 30 per cent, depending on the toxicity of the venom, the size of the snake, and the effectiveness of its bite.

The treatment of snake bite involves anti-venene (very expensive) fluid therapy and antibiotic therapy. If the horse is bitten on the leg a firm bandage can be applied and a polyvalent antivenene can be used.

Spavin

See HOCK DISORDERS.

Speedy cut

Speedy cut is a self-inflicted injury to the inner surface of the lower part of the knee joint. It is caused by a blow from the inner point of the shoe on the other front hoof. It can occur when the horse is tired, over-raced, or has an unbalanced action. It can also occur under heavy going with the wrong leg leading. Sometimes a change in gait on broken ground is liable to cause this injury. Faulty conformation may be a permanent cause.

A shoe with longitudinal corks is sometimes used with success. These corks are 7 centimetres long, 3 millimetres wide and 6 millimetres deep and are set inside the nail holes on the branches, beginning at the first nail hole.

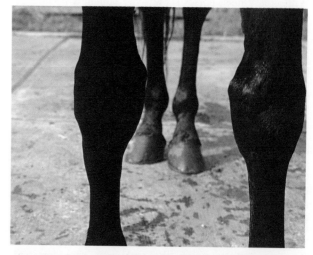

Splints are small hard bony swellings which form on the splint bone, and/or the cannon bone. The swelling on this horse's offside front leg below the knee is due to a splint.

Splints

This name is given to the bony enlargements that arise

between the large and small bones in the leg below the knee and hock. They form as a result of ossification (calcium build-up) in the ligament. This build-up of bone tissue to form the splint can also occur if the splint bone is fractured (for example, when the horse is kicked).

Splints usually develop on the inside of the foreleg and the outside of the hindleg. They vary in size from that of a split pea to that of a hen's egg, and their significance is largely dependent on their position and size, and the age of the animal. Splints most frequently develop in horses under five years of age.

The cause of the splint is often abnormal conformation, where the cannons are offset from the centre of the knee, or stress on the good leg from prolonged lameness. This puts more weight on the splint bone, causing movement between the small splint bone and the cannon bone. It is this movement that sets up an inflammation and subsequent calcification. Sometimes splints may be caused by a knock to the leg from the other leg, or more frequently they are the result of too much stress on a young horse's leg. Usually the horse walks sound but trots lame. Recent cases are painful on pressure.

When searching for a splint, lift the leg and flex the knee, then rub your thumb along the groove between the large and small bones from the knee to the button at the end of the small bone. The principle of treatment of splints is to try to get the inflammatory process to settle down and a permanent weld formed between the small and large bones. To this end the horse should be immediately rested and confined. A cold pack should be put on the area to keep the inflammation down. Provided the splint does not involve the knee, or interfere with the free action of the tendons running down the back of the cannon bone, it will not affect the usefulness of the horse. It is frequently regarded as a blemish, however. If the splint is an old one and you wish to remove it for cosmetic purposes, a blister can be applied over the area, but the best results are after the use of radiation therapy. Splints can be removed surgically.

Spondylitis
See BACK INJURIES.

Stings
See BEE STINGS. Allergic reactions, see SKIN DISORDERS: URTICARIA.

Stomach worms (Habronema)
See the section on Worming, pp. 188–94.

Straining
Straining can indicate constipation. See Illnesses of foals, p. 201.

Strangles
Strangles is an acute contagious disease of the horse. It appears as a 'pussy' nasal discharge, together with enlargement of the regional lymph nodes in the throat area. These may enlarge to the point of rupture. Occasionally the disease may spread via the bloodstream and cause abscess formation in other organs such as the lungs, kidneys, liver and intestines. The horse usually has a fever of 40–41°C increased respiratory rate, depression and loss of appetite. It begins with a mucoid discharge, followed quickly by swelling of the lymph nodes (glands). Once these burst and have discharged their creamy yellow pus, the horse's temperature drops to normal.

During an outbreak, sound sanitary measures are important to prevent spread of the disease. Affected animals should be isolated. Take their temperatures twice daily. All animals showing fevers should be isolated. Rest is essential, and affected horses should be protected from cold, draughts and inclement weather. Stables should be cleaned, and the contaminated bedding burned. The or-

ganism is a bacteria and is easily destroyed by boiling for ten minutes. Common disinfectants readily destroy the organism.

Horses respond well to antibiotics such as penicillin, streptomycin or tetracyclines. Treatment should be continued until the temperature reaches normal. (See FEVER.) A vaccine is available to prevent this disease, although its efficiency is in doubt.

Stringhalt
See HOCK DISORDERS.

Strongyles
See the section on Worming, pp. 188–94.

Sunburn
See SKIN DISORDERS.

Swamp fever
See EQUINE INFECTIOUS ANAEMIA, and SKIN DISORDERS: RAIN SCALD.

Swelling in the legs
See FILLED LEGS.

Sweeny
This term can apply to any group of wasted muscles. Its popular usage applies to the muscles over the shoulder blade. In most cases the wastage of these muscles is due to a direct blow to the point of the shoulder which damages the nerve supplying the muscles. The wasting of the muscles makes the shoulder joint appear more prominent. Sometimes there is lameness and there may be a bowing of the knee of the limb on the affected side.

There is no known treatment of any value—but heat applications may help. Final judgement should be reserved for six months.

Tail rubbing
This can be due to infestations of pinworms (see the section on Worming), lice, Queensland itch, mange, or to a dirty udder or dirty sheath.

Tapeworms
See the section on Worming, pp. 188–94.

Teeth problems
Because the grinding or molar teeth at the back of the horse's mouth do not exactly oppose, they develop sharp edges which must be filed down. Horses' teeth should be checked twice yearly and filed (floated) if necessary. Horses under six years of age may have caps to be removed from the tips of the teeth.

For information on determining a horse's age from its teeth, see the section on Selecting a horse. (See also MOUTH DISORDERS.)

Temperature
See FEVER.

Tendons, sprained or ruptured
Spraining of tendons is a well-known hazard. A sprained tendon may be the result of a slip or mis-step but more commonly it occurs at the end of an exhausting event when the muscles begin to tire. At this time propulsion is maintained through the check ligaments and tendons rather than through the muscles and tendons. The inelastic tendons are unable to cope with the excessive stretching and many of the fibres are torn. When the sprain or rupture first begins, the horse should stop work immediately, anti-inflammatory injections should be given, and the local area cold-hosed to reduce the swelling. A poultice should be applied to the area each day and left on for twenty-four hours. This procedure should continue for seven days after the swelling and/or heat has left the leg. If the tendon has been badly ruptured the leg should be plaster cast and a slightly raised heel shoe put on the leg. For the valuable animal, surgical correction is also available.

Because of the nature of the healing process, the horse will need six months' rest. Even after this rest a damaged tendon or ligament is likely to break down again under severe stress.

Tetanus

Most warm-blooded animals are susceptible to tetanus, but the horse is the most sensitive. The cost of vaccination for tetanus is very little, and there is no excuse for not giving the animal protection. All horses should be vaccinated, as the disease is usually fatal. The tetanus germ lives in most organic matter, such as manure and damp conditions around stables.

It enters the horse's body via a deep penetrating wound. The first signs are a rigidity of the forelegs and a slight tremor or tucking up of the abdominal muscles. The ears are pricked and the third eyelid may begin to protrude. As time progresses, these symptoms become much more dramatic and the horse becomes very sensitive to noise. Treatment of tetanus cases is invariably a failure.

If the horse gets a deep penetrating wound, anti-toxin and anti-toxoid should be given immediately. Booster shots of toxoid should be given a month later and then each five years.

A very nasty wound already producing granulation tissue (proud flesh).

Thinness
See MALNUTRITION.

Thirst
An abnormal desire for water is seen in fever, sugar diabetes, water diabetes, kidney disease, and diarrhoea. Salty food and very hot weather can also increase the horse's thirst. A normal horse may drink up to 45 litres of water a day, a lactating mare much more.

Thoroughpin
See HOCK DISORDERS.

Threadworms
See the section on Worming, pp. 188–94.

Thrush
See FEET DISORDERS.

Ticks
Cattle tick bites, see SKIN DISORDERS.

Tied-up
See AZOTURIA.

Tongue disorders
See MOUTH DISORDERS.

Tying-up
See AZOTURIA.

Undershot jaw
See MOUTH DISORDERS.

Urine disorders
As with most herbivorous animals, very little goes wrong with the urinary system in the horse. The colour of the urine is usually a clear light yellow; it can be very cloudy at times but this is generally of no significance. Urine of port-wine colour may indicate tying-up (azoturia). It may also indicate cystitis (inflammation of the bladder). Incontinence in the horse is usually a sign of ageing, and can be treated with hormones. The retention of urine is said to occur with colic and tetanus. This can be relieved with a catheter.

Sometimes a horse may refuse to urinate in strange surroundings—for example, new stables, at a show, on a float trip. Take the horse to a grassed area and let it eat and relax, or put it in a stable with plenty of straw bedding. 'Flooding the box' is related to water diabetes and may be caused by high grain diets. Horses will usually get over the condition, which causes no harm. (See also KIDNEY DISEASE.)

Urticaria (Allergic reaction)
See SKIN DISORDERS.

Vaginal disorders
Abnormal discharges from the vagina include pus, which indicates infection of the bladder or more commonly the uterus (metritis). Any discharge from the vulva of the mare is serious. It is important to get a vet to examine her as soon as possible. The vet will take cultures of the organism to determine which drugs to use. Antibiotics may be given by injection or in a uterine douche. Mares exhibiting such discharges are invariably infertile, at least until it is cleared. Bloody discharges may indicate a cystitis or more commonly abortion. Pustules affecting the lips of the vagina indicate skin disease such as equine coital exanthema (see SKIN DISORDERS).

Vices
Crib-biting, wind-sucking, weaving, pawing, biting, kicking stable walls, wood-chewing, and so on are all vices resulting from boredom. Many horses are locked up in a small stable, hand-fed twice daily, and given nothing else to do all day. They develop vices as a way of passing the time. The trouble is that horses are great mimics and once one starts wood-chewing, for example, a stable full of wood-chewers ('termites') soon results. Vices such as these are rarely seen in range horses.

Vitamins
Vitamin supplementation for paddocked horses is rarely necessary. Horses in heavy work (racing, polo or endurance riding) may benefit from special equine vitamin preparations, as may young growing stock, but the benefit is doubtful as the horse does produce ample of its own vitamins provided it is given good fresh food. Occasionally, horses in heavy work benefit from vitamin B12 and vitamin B complex supplements. These should always be given with folic acid. Other vitamin supplements include vitamin E for the heart and skeletal muscle. (See Feeding, p. 184, and The foal's diet, p. 205.)

Warts
See SKIN DISORDERS.

Water-gripes
See COLIC.

Weaving
This is a vice resulting from boredom. The horse stands at its stable door, head over the door, and rocks from one front foot to the other, wearing itself out and often making holes in the floor.

Ideally the weaver should be put out in a paddock and

fed only once a day, thus forcing it to forage for food for most of the day. If this is impossible, a bar or second door should be put on the stable so the horse cannot get its head out through the doorway. I have seen some trainers successfully dangle two bricks in the open space above the door to stop the horse weaving.

Windgall

Windgall (a synovial distension) is fluid distension around a joint which usually indicates that the joint has been under stress. It is commonly found on both the inside and outside of the fetlock joints between the tendons at the back of the leg and the cannon bone. It is simply a protective mechanism for an overworked joint. It is pointless draining the windgall and injecting anti-inflammatory agents as the synovial membrane has been permanently stretched and will just fill up again. Windgalls do no harm to the horse and should be left alone.

A metal device constricting the throat area to prevent wind sucking.

Wind-sucking

A wind-sucker is a horse that can crib in the air without support (see CRIB-BITING). As the wind-sucker does not use its teeth for support, the habit does not produce abnormal wear on the teeth and is only detectable when the horse is caught in the act. The head is bent towards the breast, the lips move in a peculiar manner, the head and neck are jerked upwards and air is swallowed, the act being accompanied by a grunt similar to that heard in crib-biting. Like crib-biting, wind-sucking is a definite unsoundness in a horse and can predispose to other problems—particularly colic. There is no permanent cure for such a horse, although good results can be obtained with neck straps. (See also VICES.)

The term 'wind-sucking' also refers to movement of air into a mare's vagina (carrying with it faecal debris and consequent infection) as a result of poor conformation of the mare's anus/vulva region. (See the section on Breeding, p. 196.)

Wobbler

This is a condition characteristically seen in well-developed male horses with long crested necks at yearling to two year old. It presents as a weakness in the hindlegs (a slight paralysis). Riders will complain that they feel unsafe. This condition is associated with a lesion in the neck of the horse which interferes with the nervous control of the back legs.

There are several degrees of the syndrome. In the milder form the horse should not be ridden but may lead a perfectly normal life in the paddock. In severe forms the horse may gradually deteriorate to the point where it loses the

use of its back legs and must be destroyed. There is no cure for this condition.

Wolf teeth

The wolf teeth are four redundant (vestigial) teeth which are frequently present in the horse, one in front of each of the first molar teeth in the upper and lower jaw. The two in the lower jaw rarely erupt. A wolf tooth varies in shape—usually it is tubular, but occasionally one is seen with a crown that resembles in shape a small molar. Usually the wolf teeth erupt during the first six months and may be shed about the same time as the milk teeth behind them. They may remain indefinitely. Some people claim that they interfere with the bit in the mouth and consequently horse dentists tend to remove them.

Worms

See the section on Worming, pp. 188–94.

Wounds

The chief danger for all wounds, apart from the mechanical damage, is the risk of infection and further damage—especially to joint capsules, sensitive portions of the foot, tendons, blood vessels and nerves. Lack of drainage may encourage the spread of infection. Healing of the superficial part of the wound and trapping infection underneath, may lead to abscess formation. Undetected foreign bodies such as pieces of wood or wire may be left in a wound and cause sinus tracks. Such wounds will not heal until the foreign body is removed. Conditions interfering with the healing of wounds include:

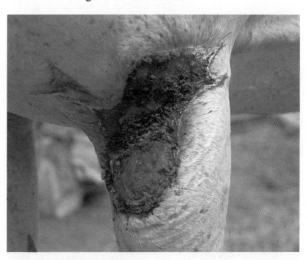

This large wound is healing satisfactorily without proud flesh. The surface is dry and will form a scab.

Interference with circulation in the vicinity of the wound. This can be caused by swelling, improper bandaging, laceration and cutting of blood vessels, prolonged infection and granulation tissue.

Invasive infection Drainage should always be established when infection is present. Failure to use sterile techniques when dressing the wounds may be the cause of infection.

Devitalised tissue Any dying tissues, particularly those that have been pulled away from their circulation, should be removed. A triangular skin flap with the apex of the flap pointed upwards or towards the incoming blood supply will usually lose the apical portion of the triangle as a result of loss of blood supply.

Inadequate drainage or collection of blood and discharges in the wound. Inadequate drainage interferes with circulation, and forms an ideal medium for growth of bacteria.

Retained foreign bodies Any foreign body left in the

wound will interfere with healing and cause a sinus track.

Continuous irritation of the wound This is usually due to lack of restaint, allowing a horse to abuse the wound area. Neck cradles and Elizabethan collars are often helpful in preventing further irritation.

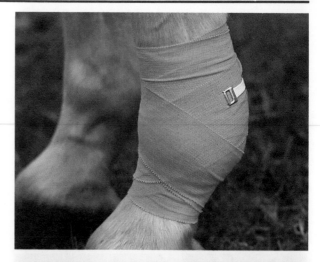

An Elizabethan collar made from wooden sticks to prevent the horse from biting at wounds or bandages.

The effect of wound medication Wound medications are often more detrimental than helpful in the healing of a wound. Irritant antiseptics and drugs should be avoided in all cases. Drugs such as copper sulphate and antimony trichloride are very irritant to new cell growth. Although these products will destroy superficial granulation tissue, they will also destroy immature, young, growing skin cells. Any granulation tissue (proud flesh) present should be surgically removed by scalpel or cautery and the wound kept under a pressure bandage with a corticosteroid and antibiotic ointment until it is healed. Powdered blue-stone (copper sulphate) in vaseline, pasted on, will reduce granulation tissue over 24 hours.

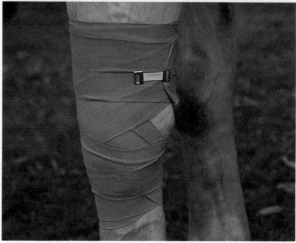

Pressure bandages replaced daily will help prevent proud flesh developing on wounds of the limbs.

wound. Infestation with parasites, bad teeth, and inadequate feeding may contribute to delays in wound healing.

(See also ABRASIONS.)

Treatment of lacerated and incised wounds

Mistreatment of wounds will result in granulation (proud flesh), scarring, blemishing and sometimes unsoundness.

Filling in a leg three days after wire cuts. Any further swelling would require antibiotic treatment.

Dirty bandages Bandages should be changed frequently to avoid irritation. Wet bandages containing wound discharges will delay healing. In most cases a bandage should not be allowed to stay in place for longer than three days. Contamination should always be avoided when applying a dressing.

Poor nutrition Poor nutrition will delay healing of a

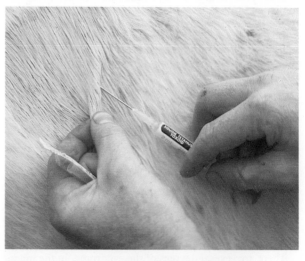

Tetanus vaccination is inexpensive and painless. Unprotected, a horse may get tetanus, a most excruciating and fatal disease.

Wounds below the carpus (knee) and the tarsus (hock) are especially sensitive and will develop proud flesh unless careful treatment is given to prevent these complications. Tetanus anti-toxin should always be administered if the horse is not on a tetanus programme.

All wounds should be cleaned carefully and tissues that have obviously lost their blood supply should be removed. Horse tissue tends to waterlog when cleansed with ordinary water, so normal saline solution should be used—that is, 1 teaspoonful of salt to 600 millilitres of water. Clean the wound using sterile gauzes or sponges.

Wounds below the knee and the hock joint that are so small that bandaging is not required should be treated daily with agents which tend to retard proud flesh development, such as 2 per cent picric acid, 2 per cent tannic acid, triple dye preparations or Socatyl paste.

Larger wounds on the limbs should be cleansed as described above and covered with Socatyl or with an antibiotic/cortisone combination cream and then bandaged firmly. The bandage should be changed daily until the seepage and discharge is minimal. Then decrease the frequency of bandage changing. Keep the wound bandaged until skin has covered the area. Keep the horse inactive until the wound has healed.

Wounds on the upper limbs and body, if not stitched, should be irrigated twice daily until pink granulation tissue has filled the hole. Then apply triple dye or commercial topical sprays.

First aid box

This should contain the following:
Twitch
Wirecutters
Sharp knife. scissors
Pliers (for pulling nails from feet)
4 adhesive bandages, 7.5 centimetres wide
4 conforming bandages, 7.5 centimetres wide
1 roll of cotton-wool
100 millilitres general antibiotic
6 (20 millilitre) syringes and needles, 19 gauge
500 grams epsom salts
1 packet of antiphlogistine
200 millilitres 5 per cent formalin
Mercurochrome, triple dye
Antibiotic lotion for topical application
Antibiotic powder
Thermometer (thick end bulbed)
Peroxide 3%
Antiseptic wash (e.g. chlorhexidine)

Yellow eggs

In autumn the bot-fly lays its yellow eggs, frequently on the horse's legs. If not removed—by shaving the hair or by wiping the area with kerosene—the eggs hatch, and the larval stages (bots) eventually find their way to the horse's stomach. (See the section on Worming, pp. 191–92.)

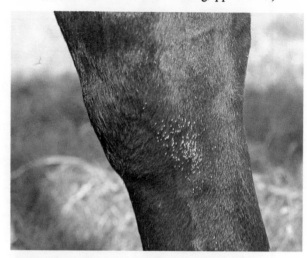

In Autumn, bot-flies lay yellow eggs in clusters along the base of the horse's hair.

MICE

Mice as pets

The mouse is timid, gentle and easily handled. It is usually more active at night than in the daytime and is a determined escaper. The presence of humans tends to inhibit activity in the mouse.

Mice are social animals and do not respond well to being kept singly. Such animals eat less food and gain less weight than those caged in groups. They tend to seek rest in dark corners and become very nervous and disturbed if compelled to remain in bright light. Male mice caged together may attack each other savagely, especially if the cage has little or no bedding to afford the weaker ones refuge. At the same time they will produce a strong odour which can rapidly penetrate a room. Mice will escape from their cage if they can and unlike rats do not often return to captivity.

The lifespan of the laboratory mouse averages between one and a half to two and a half years. However, some inbred strains may develop tumours or conditions such as leukaemia which will kill them before they are twelve months of age.

The most common species of mouse kept is *Mus musculus*, the house mouse. Although other species of mice are kept as pets, the care and feeding of them are essentially the same. Only the house mouse is available in a multitude of colours and colour combinations—more than seventy variations. The most popular colour is the white albino which is used in laboratories, but the pet mouse hobby has produced them in dark-eyed white, black, tan, evenly marked, unevenly marked, cream, beige and blue.

It is very rare for humans to contract any serious diseases from pet mice. However, the following diseases can be caught from rodents: rat-bite fever, leptospirosis, tick fever, some forms of encephalitis, and a new disease called lymphocytic chorio meningitis. This disease in man causes headaches, fever and coughs, and while it is not serious, it can be uncomfortable. It is emphasised that the above diseases are extremely rare and most can be treated satisfactorily.

Housing

Mice may be housed in shoe-box-sized cages of almost any hard-to-chew material or in cages in which the walls and floors are wire mesh. If you decide to build a cage keep it simple—complicated cages are hard to clean and hard to keep clean. Make the cage roomy. Mice are active and enjoy exercises—give them treadmills, trapezes, ladders and slippery dips. For the individual hobbyist the ideal cage is a disused aquarium, as mice cannot climb glass walls.

Mice should not be held for more than a few hours in numbers greater than thirty per cage, however big the cage, because they tend to congregate in large heaps and those at the bottom may suffocate.

You can buy a mouse cage ready-made in a pet shop—a cage with an enclosed space for nesting and sleeping. A small wooden box 12 × 6 × 22 centimetres is suitable.

The top of the box should have gaps for entry of about 2.5 centimetres at each end. Make this top easily removable for examination of the nest. There is no need to place any nesting material in the nesting box itself. Just place soft paper, cotton-wool or hemp in the bottom of the cage and the mice will build their own nest.

Bedding

Various types of bedding may be used, such as sawdust, wood shavings, cellulose, peat moss, granulated clay, dried woodchips, paddy husks and sugar beets. Whatever the material, it is important that there is enough of it to absorb the urine of all the animals in the cage because mice do not tolerate wet bedding.

Mice should be kept at a temperature of 20–25°C. They are very sensitive to noise, especially noise in the high frequencies.

A simple wire cage with shelter at one end is suitable housing.

Mice are bred in a variety of colours and colour combinations.

243

Mice have a very convenient tail by which they may be picked up.

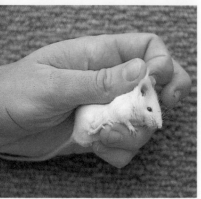

A secure but comfortable way to immobilise a mouse.

Feeding

Mice are omnivorous, but their preferred foods are cereal, seeds and many stored foodstuffs. The mouse has a simple digestive tract. A heavy-lactating female may ingest her own body-weight of food and water in twenty-four hours. This places an enormous burden on the alimentary system.

Mice are usually fed on pelleted diets which are best offered in hoppers where the animals have to eat the pellets through the wires. Mice are particularly liable to pull half-eaten pellets through the wire and let them drop to the bottom of the cage while they go back for more.

If a home diet is preferred, the best combination of foods is rolled oats, plain biscuits, mixed bird seed, bread soaked in water or milk, hay, fresh vegetables and water. An adult mouse will need a teaspoon of rolled oats and a teaspoon of moistened bread a day. Fresh, clean, raw vegetables are excellent for mice. Dandelion leaves and flowers, carrots, peas and clover are all suitable. Hay makes an important part of the mouse's diet.

Smell the hay before you use it. It should have a fresh, clean odour. (If it is musty, don't use it.) Mice will tumble through it, make a mess of it and thoroughly enjoy having it in their cages. Mice also eat insects. They love grasshoppers, crickets and cockroaches.

Mice also need something hard to gnaw on. It helps to keep their teeth in shape. A piece of rib bone or a section of shank is ideal.

Mice should have fresh water available at all times. A simple water dispenser attached to the outside of the cage with a nipple protruding into the cage is ideal.

General care
Handling

Mice are provided by nature with a very convenient tail by which they may be picked up. Even a very pregnant female comes to no harm if held by the tail. The tail, however, should be grasped at least halfway down.

To immobilise a mouse more securely, put it on a rough surface such as the top of the cage and grasp a generous fold of the skin on the scruff of its neck between the finger and thumb. The tail may be held and kept in place by the little finger of the hand holding its stump. A mouse so held can be comfortable.

Transport

Mice being small animals have a high metabolic rate and they therefore produce a lot of heat quickly. During transport their density should be low. They are much more likely to suffer from heat associated with lack of ventilation than from cold.

Mice will gnaw through most cardboard containers within a few hours.

Breeding

To differentiate the sexes of mice, lift the mouse by the nape of the neck and examine the genital region. If the mouse is male, a tiny penis will be visible. Mice breed readily all year round. Breeding is more successful if they are kept in groups, either a number of females and males or a group of pregnant females together. The usual maternal group is three females with their litters. The young will be raised by a single nurse but may suckle indiscriminately.

Each female may produce as many as eight or ten litters if she is given the opportunity, but after the first five litters her productivity falls. The average litter size is five to eight. A breeding lifetime of up to nine months is usually enough. The male too should be retired after not more than six months of breeding. The best time to stop is when the mice are getting obese and their fertility is falling off.

The female mouse is ready and willing to mate within a day after she has given birth. If this period passes without a mating it will be six weeks before her next litter could arrive, because she will not again be capable of mating until the young are weaned. If you wait until the young are twenty-eight or thirty days old before they are weaned, they will be better mice, and will live longer.

Development

Although the young are born hairless with their eyes and ears closed, they are very active and vocal from the time they are born. If they are not active they are likely to be rejected by the mother. At twelve days of age the babies open their eyes; by then they are very active and are able to run around. They will eat any solid food they can reach. They will also learn to drink water from a bottle or drinking utensil.

Mice are sexually mature at three and a half to four weeks of age, although females can be wooed at any time from sixteen days onwards. The female comes into oestrus about every four days and is receptive for twelve hours. The gestation period is seventeen to twenty-two days.

Mating by an infertile male will develop a pseudo-pregnancy which lasts nearly three weeks. A male laboratory mouse will successfully mate two or three females in one night, but may become infertile through exhaustion of sperm while still able to copulate. It is in these circumstances that pseudo-pregnancies are induced.

Disease control

Poor nutrition, overcrowding, lack of hygiene, inadequate ventilation, violent handling and exposure to mice suffering from infectious diseases, particularly wild mice, will all favour an outbreak of disease in the colony. A wild mouse is probably the greatest risk to the mouse colony. The mouse house must therefore be absolutely proof against mice (and rats) getting in as well as getting out and should also be protected against insects and other pests. Pellet feeds are unlikely to contain dangerous organisms.

Caring for the sick mouse

A sick mouse needs special attention and it is best to isolate it from the others. A shoe box will provide a spacious, draught-free, clean environment.

Punch some holes in the top (but not the sides) for draught-free ventilation and provide some dry grass or shredded newspaper for bedding. Change the water daily and provide fresh food, particularly fresh vegetables and bird seed. Place the box in a warm room.

One female mouse can produce up to 135 young mice annually. If each of these females were allowed to breed uncontrolled, 30,000 mice per year could emerge from one original female.

Common ailments

Bald spots, scaliness, itch

Bald spots, scaliness and itching usually indicate ringworm. It is best treated with ringworm ointment or with griseofulvin at the rate of 2 milligrams per 100 grams body-weight. (See also RINGWORM.)

Congenital absence of tail

This condition is noticed at birth and is a hereditary problem. Nothing can be done to change it. However, it will not adversely affect the mouse.

Death

Sudden death in mice is often preceded by an acute enteritis with diarrhoea. Separate ill animals and commence antibiotic therapy (Tetracyclines 2–5 milligrams per ml drinking water) in *all* survivors.

Depression

Depression in mice is often accompanied by hunched-up posture, roughened coat, conjunctivitis, loss of appetite, lethargy, death or stunting in surviving mice. Young mice are more commonly affected.

There are non-specific signs of septicaemia, and any latent disease can develop if the animal is stressed. The usual causes are Salmonella, mouse hepatitis virus, neovirus and heavy parasitism.

Treat with antibiotics such as Chloromycetin (at the rate of 2 milligrams per 100 grams body-weight) and hyperchlorinate the drinking water (10 p.p.m.).

Diarrhoea

Diarrhoea when accompanied by dark eyes and crust around the nose is usually caused by bacteria or viruses. Bacterial diarrhoea can be treated with Gentamycin injection 2 milligrams per 100 grams body-weight daily for seven days. The cage should be cleaned twice daily.

Another treatment is with a bland medication such as Kaomagma used at a rate of 0.5 millilitre three times daily, but this is not generally as effective.

Chronic diarrhoea is usually caused by coccidia or intestinal parasites. Coccidiosus (a protozoan disease) is diagnosed by examining the droppings under a microscope. Treatment is by adding sulphur drugs to the drinking water (see Common Ailments of Rabbits).

Worms can be eradicated by dosing with Thiabendazole, 5 milligrams per 100 grams body-weight once weekly for three weeks.

Head tilt

Head tilt is usually caused by middle ear infection. The best treatment is Gentamycin at the rate of 2 milligrams per 100 grams body-weight.

Nose

Pneumonitis causes sneezing, a runny nose, pawing at the nose, and a loss of hair on the chin. The mouse has a faster respiratory rate. Hair is unkempt, back is arched, and there is generalised depression. Treat with Chloromycetin orally, 2 milligrams per 100 grams body-weight twice daily for five days or Clavulox. Keep the cage clean. (See also SNEEZING.)

Prolapsed rectum

Usually mice are three weeks or older. It is caused by parasites. Dose with Ivermectin, at the rate of 50–100 milligrams per kilogram body-weight, in the drinking water. Use medication seven days on, seven days off, seven days on.

Ringworm

This fungal skin condition is characterized by loss of hair. It is highly contagious and affected mice should be either destroyed or separated for treatment. The treatment involves oral administration of griseofulvin (2 milligrams per 100 grams body-weight) for 42 days and the application of ringworm ointment to all affected areas of the skin.

In addition all bedding should be destroyed and the mouse-house washed with an anti-fungal solution.

Ringworm is a contagious fungal skin condition.

Salivary gland enlargement

The most obvious sign is swelling of the neck area. The most common cause is a virus and the treatment is with cortisone and antibiotics to prevent secondary infection.

Scratching

Scratching around the head and ears usually results in abrasions, sores, scabs and bald spots. For a definite diagnosis the vet will need to do a skin scraping to detect the most common cause which is microscopic mites. These can be treated by hanging a Dichlorvos pest strip in the cage or powdering the mice daily with pyrethrum flea powder. Ivermectin or Ectodex dips at low concentration.

Septicaemia

This presents non-specific signs, but may include depression, hunched-up posture, roughened coat, conjunctivitis, loss of appetite, lethargy, death, and stunting in surviving animals. It can occur in any age group but the young are more commonly affected. The most common cause is salmonella bacteria. Treatment includes hyperchlorination of drinking water (10 p.p.m.) and Tetracyclines (2–5 milligrams per ml of water).

Skin disorders

Scaly patches on the skin, or grey warty lesions on the tail, ears or nose are caused by mange from mites. Administer a benzylbenzoate lotion or dip the mouse completely in a Malathion solution diluted as per directions. Repeat weekly for three occasions. Hang a Dichlorvos pest strip on the cage for three days on, three days off, three days on. Ivermectin or Ectodex dips at low concentration.

Hairless areas with an associated dermatitis can be treated by washing with a medicated shampoo to remove surface debris and then apply either an antibiotic skin cream three times daily, or a gentian violet, mercurochrome dye twice daily until symptoms resolve. Affected mice are best quarantined to prevent disease from spreading.

In some cases, it is best to eradicate individual affected mice because of the expense of diagnosis and the difficulty of effectively treating the complaint.

Sloughing

Sloughing of a dead tail or dead digits, sometimes accompanied by small pustules, indicates a pox virus. In large colonies a vaccine can be made. Otherwise, place the mice on antibiotics (chloramphenicol at the rate of 2 milligrams per 100 grams body-weight).

Sneezing

Sneezing, chattering, laboured breathing, nasal discharge, pawing at the nose, bleeding from the nose, an unkempt coat, arching of the back, generalised depression and conjunctivitis can all be part of the one disease syndrome. It is important to seek veterinary advice and treat with long term antibiotics. The preferred antibiotics being Tetracycline 2–5 milligrams to each ml of water or a Sulphamethazine 0.02% solution. Gentamycin or Chloromycetin. (See also NOSE.)

Sores

Sores around ears and scabs and wounds randomly positioned on the last two-thirds of the tail are usually caused by fighting. Prevent these by separating the males. Sores can be treated with an antibiotic skin cream.

Tail disorders

A red or swollen tail usually indicates gangrene caused by insufficient humidity. The treatment is to amputate the tail above the constriction and increase humidity in the cage to 50 per cent. The humidity can be raised by placing shallow bowls of water or wet absorbent paper in the mouse cage.

Teeth disorders

Overgrowth of incisor teeth is caused by insufficient roughage. Trim the teeth to allow for normal wear and add roughage to the diet. Add a wood block to the cage for chewing.

Wounds

If a cage is too small for the number of occupants, fighting and injuries may occur. Male mice caged together may attack each other savagely, especially if there is inadequate bedding to supply a refuge for the weaker animals. Overcrowding in the cage must be reduced, and fighting can be prevented by separating the male mice. Where minor cuts and scratches occur apply mercurochrome or triple dye to the affected areas. Sores and wounds can be treated with an antibiotic skin cream. Veterinary attention may be necessary if the wound is of a more serious nature.

Like most active animals kept in confined spaces, mice have fights. Male mice may attack each other savagely and cause nasty wounds.

RABBITS

Rabbits as pets

In many states and countries it is illegal to keep rabbits as pets. Potential pet rabbit owners should enquire from local government or Department of Agriculture offices whether any restrictions apply in their area.

Rabbits have been pets and laboratory animals for many years. They can be playful and very tame, but only rarely can they be house-trained. Despite this, they are very clean animals and are most unlikely to transmit disease to humans.

Rabbits, like mice, have been developed with many interesting and varied coat colours, but the most popular, as with mice, is the white albino. The range of colours is white albino, white with black extremities, silver with black under, silver with yellow under, black, blue, grey, red or varied.

Housing

Each rabbit should be kept in a cage made of wood or metal, measuring at least 1 metre by 2 metres by 0.3 metres in height. The cage should preferably be made of wire mesh. One end of the cage should be enclosed, with wooden roof, floor and walls. With a small doorway onto the rest of the cage, such an enclosure ensures that the rabbit has somewhere to nestle away from cold winds and rain. For long-term use, metal cages might be better than wood because the rabbit will chew at wood. However, as rabbit urine is very corrosive, iron must be galvanised in order to avoid rapid corrosion.

The whole cage can be set on the ground and periodically moved around so that the rabbit can eat fresh grass. Faeces and urine will pass through the wire mesh on to the grass, leaving the cage hygienic.

Additional food should be kept in pellet hoppers affixed to the cage so that small quantities are always available to the rabbit without risk of their being soiled or spoiled. Rabbits are watered using nipples attached to 600 millilitre water bottles.

In this type of cage, bedding is not necessary except in the wooden nesting box. Sawdust and hay are satisfactory there. Cages should be disinfected with lysol each three months or between litters.

Although rabbits respond to fairly wide fluctuations in temperature, the desired range is between 10°C and 18°C.

A movable wire-bottomed cage with shelter at one end makes an ideal home.

Rabbits have now been developed with many interesting and varied coat colours.

Rabbits can be held by grasping a fold of skin over the shoulder, while supporting the body-weight with the other hand.

Feeding

Under natural conditions the rabbit's diet consists mainly of green herbage and other plant material. Natural diets include cereals, freshly cut grass, lucerne, vetches, cabbage, carrots, herbs and hay according to the season and availability.

Pelleted balanced diets are produced commercially (usually going by the name of rabbit pellets) and are the most sensible form of feed for the pet owner. They have been fed for long periods with no ill effects and only need to be supplemented by green feed three to four times per week. Pellets are not sufficient to maintain lactating does in good condition.

General care

Grooming

Rabbits can be groomed just like a dog or cat. Brush with a soft hair brush and smooth the hair afterwards to add extra lustre. If claws are sharp and annoying they can be trimmed as you would a cat.

Handling

When handling a rabbit be firm but gentle. A rabbit that feels insecure when you are holding it is more likely to struggle. Young rabbits can be lifted by grasping them firmly over the loins, your fingers on one side and your thumb on the other. Larger animals can be lifted or carried by holding a fold of skin over the shoulder with the right hand while the left hand is placed under the rump to support the animal's weight. Rabbits can break their backs unless held firmly, if they struggle or are released quickly.

Transport

Rabbits are quite robust animals and no special care is needed when transporting them. A wire cage with a raised mesh floor (1-centimetre squares) which allows urine and faeces to fall through is ideal. A cat-carrying cage (see p. 49) is perfect.

In an emergency, the rabbit can be carried in a pillowslip or a hessian bag, with a small hole for the head. Always avoid carrying the rabbit loose in unfamiliar places. If it is frightened, it will use its claws to make even the most determined person release it—and rabbits can run!

The mother rabbit will suckle the young ones for up to 6 weeks and may then fall pregnant again.

Breeding

Under favourable conditions sexually mature does remain on heat for long periods. During lactation or if nutrition is poor, or when in moult, does may show no desire to mate. Bucks and does can be first mated at four to five months of age. The gestation period of the rabbit is thirty days. One buck mated with four or five does will breed 200 or more rabbits per year.

The doe ovulates only after copulation with the male. It takes 10 hours for ovulation to occur after mating. This peculiar aspect of rabbit reproduction has made it popular as a laboratory animal because it is then possible to time fertilisation within an hour. When the female is in oestrus, the vulva may become swollen and slightly purple; however, there are no *consistent* external signs of oestrus. The doe becomes listless, nervous, and rubs her head and body against the cage.

If you are not interested in breeding a large number of rabbits, it will be wise to separate the sexes. When the female is ready to breed, she can be taken to the male's pen. The buck has defined this territory, and if he is taken to the doe he will be more interested in defining and exploring the new territory than in mating. If the doe is in oestrus, mating usually occurs immediately she is placed in the cage. The mating is successful if the buck falls on his side during coitus. One mating is sufficient to ensure fertilisation and the female should be removed after copulation has been completed.

Rabbits usually have their young without any problems. The newborn kittens may be handled at birth, and may be transferred to foster mothers within the first forty-eight hours after birth. The mother will suckle the young ones for up to six weeks and may then fall pregnant again. Does will mate readily shortly after giving birth, but if their feed intake is not sufficient to support lactation and pregnancy the pregnancy will fail about seven days after mating. They can have up to eight young ones per litter.

Breeding is most successful in the spring if the rabbits are kept out of doors. In some species the female may remain receptive during the cold winter months, but others will not.

All young stock should be separated into sex groups before three months of age, when males may need to be moved into individual cages. To determine the sex of a rabbit, simply press open the genital opening with thumb and forefinger. If the opening is a long slit, the rabbit is female (a doe). If the opening is round with a tiny penis, the rabbit is male (a buck).

At about three months, the bucks begin to show aggressive behaviour and attack each other, particularly in the scrotal region, causing destruction of the testes, so that ultimately only one intact male remains. This provides a severe example of natural selection. Does, on the other hand, may be left together for the rest of their lives.

Caring for the sick rabbit

The sick rabbit needs a draught-free clean hutch, preferably separated from the others. Provide fresh clean water daily together with fresh rabbit pellets and a good source of greens. Carrots and green lettuce are ideal, but in excess may cause diarrhoea.

Greens are essential for the sick rabbit as they are a good source of vitamins A and C. Supply them fresh in the late afternoon or evening as rabbits are more active at night. Sometimes oats will perk up a rabbit who is unwilling to eat. If the rabbit's complaint cannot be easily diagnosed, be sure to see your vet.

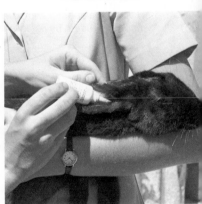

Administering ear drops.

Common ailments
Abortion

Abscesses
Abscesses are most commonly found around the jaw, neck and feet. They usually need to be lanced and hence require veterinary treatment with antibiotics.

Constipation
Constipation is a frequently encountered problem. Feed only moist greens for two or three days and add liquid paraffin.

Cystitis
The most common urinary problem is cystitis, evidenced by pus and blood passed when the animal's bladder is pressed. The rabbit is slightly lethargic and may be off its food and be drinking more water than usual. The cystitis does not seem to cause pain and responds well to veterinary treatment with Penicillin/Clavulox.

Diarrhoea
It may be caused by too many greens in the diet, but is usually the result of coccidiosis. Treat with Thiabendazole (injection) 5 milligrams per 100 grams body-weight, or 0.1 per cent Sulphamethazine in drinking water for two weeks or preferably a coccidiocide.

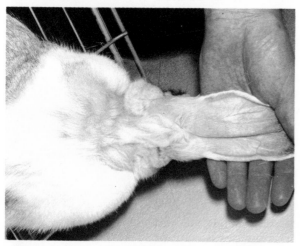

Hair loss (alopecia) and scaly skin in this position are usually caused by mites in the ears.

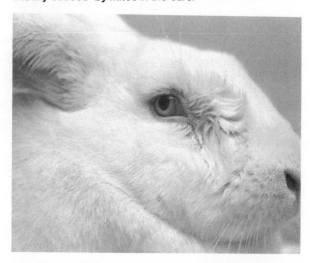

A red and runny eye signifies conjunctivitis; a common cause is the fatal myxomatosis.

Ear disorders
The usual sign of an ear problem is that the rabbit is shaking its head and scratching its ears. Sometimes the base of the ear will have a red, yellow or whitish scale on the skin surface, and it may smell because of a discharge from the ear. The ear infections are usually caused by mites. If you can, clean the rabbit's ears out with cotton buds and syringe them with a lukewarm 50 per cent peroxide and water solution before using ear drops containing a miticide available from your veterinarian. (See also HEAD TILT.)

Eye disorders
A reddened and protruding eye is usually caused by an infection (or abscess) below the eye or by conjunctivitis. Treatment includes lancing and antibiotics.

Head tilt
The cause is trauma or middle ear infection. If due to infection, treatment is by cat or dog ear drops and injection of Gentamycin 5 milligrams per kilogram body-weight. (See also EAR DISORDERS.)

White skin is prone to staphylococcal dermatitis which appears as a wet, moist area with a yellow crusty scab.

Mange
Skin mange is also caused by mites. The rabbit will scratch itself continually about the infested area until raw patches appear. The lesions can take various forms; sometimes there will be a wet, moist area with a yellowish crusty scab, or there may be just loss of hair with no apparent infection of the skin. These areas can be treated with benzylbenzoate lotion to a third of the body daily until the whole body has been treated. Repeat weekly for two or three weeks. It is best to clip away the hair for at least 2 centimetres around the lesions. A new product called Ectodex is proving very successful. In serious cases the veterinarian will take a skin scraping to determine the type of mite causing the problem. A greyish or yellowish crust on nose, face and ears can also be caused by ringworm. Apply Thiabendazole in solution twice daily for ten days. Griseofulvin tablets (at the rate of 2 milligrams per 100 grams body-weight) in the feed give good results. Ivermectin is also useful.

Mastitis
Mastitis is inflammation of the mammary glands. Treatment with antibiotics can be administered under veterinary supervision.

Myxomatosis
This is a highly fatal viral disease which is transmitted by mosquitoes and the rabbit flea. After a short incubation period there is a fever, followed by a reluctance to eat. The ears become hot and swollen. The eyes become swollen

Myxomatosis: Note *the languid look, the red eyes and ears.*

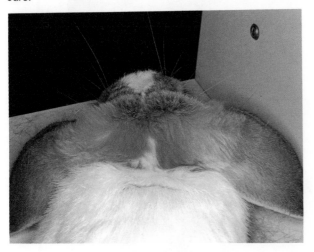

Myxomatosis: Note *the hot, red swollen ears.*

and red and begin to weep. Death invariably occurs within seven days.

Pregnancy toxaemia
This can account for deaths occurring suddenly during late pregnancy. The toxaemia is usually nutritional in origin and may be caused by the intake of food failing in quantity or quality or both towards the end of pregnancy.

Respiratory diseases
When the rabbit develops a cold it sniffles and sneezes just like a human being with a cold. To identify cases early, put your ear to the rabbit's chest and listen for the typical rattling sound. Take the rabbit to the vet at this stage.

Sometimes pneumonia may develop in very young rabbits or nursing does. If this happens, the rabbit will lose its appetite, be very thirsty and have a fever. The normal body temperature is 39°C. Fever temperature is above 40°C. The breathing will be laboured and heavy in near terminal cases. The pneumonia may be complicated and associated with diarrhoea. In these cases it is best to take the rabbit to a vet who will prescribe an antibiotic. A good antibiotic is Ampicillin orally 10 milligrams per kilogram body-weight twice daily for seven days.

Slobbers
Excess production of saliva, difficulty in eating and getting overgrown teeth caught on the wire cage are all signs of overgrown or ingrown incisors or molars.

It usually occurs in mature rabbits who are not provided with hard objects to gnaw. However, the greatest cause is malocclusion or failure of the opposing teeth to meet. The only effective treatment is to cut overgrown or ingrown incisors or molars.

Sores
Sores can be a consequence of keeping bucks in overcrowded conditions. Fighting breaks out between the bucks and even the strongest male may suffer scratching and subsequent sores.

Pressure sores on hocks are common in rabbits housed in cages with wire flooring.

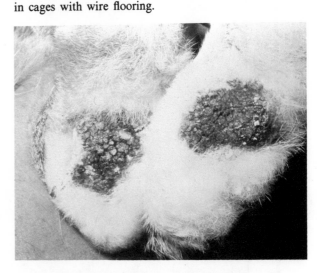

Pressure sores caused by hard floors and inadequate bedding.

Teeth disorders
Overgrowth of incisor teeth is caused by insufficient roughage in the rabbit's diet. The teeth should be filed down with an emery board or file. Add roughage to the diet and a wood block to the cage for chewing, so that the teeth are subjected to normal (and necessary) wear.

Vaccinations
Vaccination against myxomatosis—a viral disease which in certain areas has been introduced to eradicate the wild rabbit—is available in some areas for pet rabbits. Otherwise rabbits do not require vaccination.

Weight loss
Weight loss or poor weight gain, loss of strength, or stiffness in hindlegs are all caused by a vitamin E deficiency. Add vitamin E to the rabbit's diet at the rate of 1 milligram per kilogram body-weight until symptoms disappear.

REPTILES

Reptiles and amphibians as pets

Reptiles vary enormously in shape and form, and include such creatures as turtles, lizards, crocodiles and snakes. However, all reptiles have a skeleton, breathe air, and have dry skins covered with some form of scale. The dry scaly skin enables the reptile to hold in its body water, so that (unlike amphibians) it requires no water except for what it drinks.

The salamander (axolotl), which looks so much like a lizard, is actually an amphibian (the group to which frogs and toads belong). In contrast to reptiles, it has a thin moist skin through which it loses body water. Most amphibians have to dunk themselves in a river or pond to restore water to their bodies.

Amphibians and most kinds of reptiles lay eggs (although some lizards and snakes give birth to live young). Amphibian eggs are soft and jelly-like and must be laid in wet or moist places so that they will not dry out and die. Most young amphibians hatch in water and breathe with gills (like fish).

Reptiles, on the other hand, lay eggs with tough shells which protect the contents of the shell from drying out. A reptile egg can be laid in a desert and still hatch. In fact all reptiles, even those which live in the sea, come onto land to lay their eggs.

The keeping of reptiles and amphibians as pets is becoming very popular. Before acquiring your pet it is important to familiarise yourself with the particular requirements and possible problems. Reptiles and amphibians, more than any other pets, require very particular attention to their environment and feeding if they are to be kept in captivity.

In addition, most countries have fauna laws covering the collection, sale and keeping of these animals. Certainly, to have a collection of any size requires a licence from your wildlife authority.

Some reptiles, particularly snakes, can be venomous. All snakes can bite and there is no easy way for the lay person to distinguish between venomous and non-venomous species. Venomous snakes should not be kept unless the owner has had vast experience in handling and keeping other non-venomous reptiles. In fact, most experienced herpetologists recommend that venomous snakes be kept only in zoos or research institutions.

Advice on treatment for snake bite is the same as that contained in the section on Dogs (see p. 145).

Some children are fascinated by snakes. Before acquiring your pet make sure it is non-venomous.

Housing

The type of housing you should provide for a pet reptile depends, of course, on the species you plan to keep. However, there are essential features common to all.

Housing for reptiles must provide a healthy environment, enough space and ventilation for the type and number of specimens and it must be escape-proof. The enclosure must provide privacy and yet be easily accessible for cleaning. Provision should be made for heating and adequate lighting.

Temperature

Temperature is one of the most important aspects of herpetology. All reptiles are ectotherms—that is, they depend on an outside heat source to regulate their body temperature. This is why they are called 'cold blooded'.

A simple method of providing heat is a 100 watt light globe suspended in or near the enclosure. In the housing for snakes, keep the light globe outside the enclosure or they will attempt to coil around it and get burnt. With lizards, the light globe should be suspended within the enclosure.

By placing the heat source at one end of the enclosure, a range of temperatures is provided.

More sophisticated and expensive heating devices are available—including underwater coils—for certain tortoises or crocodiles.

The temperature of the enclosure should be monitored, especially in sum-

The Salamander, or Mexican Walking Fish, is an amphibian.

The Blue-tongue Lizard is a common reptile garden pet in Australia.

An enclosed meshed reptile pond.

An open tortoise pond at Taronga Zoo.

This reptile enclosure provides the correct environment for smaller reptiles: Note the shelter, water, light and heat source.

mer. Overheating or dehydration can be fatal, or at least cause damage to the nervous system. Subzero temperatures, on the other hand, can result in death from freezing of body fluids. Different species have different optimal temperatures—but the general range is between 20 and 39°C.

Humidity

Incorrect humidity often causes disease. It is important that all reptile housing be kept as dry as possible, particularly the floor. Too much humidity leads to fungal and bacterial infections, particularly amongst crocodiles and tortoises. A continually damp surface will lead to blisters and ventral infections in snakes and lizards.

Too little humidity prevents the natural periodic shedding of skin—a light spray of the enclosure every so often usually provides enough humidity. Water should be available at all times for drinking and to help the reptile slough its skin. The ideal range of humidity is 33–60 per cent.

Enclosures

Most reptiles will live in an unadorned enclosure with absorbent paper on the floor and a branch and a water bowl. However, if you do wish to make a reptile's environment more natural, a wide variety of substances can be used—such as coarse sand, gravel, large pebbles, pieces of bark, leaf litter, bracken, hollow logs or small branches (to provide privacy). Plants can either be growing in the enclosure or can be growing in pots outside it (and therefore can be rotated). Make sure plants are non-toxic. *Monstera* and *Phylodendron* are quite suitable.

Water containers should be wide based and of a depth appropriate to each animal. Keep the water clean and well away from the heat source.

Have on hand some implements for removing such things as dishes, faeces and uneaten food from the enclosure—such as long tongs or a scoop.

A glass aquarium is very suitable as a reptile enclosure and can be acquired in various sizes to suit the smaller reptiles. Enclosures made of metal or wood are also suitable, though wood (including chipboard and hardboard) should be coated with a waterproof varnish for ease of cleaning.

An outside pit gives reptiles some variety. For snakes or monitors the walls should be 1.5 metres high with a 30-centimetre overhang (of tin, for

example) projecting horizontally into the centre of the pit. The walls can be made of any material that is escape-proof, such as bricks, concrete, metal or wood. They must be vertical and smooth. To prevent snakes or lizards escaping by burrowing underneath, the walls should extend 60 centimetres into the ground.

Always have a portable cage for quarantining new or sick animals.

Since most reptiles will bathe, the ideal situation is an enclosure containing a large removable shallow dish that will accommodate the whole body of the reptile without overflowing. This may also provide drinking water.

Light

Light is very important in the control of activity and physiological function, especially of reproduction, as is explained below.

Hibernation

Those reptiles which hibernate should be supplied with as much food as they can eat before hibernation. After they stop eating they should be moved to a darkened area among sacks or leaves in an out-of-the-way place; depending on its size, move their enclosure into a box or a darkened shed.

They must be left undisturbed until hibernation ceases naturally. If woken before, their temperature may be enough to maintain activity, but not enough to stimulate feeding. High mortalities occur after hibernation and before eating.

Feeding

Healthy reptiles can fast for long periods without effect. In good condition, they may fast for several months. Reptiles are normally intermittent feeders. Snakes eat twice weekly or less. Lizards eat daily. Scent, particularly for snakes, is important in food selection.

Feeding activity is temperature dependent, and sub-optimal conditions are commonly the cause of fasting. To rectify the situation, increase the environmental temperature or give the reptile warm baths. Or change the diet, change the environment or increase the light. Temperature reduction, vibrations or disturbance of any kind will cause regurgitation.

For carnivores the best diet is a whole animal, since this reproduces their natural diet in the wild.

The Shingle-back Lizard has big rough scales on the upper side of its bulky body. It can inflict a nasty bite so treat with care.

Tortoises

Lettuce, clover, grass, tomatoes, fruit and cucumber are suitable foods. Some will eat raw fish and meat, which should be supplemented with calcium carbonate at the rate of ½ teaspoonful (0.5 gram) per 100 grams of meat fed. Cereals, bread, Farax and tinned dog foods can be tried. However, bread and other cereals should not form the major part of the diet of land tortoises, as they might cause liver disease.

Terrapins

Terrapins will eat chopped meat, heart, liver, fish (whole or in pieces), snails, shrimps, worms, insects, frogs, tadpoles, mealworms and baby mice. Vegetables such as lettuce can be given on alternate days. As with tortoises, meat should be supplemented with calcium.

Small lizards

The usual diet is earthworms, grasshoppers, slugs, fly larvae and mealworms.

Large lizards

Feed young mice, small lizards, chopped meat, dog food and raw egg.

Herbivorous lizards

Provide lettuce, fruit, plants and insects.

The common Australian Long-necked or Snake-necked Tortoise.

An Australian Python. All snakes bite so always support the body evenly, and never make sudden movements near the head.

How to hold a tortoise.

Fight wounds on a snake following a feeding frenzy.

Snakes

All snakes are carnivores, and most eat small vertebrates. Some will eat only live prey.

Force feeding

When force feeding is called for, use a small, 2-millimetre-diameter, oiled, polythene tube attached to a syringe. Gently introduce it into the mouth and pass it into the food pipe. (It is impossible to go into the windpipe by mistake.) In this way you can feed pulverised whole animal, or canned dog food, minced with egg, or infant foods.

General care

Tortoises

When handling tortoises, beware of the sharp claws. Most small tortoises can be picked up as you would hold a sandwich.

To transport a tortoise, put it in a moist cloth bag or in a box lined with moist towels. Avoid overcrowding. Always give the tortoise a good soaking before and after the trip to avoid dehydration.

Lizards

All lizards can and will bite. If bitten by a lizard, do not pull away—wait until the lizard releases its grip. To avoid being bitten, hold the lizard behind the head with one hand and the base of the tail and hindlegs with the other.

Give lizards a good drink before transporting them, so that they do not dehydrate. When transporting a lizard long distances, place it in a calico bag in a box, with absorbent padding between the bag and the box. Secure the box firmly after making sure that it has adequate ventilation holes.

If transporting the lizard by any kind of public transport, label the box with the name, address and telephone number of both the sender and the receiver. Attach another label describing the contents of the box, and giving any special instructions for care during the trip.

Snakes

All snakes bite. When handling a snake, support the body evenly, and never make any sudden movements near the head. When picking up a snake, always pin its head down with a forked stick, then grasp it behind the head from above. Remember, when a snake decides to strike and bite, it does so with extreme rapidity.

If a snake wraps itself around your arm, unwind it while continuing to hold the head. When releasing a snake, always let its head go last and withdraw your hand quickly.

Snakes should be transported in the same manner as lizards.

Breeding

Breeding seldom occurs in captivity because the reptile never truly adapts. Breeding activity is dependent on normal environment for that species—light, correct temperature, absence of stress and balanced nutrition are all important.

Special requirements for amphibians

Most amphibians are small animals with smooth, moist skins which reproduce by laying eggs in water or moist areas. The eggs hatch from their soft gelatinous covering to a larva stage and later undergo metamorphosis to the adult stage. The commonly kept amphibians include frogs, toads, newts and salamanders (axolotl).

The axolotl is actually the larval form of the Mexican salamander. It is chunky in build with a broad head and well developed gills, and averages

20 centimetres in length. It ranges in colour from pink to brownish-black. When purchasing an axolotl, ensure that it swims upright and that it uses its gills actively.

Most amphibians do not like to be handled and can be very slippery. The best way to handle them is to place your middle finger between the hindlegs and wrap the rest of your hand around the body. Axolotls should be grasped around the head and forebody.

The skin of amphibians should be kept moist and the animal should have access to water at all times. Many amphibians, especially toads, secrete poisonous substances, so it is important to wash your hands after handling.

If amphibians are to be transported it is important that they are kept damp, and have plenty of space and adequate ventilation. Polystyrene boxes containing dampened pieces of moss, grass or foam will retain the moisture and provide protection. Axolotls can be transported in a sealed plastic bag containing one-third water, two-thirds air.

Axolotls can be kept in an aquarium filled to a depth of 20 centimetres with fresh water and kept at 23°C. The aquarium should also contain some rocks or vegetation to make the axolotl feel secure. Newts and frogs can be kept in the same sort of environment, but it should also contain a half submerged stone, piece of bark or sturdy vegetation for them to climb on.

Diagram shows an easy way to capture insects.

Axolotls will only feed in the water. Axolotls and newts will eat worms, insects or dog food. Young ones will eat water fleas, white worms, tubifex and sometimes fish food.

Frogs and toads usually like their prey to be moving. They love insects and worms.

A good supply of insects can be caught by hanging a light globe over a funnel which has been placed in a jar. The insects are attracted by the light and fall into the jar via the funnel. (This method is particularly effective on summer nights.)

Caring for sick reptiles and amphibians

When treating sick reptiles or amphibians it is important to ensure a clean environment, with fresh, appetising food and clean water.

Proper temperature and humidity are crucial. It is often advisable to raise the temperature slightly to increase the animal's metabolism, thus stimulating a more rapid effect of any medications. (See HOUSING, TEMPERATURE and HUMIDITY.) Sometimes force feeding, via a 2-millimetre-diameter polythene tube introduced into the stomach, is helpful to the recovery of the animal. (See FEEDING.)

Common ailments

Acute stress syndrome

The signs are dilation of the pupil, tremor, loss of righting reflex, with terminal convulsions and death. This condition is more common in newly acquired animals or those placed in a new environment.

Oral glucose at 3 grams per kilogram body-weight helps the condition, but the causative agent should be removed, whether it is competition, high population density, or other stress-inducing conditions.

In the chronic form of this disease the reptile fails to heal and becomes secondarily infested by bacteria, fungi and parasites. Treat for any infestation/infection, then provide satisfactory environment for that species. In the meantime, force feed.

A brown snake with blister disease.

Blister disease

This is caused by excessive humidity and is common in winter. Skin (cutaneous) blisters first appear, which are sterile. These become infected and filled with pus. Blisters should be excised, flushed with 50 per cent peroxide and water and swabbed with iodine, three times daily for four days.

Calcium deficiency

See NUTRITIONAL DISEASES.

Canker, mouth rot, necrotic stomatitis

This condition is very common in snakes, lizards and tor-toises. Initially there is redness and swelling of the membranes of the mouth. Marked swelling occurs and death by suffocation is possible. As the disease progresses there is continued inflammation and ulceration and increasing quantities of dead peeled skin. The infection may spread to bones of the jaw, causing osteomyelitis. As the disease spreads further it may cause pneumonia, gastrointestinal infection or septicaemia. Vitamin C deficiency is a factor in the disease. Additional quantities during the illness help.

Treatment is to flush the area with 50 per cent peroxide and water and gently remove all dead tissue. Rinse the area with a warm saline solution (1 teaspoon salt per litre water). Then apply topical sulphadimidine or chloramphenicol. Give 10–60 milligrams of vitamin C orally daily and injections of multi-vitamins twice weekly. It is necessary to use antibiotics for at least eight days. Increase room temperature to 32°C. Don't attempt to feed the reptile. After a week if there is no improvement change the antibiotic.

Cannibalism

Cannibalism may sometimes occur as a result of over-crowding or when there is no supervision during feeding. One animal may accidentally swallow another. It may also occur when the wrong species or greatly different sizes of animals are kept together. Lizards of greatly differing sizes should never be kept together because of the danger of cannibalism. The risk is not as great as when snakes of different sizes are kept together.

Constipation

As in all animals constipation is caused by incorrect diet. It is particularly common when reptiles are constantly fed feathered or furred animals. Lack of exercise and dehydration also predispose. Signs are decreased appetite, discomfort and sluggishness; snakes are unable to coil normally. The mass may be palpable and visible in X-rays.

The best treatment is to give faecal softeners or oil orally. Enemas with gentle palpation help.

Dermatophilus

This skin disorder can affect lizards, especially skinks, and presents as multiple raised nodules or as small abscesses 7 millimetres under the skin. Treatment is with antibiotics. Oral antibiotics do not reach therapeutic levels, but long-acting penicillin intramuscularly is effective.

Dysentery (Amoebiasis)

A very important disease in larger collections. Signs include bloody diarrhoea, depression, lethargy and loss of appetite. Often the first sign of disease is sudden death.

The most effective treatment is metronidazole (Flagyl) as

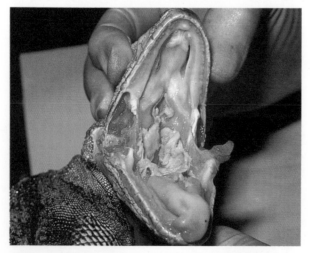

Canker (Mouth rot): Note *the dead, peeled skin in the centre of the mouth.*

In snakes the eyelids are immovable; the eye is covered by a transparent scale.

a single dose of 275 milligrams per kilogram body-weight, administered orally by stomach tube. Ampicillin should be used concurrently.

Eye disorders

In snakes the eyelids are immovable; the eye is covered by a transparent scale (the spectacle). In conjunctivitis there is a marked distension because of a build-up of pus. If this is left, permanent damage can be done to the eye. The area must be drained and flushed via a small incision at the base of the eye—a job for the vet. Suitable eye antibiotic ointments are then applied.

A few days before skin shedding, the spectacle becomes opaque and this should not be confused with infection. If humidity is too low, shedding may be incomplete and commonly the spectacle will be retained, again confusing the diagnosis. Soak with a moist compress and remove with forceps. Sometimes vitamin A deficiency can cause swellings of the eyelids.

Iodine deficiency (Goitre)

Seen in herbivorous reptiles, particularly land tortoises. Signs are lethargy and limbs with fluid in them (oedema). Generalised herbivore diets should be supplemented with 0.5 per cent iodine salt.

Kidney disease

This is often recognised as the cause of death on postmortem. Unfortunately it is usually overlooked because the only signs—loss of appetite and sluggishness—fit so many diseases.

Mouth rot

See CANKER.

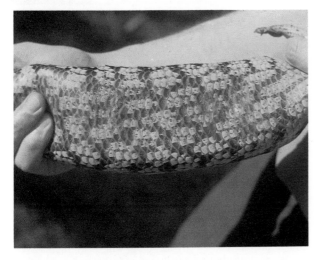

Ulcerative dermatitis (skin rot) in a Blue-tongue Lizard.

Necrotic dermatitis (Ulcerative dermatitis, 'skin rot')

In this disease expanding dark areas of dead tissue are seen beneath the scales, most commonly on the underside near the cloaca. In lizards the limbs can be affected with eventual loss of digits. Initially the animal is normal, but then develops loss of appetite and lethargy. Factors such as excessive humidity, sub-optimal temperatures, faecal contamination, blister disease and ectoparasites all predispose the disease. It is a common winter problem.

Treatment initially is conservative, to avoid defects. Use chlortetracycline orally at the rate of 200 milligrams per kilogram body-weight for ten days and use antibacterial baths. Also dose with vitamin C (10–60 milligrams). If this treatment is unsuccessful, scales and dead skin should be removed from affected areas and different antibiotics used. Correct hygiene, temperature and humidity are important.

Nutritional diseases

Vitamin A deficiency is seen, especially in terrapins, on a raw meat and green vegetable diet; the initial sign is swelling of the eyelids. Secondary infection is common. Sometimes there may be respiratory disease evident. Vitamin A additives, especially in the form of liver three times weekly, will clear the condition.

Vitamin D deficiency causes typical rickets in all reptiles. There is skeletal deformity and softening of shells. Depression, lack of appetite and weakness in the legs are also signs. Some lizards appear to utilise ultra-violet light. Supplement the diet with cod liver oil, egg yolk or day old chicks. Injections of calciostelein are helpful.

Vitamin E deficiency is due to feeding oil-laden fish or obese laboratory rodents to carnivorous reptiles. The signs are decreased appetite, inco-ordination and death. Vitamin E supplement will cure the disease.

Calcium imbalance due to incorrect feeding: Note *swollen limbs.*

Calcium imbalance is common in carnivorous reptiles fed whole meat or whole insect diets, and also in herbivorous reptiles. The reason is that the calcium levels in their diets are very low. The signs include shell deformities in tortoises and terrapins, fractures, other symptoms of nutritional secondary hyperparathyroidism, and osteodystrophies characterised by firm swollen limbs and tail. On examination, the lizard suspected of suffering from calcium imbalance appears well fed, chubby but lame. Limestone, oyster shell or cuttlefish may be placed in the water. Always add calcium carbonate at the rate of ½ teaspoon (0.5 gram) per 100 grams of red meat; to fish add 1.5 grams. The better treatment is to change to a whole-animal diet.

Obesity

Obesity is common in some reptiles, particularly the larger pythons which may feed often and exercise infrequently. In these cases the only option is to reduce the quantity of food.

Oedema

Oedema (filling of the limbs with fluid) is reported in overcrowded lizards. Reduction of the density reverses the condition. Sometimes generalised oedema may accompany vitamin A deficiency. The condition may also occur in parasitism, renal failure or goitre.

Parasites

Recently caught reptiles should be isolated until parasites are eradicated.

Mites

Mites are found only on snakes and lizards, particularly

around their eyes and anal region. The reptile's scales will be slightly raised in the infested area and the animal may be covered with tiny white spots which are the mites' faeces. Mites can be eradicated by suspending a pest strip (dichlorvos compound) from the top of the enclosure for twelve hours. If the infestation is serious take the reptile out, destroy the contents of the enclosure, scrub the enclosure thoroughly with a Malathion solution of 30 millilitres per 5 litres of water, and leave for thirty minutes, then rinse out with copious quantities of water. Leave the pest strip over the reptile for a longer period.

Roundworms
Roundworms may cause obstructions and regurgitation. In pythons they also cause severe gastric ulceration and perforations of the bowel wall. They are easily treated with piperazine orally 110 milligrams per kilogram body-weight.

Skin worms
Skin worms present as small soft swellings which if incised with a sharp blade reveal a long, flat, white worm which may be as long as the snake itself. These are immature tapeworms. Drugs are not effective against this intermediate stage and surgical excision is the routine.

Ticks
Ticks are usually harmless to reptiles but may interfere with their feeding habits. Where there are only a few ticks, remove them with tweezers. Heavy infestations require 0.2 per cent solution of Neguvon as a spray or bath, which is effective against ticks and their eggs.

Tongue worms
Tongue worms are found in the lungs and air-sacs of snakes, lizards and crocodiles. They require two hosts, and the intermediate host may be a small mammal, a frog or another reptile. They are best not treated because the dying worm may cause fatal obstruction of the airway.

Red disease
Red leg disease in frogs is thought to be of bacterial origin and is extremely contagious. It can be treated with antibiotics. A daily bath in a weak salt solution has been found to be beneficial.

Regurgitation
This phenomenon in snakes is not clearly understood but it is known to be caused by stress such as handling or disturbance after feeding. Sharp fluctuations in temperature, overcrowded conditions, internal parasites or various bacterial infections will also cause regurgitation. Sometimes a snake will do this anyway, and then it is necessary to vary its diet, the manner of feeding or the environment. It is not serious— providing it does not go on for weeks.

Respiratory disease ('Pneumonia')
Respiratory troubles usually result from a sudden decrease in temperature, or may be brought on by overcrowding or stress conditions when the animal's resistance is low. The symptoms are usually difficulty in breathing, nasal discharge, wheezing and gaping.

Raise the temperature of the environment. Give chloramphenicol intramuscularly at the rate of 3 milligrams per 100 grams body-weight. Give vitamins A and C daily. Check for parasites.

Salmonella infection
Clinical disease is rare in reptiles— but they are common carriers of rare Salmonella types not commonly associated with human infection. Signs of this infection include greenish faeces with green or yellow-stained wet uric acid. Regular observation will detect infection, which is treated by chlortetracycline orally at the rate of 200 milligrams per kilogram body-weight.

Sloughing ('Shed stop')
Trouble in sloughing old skin is often caused by an en-

vironment that is too dry. The old skin may remain on the back, stomach and head regions or on the ends of the toes and tails in lizards.

A close watch should be kept on lizards when they are sloughing, as a build-up of old skin on one of the legs or on the tail can cause it to dry and break off and the blood supply will be greatly restricted.

If a reptile has a problem with sloughing, an overnight soak in a large escape-proof container filled with water and mild disinfectant will usually remove the pieces of old skin. If not, the water will soften the skin so that it can be removed by hand.

Shell-crack in a tortoise can be repaired with fibreglass.

Trauma
Some of the commonest problems of reptiles are cracked shells in tortoises, skin sores from overheating or rough handling, abrasions of the nose and head region (particularly in snakes) and to a lesser extent, fights caused by other animals.

Tortoises are very hardy animals and in most cases a bite wound will heal by itself if kept clean. If a shell-crack is serious, it can be patched using fibreglass fabric or an epoxy resin-based adhesive such as Araldite. Wounds should be treated with 50 per cent hydrogen peroxide and water, all dead tissue should be removed and local antibiotics applied to the area. Sores resulting from overheating should be treated in the same way.

Most reptiles are quite hardy animals and minor cuts and abrasions caused by rubbing will heal themselves. Frogs are also subject to badly rubbed noses. Keep the frog warm and treat quickly with antiseptic cream to reduce infection.

Ulcerative shell disease of turtles ('Shell rot', 'rust', 'spot disease')
This very common disease was originally thought to be caused by a fungus—but is now known to be caused by bacteria. It is responsible for a fatal shell disease in crustaceans. Early lesions are blotchy, dark, focal discolorations of the shell, which later slough, leaving ulcerations up to 1 centimetre in diameter. Secondary infection may cause death. Affected animals should be isolated, their lesions scraped and treated with chloramphenicol ointment or spray, plus chloramphenicol at 40 milligrams per kilogram body-weight intramuscularly twice daily for ten days.

Wounds
Minor cuts and scratches may be treated by applying mercurochrome or triple dye to the affected area.

BIBLIOGRAPHY

The following is a list of books and articles to which reference should be made by those seeking more detailed information about specific aspects of pet care.

Adams, O. R. *Lameness in Horses*. 3rd ed. Lea and Febiger, Philadelphia, 1974.

American Association of Equine Practitioners *Proceedings* 1972–81.

Animals in the Classroom. A Guide for Teachers. McGraw-Hill, New York, 1970.

Axelrod, H. and Shaw, S. *Breeding Aquarium Fishes*. TFH Publications, Jersey City, 1971.

Baird, E. *Horse Care*. MacDonald and Jane's, London, 1977,

Banks, C. B. *Keeping Reptiles and Amphibians as Pets*. Thomas Nelson, Melbourne, 1980.

Catcott, E. J. and Smithcors, J. F. editors *Equine Medicine and Surgery*. 2nd ed. American Veterinary Publications, Inc., Wheaton, Illinois, 1972.

Conant, R. A. *Field Guide to Reptiles and Amphibians*. Houghton Mifflin, Boston, 1958.

Current Veterinary Therapy, Small Animal Practice. W. B. Saunders, Philadelphia, 1975.

DeRoss, Les. *Parrots in Australian Aviaries*. Lansdowne, Melbourne, , 1975.

Dolensek, E. P. *The Penguin Book of Pets*. Penguin Books, London, 1976.

Emery, L., Miller, J. and Van Hoosen, N. *Horseshoeing Theory and Hoof Care*. Lea and Febiger, Philadelphia, 1977.

Fitch, H. S. *Reproductive Cycles in Lizards and Snakes*. University of Kansas, Museum of National History, Lawrence, 1970.

Forshaw, J. M. *Parrots of the World*. Doubleday, Garden City, N.Y., 1973.

Hayes, M. H. *Points of the Horse*. 7th ed. Stanley Paul & Co. Ltd., London, 1969.

Hofstad, M. S. ed. *Diseases of Poultry*. 7th ed. Iowa State University Press, Ames, Iowa, 1978.

Hungerford, T. G. *Diseases of Poultry*. 4th ed. Angus and Robertson, Sydney, London, 1969.

Kelly, J. D. 'Canine Parasitology.' *Vet. Review* No. 17, The University of Sydney Post-Graduate Foundation in Veterinary Science, 1977.

Kirk, D. H. *Horse Breaking Made Easy*. D. H. Kirk, Zillmere, Qld., 1978.

Klee, A. J. *Know How to Breed Livebearers*. The Pet Library Ltd.

La Corte, Rosario. *Know How to Breed Egg-Layers*. The Pet Library Ltd.

Lapage, G. *Mönnig's Veterinary Helminthology and Entomology*. 5th ed. Bailliere, Tindal and Cox, London, 1962.

Lavelle, R. B. *Bone Problems of Growing Dogs*. Uncle Ben's of Australia, 1979.

Leighton Hardman, A. C. *A Guide to Feeding Horses and Ponies*. Pelham Books Ltd., London, 1977.

Low, R. *Aviary Birds*. A. S. Barnes, South Brunswick, N.J., 1970.

Males, R. and Males, V. *Foaling, Broodmare and Foal Management*. Ure Smith, Auckland, Sydney, 1977.

Martin, R. M. *Cage and Aviary Birds*. Collins, 1980.

Petnak, M. L. *Diseases of Cage and Aviary Birds*. Lea and Febiger, Philadelphia, 1969.

Pillsbury, E. W. *First Aid and Care of Small Animals*. Animal Welfare Institute, New York, 1955.

Porter, K. R. *Herpetology*. W. B. Saunders, Philadelphia, 1972.

Prescott, C. W. 'Parasitic Diseases of the Cat in Australia.' *Vet. Review* No. 12, The University of Sydney, Post-Graduate Foundation in Veterinary Science, 1972.

Rooney, J. R. *Biomechanics of Lameness in Horses*. Robert E. Krieger Publishing Company, Huntington, N.Y., 1977.

Rossdale, P. *Seeing Equine Practice*. William Heinemann Medical Books Ltd., London, 1976.

Sutherland, S. K. 'Treatment of Snake Bite and Arachnid Poisoning.' Commonwealth Serum Laboratories, 1978.

The UFAW Handbook on the Care and Management of Laboratory Animals. E. & S. Livingstone, Edinborough and London, 1966.

The University of Sydney, Post-Graduate Foundation in Veterinary Science. Various publications, articles, cassettes and courses.

Van Duijn, C. *Diseases of Fish*. 3rd ed. C. C. Thomas, Springfield, Ill., 1973.

Vogel, Zdenek. *Reptiles and Amphibians: Their Care and Handling*. Viking, New York, 1964.

INDEX

MICE

RABBITS

REPTILES